THE A TO Z OF
CORPORATE SOCIAL
RESPONSIBILITY

THE A TO Z OF CORPORATE SOCIAL RESPONSIBILITY

A Complete Reference Guide to Concepts, Codes and Organisations

Wayne Visser
Dirk Matten
Manfred Pohl
Nick Tolhurst

BICENTENNIAL
1807
WILEY
2007
BICENTENNIAL

John Wiley & Sons, Ltd

Copyright © 2007   John Wiley & Sons Ltd, The Atrium, Southern Gate, Chiches
West Sussex PO19 8SQ, England

Telephone (+44) 1243 779777

Email (for orders and customer service enquiries): cs-books@wiley.co.uk
Visit our Home Page on www.wiley.com

Other Wiley Editorial Offices

John Wiley & Sons Inc., 111 River Street, Hoboken, NJ 07030, USA

Jossey-Bass, 989 Market Street, San Francisco, CA 94103-1741, USA

Wiley-VCH Verlag GmbH, Boschstr. 12, D-69469 Weinheim, Germany

John Wiley & Sons Australia Ltd, 42 McDougall Street, Milton, Queensland 4064, Australia

John Wiley & Sons (Asia) Pte Ltd, 2 Clementi Loop #02-01, Jin Xing Distripark, Singapore
129809

John Wiley & Sons Canada Ltd, 6045 Freemont Blvd, Mississauga, ONT, L5R 4J3, Canada

Wiley also publishes its books in a variety of electronic formats. Some content that appears in
print may not be available in electronic books.

Anniversary Logo Design: Richard J. Pacifico

Library of Congress Cataloging in Publication Data

The A to Z of corporate social responsibility : a complete reference guide to concepts, codes
    and organizations / edited by Wayne Visser, Dirk Matten, Manfred Pohl, Nick Tolhurst.
        p.   cm.
    Includes bibliographical references and index.
    ISBN 978-0-470-72395-1 (cloth : alk. paper)   1. Social responsibility of business.
    I. Visser, Wayne.   II. Matten, Dirk.   III. Pohl, Manfred.   IV. Tolhurst, Nick.
    HD60.A22 2007
    658.4′08—dc22

                                                                    2007041621

British Library Cataloguing in Publication Data

A catalogue record for this book is available from the British Library

ISBN 978-0-470-72395-1 (HB)

Typeset in 11.5/15pt Bembo by Integra Software Services Pvt. Ltd, Pondicherry, India
Printed and bound in Great Britain by TJ International Ltd, Padstow, Cornwall, UK
This book is printed on acid-free paper responsibly manufactured from sustainable forestry in
which at least two trees are planted for each one used for paper production.

CONTENTS

FOREWORD

The original idea for an encyclopaedia of Corporate Social Responsibility (CSR) came from the founder of the Institute for Corporate Culture Affairs (ICCA), Professor Manfred Pohl, and its Chairman Takis Arapoglou at the September 2004 ICCA annual meeting and conference on Corporate Ethics in Frankfurt am Main. During the course of this event, it became clear that debates on CSR, corporate ethics and sustainability had moved beyond the stage of a specialist or *niche* subject and had now become an integral part of global business and society. Yet, despite this, much writing on CSR and related themes seemed to concentrate on the parochial or in specialised areas. Another problem is the lack of a 'common language' between business and academia in this field. Indeed, debates on CSR often involve communication between vastly different groups in society: from international NGOs to national governments to global companies and the local communities in which they operate. The very scope of the debates involved, and the actors participating, leads to the necessity of a 'common language'. Yet it is this fundamental aspect which is at present missing – and it is this lacuna that this book intends to fill. What is even meant by corporate social responsibility? In what way are corporations viewed as citizens of the countries in which they operate? How does a company know when it is operating in a sustainable way? And what is ethical investment? As well as providing definitions to these questions, the *A to Z of CSR* also lists and describes the most important organisations and landmarks in the field of CSR. What, for example, are the Global

Compact Principles and how did they come about? Which are the most respected ethical business indices and what do they measure?

From the autumn of 2005, members of the editorial board and working group of the *A to Z of CSR* started to draw up a list of the concepts, codes and organisations to be included. In 2006 and 2007 the editors identified those people in the relevant area to be approached and collated all definitions, working with over 100 experts and opinion formers around the globe. With the completion of this volume we are convinced that the publication will make a timely and innovative contribution to the literature. The book is ultimately intended to constitute the definitive terminological encyclopaedia on CSR, Sustainability, Business Ethics and the organisations and standards in this field.

The ICCA would like to thank all participating authors as well as all those who contributed towards the realisation of this project, in particular the following: Malcolm Macintosh, Andrew Dunnett, Peter Lacy, Andrew Crane, Jeremy Moon, Bryan Cress, Judy Muthuri, May Seitanidi and John Luff, who have so generously contributed towards this publication. We greatly appreciate your time, commitment and good advice. We would also like to thank all those involved, both our members and our partners, whose inspiration and hard work contributed towards the realisation of this book. In particular, we would like to thank Deutsche Bank and ICCA's Chairman Takis Arapoglou from the National Bank of Greece whose steadfast support of this project made this publication possible.

Editorial board:

Katja Böhmer	Dirk Matten
Aron Ghebremariam	Manfred Pohl
Judith Hennigfeld	Nick Tolhurst
Sandra S. Huble	Wayne Visser

1 May 2007
Frankfurt am Main

THE A TO Z OF CSR – INTRODUCTION

Wayne Visser and Dirk Matten

This *A to Z of CSR* has been compiled to help managers, consultants, teachers and researchers navigate their way through the plethora of terms, codes and organisations associated with CSR. We like to think of it as a jargon-busting guide to CSR. By way of introduction, we would like to comment briefly on four aspects of the publication, namely the context, scope, contributors and structure.

CONTEXT

'CSR has won the battle of ideas' – even the sceptical survey on CSR in the *Economist* in January 2005 conceded this much. And it is true. While the idea has been around for some five decades by now, the last 15 years have seen an unprecedented rise of CSR language, tools, actors, strategies and practices in industry all over the world. With the fall of the iron curtain and the advent of globalisation, it is business, rather than nation state governments, that have faced growing demands to address issues of societal concern and to be responsible and accountable members of our global society. Next to these developments, it is somewhat ironic to see that the very doctrines of Milton Friedman and his liberal friends – who severely criticised CSR – have led us to a situation of increased demand for CSR. The implementation of their ideas in most industrialised countries over the last two and a half decades has resulted in a situation where deregulated free markets, privatised public services and a liberalised global economy have put corporations right at the centre of public concern.

But CSR as an approach to responsibly managing an organisation is not just a topic for the business community. Increasingly, we see governments involved in promoting and fostering CSR, most notable the UK government with its CSR minister and the EU with its White Papers and the recent European Alliance for CSR. Furthermore, governments themselves, which are still responsible for roughly half of the GDP in most developed democracies, increasingly face calls for more responsible, accountable and transparent behaviour very similar to those addressed at corporations. Hence, governments all over the world are deeply involved in developing and implementing many of the CSR ideas explained in this volume.

Non-governmental organisations (NGOs), for a long time the independent 'conscience' or 'police' which played a role in translating the concerns of civil society to corporations, have recently also become engaged in the CSR agenda. This has happened in part because growing CSR practices have involved various forms of collaboration, partnerships and joint initiatives between the corporate and NGO sectors. Another reason, however, is the rise in membership, budgets and global reach of these often multinational organisations. As such, NGOs face questions similar to those on the corporate CSR agenda: In whose interest do they act? To whom are they accountable? What practices are they using?

CSR then is not only a topic for business, but equally a subject for government and civil society or the NGO sector. And it is by no means confined to the developed world, or even its Anglo-American origins. Indeed, in some ways, the current growth in CSR is more marked in Europe, Japan, South Korea or Taiwan, while the rise of India and China as key players in the global economy has given CSR a firm place on their agenda as well. The presence of big business in the developed world is even argued by many to be one of the strongest drivers for CSR, not only for Western multinationals, but also for indigenous companies. In fact, companies are increasingly viewed as a beacon of hope with regard to fighting poverty, promoting economic development and showcasing an alternative in otherwise often poorly governed economies and societies.

SCOPE

You will notice that, as an encyclopaedia of CSR, we have adopted a wide and inclusive interpretation of CSR, to include related terms which all deal in different ways with the role of business in society – from corporate governance, environmental management and human rights, to development, globalisation and waste management, to mention just a few examples. By doing this, we acknowledge that CSR is an essentially contested idea and more of a cluster concept, which forms only one strand in a web of related terms, concepts and subjects.

All in all, the *A to Z of CSR* features around 350 entries, including 10 Core terms, 85 Key terms, and 250 Definition terms. The Core terms – which include accountability, business ethics, corporate citizenship, corporate environmental management, corporate governance, corporate social responsibility, corporate sustainability, health and safety, poverty and stakeholder theory – are the most extensively discussed, including a definition of each term, how they emerged in popular discourse, the key debates surrounding their use and any related trends. The Key terms cover similar issues, but in less detail, while the Definitions are short statements that encapsulate the essence of each given term.

We had long discussions in particular about the scope of organisations to include, as the sheer number of NGOs, think tanks, business groups, academic units and consultancies on CSR globally would have made it impossible to include all actors. We have confined ourselves to the following criteria: we included (1) organisations that issue a standard or a code, (2) key organisations that represent CSR regionally, and (3) a number of organisations that historically or by degree of their impact can be regarded as key players in CSR – the latter criterion admittedly reflecting the subjective assessment of the editors.

CONTRIBUTORS

What makes the *A to Z of CSR* distinctive, apart from its holistic and inclusive approach to CSR, is the quality of its contributors. We are fortunate to have secured the participation of most of the world's leading academics and practitioners on CSR. As a result, we have adopted a very 'light touch' to editing their contributions, since they are, after all, among the foremost experts on their given subject areas. Some are widely known for having either introduced, popularised or defined certain terms – such as Professors Archie Carroll on CSR, Ed Freeman on stakeholder theory, Stuart Hart on poverty and the base of the pyramid model, and Richard Welford on environmental management. Others are individuals who have had an enormous influence on the implementation of CSR – such as John Elkington on corporate sustainability, Mary Robinson on human rights, and Judge Mervyn King on corporate governance. With contributors based on all five continents the A to Z also aspires at representing the global debate on CSR rather than just a narrow Anglo-American viewpoint.

Many contributors are leaders of organisations that are doing tremendous work related to CSR – such as Björn Stigson of the World Business Council for Sustainable Development, David Nussbaum formerly of Transparency International and Valli Moosa of the World Conservation Union (IUCN). We are also delighted to have secured the participation of the heads of regional CSR organisations – such as Aron Cramer of Business for Social Responsibility

(North America), Hugo Vergara of Forum Empresa (Latin America), Paul Kapelus of the African Institute for Corporate Citizenship and Richard Welford of CSR Asia. With more than 100 contributors of similarly high calibre, to whom we are most grateful for their time and effort, we are confident that the *A to Z of CSR* is the most authoritative international reference guide on CSR to date. Note that any terms without a specified author have been written by the editors, or extracted from the relevant organisation's website and referenced accordingly.

STRUCTURE

The *A to Z of CSR* begins with a comprehensive list of contributors, which states their relevant title and/or organisational affiliation. The body of the *A to Z of CSR* contains all the terms arranged in alphabetical order. And finally, several indexes allow the reader to search the *A to Z of CSR* in different ways. The *Terms Index* lists terms under the broad headings of Core Terms (which tend to be around 2000 words in length), Key Terms (between 500 and 750 words), and Definition Terms (100 to 250 words). The *Categories Index* lists terms under the following headings: CSR Terms, Regional Perspectives on CSR, Sectoral Perspectives on CSR, CSR Codes, and CSR Organisations. And the *Authors Index* lists terms by author, since many contributors have written multiple entries. Each term is also *cross-referenced* to related terms in the encyclopaedia, so that readers can obtain diverse perspectives and build up a fuller picture of the subject of their interest.

It is important to note that the content of the *A to Z of CSR* represents the views of the individual authors as they relate to each term, rather than those of the editors. Hence, each term credits its author or other relevant source (some organisational definitions are taken from their websites). As acting editors we were concerned, on the one hand, to ensure that all terms are represented in an accurate and, as much as possible, balanced way. On the other hand, CSR as an emerging field of practice and thought is rather dynamic. We therefore felt it appropriate to apply a rather light editorial touch on shaping the contents, in order to keep the character of this volume as a representation of the ongoing discourse in a contested area of business practice and theory.

We trust that you will find the *A to Z of CSR* a useful reference guide in your work and welcome your feedback at w.visser@cca-institute.org and n.tolhurst@cca-institute.org

ABOUT THE EDITORS

Dr Wayne Visser is Research Director at the University of Cambridge Programme for Industry and is responsible for spearheading a programme of research into sustainability leadership, learning and change. He is the author of four books, including three on the social, environmental and ethical responsibilities of business, one of which was also made into a leadership training video, as well as numerous articles and conference papers. He has lectured on corporate responsibility and sustainability at universities in Finland (Turku), South Africa (Cape Town, Rhodes and Stellenbosch) and the UK (Cambridge, Cardiff and Nottingham), including teaching a module on CSR in Developing Countries. Prior to joining Cambridge Programme for Industry, Wayne was Director of Sustainability Services for KPMG and Strategy Analyst for CAP Gemini in South Africa.

Professor Dirk Matten holds the Hewlett–Packard Chair in Corporate Social Responsibility and is a Professor of Policy at the Schulich School of Business, York University, Toronto. Until 2006, he had a chair in business ethics and was director of a research centre on sustainability issues at the Royal Holloway College of the University of London, UK. He has 12 books and edited collections and more than 150 journal articles, book chapters and conference papers to his name. Professor Matten has taught and undertaken research at academic institutions in Australia, Belgium, Britain, Canada, the Czech Republic, France, Germany, Italy and the US. His work has won numerous international awards, most recently the 'Max Weber Textbook Award' of the Institut der Deutschen Wirtschaft, awarded by Germany's deputy chancellor Franz Müntefering in November 2006 in Berlin.

Professor Manfred Pohl is the founder and CEO of the Institute for Corporate Culture Affairs (ICCA). Born in Bliesransbach, Germany, in 1944, he received his PhD in History from the University of Saarbrücken, Germany, in 1972. Since 1972 he has been an Honorary Professor at the University of Frankfurt. He is currently the Deputy Chairman of the European Association for Banking History e.V. and of Konvent für Deutschland e.V. In October 2001 he received the European Award for Culture at the European Parliament in Strasbourg. From June 2002 Manfred Pohl was head of the Corporate Cultural Affairs department at Deutsche Bank in Frankfurt, responsible for all cultural activities as well as charitable donations and sponsoring within Deutsche Bank globally before retiring in May 2006. Professor Pohl has written over a hundred books, articles and monographs on topics as varied as business history, culture, politics, ethics and travel.

Nick Tolhurst is Managing Director of the Institute for Corporate Culture Affairs (ICCA) which he joined in April 2004. Before joining ICCA, Nick Tolhurst worked for the British Foreign Ministry in Germany, advising British companies in Germany and German companies investing in the UK. Previously, Nick Tolhurst worked for the European Commission at DG II (Economics and Financial Affairs) preparing for the introduction of the Euro in differing cultures and economic systems. Nick Tolhurst studied at London Metropolitan University (UK) and completed a Masters' Degree at Osnabrück University (Germany) both in European Studies specialising in Economics and in Cultural Studies. His thesis dissertation was on the role of differing cultural and economic contexts with regard to the European Monetary Union process. Nick Tolhurst has written and edited publications on CSR, Corporate Culture, Sustainability and Economics including, most recently, the *ICCA Handbook on CSR*.

OTHER MEMBERS OF THE EDITORIAL BOARD

Katja Böhmer has been Project Manager at ICCA since 2004. She is editor of ICCA's CSR Globe – global database and communication platform for companies' CSR activities and is responsible for content management in ICCA's communications. Katja Böhmer studied international business at the accadis Bad Homburg Academy in Germany and at Northumbria University, Newcastle in the United Kingdom.

Aron Ghebremariam has been CSR project advisor at ICCA since 2005. Aron Ghebremariam received his MBA from the University of Natal in South Africa after obtaining his first degree at Asmara University in Eritrea where he also worked for two years as part of the academic staff. He is currently completing his on PhD at Frankfurt University, Faculty of Economics and Business Administration, focusing on Corporate Social Responsibility and business strategy.

Judith Hennigfeld is a Senior Advisor focusing on social and environmental sustainability issues in the area of international relations, a field in which she has worked for more than ten years in total. Her clients have included the United Nations, the European Commission and the German Technical Cooperation. From 2004 until the end of 2006 she was the Managing Director of the Institute for

Corporate Culture Affairs (ICCA). Previously she served for more than four years on the UN Development Programme in New York, where she was Programme Officer in the Bureau for Development Policy. From 1991 to 1993 Ms. Hennigfeld was a Fulbright scholar, graduating with an MSW from Hunter College, School of Social Work at the City University of New York. Judith Hennigfeld is co-editor of The *ICCA Handbook on Corporate Social Responsibility*, published in 2006 by Wiley.

Sandra Silvia Huble holds a degree in business administration from the Johann Wolfgang Goethe University, Frankfurt am Main, Germany. In 1992, Sandra Huble joined Deutsche Bank working in both the Private Wealth Management and Corporate Social Responsibility Departments. Between 2003 and 2005 she was Managing Director of the Konvent für Deutschland in Berlin.

LIST OF CONTRIBUTORS

Charles Ainger, PhD
Sustainable Development Director, Montgomery Watson Harza
(MWH) UK
Visiting Professor, Centre for Sustainable Development,
Department of Engineering, and Senior Associate, Cambridge
Programme for Industry, University of Cambridge, UK

Maritza Baca
Communications Director, Forum EMPRESA, Chile

Jane Batten
Business Support Team Manager, University of Cambridge
Programme for Industry, UK

Jem Bendell, PhD
Adjunct Associate Professor, Griffith Business School, Australia
Visiting Fellow, UN Research Institute for Social Development
(UNRISD), Geneva

David Ian Birch, DPhil
Professor, School of Communication and Creative Arts, and
Deputy Director, Corporate Citizenship Research Unit, Deakin
University, Australia

Mick Blowfield, DPhil
Director of Programme Development, University of Cambridge
Programme for Industry, UK
Associate Professor, University of Middlesex, UK

Jorge E. Reis Cajazeira, PhD
Chair, ISO 26000 Social Responsibility Working Group
Corporate Head of Competitiveness, Suzano Pulp and Paper,
Brazil

Jenny Cargill
Director, Business Map Investment Strategy Advisers, South Africa

Archie Carroll, PhD
Director, Nonprofit Management Program and Professor
Emeritus, Terry College of Business, University of Georgia, USA

Jonathan Cohen
Principal, Stakeholder Consulting, Washington DC, USA
Author, Business-Watch blog

Rebecca Collins
Executive Assistant, University of Cambridge Programme for
Industry, UK

Susan Cote–Freeman
Program Director, Transparency International Ltd

Polly Courtice
Director, University of Cambridge Programme for Industry, UK
Co-director, Prince of Wales's Business and the Environment
Programme, UK

Aron Cramer
President and CEO, Business for Social Responsibility (BSR),
USA, Europe and China

Andrew Crane, PhD
George R. Gardiner Professor of Business Ethics, Schulich School
of Business, York University, Canada

Bruce Davidson
Partner, ERM, UK

Theo de Bruijn, PhD
Senior Researcher, Center for Clean Technology and
Environmental Policy, University of Twente, The Netherlands
Coordinator, Greening of Industry Network Europe

Duncan Duke
Center for Sustainable Global Enterprise, Johnson Graduate
School of Management, Cornell University, USA

Dermot Egan
Research and Knowledge Manager, Business Taskforce on
Sustainable Consumption and Production, University of
Cambridge Programme for Industry, UK

John Elkington
Founder and Chief Entrepreneur, SustainAbility, UK

Ruth Findlay-Brooks
Programme Manager, Postgraduate Certificate in Cross-Sector
Partnerships, University of Cambridge Programme for Industry,
UK
Associate Lecturer, Open University, UK

R. Edward Freeman, PhD
Elis and Signe Olsson Professor of Business Administration, and
Director of the Olsson Center for Applied Ethics, Darden School
of Business, University of Virginia, USA

Aron Ghebremariam
Project Adviser, Institute for Corporate Culture Affairs (ICCA),
Germany

Kate Grosser
Researcher, CSR and Gender Project, International Centre for Corporate Social Responsibility (ICCSR), Nottingham University, UK

Lars H. Gulbrandsen
Senior Research Fellow, The Fridtjof Nansen Institute, Norway

Stirling Habbitts
Vice President: Emissions Products, ING Wholesale Banking, The Netherlands

David Halley
Head of International Partnerships, Business in the Community, UK

Stuart L. Hart, PhD
S.C. Johnson Chair in Sustainable Global Enterprise, and Professor of Management, Johnson Graduate School of Management, Cornell University, USA

Axel Haunschild, PhD
Professor of Human Resource Management, University of Trier, Germany Guest Professor, Royal Holloway, University of London, UK

Andreas Hermann, LLM
Scientist, Environmental Law and Governance Division, Öko-Institut e.V. (Institute for Applied Ecology), Germany

Kai Hockerts, PhD
Associate Professor, Department of Intercultural Communication and Management, Copenhagen Business School, Denmark

Kara Hartnett Hurst
Managing Director: Advisory Services, Business for Social Responsibility (BSR), USA

Jennifer Iansen-Rogers
Senior Manager, KPMG Global Sustainability Services,
The Netherlands
Non-executive Director, AccountAbility, UK

Paula Ivey
Founder, The CSR Group, UK

Matt Jeschke
Director, Energy and Extractives, Business for Social
Responsibility (BSR), USA

Aled Jones, PhD
Director, Climate Leadership Programme, University of
Cambridge Programme for Industry, UK

Paul Kapelus
CEO, African Institute of Corporate Citizenship (AICC), South
Africa

Mervyn King
Chairman, King Committee on Corporate Governance in South
Africa, South Africa
Chairman, Global Reporting Initiative, The Netherlands
Professor Extraordinaire, Centre for Corporate Citizenship,
University of South Africa (UNISA), South Africa

Debbie Kobak
Market Strategist, Mission Based Deposits, ShoreBank, USA

Philip Kotler, PhD
S.C. Johnson & Son Distinguished Professor of International
Marketing, Kellogg School of Management, Northwestern
University, USA

Peter Lacy
Executive Director
European Academy of Business in Society

Harriet Lamb, CBE
Executive Director, Fairtrade Foundation, UK

Melissa Lane, PhD
Senior Lecturer, Faculty of History, Cambridge University, UK
Doctoral Fellow in Philosophy, King's College, Cambridge, UK

Kelly Lavelle
Programme Manager: Alumni Services, University of Cambridge
Programme for Industry, UK

Zoe Lees, PhD
Strategic Adviser – Sustainable Development, South Africa

Margaret Legum
Chairperson, South African New Economics Foundation (SANE),
South Africa

Deborah Leipziger
Managing Director, The Anders & Winst Company,
The Netherlands
Director, Stichting Social Accountability International, USA

Klaus M. Leisinger, PhD
President and CEO, Novartis Foundation for Sustainable
Development, Switzerland
Professor for Development Sociology, University of Basel,
Switzerland

Mark Line
Director, csrnetwork, UK

Hunter Lovins
President and Co-founder, Natural Capitalism Inc., USA

Steve Lydenberg
Chief Investment Officer, Domini Social Investments LLC, USA

Antoine Mach
Co-founder and Director, Covalence, Switzerland

Daniel Malan
Associate Director, KPMG Sustainability Services, South Africa
Senior Lecturer in Ethics and Governance, University of
Stellenbosch Business School, South Africa

Petrus Marais, Adv
Managing Director, KPMG Forensic Africa, South Africa

Dirk Matten, PhD
Hewlett-Packard Chair in Corporate Social Responsibility,
Schulich School of Business, York University, Canada

Malcolm McIntosh, PhD
Professor of Human Security, and Director of the Applied
Research Centre in Human Security (ARCH), Futures Institute,
Faculty of Business, Environment and Society, Coventry
University, UK

Mark B. Milstein
Center for Sustainable Global Enterprise, Johnson Graduate
School of Management, Cornell University, USA

Anupama Mohan, PhD
Belgacom Fellow in CSR, Solvay Business School, Belgium
Independent consultant and researcher in corporate responsibility
and sustainability, UK

George Molenkamp, PhD
Chairman, KPMG Global Sustainability Services, The Netherlands
Special Professor of Business Studies, Economics Faculty,
University of Amsterdam, The Netherlands

Johann Möller
Ferret Mining & Environmental Services, South Africa
Former Head of Certification Services, KPMG Sustainability
Services, South Africa

Valli Moosa
President, The World Conservation Union (IUCN), Switzerland
Former Minister of Environmental Affairs and Tourism, South
Africa

David F. Murphy, PhD
Senior Associate, Development Cooperation Resident
Coordinator System Learning Support, United Nations System
Staff College
Tutor, Post-graduate Certificate Programme in Cross-sector
Partnerships, University of Cambridge Programme for Industry,
UK

Judy N. Muthuri
Doctoral Researcher, International Centre for Corporate Social
Responsibility (ICCSR), Nottingham University Business School,
UK

Jane Nelson
Director, Corporate Social Responsibility Initiative (CSRI) and
Senior Fellow, Kennedy School of Government, Harvard
University, USA
Director, Business Leadership and Strategy, the Prince of Wales
International Business Leaders Forum (IBLF), UK

Karsten Neuhoff, PhD
Senior Research Associate, Faculty of Economics, University of
Cambridge, UK

Jan Noterdaeme
Senior Director, EU and Stakeholder Relations, on behalf of CSR
Europe, Belgium Maître de Conférence:
Université Catholique de Louvair, Belgium

David Nussbaum
Chief Executive, WWF-UK, UK
Formerly Chief Executive, Transparency International, Germany

David Owen
Professor of Social and Environmental Accounting, International Centre for Corporate Social Responsibility (ICCSR), Nottingham University Business School, UK

John Owen
Corporate Secretary, International Accreditation Forum (IAF), USA

Bidhan Parmar
Doctoral Candidate in Business Ethics, Entrepreneurship and Strategy, Darden School of Business, University of Virginia, USA

Ken Peattie
Professor of Marketing and Strategy, and Director of BRASS (Centre for Business Relationships, Accountability, Sustainability and Society), Cardiff University, UK

Manfred Pohl, PhD
Founder and CEO, Institute for Corporate Culture Affairs (ICCA), Germany

Chris Pomfret
Board Member of Food Standards Agency, UK
Senior Associate, University of Cambridge Programme for Industry

Jonathon Porritt, CBE
Founder Director, Forum for the Future, UK
Chairman, UK Sustainable Development Commission (SDC), UK

Scott J. Reynolds, PhD
Assistant Professor of Business Ethics and Helen Moore Gerhardt Faculty Fellow, University of Washington Business School, USA

Klaus Richter
Coordination CSR and Sustainability, Volkswagen Group, Germany

The Honorable Mary Robinson
Founder and President, Realizing Rights: The Ethical
Globalization Initiative, USA
Former United Nations High Commissioner for Human Rights
and Former President of Ireland

Dick Robson
Former Director, Sustainable Development and Responsible Care,
European Chemical Industry Council, Belgium

Catherine Rubbens
Director, Products and Services, CSR Europe, Belgium

John Sabapathy
Senior Associate, AccountAbility, UK
Editor, Accountability Forum, UK

Andreas Georg Scherer
Chair of Foundations of Business Administration and Theories of
the Firm, and Head of the Institute of Organization and
Administrative Science, University of Zurich, Switzerland

Katharina Schmitt
Scientist, Environmental Law and Governance Division,
Öko-Institut e.V. (Institute for Applied Ecology), Germany

Jan Aart Scholte, PhD
Professor in the Department of Politics and International Studies
and Co-director, Centre for the Study of Globalisation and
Regionalisation, University of Warwick, UK

Maria Sillanpää
Director, SMART Company
Former Managing Director, AccountAbility, UK

Erik Simanis
Co-director, Base of the Pyramid Protocol, and Senior Research
Associate, Center for Sustainable Global Enterprise, Johnson
Graduate School of Management, Cornell University, USA

Timothy Smith
Senior Vice President, Walden Asset Management, USA
Chair, Social Investment Forum, USA

Telita Snyckers
Senior Manager, South African Revenue Service, South Africa

Laura J. Spence, PhD
Reader in Business Ethics and Member of BRESE (Brunel
Research in Enterprise, Innovation, Sustainability and Ethics),
Brunel University West London, UK

Björn Stigson
President, World Business Council for Sustainable Development
(WBCSD), Switzerland

Satish Sule, PhD, LLM
Case Handler, European Commission, DG Competition, Belgium

John E. Tedstrom, PhD
Executive Director, Global Business Coalition on HIV/AIDS,
Tuberculosis and Malaria (GBC), USA

Nick Tolhurst
Managing Director, Institute for Corporate Culture Affairs
(ICCA), Germany

Hugo Vergara
Executive Director, Forum EMPRESA, Chile

Wayne Visser, PhD
Research Director, University of Cambridge Programme for
Industry, UK

Sheila von Rimscha
Programme Manager, CHRONOS E-learning, University of
Cambridge Programme for Industry, UK

Halina Ward
Director, Business and Sustainable Development Programme, Sustainable Markets Group, International Institute for Environment and Development (IIED), UK

Nicki Websper
Associate Marketing Consultant, csrnetwork, UK

Richard Welford, PhD
Co-founder and Director, CSR Asia, China (Hong Kong)
Professor, University of Hong Kong, China (Hong Kong)

Peter Wilkinson
Project Adviser, Transparency International, Secretariat Business Principles for Countering Bribery, Germany

Emma Wilson
Senior Researcher, Business and Sustainable Development Programme, Sustainable Markets Group, International Institute for Environment and Development, UK

Franziska Wolff
Research Fellow, Environmental Law and Governance Division, Öko-Institut e.V. (Institute for Applied Ecology), Germany

Donna Wood, PhD
David Wilson Chair of Business Ethics and Professor of Management, Philosophy and Religion, University of Northern Iowa, USA

Stephen B. Young
Global Executive Director, Caux Round Table, USA

Betsy Zeidman
Research Fellow and Director, Center for Emerging Domestic Markets, Milken Institute, USA

CONTENTS OF THE A TO Z

THE A TO Z

3Rs
→ Recycling, Waste management

AA 1000 SERIES OF STANDARDS ON ACCOUNTABILITY
→ Accountability
🖰 www.accountability21.net

The AA 1000 Series are principles-based standards offering a non-proprietary, open-source series of standards applicable to all organisations, covering the full range of an organisation's sustainability performance and reporting. The AA 1000 Series is comprised of:

- AA 1000 Purpose and Principles (under development)
- AA 1000 Framework for Integration (under development)
- AA 1000 Assurance Standard
- AA 1000 Stakeholder Engagement Standard

In 1999 the London-based AccountAbility published the first document in the series, the AA 1000 Framework. This included sections on purpose and principles, framework for integration, → assurance and stakeholder engagement. After its publication the decision was made to publish revisions of these sections as individual standards. These four standards now make up the AA 1000 Series. As each standard in the Series is published, it replaces the information in the original Framework on that topic. When all four standards have been developed, the Framework will be withdrawn.

AA 1000 Framework – the AA 1000 Framework was developed to help organisations build their social responsibility and → accountability through high quality accounting, → auditing and reporting. It is driven by inclusivity and requires organisations to integrate stakeholder engagement processes into their core management activities.

The Framework provides guidance on how to establish a systematic stakeholder engagement process that generates the indicators, targets, and reporting systems needed to ensure greater → transparency, effective responsiveness to stakeholders and improved overall organisational performance.

AA 1000 Assurance Standard (AA 1000AS) – following an extensive international consultation process and drawing on the practical experience and perspectives of the business, public and civil society sectors, the AA 1000AS was launched in 2003. It is the first → assurance standard that covers the full range of an organisation's sustainability performance. It has been designed to complement the → Global Reporting Initiative's Sustainability Reporting Guidelines and other standardised approaches.

The standard addresses the need for an approach that effectively deals with the qualitative as well as quantitative data that reflects sustainability performance together with the systems and competencies that underpin reported data and organisational performance.

The AA 1000AS is based on assessment of reports against three principles:

- Materiality – does the sustainability report provide an account covering all the areas of performance that stakeholders need to judge the organisation's sustainability performance?

- Completeness – is the information complete and accurate enough to assess and understand the organisation's performance in all these areas?
- Responsiveness – has the organisation responded coherently and consistently to stakeholders' concerns and interests?

In addition to the above principles, AA 1000AS covers the essential elements of a public → assurance statement, and the independence, impartiality and competency requirements for → assurance providers.

The AA 1000 Stakeholder Engagement Standard (AA 1000SES) – the stakeholder engagement standard, launched in 2003 as an exposure draft, is a generally applicable framework for improving the quality of the design, implementation, assessment, communication and → assurance of stakeholder engagement. It is based on the same three principles as AA 1000AS.

The AA 1000SES is applicable to the full range of engagements, including functional (e.g. customer care), issue-based (e.g. → human rights), and organisation-wide engagements (e.g. reporting and → assurance).

The AA 1000SES is designed for all those initiating, participating in, observing, assessing, assuring or otherwise communicating about stakeholder engagement. It aims to enable, among other things:

- Organisations to design and implement stakeholder engagement in accordance with clear principles and criteria and inform stakeholders of their approach.
- Stakeholders to identify, assess and comment on the quality of an engagement using clear principles and associated criteria.
- → Assurance practitioners to assess and comment on the quality of stakeholder engagement, both in its own right and as a means of assessing an organisation's determination of what is material, how it manages and understands material issues, and how it responds to stakeholder expectations.

The AA 1000SES complements AA 1000AS, and is also intended to complement other standards in which stakeholder engagement is an important element, such as those covering reporting, → assurance and governance, as well as issue-specific standards on, for example, labour, → human rights and → corruption (e.g. → Global Reporting Initiative Sustainability Reporting Guidelines, ISO standards, SA 8000, IAASB standards and → ISEAL member standards).

AA 1000PP Purpose and Principles (under development) – this standard will address the need for a systematic, legitimate approach to → accountability and the role for standards. It will explain AccountAbility's principles-based approach and defines the principles of inclusivity, materiality, completeness and responsiveness as they apply to the Series as a whole.

AA 1000FI Framework for Integration (under development) – this standard will address the need for organisations to integrate their non-financial → accountability practices into their core management processes. It will provide guidance on systems and processes and links the AA 1000 Series to other key standards.

Maria Sillanpää

ACCOUNTABILITY

Accountability is a concept in ethics with several meanings, often used synonymously with such concepts as answerability, responsibility, liability and other terms associated with the expectation of account-giving. AccountAbility has defined the term as having three dimensions: first, 'compliance', which implies the compliance with rules, norms, regulations etc. agreed or applicable between the agent to whom certain responsibilities or power has been assigned; second, '→ transparency', which implies account-giving by the agent to the applicable principle(s); and third, 'responsiveness', which implies the agent's willingness and ability to respond to legitimate expectations and rights of the principle(s).

As an aspect of governance, accountability, or its lack, has, especially during the last two decades, risen to be one of the central debating points in the political, civil society and corporate arenas.

Concerning corporations, the classic text exploring accountability was written by A. Bearle and G. Means in 1933. Their article 'Traditional Theory and the New Concept of the Corporation' is one of the first explorations of corporations as a dominant institution of our modern world and how the depersonalisation of corporate ownership and the emergence of professional management should affect our thinking and practices on who is accountable to whom, on what and how. Bearle and Means, as well as many others who followed suit, were deeply concerned about how the emerging powerful corporate machines of their day could be controlled as societal players – in essence they saw accountability as a tool for civilising power whether political or corporate. Their thinking has fundamentally influenced our notions, codes and laws concerning → corporate governance. However, now these prevailing notions of → corporate governance and the related accountabilities they assign to corporate directors as stewards of their shareholders' capital interests are seen as seriously wanting in the eyes of many – especially in the eyes of those wishing to revitalise our democratic processes, those advocating → sustainable development and those calling for increased → corporate social responsibility.

Focusing mostly on the attack on traditional notions of accountability by corporate social responsibility and → sustainable development advocates, we can outline two interrelated arguments why new definitions, or innovations, of accountability are needed.

First, the power and influence of today's business is such that it appears increasingly challenging to hold large corporates to account even on their currently defined legal and fiduciary responsibilities. Witness the recent spectacular → corporate governance scandals from the Enrons in the US, to the Parlamats in → Europe and Hyundais of Korea among many others and the repulsion felt internationally (especially by those pension fund members that many of these scandals have left with an impoverished old age) following the realisation that very few corporate officials have been held to account for blatant failures in basic compliance or stewardship responsibilities.

→ Globalisation has tremendously amplified corporate power – shrinking the state and making the global corporation arguably the most powerful of our modern institutions (according to the World Bank, 95 of the world's 150 largest economic entities are corporations) and increased its sway in public policy and law making. Businesses now have a profound impact on elected governments, but are accountable, beyond being obliged to comply with the laws of the countries in which they operate, only to their shareholders. This, according to critics, is intolerable and has been one of the key causes leading to the birth of the corporate social responsibility movement holding big business to account in the courts of public opinion, seeking to put pressure and shame on those perceived not to behave according to agreed norms of lawfulness or basic tenets of governance and accountability.

The second concern about the current state of accountability goes beyond the one discussed above in that its advocates don't see the solution lying in 'more compliance' with existing rules, but calls for a reinvention and renegotiation of existing accountability boundaries. This faction sees our world full of accountability gaps – issues of global, national and local challenges and concern that no one appears to be responsible for and therefore no one can be held to account for their proper management or otherwise. Some of the arguments here are based on the familiar notion of '→ externalities' – the inability of the market system to account for vast areas of corporate impact and behaviour on society and the planet. Other arguments emphasise the factually different nature of our global order compared to the pre-globalised world where sovereign states still had the power to control pre-globalised businesses. In the new reality corporate power is not only greater, but is exercised differently across national, legislative and sectoral boundaries. The barriers between the old Newtonian societal 'atoms' – independent and autonomous – have disappeared and the boundaries between what is public, private or societal are becoming increasingly blurred. As power is being exercised differently, the argument goes, our understanding of accountability needs to be redefined.

Both would call for an expanded basis on which companies are held to account – from shareholder to a pluralistic stakeholder model that would vastly expand directors' duties from being solely the stewards of the capital interests of owners.

As one of the solutions, both of these groups have vigorously argued for expanded corporate → transparency, arguing that the current corporate obligation to render an account only on its financial performance and only to the owners of capital is vastly inadequate and so the concept and practice of CSR and sustainability reporting (→ non-financial reporting) was born.

Another key demand advanced by both is the call for greater inclusivity in corporate decision-making – the right of those affected by corporate impacts and behaviour to be heard and the related obligation of business to respond to legitimate concerns. The concept of stakeholder engagement surfaced in the mid-1990s as a proposed process for greater inclusivity. The early advocates of stakeholder engagement first struggled to get their messages across, but the practice has now spawned into a veritable industry with its consultants, think-tanks, manuals etc. Try Google and you get just under 4 million 'hits' on stakeholder engagement.

Going further, the calls for inclusivity have more recently translated into calls for business not only to accept expanded accountabilities for their own, micro-level behaviour and impacts but also to proactively play its part in finding positive solutions to pressing global issues such as poverty, → climate change, health, female → empowerment etc. This has caused cries of protest in some corporate and political quarters wishing to hark back to the

Friedmannian world of 'business of business being business', but on the other hand has successfully been embraced by some pioneering companies as a new source of → competitive advantage and societal legitimacy – a space for 'win–win' outcomes and a contributor to a more sustainable future where a company can also better ensure its own longevity.

Accountability as a performance driver – what we are witnessing is a shift from static notions of accountability as a function of compliance with institutionalised norms, standards and laws (including those that define common sets of financial performance indicators for companies to render an account on) agreed somewhere 'outside' corporate entities to a more dynamic understanding of accountability as a phenomenon that requires constant renegotiation between societal actors as well as businesses and their stakeholders – in effect, a social contract that is constantly being rewritten as new issues and challenges appear on our societal or stakeholder radars. In this world, the assessment of how accountable any given company is will be based on stakeholder perceptions first on the company's openness to the renegotiation process itself and second on the quality of their response to the concerns and expectations raised.

A small but growing number of companies have accepted this and would now see accountability – and the processes of discovering new societal accountability expectations – as a driver of performance, not as a necessary evil to be complied with and costed in as governance expenditure. The discovery process is bringing in new ways of corporate → learning, mostly via stakeholder engagement, and leading to unexpected new sources of innovation. These companies seek to belong to new ecosystems, forcing cross-sectoral partnerships and multi-stakeholder initiatives that are co-creating new tools and definitions of accountability and in that process finding new ways of creating value.

New tools for the trade – our corporate accountability definitions and practices are gradually changing to reflect the new realities. During the last 10 years or so, we have witnessed a veritable maelstrom of new standards, codes and guidelines being proposed as new islands of clarity in the murky waters of accountability. They seek to propose new ways of operationalising expanded stakeholder rights and/or company obligations.

Perhaps not surprisingly, considering that one of the corner-stones of accountability has always involved the expectation of 'account-giving' as a way of discharging accountability, one of the first significant innovations emerging from the 'new wave' accountability movement has focused on reporting. The → Global Reporting Initiative has sought to become the hub for 'sustain-ability reporting (→ non-financial reporting)' and its design process (to which some 1000 companies subscribe at the last count) is based on multi-stakeholder dialogue, a collaboratively governed conversation between representatives from business, accountancy, investment, environmental, → human rights, research and labour organisations from around the world to produce the 'sustainabil-ity reporting guidelines'. The third generation guidelines were introduced in October 2006 and welcomed as the definitive set of globally applicable measures relevant to the majority of companies.

Sustainability reporting (→ non-financial reporting) – driven by voluntary initiatives – has leaders and laggards. Companies such as Nike, McDonald's, Gap, Novo Nordisk and Shell, all of which have felt both the pain of external attacks as well as the inspiration of visionary → leadership, have forged ahead in making their busi-ness practices transparent and responsive to their stakeholders. But this, by no means, applies across the corporate spectrum, leaving good quality sustainability reporting (→ non-financial reporting) still a playground for the few. Many have concluded from this that voluntary initiatives will never deliver the goods of increased cor-porate → transparency – it needs to be mandated and enforced by governments.

If the → Global Reporting Initiative is the trailblazing tip of the CSR and sustainability standards iceberg, then AA 1000 Series is perhaps the definitive standard designed to sort out what lies beneath the surface – the management systems, processes and competencies required for accountable and inclusive organisational management and credible reporting. AccountAbility's AA 1000 Series with its current standards modules on sustainability → assurance (AA 1000AS) and stakeholder engagement (AA 1000SES) has been in development since 1999 and currently offers the only internationally applicable open-source, non-proprietary standards for assuring the quality and accuracy of sustainability reports and for engaging with stakeholders to determine what really is important, or material, to an organisation's stakeholders about the company's sustainability performance and where it wishes to draw its accountability boundaries. Like the → Global Reporting Initiative, the design process behind the Series is based on multi-stakeholder dialogue.

Trading accountability – advancing responsible practices and adopting wider accountabilities does not come easy to individual leaders regardless of their wish to adopt and comply with new forms of what might be called '→ civil regulation'. Fickle consumers and investors obsessed with quarterly returns and their own incentive schemes often fail to reward, and have the power to penalise, companies for doing the right thing. As AccountAbility's → Responsible Competitiveness work has highlighted, markets and free riders can undermine responsible first movers requiring systemic innovations and public policy interventions to advance market-based, social and environmental and long-term financial accountability. Standards matter, but on their own are only a part of the solution – without public policy support from governments, which enables responsible behaviour and penalises the reverse, the playing field will never be level.

Innovating accountability – beyond the standards discussed above there is a myriad of diverse initiatives working to advance new forms of corporate accountability or, indeed, shaming those whose accountability practices are perceived wanting. However, what tends to characterise these initiatives of the nascent accountability movement, in a similar way as we have seen in the sustainability movement of the last 30 years or so, is its tendency to focus on narrowly compartmentalised issues or targets. AccountAbility's conference in 2005 on 'reinventing accountability for the 21st century' concluded that the accountability innovations that we so desperately need not only to ensure our survival but to advance our progress are unlikely to come from those institutions that moulded and stewarded today's approaches to accountability, whether in and for government, business or individual citizens, but will be rooted in today's experimentation in collaborative governance, peer-to-peer networks and new forms of → civil regulation crossing sovereign, cultural and sectoral boundaries. Cross-fertilisation of ideas is urgently needed – and some of the lessons for how to go about this come from the winning multi-stakeholder initiatives and partnerships now operating under the banner of CSR and sustainability.

Maria Sillanpää

ACCOUNTABILITY
→ AA 1000 Series of Standards

ACCOUNTING
→ Social and environmental accounting

ACCREDITATION
→ Certification

ACTIVISM
→ Anti-globalisation, Non-governmental organisations (NGOs), Shareholder activism, Stakeholder theory

The term activism is often used to describe political activities outside the regular political system. These activities address controversial political or social issues and attempt to bring about political or social change by creating public awareness and political pressure to change conditions. Activism establishes a new form of sub-politics, often driven by social movements, civil society groups or non-governmental organisations, outside the official political system. There are various forms of activism such as civil disobedience, strikes, protest marches, political campaigning, → lobbying, media and internet activism, boycotts and disinvestments. Activism often addresses actors and institutions within the official political system (e.g. politicians, nation state governments, international govern-mental organisations) in order to make use of the political steering capacity of official institutions to bring about social change. The activists, for example, lobby for the passing of new laws or stricter regulations or demand official action to address → human rights abuses, social miseries, or environmental problems. Today, activism also targets the economic system and its main protagonists directly, i.e. the corporations and their managers. Both activists and corporate managers have become aware that even powerful companies will be very vulnerable if activists successfully communicate their case to a wider public or the relevant consumers (see, for example, the famous Brent Spar case of Royal Dutch Shell). As a consequence, many companies have started to directly communicate with stake-holder groups in order to address issues of public concern before anti-corporate activism emerges.

Andreas Georg Scherer

ADVERTISING
→ Marketing ethics

AFFIRMATIVE ACTION
→ Diversity

AFRICA

→ African Institute for Corporate Citizenship (AICC)

Companies have a long history of being deeply involved in the lives of African communities, dating back to the early days of the Dutch East India Company and other colonial era companies. Business impacts have been both positive and negative. For example, the massive mining industries that spawned the city of Johannesburg illustrate both the economic benefits of business investment and the social and environmental costs, while the role of companies operating under dictatorships or regimes such as apartheid raise many ethical dilemmas.

The governance role of business in Africa is also highly contested in the CSR debate. For example, historically, many companies in the extractive, forestry and agricultural industries in Africa have taken on the roles of government, such as provision of health services, → water, sanitation, roads, → telecommunications, power supply and housing. On the one hand, these can be seen as examples of good corporate social investment, but there are clearly issues of dependence when towns in Africa become *de facto* company towns.

In addition to community investment, key CSR issues in Africa include:

- Working conditions – in many countries, new legislation has improved the working conditions of employees and the role of the International Labour Organisation has been paramount in these efforts.
- → Human rights – issues around → child labour, especially on farms, remain a concern, as do dilemmas involving child-headed households in countries with a high incidence of HIV and AIDS.
- → Health and safety – in sectors such as mining, there are still high numbers of fatalities and incidences of lung infections. → HIV/AIDS and malaria are also a top priority for companies due to their devastating human and economic cost.

Other CSR issues which are important but often get less attention are:

- Community poverty;
- Lack of trust in companies;
- Environmental impacts, → conservation and land rehabilitation;
- Corrupt business practices;
- → Water usage and impacts on scarcity; and
- → Climate change and → biodiversity impacts.

In the face of these issues, African CSR practices have been influenced by various factors:

- The Western CSR and ethical consumerism movements that have promoted a → business case for CSR in Africa.
- The work of the United Nations, including the World Summit on Sustainable Development and the → UN Global Compact, which have been an important catalyst for many initiatives in Africa.
- The African Union, which provides for a focus on → corporate governance and CSR through the New Partnership for Africa's Development (NEPAD) African Peer Review Mechanism.
- The growing importance of foreign direct investment and the CSR policies of multinational companies, as well as global principles like the OECD Guidelines for Multinationals.
- The rise of the international NGO movement focusing on the ethical practices of companies in Africa, including ongoing challenges to companies on → human rights, → corruption, governance and environmental impacts.
- The increase in multilateral interest in social and environmental impacts, including by the World Bank and International Finance Corporation.
- The growing importance of indigenous CSR-related initiatives such as Black Economic Empowerment (→ empowerment) or affirmative action.

- The supply chain → codes of conduct, → fair trade initiatives and related instruments such as the SA 8000, driven largely by concerned Western consumers.
- And the small but growing driver of Socially Responsible Investment (SRI) funds.

Despite this increasing attention paid to CSR in Africa, it has still had a limited impact on the marketplace. The types of products and services that could help solve Africa's → sustainable development challenges are seldom given a high priority. Nevertheless, a few examples highlight the potential for the market to be an important driver for CSR, including: the accessible pricing of medicines for diseases such as → HIV/AIDS, malaria and drug-resistant TB; the massive uptake of mobile telephony and the positive impact it can have on the → digital divide; and innovative → banking products for the poor. It is critical that these and other kinds of CSR opportunities are taken up, in collaboration with the government and NGO sectors, to promote effective solutions to Africa's social, ethical and environmental challenges.

Paul Kapelus

AFRICAN INSTITUTE FOR CORPORATE CITIZENSHIP (AICC)
→ Africa
🖰 www.aiccafrica.org

The African Institute of Corporate Citizenship (AICC) is a non-governmental organisation committed to being a centre of excellence in promoting the role of business in building sustainable communities in → Africa.

AICC was established in 2001 to define the role of → corporate citizenship in → Africa's → development and to enhance African governments' and organisations' engagement at the international level. The AICC endeavours to unite business, government and civil society in the promotion of economic development initiatives that encompass social and environmental performance and the development of social enterprises in → Africa.

The AICC believes → development requires the evolution of responsible business practices and that solutions to → Africa's complex challenges can be achieved with the active involvement of the private sector through the promotion of → corporate citizenship in encouraging businesses to engage with society in a more substantial manner.

With offices in South Africa and Malawi, the organisation is involved with projects in a number of African countries working with partners and networks. The AICC is developing a collaboration platform to promote Pan-African dialogue on the role of business in society.

Paul Kapelus

AGENDA 21

→ Rio Declaration on Environment and Development, Sustainable
  development

⌨ www.unep.org

Agenda 21 is the programme of commitments on → sustainable development adopted by almost all of the world's nation states at the United Nations Conference on Environment and Development in Rio de Janeiro in 1992. According to UNEP, Agenda 21 represents a 'global consensus and political commitment at the highest level on → development and environment cooperation'. Its successful implementation is first and foremost the responsibility of governments, through the adoption of national strategies, plans, policies and processes. However, international cooperation, public participation, and involvement of NGOs and other international, regional and sub-regional organisations are also encouraged. Virtually all aspects of Agenda 21 are likely to impact on business and to be relevant to CSR practice. There are, however, also specific chapters in Agenda 21 on strengthening the role of workers, their trade unions, business, industry, the scientific and technological community, and farmers.

The programme areas that constitute Agenda 21 are described in terms of the basis for action, objectives, activities and means of implementation, and include the following: combating poverty; changing consumption patterns; demographic dynamics and sustainability; protection and promotion of human health; promoting sustainable human settlement development; integrating environment and → development in decision-making; protection of the atmosphere; an integrated approach to the planning and management of land resources; combating deforestation, desertification and drought; sustainable mountain development; promoting sustainable agriculture and rural development; → conservation of biological diversity; environmentally sound management of biotechnology; protection of the oceans and the rational use and development of their living resources; protection of the quality and supply of freshwater resources; environmentally sound management of → waste; global action for women towards sustainable and equitable development; children and youth in → sustainable development; recognising and strengthening the role of → indigenous people, their communities and non-governmental organisations; local authorities' initiatives in support of Agenda 21 (also called Local Agenda 21); strengthening the role of workers, their trade unions, business, industry, the scientific and technological community, and farmers; financial resources and mechanisms; transfer of environmentally sound → technology, cooperation and capacity-building; science for → sustainable development; promoting education, public awareness and training; national mechanisms and international cooperation for capacity-building; international institutional arrangements; international legal instruments and mechanisms; and information for decision-making.

AGRICULTURAL SECTOR
→ Food and beverage sector

AIDS
→ HIV/AIDS

AIR POLLUTION
→ Pollution

ANIMAL RIGHTS
→ Animal welfare

ANIMAL TESTING
→ Animal welfare

ANIMAL WELFARE
→ Personal and household goods sector, Pharmaceutical sector

Animal welfare is concerned with minimizing or avoiding suffering for animals while being subject to human care. There are various religious, philosophical or cultural ways of justifiying a concern for animal welfare. An influential voice in the debate is the philosopher Peter Singer who considers an animal's capacity for experiencing suffering as the starting point of the debate and subsequently suggests a human responsibility to reduce and at best avoid causing suffering to animals on similar grounds as one would argue to avoid suffering of human beings. Animal welfare is a particular issue for the agricultural and → food industry, where concerns about the production, raising, transport and slaughter of animals are considered increasingly as CSR issues. Similarly, the cosmetics and pharmaceutical industry have faced questions about their use of animals for product development, most notably the legitimacy of the suffering this inflicts on animals. There are a number of activist groups concerned with animal welfare and in some countries, such as the UK, animal welfare is part of the legal framework for corporations.

Dirk Matten

ANTI-CAPITALISM
→ Anti-globalisation

ANTI-GLOBALISATION
→ Globalisation

Globalisation can be understood as the growing economic and social dependency and interconnectedness of regions. This process is the result of multilateral deliberate political decisions in the GATT and → World Trade Organisation (WTO) to break down trade barriers and to establish a free trade regime worldwide. These decisions are supported by economic theory and its assumption that under conditions of free trade and economic exchange in perfect markets social welfare can be enhanced. Consequently, in this view, market forces have to be set free while bureaucratic and regulative restrictions set by the state have to be limited. Thus the → globalisation process is accompanied by deregulation and liberalisation policies in many industries (e.g. telecommunication, public transport, public supply etc.) and is further intensified by lower costs in transportation and technological achievements in communication technologies.

Anti-globalisation, by contrast, is the rhetoric of the critics of → globalisation and emphasises the negative consequences of the → globalisation process, such as unequal access to resources and public goods, the unjust distribution of → globalisation gains, → externalities, → human rights abuses, social miseries, and environmental disasters. Anti-globalisation → activism can be observed in different forms, reaching from violent protests (such as at the WTO meetings in Seattle 1999 or the G8 summit in Genoa 1999), over spontaneous peaceful initiatives by activist groups (e.g. internet and media campaigning) to institutionalised forms such as NGOs (e.g. Human Rights Watch, Greenpeace) or political parties (e.g. the green parties in many countries) that try to push their concerns into the official political agenda in nation state or international governance. International organisations such as the UN, the ILO or the WTO have begun to create discourse arenas for dialogue with critics in order to focus on problems of public concern, to develop appropriate solutions, and to avoid the explosion of disguise in violent actions.

Next to official political institutions, multinational companies have been targeted by anti-globalisation critics as well. For example, → human rights groups argue that working conditions in the supplier factories in the emergent and → developing countries are like those of '→ sweatshops' and that there are repeated cases of → child labour in the third world. Regular reports are published on the internet by various → human rights organisations, for example Clean Clothes Campaign, Global Exchange, and Human Rights Watch. These organisations demand that the multinational companies ensure adherence to → human rights and the labour and social standards of the International Labour Organisation (ILO) in their own factories and in those of their suppliers. Other NGOs point to the environmental problems of → globalisation and the threats to the earth's ecosystem. They pressure multinational companies to comply with available environmental standards, to use resources in a sustainable way, and to stop destroying the natural environment.

On the theoretical and intellectual level there is a wide and intensive interdisciplinary discourse on the achievements and problems of → globalisation. The contributions range from more popular writings (e.g. Klein: 'No Logo') to scholarly elaborations on the consequences of → globalisation (e.g. Beck: 'What is Globalisation?', Stiglitz: 'Globalisation and its Discontents') and the possibility of new forms of governance (e.g. Habermas: 'The Post-National Constellation'). From these discussions a critical position on → globalisation has evolved which holds that rejuvenating political regimes would reduce the negative consequences of → globalisation. Critics of → globalisation believe that the market can only fulfil its function as a tool of coordination for society within a politically defined framework. This framework has to ensure that the economy does not serve any minority interests (such as the interests of financial investors or company owners) but rather prioritises the interests of global society as a whole – prosperity and social peace. The critical position on → globalisation holds that market and competition alone cannot create the conditions for social justice and welfare. A strong political power is necessary for this, a powerful institution where the framework of the economy is politically defined through dialogue and cooperation on many levels. National governments and the available international governmental institutions do not yet have the capacity to take care of global problems such as global warming, global poverty, → human rights abuses and others. Therefore, an active civil society is addressing these issues of public concern and is compensating for the lack of regulation capacity on a global level. In political theory these developments are analysed and a new theory of → global governance is emerging with special emphasis on the role of non-governmental actors and institutions such as civil society groups, social movements, NGOs, and multinational companies. The analysis of the anti-globalisation movement and its contribution to → global governance plays an important part in these new theoretical developments.

Andreas Georg Scherer

ANTI-SLAVERY INTERNATIONAL
→ Labour issues
🖰 www.antislavery.org

The London-based NGO Anti-Slavery International is one of the world's oldest international → human rights organisations. Its roots stretch back to 1787 when the first abolitionist society was formed. This broad-based society was at the forefront of the movements to abolish the slave trade (achieved in Britain in 1807) as well as slavery throughout the British colonies (achieved in 1833). Today, the organisation campaigns for the rights of people who work in modern forms of what Anti-Slavery International considers slavery: people who are forced to work; owned or controlled by an 'employer', usually through mental or physical abuse or threatened abuse; dehumanised, treated as a commodity or bought and sold as 'property'; are physically constrained or have restrictions placed on his/her freedom of movement. Key campaign issues include the enforcement of labour standards in → developing countries, the verification of fair and ethical trade labels and the issues of human trafficking, in particular in the context of the global sex industry.

APPAREL INDUSTRY PARTNERSHIP (AIP) CODE
→ Supply chain
⌐ www.itcilo.it

The Apparel Industry Partnership (AIP) Code represents one of the most important international steps to address the issue of labour standards and working conditions in the apparel industry. It is a voluntary standard which was developed under the leadership of the US Department of Labour during the Clinton administration and mainly targets and includes US companies. The AIP Code was launched in 1997 and is a code of conduct that individual companies voluntarily adopt and require their contractors to adopt. Main contents of the Code are:

- The prohibition of employing any persons under the age of 15 (unless permitted by the country of manufacture to be 14);
- Prohibitions against any worker abuse or harassment and → discrimination;

- The recognition and respect for workers' rights of freedom of association and collective bargaining;
- The requirement that employers pay at least the minimum or prevailing industry wage, whichever is higher, and provide mandated benefits;
- The requirement that workers are provided with a safe and healthy working environment;
- A cap on mandatory overtime to 12 hours per week and the regular working week of the country (or 48 hours, whichever is less); and requiring a day off in every seven day period; and
- The requirement that overtime be compensated for at the premium rate required in the country or at least equal to their regular hourly compensation.

An important element is that independent external monitors conduct independent reviews of participating company policies and practices; provide company employees and contractors' employees with secure communication channels to report concerns of non-compliance; make available audit production records and practices to ensure compliance; conduct employee interviews and site visits; and verify that the company is in compliance with its obligations and commitments under the Code.

It also includes an internal monitoring system that outlines the obligations each company will undertake to ensure that the Code is enforced in its facilities and its contractors' facilities both domestically and internationally.

ASIA
→ CSR Asia

In the Asia-Pacific context, it would be wrong to assume that all CSR practices are less developed than in the West. Nevertheless it is clear that many aspects of CSR are less well developed. These would certainly include the internal human resource and employment practices, policies on → diversity, environmental initiatives and local community engagement commonly seen in the West. However, Asia is increasingly the workshop of the world and is central to manufacturing of outsourced products for most of the world's large brands. Consistent with this, much of the attention for CSR is in examining the operations and activities of → supply chains in the region.

Many large firms have been subjected to accusations of running → sweatshops in Asia over the last two decades. Since this is hugely damaging to brands (particularly when they involve allegations about the use of → child labour) most have put in place sophisticated → codes of conduct relating to the conduct of factories from which they source and regularly inspect and audit those factories. Thus much of the emphasis for CSR in Asia has been on dealing with labour standards in factories, the accommodation provided for workers, appropriate training, proper wage payments being made to workers, → health and safety practices, the protection of the rights of migrant workers and dispute resolution.

Recently, it has become clear in the region that companies sourcing offshore have started to rationalise their supply chains. In part this is because of a wish to work with fewer, larger and more trusted suppliers to ensure better CSR practices based on shared → values rather than audit and inspection approaches.

For supply chains in Asia the biggest (but not the only) driver of CSR practices tends to be the big buyers who are keen to protect brands and reputations. This has led to one of the most common CSR practices being related to → codes of conduct and the implementation and checking of them through → auditing. However, → auditing and inspections are increasingly being seen as expensive and ineffective and many factories simply cheat to appear to be abiding by both → codes of conduct and the law. There is therefore a new emphasis on moving beyond such approaches and towards building relationships with suppliers based on shared → values, trust and the provision of consultancy services instead of inspections.

There are many examples of good CSR practices in the region that may even be absent in more developed economies. Examples include training and capacity-building initiatives among workers who have received little formal education, empowering women workers, promoting good practice in industry-wide factory initiatives, establishing factory cooperatives, developing multi-stakeholder initiatives, creating worker committees and promoting → human rights.

While international standards linked to CSR practices have a role to play in supply chains, an interesting recent development has been the establishment of home-grown social responsibility standards in Asia. It is perhaps in the debates surrounding → discrimination, freedom of association, employment practices, trade unions, collective action, dispute resolution, migrant workers, bonded labour and → child labour that we see the most activity.

Nevertheless, some CSR practices in Asia also extend to community investment, the → environment, → conservation and broader health initiatives. Stakeholder dialogue, reporting and disclosure, all central to CSR, are being seen as tools to be used by businesses but also by local authorities keen to promote better practices in the private sector. Increasing attention is also being paid to issues of → corporate governance.

Many good CSR practices are not achieved by businesses working alone, but with other businesses, civil society organisations and government. A number of tripartite partnerships in the region have been developed to promote good CSR practices in the future.

Despite there being clear benefits, in many countries progress on CSR has been slower than elsewhere. The main problems are associated with a lack of awareness of CSR issues and practices, costs of engagement, a lack of suitably trained and skilled human resources, inefficient management systems, competing → codes of conduct, an overemphasis on factory inspections, → corruption and poor procurement practices. There is a need for more training programmes, engagement and awareness-raising activities with civil society groups, demonstration projects, industry-wide stakeholder dialogues, good practice guides, and better links with business associations, NGO groups and government.

Richard Welford

ASSURANCE
→ Auditing, Report verification

Assurance is usually used to describe evaluation methods which are employed to assess the performance of an organisation and/or the quality of the organisation's communications on its performance, for example in → non-financial reporting in an 'assurance engagement'. It includes the communication of the results of the process to add credibility for users. It may also be used to refer to the outcome of this process in which users or stakeholders feel 'assured' and can therefore take decisions based on the information provided with confidence.

CSR means not only taking responsibility, but also being held accountable for the economic, environmental and social impacts of the organisation and communicating this to stakeholders. One way to achieve this is to provide credible information to stakeholders on how the organisation manages these impacts and ultimately performs over time. Organisations have developed different approaches to satisfy the need for relevant and reliable information from a variety of stakeholders such as investors, employees, consumers and regulators as well as management. Auditing, → certification and verification are some of the tools by which assurance is obtained. Stakeholder engagement can also provide assurance through dialogue and building trust.

CSR assurance may be provided by audit and advisory firms, → certification bodies, NGOs or recognised individual experts or opinion leaders. Their work may be governed by generic assurance standards such as the International Standard for Assurance

Engagements ($\rightarrow$ ISAE 3000) issued by the International Auditing and Assurance Standards Board of the International Federation of Accountants (IFAC) or specific assurance standards for CSR such as the $\rightarrow$ AA 1000 Assurance Standard.

Jennifer Iansen–Rogers and George Molenkamp

ATTAC
$\rightarrow$ Anti-globalisation
🖰 www.attac.org

ATTAC (Association for the Taxation of Financial Transactions for the Aid of Citizens) is one of the first NGOs set up against the backdrop of growing unrest about the undesired consequences of $\rightarrow$ globalisation in France in 1998. It is probably the most well-known player in the growing $\rightarrow$ anti-globalisation movement. It consists of a network of independent national and local groups in many countries all over the globe, and claims a membership of some 80 000 worldwide. The initial and main aim of the group was to promote the idea of an international tax on currency speculation ($\rightarrow$ Tobin tax), against the backdrop of the 1997 crisis in Asian financial markets and its detrimental effects on many $\rightarrow$ developing countries. ATTAC also campaigns on broader issues of perceived injustices of $\rightarrow$ globalisation such as to end tax havens, replace pension funds with state pensions, cancel Third World debt, or reform the insitutions that govern the global economy, such as the World Bank or the $\rightarrow$ World Trade Organisation.

AUDITING
$\rightarrow$ Environmental auditing, Social auditing, Report verification

An audit is an objective, systematic and documented process of collecting and evaluating evidence in relation to systems, information or behaviour against predetermined audit criteria.

The audit criteria may be determined by: independent standards (e.g. International Auditing and Assurance Standards Board standards for financial reporting); the organisation's internal policies, practices or controls; conventions, laws, regulations or codes of practice; the requirements of a recognised management system (e.g. → ISO 14001); and internal or external reporting guidelines.

Although → auditing has a long established meaning in relation to independently verifying the accuracy and completeness of financial accounting records, in the context of CSR the term is used to encompass many different types of audit by independent experts who are used to measuring and reporting on an organisation's sustainability impacts, policies, management systems or performance. These include → environmental auditing and social auditing as well as those relating to health, safety, economic, human resources or community aspects. In some cases the audit may be very specific, for example checking compliance with a specific law or regulation (compliance audit), confirming the reliability of data for greenhouse gas emissions in relation to → emission trading or establishing the energy use of a building or installation in the context of → energy management. The term audit is also used in relation to the verification by independent experts of the information published by an organisation on its CSR performance, usually in the form of a printed or web-based non-financial report. It is designed to test the reliability (accuracy and completeness) of management assertions in the report.

Certain types of CSR audit are governed by generally accepted → auditing standards, for example those directed at report verification such as the International Auditing and Assurance Standards Board → ISAE 3000 Standard for Assurance Engagements as used by accounting firms, or those designed for management systems audits such as ISO 19011:2002 Guidelines for Quality and/or Environmental Management Systems Auditing. The standards are designed to ensure the independence and professional competency of the audit firm, audit team or individual auditor, and a standard approach, set of procedures and report in line with the → auditing standard adopted.

During an audit the auditor needs to obtain sufficient reliable and relevant evidence to achieve the audit objectives. An audit programme is therefore designed to gather different types of (audit) evidence:

- Physical (direct observation of materials and equipment, buildings and installations, attitudes and behaviour);
- Documentary (printed outputs such as internal reports, minutes of meetings, policy statements, business plans, or procedures, invoices, or publicly available materials);
- Testimonial (interviews/representations with internal/external parties); and
- Analytical (relational, e.g. energy use or production and emission data).

CSR systems audits and information audits are, in general, able to rely largely on documentary, physical and analytical evidence. Audits of behaviour, for example whether managers observe → discrimination policies when recruiting new staff, tend to require a larger degree of corroborative testimonial evidence.

The evidence collected during an audit should fulfil certain quality criteria:

- Origination (from appropriate, credible and reliable sources);
- Authenticity (based on or approved by the source);
- Not subject to bias (from a suitably 'independent source' or, if not, corroborated from other sources);
- Current (timely in relation to the subject); and
- Relevant (complete, consistent, balanced).

The audit evidence, findings, and the analysis and interpretation of these, must be documented and support the final conclusions. All audits require a lesser or greater degree of professional judgement and scepticism on the part of the auditor.

An audit may be undertaken by the organisation itself (internal audit) or by an external team of specialists (external audit). In both cases the audit team should be independent of the operations being audited. An internal audit is usually designed to improve an organisation's operations through a systematic evaluation of its risk management, control and governance processes. The report of the audit team is aimed at management and is not made public. An external independent audit usually results in reporting the main conclusions to a third party, for example in a verification statement or assurance report for stakeholders (report verification), or a certificate (e.g. → ISO 14001) directed at customers and clients. In both these cases the auditors normally prepare a separate report to management documenting findings and identifying weaknesses and opportunities for performance improvement.

Jennifer Iansen-Rogers and George Molenkamp

AUSTRALIA

For a number of years it was proposed that Australia is/was anywhere between 10 and 20 years behind the major European and American CSR initiatives. While this may well have served some journalistic conceits (and still does), and may well be true with respect to formal CSR → reporting (compared to the UK) and levels of → philanthropic giving (compared to the USA), it is not, nor has ever really been, the case overall.

In some respects, Australia has led the way, globally, in a number of important CSR-related areas, not least of which have been in corporate social and cultural engagement with → indigenous communities and in the forging of long-term cross-sector corporate community partnerships.

Global CSR paradigms changed dramatically, for example, in the mining and resource industries when in 1995 Leon Davis, then CEO of CRA (now Rio Tinto) speaking to the Securities Institute in Australia said, 'In CRA, we believe there are major opportunities for growth in outback Australia which will only be realised with the full cooperation of all interested parties.'

In support of the Native Title Act (significantly opposed by Australian business at this time), Davis effectively redefined CSR from its comfortable sponsorship and philanthropic mould to a strategic → business case driven set of policies and practices, the ramifications of which have been dramatic worldwide. He argued that the Native Title Act 'laid the basis for better exploration access, and thus increased the probability that the next decade will see a series of CRA operations developed in active partnership with Aboriginal people'.

When this appeared in the press the secure foundations of the then corporate world were significantly shaken. Davis called for new competencies to be developed in social, environmental and cultural domains and it is this emphasis on new competencies (rather than specific CSR practices) which really best defines CSR in Australia. It is a fundamental, strategic, business driven approach to CSR and is increasingly at the core of what defines CSR in most Australian companies and industries. In effect, the history of CSR in Australia in recent years can be mapped against both the developing support for Leon Davis's position in 1995 (and now) and the resulting changes to the massive corporate opposition that he was faced with at the time.

If 1995 is a watershed moment in CSR in Australia, then this was followed in 1998 by another in the form of the first ever national conference on → corporate citizenship to be held in Australia organised by the newly established Corporate Citizenship Research Unit at Deakin University. This conference brought together leading corporates, government, NGOs, unions, and cultural groups in a way which developed a new agenda for CSR in Australia, moving beyond the then dominant view of CSR as corporate philanthropy to a view of CSR which sought significant long-term behavioural change. In this same year the Liberal Government under the leadership of John Howard developed the Prime Minister's Business

Community Partnership following a series of round tables, an entity still in existence today, which sought to mobilise debate on CSR, award companies and community groups for their engagement and partnerships and increase educational opportunities in a variety of ways to ensure that CSR remained firmly on the Australian agenda.

Government then, in 1998, and now, has not necessarily kept pace with the CSR developments within corporates and large NGOs, but for the most part, government has not been overly interventionist in terms of legislation and compliance regimes. This is an important marker of the state of CSR in Australia compared to some other countries in the world. There are few legislative requirements with respect to CSR in Australia either at a federal, state or local government level, with the exception that the Corporations Act (2001 and 2004) requires companies to include details of breaches of environmental laws and licences in annual reports, while the Financial Services Reform Act (2001) also requires providers of financial products with an investment component to disclose the extent to which labour standards or environmental, social, or ethical considerations are taken into account in investment decision-making. Such an overall lack of legislative requirements may well mean, for some, that Australia lags behind other countries, but for the majority of Australian companies this overall lack is a very clear marker of Australia's own distinctiveness in the field.

Initiatives like the → UN Global Compact have also been slow to take off in Australia, although more and more companies are using, in one degree or another, codes and guidelines like the → Global Reporting Initiative's Sustainability Reporting Guidelines (2002), and similarly the → World Business Council for Sustainable Development's metrics, the → Dow Jones Sustainability Index, the OECD Guidelines for Multinational Enterprises, SA 8000 and the ILO Core Labour Standards. 'Home-grown' codes, like the Australian Stock Exchange's Principles of Good Corporate Governance, are also widely used. However, what we are seeing more and more in Australia is a move from terms like

→ corporate citizenship and CSR to a more overarching under-standing of these developments within the broader umbrella of sustainability, and most specifically, that such moves are increasingly defined in Australian, rather than European or American, terms.

For example, non-mandatory, stand-alone, sustainability social and environmental reports have increased in the last 10 years in Australia, although compared globally to the 52% or so of major companies globally that produce them, approximately only 24% of Australian companies do, and these tend to be companies either headquartered, or with significant operations, overseas. However, more and more companies are increasingly reporting on their CSR-related activities in their annual reports and on their websites.

Controversy still exists in Australia with respect to the CSR indices and reputation ratings associated with CSR which exist (e.g. Reputex and the Corporate Responsibility Index), both of which rate Australian companies with respect to CSR and publish the results, but overall, the trend within Australia is very clear – cautious growth in sustainability reporting (→ non-financial reporting); a reluctance to encourage government legislation and compliance regimes, and in fact strong opposition when governments suggest the creation of legislation to 'force' the CSR agenda in some form or another; a growing recognition by governments legitimising CSR as an important part of business (e.g. a recent government enquiry into CSR by the Parliamentary Joint Committee on Corporations and Financial Services); and a steady increase in CSR activities and programmes, ranging from straightforward philanthropy, through → volunteering schemes and matched giving, to long-term cross-sector partnerships.

CSR in Australia is well and truly on the agenda, and is considered to be a non-negotiable item by most businesses, though corporate realisation of specific CSR practices and policies may differ widely. Given that Australia has one of the most active share-owning populations in the world (well over 50% of Australians own shares), close attention will continue to be paid to CSR in one way or another, not generally as some form of altruism, but because it makes simple business sense and is in the interests of these shareholders.

Overall, then, CSR in Australia is in a healthy state, but should not be simplistically compared with CSR in other countries. The February 2005 OECD economic survey of Australia indicated that 'in the last decade of the 20th century Australia became a model for other OECD countries'. Some aspects of Australian CSR could also be included in that assessment, not least of which is a greater worldwide recognition of the distinctiveness and culturally specific nature of Australian CSR.

David Birch

AUTOMOTIVE SECTOR

CSR in the automotive industry means actively safeguarding jobs while assuming social and ecological responsibility at every production site. The automotive industry manufactures a product that is associated with various environmental, social, → health and safety impacts. All manufacturers, regardless of their country of origin, thus face a number of challenges if they wish to manage such a product responsibly.

The foremost CSR-mandated duty of many car companies in North America, → Europe and Japan is to deal with the option of outsourcing production in low wage countries, either in → Latin America, Eastern Europe or China and other Asian countries. Because of the relatively high number of employees in the automotive industry, both their skills and their integration into the company's plans take on a vital role. As transnational actors, enterprises assume responsibility mainly in the regions in which they produce, whether in → Europe, → Asia, Australia, North or South America, or → Africa. They play a central role not only in job creation but also in infrastructural and regional development, because for every job at large manufacturing sites, there is least one more job at a supplier company as well as infrastructural jobs in, for example, the fields of education, public transportation, commerce, civil service and gastronomy. The outsourcing decision in the past has proven to be deeply intertwined with the social responsibilities of a car manufacturer, either negatively when jobs are outsourced, or positively when communities benefit from car companies investing in existing or new sites.

A crucial aspect of long-term enterprise management is the respect for the rule of law, a respect that is not only an obligation in industrialised countries but also a continuing challenge in the developing world. Since the automotive industry consists of a complex network of globally active suppliers, uniform standards must prevail for all suppliers within the entire supply chain.

The issue of fuel economy takes on increased significance against the backdrop of → climate change, rising oil prices and the growing dependency on politically unstable oil-exporting countries. The industry's own goal is to reduce the average fuel consumption of new passenger vehicles in → Europe to 5.5 l per 100 km by 2009, which corresponds to roughly 43 mpg. The target is lower in the United States: 24 mpg – or 9.75 l per 100 km – by 2011. In addition, the European Automobile Manufacturers Association has voluntarily promised to lower the average CO_2 emissions of its new-car fleet to 140 g/km by 2008. However, the manufacturers face a challenge in achieving these reductions by 2008. In addition to fuel economy and CO_2 emissions, other key ecological measures include: equipping vehicles with particulate filters; climate-protection strategies; driver training to promote fuel-efficient driving; product recovery and recycling systems; and alternative ways of fuelling a car. By now, every company is in some way or other conducting research into alternative fuels. The industry covers a broad spectrum: biofuels, natural gas, electric and hybrid vehicles, hydrogen power and fuel cells. But there is still a significant step to be taken between research and mass production.

The automobile manufacturers, oil companies and automotive suppliers taking part in the → World Business Council for Sustainable Development's (WBCSD) Sustainable Mobility project (completed in 2004), developed a common vision for worldwide mobility in the year 2030 as well as ways to achieve it. The network has since grown from a → learning and dialogue forum into a facilitator for joint projects (such as Sustainable Mobility 2030, the → Greenhouse Gas Protocol, Energy and Climate Change – Facts and Trends 2050, and Global Road Safety). Participation in the Mobility Forum of the United Nations Environment Program (UNEP) also serves as a way to exchange experiences in order to learn together with others. One result of this work is the Automotive Supplement to the → Global Reporting Initiative (GRI), which sets forth indicators for sustainability reporting (→ non-financial reporting) in the automotive sector.

In addition, most automotive enterprises adapt their conduct to the → UN Global Compact Guidelines, the ICC Charter, the → OECD Guidelines for Multinational Enterprises, the → Global Reporting Initiative Guidelines and ILO Core Labour Standards – not least because they recognise the benefit of a positive listing in the sustainability-oriented rating indices. The most important such indices include the → Dow Jones Sustainability Index, → FTSE4Good and Stoxx Sustainability.

Whether motor companies succeed in the future will depend largely on how well they perform the balancing act that pits conventional product requirements such as performance, safety and comfort on one side against ecological and social challenges on the other. The rising demand in newly industrialising countries underscores the need for automotive enterprises to follow a sustainable strategy in order to survive in the market.

Klaus Richter

BANKING SECTOR

→ Equator Principles, UNEP Statement by Banks on the Environment and Sustainable Development

Financial services companies deal with the management of money and include retail banks, investment banks, commercial banks, asset management companies, insurance companies, credit card companies and stock brokerages.

The industry is associated with a range of specific CSR-related issues, not only arising from management of their own business practices, but also because of the potential impact of the capital they supply and the provision of access to financial resources. As a result, financial services companies are becoming increasingly heavily regulated internationally, in response to specific instances of impropriety and a general groundswell of concern.

Key CSR issues include:

- Misselling – as new products are developed and brought onto the market, a responsible approach to sales and marketing requires high standards of → transparency by banks and insurance providers regarding sales literature, advertising and the sales process itself. Allegations of misselling occur where these processes are not effective, particularly with more vulnerable consumers.
- Personal indebtedness – ready access to credit and other forms of borrowing has steadily increased over the last decade, inevitably resulting in a rise of a range of problems for consumers from financial difficulty to bankruptcy and even related suicide. A responsible approach to lending places a burden on lenders to have embedded processes that enforce an ethical position on lending within commercial policies.
- Access to banking services – in some more developed economies there have been recent cycles of consolidation in financial services, for example, in response to the emergence of internet-based services. Concern has been expressed that bank branch closures have occurred more frequently in poorer communities,

potentially increasing a local pattern of economic decline and leading to financial exclusion. Banks are also under pressure to provide services to customers who are not able to show the traditional forms of proof of identity (to combat money laundering) such as utility bills and information from employers, where these customers are not in permanent accommodation or employment.

- Capital financing – when providing funds for major commercial projects, project financiers encounter social and environmental issues that are both complex and challenging, particularly with respect to projects in the emerging markets. These are addressed by initiatives like the → Equator Principles and the → UNEP Finance Initiative. Some project financiers and commercial lenders taking an ethical position state explicitly that they will not invest in projects that are associated with → human rights violations, the arms trade and genetic modification.

- Insurance – insurance providers allocate different premiums depending on the level of risk involved when providing insurance. Fair pricing and access to insurance services by marginalised communities are key CSR issues for the insurance industry, as is the growing issue of how to insure against the spiralling impacts of → climate change.

- → Microfinance – microfinance is the provision of financial services to those who are excluded from the traditional financial system on account of their lower economic status. These will most commonly take the form of loans (micro-credit) and micro-savings, though it can include other services such as micro-insurance and payment services. Certain banks specialise in banking in emerging economies.

- → Socially Responsible Investment (SRI) – many investors are becoming more and more interested in the corporate practices of the companies in which funds are invested. SRI combines the intentions to maximise financial return and the consideration of the social, environmental and wider economic impacts of the investment. The → UN Principles for Responsible Investment address these issues.

- Money laundering – money laundering is the disguising of funds from criminal activity to give them legal respectability. It has been estimated by the International Monetary Fund that such financial flows are equivalent to between 2% and 5% of global GDP.
- Islamic banking – under certain faiths it is not permissible to earn interest on invested funds. This is a feature of so-called Islamic banking which also prohibits gambling, the dealing in liquor, pork, pornography and anything else that the Shariah (Islamic law) deems unlawful.

Guidelines that have been developed for the financial services sector to address global CSR issues include:

- The → Equator Principles – a set of voluntary environmental and social guidelines for ethical project finance. These principles commit commercial lenders and other signatories not to finance projects that fail to meet these guidelines.
- The → UNEP Finance Initiative (UNEP FI) – a global partnership between UNEP and the private financial sector. UNEP FI works closely with over 160 financial institutions and a range of partner organisations to develop and promote linkages between the → environment, sustainability and financial performance.
- The → UN Principles for Responsible Investment – a framework for investors that enable them to give appropriate consideration to social, environmental and → corporate governance issues when making investment decisions.
- The → Global Reporting Initiative (GRI) financial services – a sector supplement that can be used in conjunction with the GRI guidelines.

Nicki Websper

BASEL CONVENTION

→ Waste management

⌨ www.basel.int

The Basel Convention is a global agreement, which entered into force in 1992 and included 168 countries as at May 2006, for addressing the problems and challenges posed by hazardous → waste. Hazardous waste is a problem because, when it is dumped indiscriminately, spilled accidentally or managed improperly, it can cause severe health problems, even death, and poison → water and land for decades. The Basel Convention was originally designed to address the global problem of the uncontrolled movement and dumping of hazardous wastes, including incidents of illegal dumping in developing nations by companies from developed countries.

During its first decade (1989–1999), the Convention also developed the criteria for environmentally sound management, which it defines as taking all practical steps to minimise the generation of hazardous wastes and strictly controlling its storage, transport, treatment, reuse, recycling, recovery and final disposal, the purpose of which is to protect human health and the → environment. During the present decade (2000–2010), the Convention's activities are focused on: active promotion and use of cleaner technologies and production methods; further reduction of the movement of hazardous and other → wastes; the prevention and monitoring of illegal traffic; improvement of institutional and technical capabilities – through → technology when appropriate – especially for → developing countries and countries with economies in transition; and further development of regional and sub-regional centres for training and → technology transfer. The Secretariat is administered by UNEP.

BASE OF THE PYRAMID (BOP) MODEL

→ Development, Poverty

A recent concept developed in the late 1990s within the management literature, the base (bottom) of the pyramid (or BOP) refers simultaneously to the socio-economic demographic representing the 3–4 billion poorest people inhabiting the globe as well as private sector business models meant to address poverty.

The idea of the BOP as a business opportunity came about as a convergence of two streams of thought within strategic management. The first is premised on a new model of global economic expansion through innovation and → technology management within international business. This perspective challenges assumptions regarding the source of innovation and creativity – shifting it from home offices and headquarters based in developed nations to subsidiaries and competitors based in → developing countries.

The second is a model of the global economy that emerged from work on organisations and sustainability. This view describes the global economy as consisting of three distinct demographic categories that transcend geographic boundaries, organised by the sustainability challenges being faced by each. The first group is comprised of the 'mature' economy made up of the world's wealthiest individuals that represents about 15% of the global population. These individuals are able to afford all the goods and services they need as well as any or most of what they might want. The challenge and opportunity for business is to develop goods and services that reduce the large environmental footprint that occurs through consumption in this market.

The second group represents the aspiring middle class that comprises approximately 20% of the global population. These individuals are able to afford most goods and services they need and some of those they want. The challenge for business here is to develop innovative products and services that prevent further contributions to environmental degradation as the aspiring economy develops. Most efforts by companies to penetrate emerging economies are attempts to adapt expensive products and services for the mature economy to make them more affordable.

The incremental revenue generated from sales of such products is often lower than expected and the impact on the → environment high.

The third group represents the 'survival economy' made up of nearly two-thirds of humanity that earn between $1 and $3 a day. Demographically, this is the BOP. These individuals are barely able or unable to meet their most basic of needs, such as clean → water, health care, education, housing and nutrition. For the most part, the economic system has overlooked, ignored, or even exploited this market segment. Existing business models, products and services have little relevance in this market because logistical, cultural, technical, and political characteristics are so different from the mature economy for which they were developed. What goods do exist are usually more expensive and of lower quality than comparable items available to the wealthy.

These two perspectives have merged into a paradigm of BOP as business opportunity where poverty is addressed and low income markets become engines for entrepreneurship and business growth. This view is very contentious for those suspicious of the motivations of companies pursuing BOP initiatives. Their concern is that such initiatives are simply another way to sell unnecessary goods to poor people in a way that extracts what little wealth exists in those markets. There is also concern that successful BOP strategies will lead to increased consumption patterns that place even more pressure on critical ecosystem services, furthering environmental decline.

However, another viewpoint promotes BOP ventures as a way to unlock the latent vitality and ingenuity of robust, informal markets, thus releasing the poor from economic imprisonment. This view rejects the idea of the poor simply as a source of revenue for new business growth and instead sees the poor as capable partners and resources for → technology development and innovation. The BOP is not advocated as simply the opportunity for increasing sales through the marketing of existing products and services in forms that are smaller and cheaper than their upmarket cousins (e.g. sachets, single servings). Instead, BOP is conceptualised as a holistic, long-term investment process in business model innovation based on partnerships and need-based product and service development as articulated by the poor themselves and built on the local resource base, → infrastructure, and cultural institutions.

Mark B. Milstein, Erik Simanis, Duncan Duke and Stuart Hart

BENCHMARKING
→ Reporting, Best practice

Benchmarking is a tool whereby a company measures one of its performances or processes against other companies' → best practices, determines how those companies achieved their performance levels, and uses the information to improve its own performance.

Essentially, there are two ways to benchmark CSR initiatives. Evaluative sustainability assessments measure performance for a non-specialist audience. These are often done by organisations and initiatives related to the financial markets, such as the → Dow Jones Sustainability Indexes and FTSE4Good.

Diagnostic sustainability benchmarking is oriented toward detailed information rather than an overall score, and focuses on tasks such as understanding how companies perform in different sustainability areas, what their strengths and weaknesses are, and how variations can be explained.

Because results tend to remain confidential, much of the benchmarking information in the public domain is circumstantial and issue specific. More systematic comparisons tend to be owned by specialist consultancies, sector bodies, companies and regulators.

Some of the different international norms and standards available to promote CSR benchmarking include: the → UN Global Compact, the → OECD Guidelines for Multinational Enterprises, the → Global Reporting Initiative and the Green Paper 366 (issued by the European Commission to promote CSR practices at the EU level). The → World Business Council for Sustainable Development also helps its members benchmark through its Learning by Sharing meetings on different topics for different sectors.

Björn Stigson

BEST IN CLASS INVESTING
→ Socially responsible investment

BEST PRACTICE
→ Benchmarking

A best practice is a technique or methodology that, through experience and research, has proven to reliably lead to a desired result. A commitment to using the best practices in any field is a commitment to using all the knowledge and → technology at one's disposal to ensure success. A best practice tends to spread throughout a field or industry after a success has been demonstrated.

Best practice tends to be fairly easy to define as regards environmental impacts and management, and technological processes with clearly measurable results. It is harder in areas such as corporate responsibility. Global companies are expected to meet global standards of corporate → accountability, responsibility and sustainability. Yet many of these standards are complex and contradictory. Tools and guidelines include the OECD Guidelines to Multinational Enterprises and Corporate Governance, and the → Global Reporting Initiative (GRI).

The field of corporate responsibility is still developing, and the analytical tools needed to assess the → business case for CSR are as yet quite rudimentary. Further, few companies have deep experience in the field.

The sharing of best practices among companies and industry sectors can help them avoid unnecessary mistakes and find shortcuts to achieving tangible success.

Björn Stigson

BIODIVERSITY

Biodiversity is the shortened term for biological diversity, which is defined by the 1992 Convention on Biological Diversity as 'the variability among living organisms from all sources including, inter alia, terrestrial, marine, and other aquatic ecosystems and the ecological complexes of which they are part; this includes diversity within species, between species and of ecosystems'. Numerous other definitions exist, but they all concern the variety of life on our planet. The components of biodiversity are biological resources, which include genetic resources, organisms, populations, or any other biotic component of ecosystems with actual or potential use or value for humanity. The guiding objectives of the Convention are the → conservation, sustainable use, and equitable sharing of benefits of biological resources. The Convention particularly encourages the engagement of the private sector in developing methods for biodiversity objectives. A critical element in CSR is to ensure business operations do not have negative impacts on biodiversity. Some industries, notably oil, gas and mining, have gone beyond this minimum to seek to improve biodiversity in the regions where they are working, or to fund appropriate → conservation activities elsewhere to compensate for the residual, unavoidable harm to biodiversity caused by their development projects, otherwise known as biodiversity offsets.

Valli Moosa

BIOREMEDIATION

Bioremediation is defined as the process whereby substances hazardous to human health and/or the → environment are biologically degraded, under controlled conditions, to an innocuous (harmless) state, or to levels below concentration limits established by regulatory authorities. It is a → technology used for the clean-up of contaminated land and groundwater. It uses naturally occurring bacteria and fungi or plants to degrade or detoxify. The microorganisms may be indigenous to a contaminated area, or they may be isolated from elsewhere and brought to the contaminated site (bioaugmentation). Bioremediation is effective only where environmental conditions permit microbial growth/activity. Thus, its application often involves the manipulation of environmental parameters such as soil temperature, oxygen, and nutrient content to allow microbial growth and degradation to proceed at a rapid rate. Different microorganisms degrade different types of compounds and survive under different conditions, and biodegradation of a compound is often a result of the actions of multiple organisms. Therefore, the use of bioremediation at a site is based upon: the existence of a microbial population capable of degrading the pollutants; the availability of contaminants to the microbial population; and the environmental factors (type of soil, temperature, pH, the presence of oxygen or other electron acceptors, and nutrients), or the ability to manipulate these factors. As with other technologies, bioremediation has its limitations. Some contaminants, such as chlorinated organic or high aromatic hydrocarbons, are resistant to microbial attack; and heavy metals such as cadmium and lead are not readily absorbed or captured by organisms.

Zoe Lees

BLACK ECONOMIC EMPOWERMENT
→ Empowerment

BLUEWASH
→ Greenwash, UN Global Compact

Corporations that claim to abide by internationally agreed-upon standards of the United Nations when they actually do not, in order to enhance their brand reputation, are engaged in bluewashing. Corporations seek to associate with the international credibility of the blue flag of the United Nations and its work concerning humanitarian need and peace. The term bluewash is a variation on the term → greenwash – an Orwellian posturing by corporations in an effort to be perceived as environmental and trade on their positive connotation with the public.

Based on the 1876 classic American novel *The Adventures of Tom Sawyer* by Mark Twain, the phrase whitewash started a trend akin to Watergate being the root of American scandals ending in the suffix 'gate'. The protagonist Tom Sawyer persuaded other boys that his task of whitewashing a fence was in fact not work but enjoyable play and they were deceived into paying for the privilege as Sawyer watched idly by.

Jonathan Cohen

BOYCOTTS
→ Ethical consumption

BRANDING
→ Marketing ethics, Reputation

Understanding brands or brand social responsibility is imperative if we are to understand corporate social responsibility. Brands can be used as a hostage by stakeholders as associating brands with activities perceived as irresponsible can have a significant impact on the brand value.

Where transgressions of → human rights, labour standards and environmental protection have been detected, corporations have been targeted as easily identifiable culpable parties in the supply chain from producers, often in → developing countries, to consumers, often in developed countries.

Brands are a part of everyday life. In any one day, the average person will come into contact with some 1500 brands and when they go to the supermarket (in a developed economy) they will be confronted with up to 50 000. Brands are existential; they are here and everywhere. Brands are the way we live; the way we identify ourselves. They are amorphous and 'belong' to all of us and no one. Brands that have a direct interface with consumers are more valuable than the corporations that nominally own them. The world's most valued brands are Coca-Cola, Microsoft, IBM, GE, Intel, Disney, McDonald's, Nokia, Toyota, and Marlboro. The vast majority of people in the world, whether rich or poor, come into contact with one or more of these brands on a daily basis, or are regularly impacted by their use.

Viewing the corporate social responsibility debate from the perspective of brands paints a new picture of a complex network of relationships between ideas, interest groups, products and consumption and global supply chains, global trade issues and the interface between government, corporations and NGOs. And it shifts some of the responsibility for change to a range of stakeholders.

Malcolm McIntosh

BRIBE PAYERS INDEX
→ Corruption
⌐ www.transparency.org

The Transparency International Bribe Payers Index ranks leading exporting countries according to the reported propensity of companies headquartered in those countries to pay bribes when doing business abroad. The Index measures the 'supply' side of bribery in countries where the bribes are paid. Countries are ranked on a mean score from the answers given by respondents to the question: 'In the business sectors with which you are most familiar, please indicate how likely companies from the following countries are to pay or offer bribes to win or retain business in this country?'

David Nussbaum and Peter Wilkinson

BRIBERY
→ Corruption

BRUNDTLAND COMMISSION
→ World Commission on Environment and Development

BUSINESS AND HUMAN RIGHTS RESOURCE CENTRE
→ Human rights
⌨ www.business–humanrights.org

The Business and Human Rights Resource Centre is an independent non-profit organisation, in a collaborative partnership with Amnesty International and academic institutions. Its International Advisory Network is chaired by Mary Robinson, former UN High Commissioner for Human Rights.

The Resource Centre runs an online library on companies' → human rights and environmental impacts. This website is updated hourly and tracks the conduct of over 3500 companies worldwide, highlighting positive steps as well as concerns. Its sources include local and international media, NGOs, companies, governments, and intergovernmental organisations.

The Centre invites companies to provide responses to allegations of misconduct. It includes the allegations and responses on its website and in its weekly email updates, sent to thousands of opinion formers worldwide. This process creates an impartial forum that brings together diverse perspectives on specific → human rights issues, helping to encourage constructive decision-making and practical change on the ground. The Centre seeks responses from companies based in all regions, ranging from well-known multinationals to small manufacturers.

The Resource Centre has offices in the UK and the USA, with researchers based in other regions including Hong Kong and South Africa.

BUSINESS CASE

→ Value creation, Competitive advantage

According to the 1987 Brundtland Report, Our Common Future: 'Far from requiring cessation of economic growth, → sustainable development recognizes that the problems of poverty and under-development cannot be solved unless we have a new era of growth in which → developing countries play a large role and reap large benefits.'

According to this perspective, → sustainable development is dependent on responsible economic growth, with business as the engine of such growth. Hence, it is critical for the planet and its people that there be a business case – as opposed to only an ethical or a societal case – for → sustainable development.

The business case for → sustainable development was first advocated by the Business Council for Sustainable Development, the predecessor of the → World Business Council for Sustainable Development (WBCSD). In the run-up to the Rio Earth Summit in 1992 it argued that there are a number of actions that companies should pursue because they make business sense, while at the same time improving the environmental performance of a company.

Its first example was → eco-efficiency – doing more with fewer inputs, → waste and pollution – thus saving money while better managing the → environment.

The business case for → sustainable development includes the following elements:

- Operational efficiency;
- Risk reduction;

- Recruitment and retention of talent;
- Protecting the resource base of raw materials; and
- Creation of new markets, products and services.

The business case is partially founded on the notion that business cannot succeed in societies that fail, and that companies should behave responsibly in order to earn and retain public trust, and thereby secure their licence to innovate, operate and grow.

The business case is not just about avoiding risks, but also about taking advantage of opportunities. Sustainable development can make firms more:

- Competitive;
- Resilient to shock;
- Nimble in a fast changing world;
- Unified in purpose; and
- Likely to attract and retain customers and the best employees.

As a result, relations with regulators, banks, insurers and financial markets will also run more easily.

A 2006 WBCSD report argued that the companies that will remain successful in 2020 will be those that provide goods and services in ways that address the world's major challenges, including poverty, → climate change, resource depletion, → globalisation and demographic shifts.

It argued that if action to address such issues is to be substantial and sustainable, it must also be profitable. Businesses' major contribution to society will therefore come through core business activities rather than through philanthropic programmes.

The business role in society has moved beyond a simple equation of profitability plus compliance plus philanthropy, to making responsibilities part of core businesses through deeper understanding of both business and the society in which it operates.

This approach is leading some executives to work more closely with non-governmental organisations and other citizen groups as partners, and to work more closely with governments, urging those governments to establish framework conditions which improve the business case for → sustainable development.

Business needs a stable environment and long-term goals to attract investors. Stable frameworks encourage companies to invest more in research and development, allowing them to experiment with new ways of managing environmental impacts and finding market-based opportunities that encourage low income societies to make their way out of poverty and enter into the mainstream economy.

By introducing → sustainable development into conventional business strategy, company leaders are learning to think several moves ahead in terms of social and environmental value, while continuing to focus on the economic and market values of today, an approach that embodies the business case for → sustainable development.

Björn Stigson

BUSINESS CHARTER FOR SUSTAINABLE DEVELOPMENT
→ ICC Business Charter for Sustainable Development

BUSINESS ETHICS
→ Ethical decision-making, Values

According to one of the leading textbooks, business ethics can be defined as the study of business situations, activities and decisions where issues of right and wrong are addressed (see Crane and Matten, *Business Ethics*, Oxford University Press, 2006). 'Right' and 'wrong' in this context means morally right and wrong as opposed to, for example, commercially, strategically, or financially right or wrong. Moreover, the term 'business ethics' does not confine the subject only to commercial businesses, but extends also to government organisations, pressure groups, not-for-profit businesses, charities and other organisations. For example, questions of how to manage employees fairly, or what constitutes deception in advertising, are equally as important for organisations of any kind, be they public bodies, non-governmental organisations or private businesses.

Business ethics as a sub-area of management concerned with social issues in business has probably the longest standing as a CSR-related subject of business education and research. Indeed, many CSR issues initially have been discussed under the label of business ethics. Today, after more than five decades of debate on the subject, and with business having taken up many of the issues discussed in the academic literature, we could, however, see business ethics more as being a sub-field of → CSR. While CSR describes the activities corporations undertake to live up to society's expectations, business ethics can be seen as the analytical tool that managers and others can use to understand, conceptualise and legitimise the moral status of corporate policies, strategies and programmes. For some, while CSR is about tangible corporate practices, business ethics is more about the → values driving business decisions.

Business ethics can be differentiated into two broad domains. First, there is 'normative business ethics', which – mainly based on philosophical thinking – attempts to understand what is the morally right or wrong course of action in a specific situation. Second, there is 'descriptive business ethics' which – mainly based on psychological and ethnographic research – tries to understand how ethical decisions are actually made in business, and what influences the process and outcomes of those decisions.

Normative business ethics

Having defined business ethics in terms of issues of right and wrong, one might quite naturally question whether this is any way distinct from the law. In fact, → regulation is essentially an institutionalisation or codification of ethics into specific social rules, laws and proscriptions. Nonetheless, the two are not equivalent. Perhaps the best the way of thinking about ethics and the law is in terms of two intersecting domains. The law might be said to be a definition of the minimum acceptable standards of behaviour. However, many morally contestable issues, whether in business or elsewhere, are not explicitly covered by the law. Similarly, it is possible to think of issues that are covered by the law, but which are not really about ethics. For example, the law prescribes whether we should drive on the right or the left side of the road. Although this prevents chaos on the roads, the decision about which side we should drive is not an ethical decision as such.

In one sense then, business ethics can be said to begin where the law ends, i.e. beyond → legal compliance. Business ethics is primarily concerned with those issues not covered by the law, or where there is no definite consensus on whether something is right or wrong. Discussion about the ethics of particular business practices may eventually lead to (→ self-)regulation once some kind of consensus is reached, but for most of the issues of interest to business ethics, the law typically does not currently provide us with guidance. For this reason, it is often said that business ethics is about the 'grey areas' of business.

The problem of trying to make decisions in the grey areas of business ethics, or where → values may be in conflict, means that many of the questions posed are equivocal. There simply may not be a definitive 'right' answer to many business ethics problems. And as is the case with issues such as the → animal testing of products, executive pay, persuasive sales techniques, or → child labour, business ethics problems also tend to be very controversial and open to widely different points of view. In this sense business ethics is not about finding the 'right' or 'wrong' answer in a specific situation. Rather, it is an analytical tool which could help managers to weigh different options against each other and develop some moral imagination about the consequences of their actions for the human beings affected by those decisions.

Some of the controversy regarding business ethics is no doubt due to different understandings of what constitutes morality or ethics in the first place. In common usage, the terms 'ethics' and 'morality' are often used interchangeably. In many ways, it is probably true to say that this does not pose many real problems for most managers in terms of communicating and understanding things about business ethics. However, in order to clarify certain arguments, many academic writers have proposed clear differences between the two terms. There are certain advantages in making a distinction between 'ethics' and 'morality', and the most common and useful way of distinguishing them might be the following distinction: morality is concerned with the norms, → values, and beliefs embedded in social processes which define right and wrong for an individual or a community. Ethics is concerned with the study of morality and the application of reason to elucidate specific rules and principles that determine right and wrong for a given situation.

Ethics therefore represents an attempt to systematise and rationalise morality into generalised normative rules that attempt to offer a solution to situations of moral uncertainty. The outcomes of the codification of these rules and principles are ethical theories, which are in turn often derived from philosophical theories. For instance, one popular business ethics theory is 'utilitarianism' which argues that an action is morally correct if it provides 'the greatest amount of utility for the greatest amount of people'. So, for instance, in considering the dilemma surrounding the use of new technologies such as genetic engineering, utilitarianism would look at all the different groups of people affected by the decision and try to assess in which ways and to what degrees the new → technology would harm or benefit these people. Then by using a scoring technique one might be able to determine whether on balance the action has more benefit than harm and therefore reach a conclusion about the ethical merits of the decision to use the proposed → technology.

Other philosophical approaches are based on the concept of rights and would ask whether a certain decision, for instance on working conditions in a Third World factory, would violate fundamental → human rights. More recent philosophical theories also look at the processes of decision-making and might suggest that the ethically correct business decision is one that involves the company and its stakeholders in a process of free, fair and open deliberation. This approach of 'discourse ethics' is more concerned with the process of → ethical decision-making and contends that people in general have no ethical misgivings with a decision as long as the decision-making process lives up to basic ethical standards. Applications of this approach can be found in decision-making processes that involve → stakeholder engagement, whether for the location of a hazardous → waste site or the construction of a new runway at an airport.

Business ethics is currently a very prominent business topic, and the debates and dilemmas surrounding business ethics have tended to attract an enormous amount of attention from various quarters. For a start, consumers and pressure groups appear to be increasingly demanding firms to seek out more ethical and ecologically sound ways of doing business. The media also constantly seems to be keeping the spotlight on corporate abuses and malpractices. And even firms themselves appear to be increasingly recognising that being ethical (or at the very least being seen to be ethical) may actually be good for business. Ethical issues confront organisations whatever line of business they might be in. There are therefore many reasons why business ethics might be regarded as an increasingly important area of study, whether for students interested in evaluating business activities, or for managers seeking to improve their decision-making skills.

Against the backdrop of increasingly complex demands on companies to account for their power and influence, ethical reasoning helps business leaders to frame and justify their CSR actions in response. In particular, business ethics can help to improve → ethical decision-making by providing managers with the appropriate knowledge and tools that allow them to correctly identify, diagnose, analyse and provide solutions to the ethical problems and dilemmas they are confronted with.

Descriptive business ethics

Business ethics also provides a way of looking at the reasons behind ethical infractions that occur within the workplace, and the ways in which such problems might be dealt with by managers, regulators, and others interested in improving ethical performance of companies. For example, in a recent UK survey of ethics in the workplace, one in four employees said that they had felt pressure to compromise their own or their organisation's ethical standards, and one in five had noticed behaviour by their colleagues that violated the law or did not accord with expected ethical standards.

This area of business ethics has attempted to come up with models of → ethical decision-making to understand the factors that actually have an influence on people taking morally right or wrong decisions. These factors can be differentiated into two broad categories:

- Individual factors – these are the unique characteristics of the individual actually making the relevant decision. These include factors which are given by birth, such as age and → gender, and those acquired by experience and socialisation, such as education, personality and attitudes.
- Situational factors – these are the particular features of the context that influence whether the individual will make an ethical or an unethical decision. These include factors associated with the work context, such as reward systems, job roles and → cultural issues. Other factors are those associated with the issue itself. A common example is the intensity of the moral issue: managers might be likely to bend the rules if they think no one gets hurt – often the rationale for petty → corruption or bribery while they might well recognise the moral status of a decision, if for instance the

life or health of people is threatened by a certain course of action. Another important issue-related factor is the moral framing of an issue: in the case of bribery, the moral connotations of framing it as 'handing out some positive inducements' might be very different from calling it 'active participation and promotion of → corruption' – which in turn influences significantly the moral outcome of a decision.

An understanding of these issues actually helps in addressing a host of ethical infractions which occur in business, such as → bribery, → corruption or → discrimination. The underlying assumption is that ethical misconduct does not necessarily occur in organisations because managers are inherently evil but because personal characteristics of the decision-makers and/or the specific circumstances in which these decisions are taken encourage unethical behaviour. Or to turn it positively, if we understand the factors that incentivise ethically right behaviour and those that discourage wrong decisions we are much more likely to come up with strategies, tools and organisational designs which will lead decision-makers to avoid unethical behaviour.

Business then has responded in a number of practical ways to embed ethical conduct in their operations. The most notable manifestation is the growing number of codes of ethics (or their equivalent, → codes of conduct), where companies define ethical norms and processes to which they commit themselves and their employees. In particular in the US, as a consequence of the → US Sentencing Guidelines, companies have set up → 'ethics officers' and 'ethics committees' (responsible for setting, implementing and monitoring ethical standards) and 'ethics hotlines' (where employees can call and report ethical infractions). Typical expressions are also policies for the protection of → whistleblowers (people who report ethical misconduct).

The last few years have also witnessed significant growth in what might be regarded as the business ethics 'industry', i.e. ethics consultants, ethical investment trusts, ethics conferences, ethical products and services and various activities associated with ethics → auditing, monitoring and → reporting (as have been recently developed by many of the leading consulting and → auditing firms).

Despite these actions, research has shown that businesses are often reluctant to use the language of business 'ethics' explicitly and are more comfortable with the language of → 'corporate citizenship' or 'corporate (social) responsibility'. The reason for this, according to ethicists such as Zygmunt Bauman, could be that businesses fear that basing decisions on individual moral impulses and ethical urges might undermine the organisation's bureaucratic governance structure. Hence, they prefer to codify, formalise and even, as Crane (*Organisation Studies*, 2000) has put it, 'amoralise' decisions with an ethical dimension.

To sum it up, there does seem to be some consensus about the importance of business ethics, whether by academics, governments, consumers or businesses, but there is rather less agreement on what actually constitutes ethical behaviour in business. That said, there appears to be considerable interest in the teaching and → learning of business ethics, as witnessed by the number of modules in business ethics being run in universities across the world and the outpouring of → research on the subject, as well as web pages, blogs and other electronic publications. For instance, amazon.com currently stocks more than two thousand books related to business ethics and corporate responsibility, while a Google search on 'business ethics' returned more than 4 million hits.

Business ethics then can be said to underlie the → values, decisions and processes in the context of CSR. On the one hand, it helps companies to understand, delineate and legitimise their actions as responsible corporate citizens. And on the other hand, it provides a credible label under which CSR can be practised and researched.

Andrew Crane and Dirk Matten

BUSINESS FOR SOCIAL RESPONSIBILITY (BSR)

→ North America

✆ www.bsr.org

Business for Social Responsibility (BSR) is a non-profit business association that seeks to create a more sustainable global economy by working with the business community. Founded in 1992, BSR is a leading provider of innovative business solutions to many of the world's leading corporations.

Headquartered in San Francisco with offices in Paris and Guangzhou, China, BSR serves its 250 member companies and other Global 1000 enterprises through advisory and member services, information and analysis, and convenings. BSR helps companies develop innovative strategies for integrating corporate responsibility into daily business operations. BSR also works to foster dialogue, engagement and collaboration between the business community and the public sector and civil society to realise its mission, and has engaged in and led numerous multi-stakeholder initiatives.

BSR's staff of 60 professionals focuses on → human rights, economic development, environment, and governance and → accountability. From its three offices, BSR has undertaken project work in more than 60 countries, and its annual conference is the largest event dedicated to advancing corporate responsibility.

Aron Cramer

BUSINESS IN THE COMMUNITY (BITC)

→ Business in the Environment Index, Community development, Corporate Responsibility Index

✆ www.bitc.org.uk

Business in the Community (BITC) is a member-driven organisation, a registered charity and company limited by guarantee whose mission is to encourage companies to improve and extend their positive impact in the community, to reduce their impact on the → environment, to address issues affecting them in the market-place and in their supply chain, and to encourage flexibility and → diversity in the workplace. Founded in 1982 under the presidency of HRH the Prince of Wales as a corporate response to significant social problems in the UK's inner cities, BITC is head-quartered in London and has 11 regional offices in England, Wales and Northern Ireland. In addition to over 1000 partnerships through which it works in the UK, it also is able to offer support to its international member companies through a global network of 95 partners worldwide and → benchmarking tools such as the Business in the Environment Index and → Corporate Responsibility Index.

David Halley

BUSINESS PRINCIPLES FOR COUNTERING BRIBERY

→ Corruption

⁐ www.transparency.org

The Business Principles for Countering Bribery are an initiative of → Transparency International and Social Accountability International and were developed by a multi-stakeholder group of private sector interests, non-governmental organisations and trade unions as a tool to assist enterprises in developing effective approaches to countering bribery in all of their activities. The Business Principles, which were launched in 2002, were developed to provide a model of good practice for enterprises wishing to develop comprehensive anti-bribery policies and programmes. The Business Principles have a narrow focus on bribery and, as such, constitute a subset of fuller codes of ethics that normally include broader provisions dealing with issues such as conflicts of interest, money laundering,

→ fraud and embezzlement. The Business Principles emphasise the importance of a no-bribes policy and the detailed implementation of an anti-bribery programme. They have been designed for use by large, medium and small enterprises and apply to bribery of public officials and to private-to-private transactions. The Business Principles can be used as a basis for enterprises developing an anti-bribery policy for the first time or they can be used as a benchmark against which to assess an enterprise's existing policy and practices. The Business Principles are supported by a suite of implementation tools.

David Nussbaum and Peter Wilkinson

BUSINESS SOCIAL COMPLIANCE INITIATIVE (BSCI)

⌐ www.bsci-eu.org

Acting socially responsible in a globalised economy has become a major issue for trade as tough competition and decreasing tolerance with regard to poor working conditions in production facilities represent a huge challenge for retailing companies as well as for suppliers. How can retailers and suppliers meet requirements of high quality, low prices and socially fair produced goods?

The Brussels-based Foreign Trade Association (FTA) began efforts in 2002 to establish a common platform for the various different European Codes of Conduct and monitoring systems and to lay the groundwork for a common European monitoring system for social compliance. In 2002 and 2003, retail companies and associations held several workshops to determine the framework for such a system. In March 2003 the FTA formally founded the BSCI, for the purpose of developing the tools and procedures for the European Business Social Compliance Programme. In the spring of 2004 the development phase was achieved and since then the implementation and broadening of the system is the major task of the parties involved.

The Business Social Compliance Initiative (BSCI) now claims to be the broadest business-driven platform for the improvement of social compliance in all supplier countries and for all consumer goods. BSCI has membership comprising almost 70 retailers, industry and importing companies from 10 countries. Through pooling efforts and resources, BSCI's members are promoting a common monitoring and factory development system.

CACG PRINCIPLES
→ Commonwealth Corporate Governance Principles

CARBON BALANCE
→ Climate change

The term carbon balance refers to the process of identifying and quantifying carbon in the form of carbon dioxide (CO_2) added to or removed from the earth's atmosphere, by natural and human activity. Carbon balances are increasingly used to better understand → climate change.

The main reservoirs of carbon on earth are the oceans, the atmosphere, the biosphere (living matter) and the geosphere (earth including fossil deposits such as buried coal and oil). Carbon balances model the movement of carbon between these reservoirs, and usually focus on resulting changes in the atmosphere. An activity that adds carbon to the atmosphere (mostly in the form of CO_2, the most common greenhouse gas) is referred to as a source of carbon, and an activity that removes carbon from the atmosphere is referred to as a sink of carbon. Sources and sinks can be categorised as natural or anthropogenic (human induced). Natural sources and sinks include naturally occurring plants, animals, decaying organic matter, oceans and other → water bodies and certain geological activity. Anthropogenic sources include emissions from the combustion of fossil fuels (coal, oil, gas, jet fuel etc.), chemical and industrial processes, construction, agriculture and human-induced deforestation. There are relatively few anthropogenic sinks (exceptions include some forestry and agricultural practices), and most human activity has created more sources of CO_2. This has been linked to increases in levels of CO_2 in the earth's atmosphere (of over 30% since the beginning of the industrial revolution), leading to changes in the properties of the atmosphere and associated → climate change.

Stirling Habbitts

CARBON CREDITS
→ Climate change

Carbon credits are quantified and verified reductions in greenhouse gas emissions, or avoided or sequestered greenhouse gas emissions, that are tradable and have a financial value, and are (in most cases) created under a legal framework for greenhouse gas trading such as the → Kyoto Protocol or the EU Emissions Trading Scheme, and in some cases are generated by voluntary action outside of any legal framework.

In recognition of the significant negative impacts of → climate change, legislative-based emissions trading schemes have been created in certain regions (e.g. the → EU Greenhouse Gas Emission Trading Scheme), and globally under the United Nations (the → Kyoto Protocol), based on the concept of tradable carbon credits. The word carbon refers to the element carbon in the most common greenhouse gas, carbon dioxide (CO_2). Carbon credits can also be created from → greenhouse gases other than CO_2, such as methane, but are still referred to as carbon credits. One carbon credit represents one tonne of CO_2. Carbon credits have other names depending on the scheme and region in which they were created. These are shortened to acronyms, usually three or four letters, which may be thought of as different currencies for trading in different regions. The most common include:

- European Union Allowances (EUAs), used under the → EU Greenhouse Gas Emission Trading Scheme;
- Certified Emissions Reductions (CERs), used for → Clean Development Mechanism (CDM) projects under the → Kyoto Protocol;
- Emission Reduction Units (ERUs), used for → Joint Implementation (JI) projects under the → Kyoto Protocol;
- Assigned Allowance Units (AAUs), used for International Emissions Trading under the → Kyoto Protocol;
- Verified Emissions Reductions (VERs), commonly used for voluntary action that has been verified by a third party.

Stirling Habbitts

CARBON DISCLOSURE PROJECT (CDP)

→ Climate change

🖱 www.cdproject.net

The Carbon Disclosure Project (CDP) provides a secretariat for the world's largest institutional investor collaboration on the business implications of → climate change. CDP represents an efficient process whereby many institutional investors collectively sign a single global request for disclosure of information on greenhouse gas emissions. More than 1000 large corporations report on their emissions through this website. On 1 February 2007 this request was sent to over 2400 companies.

The Carbon Disclosure Project (CDP) was launched in 2003 (CDP1) with 35 institutional investors representing $4.5 trillion in assets, and subsequently expanded in 2004 (CDP2) to 95 institutional investors with $10 trillion in assets and then again in 2005 (CDP3) to 155 institutional investors with over $21 trillion in assets. In each year, the CDP sends requests to each of the companies listed in the Financial Times 500 (FT500) list – an annual snapshot of the world's 500 largest companies. The requests consist of a letter and questionnaire, and the responses to the requests are collated and the results made available publicly in a report and on the CDP website.

The results include the percentage of companies that responded to the request, their emissions of → greenhouse gases, activities to reduce emissions, and commercial considerations such as the projected impact of carbon credit prices on net income. The Carbon Disclosure Project is a special project of Rockefeller Philanthropy Advisers, with US IRS 501(c)(3) charitable status, for the sole purpose of providing a co-ordinating secretariat for the participating funders and investors.

Stirling Habbitts

CARBON FUNDS
→ Climate change

Carbon funds are pooled funds set up to purchase → carbon credits, usually on behalf of companies and other investors that will use the credits for compliance under the rules of an emissions trading scheme (e.g. the → EU Greenhouse Gas Emission Trading Scheme) or sell the credits at a later date.

Carbon funds assist companies and governments to meet their emissions targets under regional emissions trading schemes or under the → Kyoto Protocol. The World Bank set up one of the first carbon funds in 1999, the Prototype Carbon Fund (PCF), to invest contributions made by companies and governments in → Joint Implementation and → Clean Development Mechanism credits. The investors in the PCF receive a pro rata share of the → carbon credits in return for their investment. Many other carbon funds have since been created, broadly categorised as private or government. Most European governments (and some non-European such as Japan) have set up carbon funds to assist in meeting their targets under the → Kyoto Protocol. A growing number of private funds have also been created. These funds purchase → carbon credits on behalf of companies, or on a speculative basis for selling later at a profit. Several of these funds have been listed on London's Alternative Investments Market (AIM), and others have been set up within large European banks.

Stirling Habbitts

CARBON NEUTRAL
→ Climate change

Carbon neutral means that the emissions of carbon dioxide and/or other → greenhouse gases into the atmosphere from an activity, a person, a group of people, or the manufacture of a product have been offset by removing an equal amount of carbon dioxide and/or other greenhouse gases from the atmosphere. The basic idea is that it doesn't matter where in the world carbon is reduced, since → climate change is a global problem.

To make something carbon neutral, its associated emissions are usually offset through the purchase of → carbon credits or other means (the most common being the planting of trees or investment in low carbon technologies like renewable energy projects). Examples of activities that have been made carbon neutral include recent G8 Summits, tours and albums by singers and bands, government activities, individual lifestyles, consumer products, rental car contracts and air tickets.

There is some controversy around the concept of carbon offsetting, since it is perceived by some as a way to buy peace of mind, without changing behaviour or consumption patterns which underly the problem of greenhouse gas emissions and → climate change.

Stirling Habbitts

CARBON OFFSETTING
→ Carbon neutral

CARBON SINK
→ Carbon balance

CARBON TAX
→ Climate change

A carbon tax is a tax on the use of fuels that result in emissions of carbon dioxide and other → greenhouse gases into the atmosphere, and is usually based on the quantity and type of fuel used (e.g. coal, oil or gas).

The word carbon in carbon tax refers to the element carbon in the most common greenhouse gas, carbon dioxide (CO_2). The primary purpose of a carbon tax is to create an incentive to increase the efficiency of fuel use, and thereby reduce greenhouse gas emissions from fuel and the associated contribution to → climate change. Carbon taxes also generate revenue for governments, like other taxes.

Sweden was the first country to introduce a carbon tax in 1991, on the use of oil, coal, natural gas, liquefied petroleum gas, petrol, and aviation fuel used in domestic → travel. The tax included concessions and exemptions for certain industries. Finland, the Netherlands, and Norway have also introduced carbon taxes, and they have been formally proposed (but not adopted) in New Zealand and in the USA. Carbon taxes are generally regarded as alternative mechanisms to greenhouse gas emissions trading schemes (such as the → EU Greenhouse Gas Emission Trading Scheme and emissions trading under the → Kyoto Protocol), as both share the objective of reducing emissions and tackling → climate change.

CARBON TRADING
→ Emissions trading

CAUSE-RELATED MARKETING

Cause-related marketing occurs when a company states that a small part of the purchase price will be contributed to support a specified worthy cause. One of the earliest examples is when American Express said that consumers who use their American Express credit card for charges during a specified period are assured that 1% of the charge would be contributed to repairing the Statue of Liberty. A more current example is where Avon says that it will denote a certain percentage of consumer purchases to support research on breast cancer; to date, Avon has already contributed more than $40 million to this cause. A growing number of consumers respond to cause-related marketing offers as long as they find everything else about the product or service is satisfactory.

Philip Kotler

CAUX ROUND TABLE

⌘ www.cauxroundtable.org

The Caux Round Table (CRT) is an international network of business leaders working to promote a moral capitalism. The CRT advocates implementation of the CRT Principles for Business through which principled capitalism can flourish and sustainable and socially responsible prosperity can become the foundation for a fair, free and transparent global society.

With respect to public governance, the CRT further advocates implementation of the CRT Principles for Government so that appropriate social capital can be accumulated throughout the world in a just and responsible manner. The CRT has also published a collateral set of ethical principles for the better governance of NGOs. The group was first convened in 1986 by Frederik Philipps and Olivier Giscard d'Estaing in Caux, Switzerland. In 1994 the group published a set of ethical guidelines for profitable business enterprises called the CRT Principles for Business. It subsequently developed an implemenation management process to help companies apply these Principles in their business decision-making.

Stephen B. Young

CERES PRINCIPLES

🖰 www.ceres.org

The CERES Principles, launched in 1989 by the Coalition for Environmentally Responsible Economies (CERES) as the Valdez Principles, are a 10-point code of corporate environmental conduct to be publicly endorsed by companies as an environmental mission statement or ethic. Embedded in that code of conduct is the mandate to report periodically on environmental management structures and results. In 1993, following lengthy negotiations, Sunoco became the first Fortune 500 company to endorse the CERES Principles and today over 50 companies have followed suit, including 13 Fortune 500 firms. By endorsing the CERES Principles, companies not only formalise their dedication to environmental awareness and → accountability, but also actively commit to an ongoing process of continuous improvement, dialogue and comprehensive, systematic public reporting. Endorsing companies have access to the diverse array of experts in the CERES network, from investors to policy analysts, energy experts, scientists, and others. The 10 Principles cover: Protection of the Biosphere; Sustainable Use of Natural Resources; Reduction and Disposal of Wastes; Energy Conservation; Risk Reduction; Safe Products and Services; Environmental Restoration; Informing the Public; Management Commitment; and Audits and Reports.

CERTIFICATION

Certification is a procedure where an independent and competent third party gives written → assurance, by means of a certificate, that a product, service, system, process or material conforms to specific requirements.

Certificates of conformity to specified standards are issued by certification bodies, which are independent of the organisations they certify.

Quality and → environmental management system certification assures users and customers that an organisation has a management system in place that complies with the → ISO 9001 and/or the → ISO 14001 standards, irrespective of the organisation's activities. To maintain compliance, organisations are monitored by regular surveillance.

Product certification is specific to a particular product produced by a particular business. Product certification assures users and regulators that the certified product complies with the standard(s) specified on the certificate, such as those of → fair trade or organic produce. Product certification may be limited to compliance with one or more standards even though the product may be subject to many standards.

When an authoritative body gives formal recognition that a certification body is competent to carry out its certification activities, this is known as accreditation. Accreditation reduces risk for government, business and customers by ensuring, through regular surveillance, that an accredited certification body is independent and competent, and delivers its services in the most time and cost effective way.

Accreditation bodies are established in many countries, often by government or with the encouragement of government, with the primary purpose of ensuring that certification bodies in that country are subject to oversight by an authoritative body.

Users of certification can have confidence in the credibility of the certification body they use if it has been assessed as competent by an accreditation body which is a member of the → International Accreditation Forum (IAF).

John Owen

CHARITY
→ Philanthropy

CHEMICALS SECTOR
→ Responsible Care

CSR in the chemicals sector can be thought of in terms of three historical eras: the Carson era, the Love Canal era and the REACH era.

The Carson era began with the watershed publication of Rachel Carson's 1962 book, *Silent Spring*, in which she argued that the proliferation of persistent chemicals building up in the → environment was unsustainable for all life. Carson illustrated her case with the story of Clear Lake, California, where residues of the poisonous insecticide DDT had accumulated initially in the plankton, then in the fish that ate the plankton, then in the water birds that ate the fish, at each stage increasing in concentration. The dead birds were eventually found with up to 1600 parts per million (ppm) of DDD (a form of DDT), compared to the recommended safe concentration of 0.05 ppm. The Carson era of the 1960s and 1970s was therefore characterised by the expression of health concerns about chemical build-up in the → environment by a small but vocal group of scientists and other concerned groups. By and large, these concerns were dismissed by the chemicals industry and ignored by the public who were enjoying the benefits of chemicals in everyday products.

The Love Canal era began with an explosion in 1978 at an industrial → waste site, owned by Hooker Chemicals, at Love Canal near Niagara Falls in the United States. The resulting dispersion of chemical compounds in the community, many of which were suspected carcinogens, were later claimed to have resulted in birth defects and other harmful health impacts. Love Canal, however, was only the first in a string of high profile incidents that plagued the chemicals industry in the 1980s, not least of which was the industrial accident in 1984 at Union Carbide's pesticides facility in Bhopal, India, which killed more than 2000 people. Another was the catastrophic spilling of 10.8 million gallons of oil by the *Exxon Valdez* tanker off the coast of Alaska in 1989, resulting in environmental clean-up and community liabilities exceeding $8 billion. With the sector's reputation severely tarnished, the chemicals industry responded by developing the → Responsible Care programme, a set of self-regulatory standards launched in 1988 and designed to improve chemical companies' health, safety and environmental management practices. This has become the chemicals industry benchmark for good practice worldwide.

The REACH era began with the adoption of the REACH regulations (standing for the Registration, Evaluation and Authorisation of Chemicals) by the Council of European Environment Ministers on 13 December 2006 and its entry into force on 1 June 2007. The intention of the REACH regulations is to subject the more than 100 000 chemicals that have proliferated in the past decades to rigorous testing for their environmental and health impacts. The process essentially involves registering the chemicals, including an analysis of their impacts and how best to manage these, followed by an evaluation by the government agency. Deadlines for chemical registration are staged with a deadline of June 2008 for the most hazardous substances. It is expected that over 30 000 chemicals will be registered with the agency by 2018 and of these around 1500 are likely to be considered of high concern. Substances of high concern include those that are persistent, bio-accumulative and toxic (so-called PBTs), very persistent or very bio-accumulative and endocrine disrupting chemicals (EDCs). For these, an authorisation process is then required. Hence, in the REACH era, chemicals companies will increasingly be required to be transparent and accountable for the environmental and health impacts of their products.

In summary, the main CSR issues faced by the chemicals sector include:

- Environmental impacts, including emissions to air (especially → greenhouse gases like carbon dioxide and noxious gases like sulphur dioxide), → water (especially persistent chemicals) and land (including chemical spills, soil contamination and sterilisation of land).
- Health impacts, including exposure to chemicals that are toxic, carcinogenic, affect human immune or reproductive systems and cause skin irritation.
- Safety impacts, including the loss of life or cause of injuries among employees and the public through industrial accidents at chemical plants or during transportation or consumption.
- Community impacts, including economic benefits through the provision of jobs and social investment in → infrastructure and public services, but also disruption or displacement of communities through chemical infrastructure projects or layoffs.

Wayne Visser

CHILD LABOUR
→ Labour issues

Child labour refers to the systematic use of children as part of the workforce (domestic or industrial). It is often considered exploitative, and there are international conventions that seek to protect children from economic exploitation and from performing any work that is likely to be hazardous or to interfere with their education, or to be harmful to the child's health or physical, mental, spiritual, moral or social development.

There is disagreement about what is acceptable child labour. The UN Convention on the Rights of the Child and ILO's Convention 182 focus on the worst and most harmful forms of child labour. Children's rights organisations such as Save the Children endorse these, but indicate a need to recognise that child labour takes many forms, some of which violate children's rights while others do not. Most forms of work have both good and bad elements, and for this reason, can be both harmful and beneficial to children's development and well-being.

Child labour has many causes: primarily poverty but also debt, conflict and structural adjustment. An estimated 218 million children aged 5–17 are engaged in child labour (not including child domestic labour) working as anything from factory workers, to farm labourers, to prostitutes, to armed soldiers.

Mick Blowfield

CIVIL REGULATION
→ Non-governmental organisations, Partnerships

Civil regulation theory proposes that businesses are being regulated by civil society (rather than governments), through the dual effect of negative impacts from conflict and benefits from collaboration. This approach provides new means for people to hold companies accountable, thereby democratising the economy directly. The theory was introduced in → development studies and environmental management studies to broaden the dualistic debate between advocates of business → self-regulation and greater state regulation, both by suggesting that policy responses from business could be legitimate if in response to stakeholder demands, and by highlighting how many businesses were being compelled to respond, due to the financial implications of increasingly institutionalised civil society action. Since 2000, more analysis has focused on the limitations of civil regulation, in terms of the number of companies affected, the issues covered and the questionable → accountability of the multi-stakeholder codes and → certification systems that result.

Jem Bendell

CIVIL SOCIETY ORGANISATIONS (CSOs)
→ Non-governmental organisations (NGOs)

CLEAN DEVELOPMENT MECHANISM (CDM)
→ Kyoto Protocol

The Clean Development Mechanism (CDM) is one of the mechanisms of the → Kyoto Protocol, under which projects to reduce, avoid or sequester emissions of → greenhouse gases undertaken in countries categorised as non-Annex I countries under the → Kyoto Protocol can generate → carbon credits that can be used in Annex I countries to assist these countries to meet their greenhouse gas emissions targets.

Under the → Kyoto Protocol, countries are divided into two categories, Annex I (industrialised countries and countries with economies in transition) and non-Annex I countries (typically, → developing countries). Annex I countries have targets to reduce greenhouse gas emissions, and non-Annex I countries do not. A mechanism to take action to reduce emission in non-Annex I countries is, however, provided in the form of the CDM, which allows → carbon credits generated from emissions reduction projects in non-Annex I countries to be used by Annex I countries to assist in meeting their targets.

The CDM is overseen by the CDM Executive Board, which is appointed under the United Nations Framework Convention on Climate Change. The rules of the CDM include the requirement that all CDM projects contribute to → sustainable development in the countries in which they take place, as determined by the Designated National Authority for CDM projects appointed by the government of the country. CDM projects are also required to follow a particular project cycle, including validation and verification of the project and associated emissions reductions by an appointed independent third party, and registration with the CDM Executive Board. CDM projects are also required to be additional to what would have happened in the absence of the CDM, referred to as additionality. As of June 2006, the United Nations Climate Change Secretariat noted that the CDM had generated more than one billion tonnes of → carbon credits for the period up to the end of 2012.

Stirling Habbitts

CLEANER PRODUCTION
→ Eco-efficiency

CLEAN TECHNOLOGY
Clean technology is → technology that creates less pollution. Where pollution control initially involved only end-of-pipe measures, nowadays the focus is on production processes that cause less pollution. Implementing cleaner technology is the key to achieving this. Measures include changing inputs, changing equipment, changing process parameters or changing working procedures. The use of clean technology, therefore, is an important element in → waste management. The major aim in → waste management, next to controlling waste streams, is to move up in the waste hierarchy: from pollution towards recycling, reuse and reduce. By rethinking production processes and the subsequent implementation of clean technology, less waste (useless output) can be produced, thus increasing the amount of desired output (product) per unit of raw material. In other words: the company is becoming more eco-efficient by using clean technology.

Theo de Bruijn

CLIMATE CHANGE
→ Carbon balance, Carbon credits, Carbon Disclosure Project, Carbon funds, Carbon neutral, Carbon tax, Clean Development Mechanism (CDM), Emissions trading, EU Greenhouse Gas

Emission Trading Scheme, Greenhouse gases, Greenhouse Gas Protocol, Joint Implementation, Kyoto Protocol

Climate change refers to the variation in the earth's global weather systems over time. These variations are caused by, among others, changes in the earth's orbit, variable solar activity, volcanic activity, changes in vegetation, catastrophic events such as meteor impacts, and the greenhouse effect. At the extremes they result in prolonged warm periods or ice ages.

The greenhouse effect, which keeps the temperature about 30 degrees Celsius warmer than it would otherwise be, is the process of absorption of infrared radiation by the gases in the earth's atmosphere (the so-called → greenhouse gases).

Evidence for past climate change is taken from a number of sources including vegetation, ice cores, sea level changes, glacial coverage and tree ring growth. Human historical records are sparse, but include the depth of burials in Greenland (these depend on how frozen the ground was at time of burial) and documentary evidence of harvesting times. Daily temperature records have only been taken since 1873.

Recently the term climate change has been used to describe the additional anthropogenic (human caused) variation to the climate. As this is associated with an average increase in temperature it is also referred to as global warming.

Anthropogenic climate change is caused by the additional → greenhouse gases emitted from activities such as transport, power generation and deforestation. These emissions affect the → carbon balance and this has resulted in an average temperature rise of almost 0.7 degrees Celsius since pre-industrial times. This rise in temperature has a large effect on the climate, altering weather patterns around the world.

As the concentration of → greenhouse gases increases, especially due to the increasing demands of society for fossil fuel-based energy, this temperature rise continues. Recent scientific models have shown that a rise of over 2 degrees Celsius above pre-industrial levels could lead to dangerous conditions such as the irreversible melting of the Greenland ice cap, which in turn leads to global sea level rises of about 7 metres over several millennia.

The effects of climate change on human society are increased due to our tendency to live in coastal areas and the fact that we have developed a society dependent on the current climate and access to cheap energy. The 2006 UK Government commissioned Stern Review on the economics of climate change states that the consequences of unconstrained climate change could cost as much as 5–20% of global gross domestic product (GDP) whereas action taken now to combat dangerous climate change would cost an average of 1% of GDP.

Action on climate change is divided into two areas:

1. Mitigation, i.e. action aimed at preventing emissions of → greenhouse gases to reduce future warming, including the development of technologies such as renewable energy; and
2. Adaptation, i.e. action aimed at changing aspects of current society to limit the effects of climate change, including investment in areas such as better flood defences.

Much of this action is framed against the backdrop of the work of the Intergovernmental Panel on Climate Change (IPCC), which was established in 1988 to assess the risk of human–induced climate change. The United Nations Framework Convention on Climate Change (UNFCCC) was set up as an international treaty and started a process for negotiating joint action to tackle climate change. The → Kyoto Protocol was negotiated as part of this process and came into force in 2005. It requires countries to meet emissions targets by 2012.

Current international frameworks come to an end in 2012 and negotiations are under way as to what should replace the → Kyoto Protocol. This includes possible stabilisation targets for the concentration of → greenhouse gases in the atmosphere.

In the meantime, a number of ways to stabilise emissions have been proposed in order to avoid dangerous climate change. Most famous of these are the so-called 'Socolow wedges', based on an article by Stephen Pacala and Robert Socolow from Princeton in the 13 August 2004 issue of *Science*. They proposed 15 existing technologies that, if adopted on a mass scale, could each prevent the emission of 1 billion tonnes of → greenhouse gases per year. All 15 are not mutually exclusive and their model shows how, by choosing appropriate technologies and policies, 7 billion tonnes of carbon emissions per year could be prevented and thereby stabilise concentrations below dangerous levels.

Aled Jones

CLUB OF ROME
⌂ www.clubofrome.org

The Club of Rome is a global think-tank and centre of innovation and initiative. As a non-profit, non-governmental organisation, it brings together scientists, economists, businessmen, international high civil servants, heads of state and former heads of state from all five continents who are convinced that the future of humankind is not determined once and for all and that each human being can contribute to the improvement of our societies.

The Club of Rome's mission is to act as a global catalyst of change that is free of any political, ideological or business interest. The Club of Rome contributes to the solution of what it calls the world problematique, the complex set of the most crucial problems – political, social, economic, technological, environmental, psychological and cultural – facing humanity. It does so by taking a global, long-term and interdisciplinary perspective of the increasing interdependence of nations and the → globalisation of problems that pose predicaments beyond the capacity of individual countries.

The Club of Rome raised considerable public attention with its *Limits to Growth* report, which has sold 30 million copies in more than 30 translations, making it the best selling environmental book in world history. The *Limits to Growth* essentially argued that the projected industrial trends in resource use and pollution associated with population and economic growth were ecologically unsustainable.

CODES OF CONDUCT

A code of conduct is a set of rules that guides and orients behaviour within an organisation or sector in order to promote social, environmental, and/or ethical behaviour. A code is a formal statement which encapsulates the → values and principles of an organisation. Codes of conduct are voluntary instruments that vary greatly in content, origins and enforcement mechanisms.

Some are only a short statement and others are agreed through complex multi-stakeholder consensus.

In corporate responsibility, there is a continuum from → values, through principles and codes, to norms and standards. It is useful to differentiate codes of conduct from standards. Codes are generally internal or firm specific, while standards, such as SA 8000, apply broadly across a wide range of companies and sectors. Generally, codes involve only limited → accountability, whereas standards entail a greater degree of → accountability, in terms of reporting. Codes of conduct tend to be developed through internal consensus with some consultation with stakeholders, whereas standards and norms require a greater degree of consensus among stakeholders.

Classification of codes of conduct

Codes of conduct can be classified in a variety of ways:

- Their focus, i.e. whether they are focused on process and/or performance or both;
- The way in which they were developed;

- Their scope (i.e. whether they cover → human rights, labour and/or environment), and
- Their stakeholder focus (i.e. whether they are focused on employees, buyers, investors, consumers or a combination thereof).

Focus of codes of conduct

Codes of conduct can be divided into two key categories, those that focus on performance and those that focus on process. Performance-oriented codes define minimum standards of what constitutes socially responsible behaviour. These tools relate to the focus of corporate responsibility and the outcomes that companies are working towards, such as the elimination of → child labour.

Process-oriented codes define procedures that companies or organisations should follow, such as social reporting, stakeholder consultation, and mechanisms for addressing complaints. Many codes of conduct include both performance and process elements.

The development of codes of conduct

Codes can also be characterised by how they were developed, either through unilateral, bilateral, or multi-stakeholder consultation. Unilateral codes are developed by a company or organisation. Usually there is some consultation with stakeholders, but the company has the ultimate responsibility for the code. Examples of these branded codes of conduct include Nike's Code of Conduct. Bilateral codes are signed between two parties. For example, a framework agreement is signed between a trade union and a company. The Ikea Framework Agreement and the Statoil Framework Agreement are examples of bilaterally agreed codes. Multi-stakeholder codes are developed by a network of organisations through extensive consultations and shared governance. Examples include the Ethical Trading Initiative's Base Code (→ ETI Base Code).

The scope and focus of codes of conduct

Corporate responsibility includes a wide range of issues; however, most corporate responsibility codes of conduct focus only on a portion of these issues. Some of the issues covered by codes of conduct include:

- Working conditions;
- Combating bribery;
- Environment; and
- → Human rights.

Codes of conduct can be targeted towards different stakeholders. Codes can be directed towards a wide range of stakeholders, including employees, buyers, suppliers, governments, customers, and trade unions, among others.

The uses of codes of conduct

Codes of conduct can help organisations in a wide range of ways. Codes can:

- Raise awareness about corporate responsibility within an organisation;
- Help organisations to set strategies and objectives;
- Assist organisations with implementation;
- Help organisations to avoid risk;
- Foster dialogue and partnerships between companies and key stakeholders; and
- Enhance unity and identity within an organisation or among organisations.

In the early to mid-1990s, companies began to develop codes of conduct to address working conditions within their supply chain. Companies, such as Levi Strauss & Co., Reebok, and Philips van Heusen were among the first companies to draft codes of conduct for their suppliers. As more and more companies developed their own codes, suppliers grew confused by the multiplicity of codes. In the late 1990s, multi-stakeholder codes of conduct were developed such as SA 8000 and the → ETI Base Code.

Over the past two decades, sector initiatives have continued to evolve, many of which have launched sector-wide codes of conduct, including the toy and electronic goods sectors. NGOs have also begun to develop codes of conduct, for their own suppliers and for their activities more broadly. Whenever codes of conduct are launched, they must be embedded into the organisation through training, awareness raising, and management systems to ensure that they are adhered to in a consistent manner.

Deborah Leipziger

CODES OF ETHICS
→ Codes of conduct

CODE OF LABOUR PRACTICES FOR THE APPAREL INDUSTRY INCLUDING SPORTSWEAR
→ Labour issues, Supply chain
⤵ www.cleanclothes.org

The Code of Labour Practices for the Apparel Industry including Sportswear was developed by the Netherlands-based NGO Clean Clothes Campaign, a worldwide network of organisations that focus on improving working conditions in the global garment industry. It was published in 1998 and by many experts is considered as one of the strictest and most stringent efforts to tackle labour conditions, in particular → child labour in → developing countries. Particularly strict are monitoring systems and management commitment. It envisages monitoring by an independent body consisting of trade union organisations, trade associations, employers' organisations and NGOs, and includes severe sanctions for companies and third parties.

CODES OF PRACTICE
→ Codes of conduct

COMBINED CODE ON CORPORATE GOVERNANCE
→ Corporate governance
🖰 www.fsa.gov.uk

The Combined Code on Corporate Governance applies to all companies incorporated in the UK and listed on the Main Market of the London Stock Exchange. The Combined Code comprises a combination of broad principles and specific provisions relating to → corporate governance. Listed companies are required to report annually on their application of the Code's principles, and either to confirm compliance or explain non-compliance with the Code's provisions. The Combined Code was published by the Financial Reporting Council in September 2003, and an updated version of the Code was published in June 2006. The aim of the Code is to raise the standards of → corporate governance, thereby enhancing board effectiveness and improving investor confidence. Some of the main features of the Code are:

- Stipulating more open and rigorous procedures for the appointment, induction, development and renewal of directors;
- Formal performance evaluation processes for boards, committees and individual directors;
- At least 50% of the board in larger listed companies should be comprised of independent non-executive directors;
- The separation of the roles of chairman and chief executive officer (the chief executive should not become the chairman of the same company); and

- A more prominent role for the Audit Committee, specifically in terms of monitoring financial reporting and reviewing the management of both financial and non-financial risks.

Daniel Malan

COMMON GOOD
→ Public interest

COMMONWEALTH CORPORATE GOVERNANCE PRINCIPLES
→ Corporate governance
⌨ www.cacg-inc.com

The Commonwealth Association for Corporate Governance (CAGC) is an incorporated society registered in New Zealand and was established in 1998 by 24 member countries of the Commonwealth after a technical meeting on → corporate governance was convened by the Commonwealth Secretariat. This took place in response to the Edinburgh Declaration of the Commonwealth Heads of Government meeting in 1997 to promote excellence in → corporate governance in the Commonwealth.

The CAGC Principles were published in November 1999 as guidelines to facilitate → best practice in → corporate governance in both the private sector and state-owned enterprises. They are not mandatory and are currently under review. There are 15 principles, focusing on activities that the board should engage in. According to these principles, the board should:

- Exercise → leadership, enterprise, → integrity and judgement;
- Ensure effective board appointment processes;
- Determine the corporation's purpose and → values and ensure the protection of the corporation's assets and reputation;

- Monitor and evaluate the implementation of strategies, policies, management performance criteria and business plans;
- Ensure compliance with relevant laws, regulations and codes of best business practice;
- Ensure effective communication with shareholders and other stakeholders;
- Serve the legitimate interests of shareholders and account to them;
- Identify internal and external stakeholders and agree a policy on how to relate to them;
- Ensure appropriate balance of power and authority on the board (e.g. through separating the roles of chief executive officer and chairman and a balance between executive and non-executive directors);
- Ensure effectiveness of internal systems of control;
- Regularly assess its own performance and effectiveness;
- Appoint the CEO, ensure effective training for management and employees and develop a succession plan for senior management;
- Ensure that all → technology and systems are adequate to properly run the business;
- Identify key risk areas and key performance indicators; and
- Ensure annually that the corporation will continue as a going concern.

Daniel Malan

COMMUNITY DEVELOPMENT
→ Local economic development

Community development in a CSR context is about recognising that how a company recruits, purchases and invests can create opportunities not only to build prosperous communities but also to reach out and help their most disadvantaged members of society to improve the quality and substance of their lives.

Some of the ways in which responsible business practice can have impact in addition to bringing business benefits include:

- Reflecting the local community in their workplace profile and removing barriers to employment.
- Engaging employees in community activity and aiming to support staff in → volunteering, which can include mentoring young people to improve employability skills, helping primary school children with reading and numeracy skills, and using professional skills to help improve the professionalism of charities and other organisations delivering services. Other examples of mentoring opportunities include those which use employees as job coaches to the homeless, mentors in secondary schools, support to ex-offenders, or partners to head teachers and community leaders.
- Reviewing local purchasing and supplier opportunities and building local education and training links particularly in deprived areas.
- Working in partnership with community organisations and charities to invest through employee support, expertise, skills, cash, gifts in kind and linking brands to causes.
- Listening and engaging in real dialogue with communities, the public and voluntary sector on matters of mutual concern.
- Working collaboratively with other businesses, measuring the benefit to business and the community, and communicating the impact.

David Halley

COMMUNITY INVESTING

→ Community development, Philanthropy, Socially responsible investment

Community investing deploys capital from investors and directs it to communities that are overlooked and underserved by 'traditional' financial institutions, providing access to credit, equity and basic → banking products that otherwise may not be available. Community development financial institutions (CDFIs) are the primary intermediaries who deploy capital in underserved communities. There are four basic types of CDFIs, which combined had $14 billion of total US assets in 2005 and $20 billion in 2006: community development banks, community development credit unions, community development loan funds, and community development venture capital funds. CDFIs provide critically needed financing in underserved minority areas to enable increased home ownership and the construction of affordable housing, small business lending, microcredit, and environmental → conservation.

Debbie Kobak

COMPETITIVE ADVANTAGE

→ Business case, Responsible competitiveness, Responsible Competitiveness Index

The idea that CSR creates competitive advantages is based on the assumption that CSR investments may help firms achieve sustainable, above-average performance compared with industry peers. At first this notion is counter-intuitive since social performance creates public goods while the costs are private. However, some firms can create shareholder value from seemingly philanthropic activities.

First, CSR investments can reduce firm risk by containing consumer boycotts, governmental regulation, or by protecting a firm's → licence to operate (i.e. its support in the local community).

Second, CSR can increase operational efficiency. Better → waste, energy, and → water management can reduce costs (named → eco-efficiency). Proactive CSR also motivates employees, thus reducing staff turnover and absenteeism. In some cases inclusion in socially responsible investing funds may slightly reduce a firm's cost of capital.

Third, firms may adopt social marketing for products with a higher social performance, thus increasing sales or allowing them to charge price premiums. There are an increasing number of products with labels attesting to a product's social performance ('organic', '→ fair trade', 'energy efficient', or 'no → child labour').

Finally, there are a small number of firms that have used CSR to enter or even create new markets. Typical examples are the market for → clean technology venture capital or the creation of markets for the poor (also called → Base of the Pyramid).

Kai Hockerts

CONFLICT OF INTEREST
→ Business ethics, Corporate governance

A conflict of interest exists when the independence and impartiality of decision-makers is compromised due to competing interests influencing the outcome of a decision, for personal benefit in particular. Real or perceived conflicts of interest determine a person's or institution's credibility.

Ramifications of real or perceived conflicts of interest include legal liability, decline in share price and loss of trust with shareholders, regulators, employees, investors, customers, suppliers, partners, the media and the public.

Remedies for real or perceived conflicts of interest include the transparent declaration of interests that detract from the independence and impartiality of decision-makers, removal from situations where a conflict applies and/or evaluation by independent third parties of adherence to conflict of interest standards, → codes of conduct or guidelines.

An example of a conflict of interest occurred when corporate research analysts issued recommendations to buy stock in weak → technology companies in an effort to gain investment → banking deals for their employers, which contributed to the artificial rise in and burst of a stock market bubble and loss of significant money by investors in the late 1990s. These severe conflict of interest violations resulted in a $1.4 billion research settlement by Wall Street banks, as reported by the US Securities and Exchange Commission in December 2005.

Jonathan Cohen

CONSERVATION
→ Biodiversity

Conservation can be defined as the rational and prudent management of biological resources to achieve the greatest sustainable current benefit while maintaining the potential of the resources to meet the needs of future generations. In natural resource economics, conservation is a rate of use of a biological resource which ensures that the same or a greater quantity of that resource will be available in the future. Thus conservation includes preservation, maintenance, sustainable utilisation, restoration, and enhancement of the natural environment. But conservation is far more than such a straightforward definition, as it embodies a fundamental philosophy about the relationship between people and the rest of nature. It assumes a responsibility for ensuring that the activities of people do not lead to ecological degradation, that resources are used in a sustainable manner, and that the → environment remains in a productive state even after some of the resources that were found within the ecosystem have been utilised.

The central notion of conservation and its approaches have evolved considerably. In its early days, conservation was often motivated by loss of species, with many protected areas established on a preservationist approach. According to the 2006 IUCN Red List, the latest indications are that some 24% of mammals, 12% of birds, and 33% of amphibians are threatened with extinction. However, one of the hot debates in the conservation community is whether it is more effective to focus on individual species (e.g. through species recovery plans or lists of threatened species) or through systems approaches (such as the ecosystem approach advocated by the Convention on Biological Diversity). The debate is compounded by the need to take account of local and → indigenous people affected by conservation practices, as well as incorporate → development objectives, leading to pro-poor or socially responsible conservation.

Conservation has become a profession, with training at the university level in documenting, managing, monitoring, and enhancing natural resources through appropriate forms of management. Many non-governmental organisations have been established with the objective of contributing to the conservation of nature and natural resources. These NGOs can provide important partners in CSR, helping to provide technical advice on how to incorporate conservation into corporate activities. They may also carry out a watchdog function if a corporation does not live up to its stated conservation ideals and objectives.

Conservation includes planning action aimed at preserving or protecting both living and non-living resources. It can also include avoiding actions that will threaten the resources that need to be conserved. In terms of CSR, it assumes a responsibility for future generations, contributing to clean rivers and lakes, diverse wildlife populations, healthy soils and clean air. Companies should avoid any actions that further endanger rare species, and ensure that their activities do not threaten the ecological integrity of protected areas.

While different organisations may take varying approaches to determining priorities for conservation investment, all are valid and mutually reinforcing. Conservation requires diversity in strategies, policies, and practices in order to respond to the multiple challenges. Perhaps more important, no conservation investment is likely to be effective if economic, social, and political factors are leading to → ecosystem degradation. Instead, conservation needs to build a stronger political constituency, new ways of providing knowledge for decisions, better ways of mobilising information, dynamic approaches that enable us to adapt to changing conditions, and new ways to generate funding for conservation.

Valli Moosa

CONSUMERISM
→ Consumer rights, Ethical consumption

Originally an American term describing the doctrine that a stable economy is conditional on continuous growth of goods and services, consumerism is now used far more broadly to refer to individuals' patterns of expenditure – often within market societies where particular social premiums are placed on the consumption of constantly innovated products and services. In its contemporary use the term often has a rather negative connotation as it gets associated with the belief that happiness in a modern society is inextricably linked with the number and quality of goods and services consumed. Within a CSR context the term has been linked with a variety of adjectives: such as ethical consumerism (→ ethical consumption) and can be associated with → sustainable consumption.

Consumerism raises a number of difficult questions for companies seeking to be socially responsible: are our products and services 'useful' to society; what are their impacts; do we target consumers who benefit from them; are the patterns of consumerism we promote sustainable or responsible? The relationship between consumerism and → sustainable consumption is particularly vexed.

John Sabapathy

CONSUMER RIGHTS
→ Consumerism, Ethical consumption, Stakeholder theory

Consumer rights are principles governing the interactions between organisations and consumers that protect consumers' interests to ensure that consumers are safe, informed, represented, and fairly treated.

For much of the history of business, the consumer's interests were either ignored under the principle of 'caveat emptor' (let the buyer beware!), or sometimes protected through the individual interventions of the local judiciary or clergy. In theory the principle of consumer sovereignty, which underpins both free market economics and marketing, should guarantee that company behaviour is directed by the wishes and interests of consumers. In practice, during the 19th and early 20th centuries, as the scale and influence of business grew, so did concerns about a widening power imbalance between companies and their customers. In particular concerns emerged about the power of monopolies and their impact on prices and consumer choice; the lack of information for consumers on issues like → food ingredients; the relative lack of influence consumers had on government policy-making processes; and the need to protect vulnerable consumers, particularly the poor and elderly. These concerns drove the growth of the → consumerism movement during the 20th century, and in 1962 US President John F. Kennedy made a groundbreaking declaration on consumer rights to the US Congress: 'Consumers by definition include us all. They are the largest economic group affecting and affected by almost every public and private economic decision. Yet they are the only important group whose views are often not heard.'

This declaration identified four fundamental consumer rights:

- The right to safety;
- The right to be informed;
- The right to choose; and
- The right to be heard.

Consumers International (originally the International Organisation of Consumers Unions) which represents over 100 countries, went on to extend the original list of four rights to eight:

- The right to satisfaction of basic needs – through essential goods and services like adequate → food, → water, clothing, shelter, health care and sanitation.

- The right to safety – protection against products, production processes and services that endanger health or life.
- The right to be informed – through the facts and information necessary to make informed choices.
- The right to choose – from a range of products and services of satisfactory quality, offered at competitive prices.
- The right to be heard – and to have your interests as a consumer represented in government policy.
- The right to redress – and a fair settlement of just claims, including compensation for misrepresentation, shoddy goods or poor services.
- The right to education – to acquire the knowledge and skills necessary to make informed and confident choices.
- The right to a healthy environment – to live and work in an environment which does not threaten the well-being of present or future generations.

In 1985 these eight rights were adopted by the United Nations in its Guidelines for Consumer Protection, and since 1983 the anniversary of President Kennedy's declaration on 15 March has been celebrated as World Consumer Rights Day, focusing on a different rights issue each year. They are also supported through organisations such as consumers unions, and the publications they produce such as *Which?* and *Consumer Reports* in the UK.

In practice consumer rights have mainly been protected through legislation covering competition policy; the sale, display and pricing of goods; product safety; and environmental regulations. In industries such as financial services, → food and → travel more specific rights have also been identified and legally protected. Other aspects of consumer rights, such as access to basic needs, consumer education and the right to be heard are also addressed through public policies and services. As principles of customer service have spread, so areas of public services, such as state health care in many countries, have developed additional specific principles of consumer rights, such as the right to dignity or the right to privacy.

In recent years the debate about consumer rights has been tempered by a focus on the responsibilities of consumers, including a focus on:

- The rights of non-consumers (e.g. the impacts of smoking on non-smokers);
- The rights of the current generation of consumers to consume at a level which may restrict the opportunities of future generations; and
- Poverty, and the rights of primary producers in poor countries, whose quality of life is often far worse than that of the ultimate consumer in wealthier countries.

Ultimately there has been an assumed 'right to consume' whatever one can afford. On a planet whose environmental limits are already being stretched, and on which around 3 billion people exist on under two dollars per day, and are therefore excluded from the consumer society, this assumption may be increasingly challenged.

Ken Peattie

CONTINUAL IMPROVEMENT

→ Environmental management system, Quality management

Continual improvement can be defined as the recurring process of enhancing a management system to achieve improvements in overall performance of the organisation in line with the organisation's policy.

Continual improvement is based on the 'Plan, Do, Check, Act' model which was first associated with quality management and now also environmental management. This model leads to continual improvement based upon the principles described below:

- Plan – planning, including identifying environmental aspects and establishing goals.
- Do – implementing, including training and operational controls.

- Check – checking, including monitoring and corrective action.
- Act – reviewing, including progress reviews and acting to make needed changes to the management system.

In the context of the requirements of → ISO 14001:2004 related to continual improvement, the process need not take place in all areas of activity simultaneously but clear evidence of improvement must be demonstrated.

Johann Möller

CORPORATE AFFAIRS
→ Public affairs

CORPORATE CITIZENSHIP

Corporate citizenship can be defined as extending the relationship between business and society to include an understanding of the social, environmental and political responsibilities of business. The notion of corporate citizenship sees the company as having rights, duties and responsibilities in society in the same way that citizens also have rights, duties and responsibilities. For many practitioners and activists it is a radical notion that its fulfilment means a rewriting of the rules of business.

Conceptually, the notion of citizenship exposes the fact that many of the CSR-related activities of companies today are taking place in traditionally political arenas. For example, philanthropic activities to support education or the arts often substitute dwindling governmental support. Likewise, engagement in implementing labour and → human rights standards in the developing world often steps in for governments unwilling to protect their citizens. Corporate citizenship addresses this dimension and conceputalises a company as a member of society which – like a normal citizen – is involved and participates in the governance of society in various shapes and forms.

However, in practice the term 'corporate citizenship' is often used as a synonym for → corporate (social) responsibility. It is also sometimes conflated with → business ethics and → corporate governance under the general discourse around 'business and society' or 'business in society'. Towards the end of the 20th century the term was co-opted by many businesses and management consultancies in the US and UK to show an apparent new concern for people and planet. In reality the term has been in use around the world since the beginning of the 1930s in India and 1950s in the USA. In business this language is often used to evoke notions of membership, participation and good neighbourhood and the subject area is often concerned with risk, reputation, communications and strategic management. As many have noted, it has been used rather loosely such that its legitimacy as a widely understood term has been undermined. However, in this regard it has this in common with its synonyms and other terms, with which it is related, such as → sustainable development.

The study of corporate citizenship and a new understanding of the relationship between business and society have been driven by a number of factors. First among these is the significant growth in the size, scope and power of transnational corporations in the second half of the 20th century and on into the 21st century. In 2000 it was estimated that of the world's largest 100 economies, 50 were companies not countries. Even if this is a slightly spurious notion it does point to the dwarfing of many smaller national economies by global corporations which raises issues of power and influence particularly as the largest 100 companies are based in the US, → Europe and Japan. This fact has been accompanied by a number of other issues of concern: the slow realisation of the centrality of environmental resources in social and economic wellbeing; changes in attitudes to workplace ethics; the rethinking of local, national and international community space; and fundamental shifts in global markets through radical changes in communications technology.

Even though the term corporate citizenship had been used in India and the USA as a reference to corporate philanthropy, it gained new legitimacy as a radical revision of corporate responsibility in the 1990s particularly in → Europe when the Corporate Citizenship Company was formed in 1997. Various academic centres in the UK, Germany, the US and Australia dedicated to corporate citizenship were set up and the *Journal of Corporate Citizenship* was launched in 2001. Also in 2001 initiatives such as the → UN Global Compact referred to corporate citizenship as a radical model of business which incorporated concerns for → human rights, labour standards and environmental protection as being at the heart of business strategy and operations.

The contentiousness of the term lies in several areas, the most contentious of which is the application of the idea of citizenship, which normally refers to individuals, to corporations which surely, it is argued, do not have soul, conscience and moral purpose at their heart. As Peter Drucker said in 1993, when referring to corporate citizenship: 'As a political term citizenship means active commitment. It means responsibility. It means making a difference in one's society, and one's country.' This model requires that those who run global corporations are mindful of a range of stakeholder expectations around the world and wise enough to act in the interests not just of the company but also the communities in which the company operates and the planet on which companies and communities rely for environmental resources and amenities. It is therefore a central notion in corporate citizenship that companies are cognisant of their → externalities and try as far as possible to internalise and take responsibility for them. In other words corporate citizenship is a holistic understanding of all the impacts of the corporation and an awareness that the corporation has some responsibility to a wide range of stakeholder concerns. In these respects it is somewhat more radical than CSR and other sometimes synonymous terms because corporate citizenship requires a company to understand its political situation, including the responsible use of power and influence.

In the book *Corporate Citizenship* (1998) McIntosh, Leipziger, Jones and Coleman and again in *Living Corporate Citizenship* (2003) McIntosh, Thomas, Leipziger and Coleman said that the first priority of a good corporate citizen is that it should be able to articulate its role, scope and purpose. This in turn means that it must understand all its internal and external impacts, and if necessary take responsibility for what previously may have been regarded as → externalities. In reality working to this model has required companies to investigate their own activities far more than they have hitherto felt necessary. In practical terms this has meant companies being more transparent in their decision-making and operational procedures and therefore being held more accountable for their day-to-day management, and, perhaps just as significantly investigating their relationships with suppliers and contractors involved in their supply chains and other activities. In many cases it has led to a radical remodelling of the business venture as companies realise that their greatest challenges and opportunities may lie in an area of the world or with a particular stakeholder group that they were previously unconcerned with.

Examples of consultancy and research in corporate citizenship include the US-based Boston College's four core principles which are: minimise harm – the negative consequences of business decisions on society, maximise the positive contribution of business decisions to society, be accountable and responsive to key stakeholders, and support strong financial results. Similarly the Corporate Citizenship Company in the UK sells services in management systems and risk control which means identifying the company's principles, → values and policies, identifying the company's key stakeholders and identifying their concerns, building performance measures and collecting the necessary data. This leads to → benchmarking and assessing the company's performance.

Corporate citizenship can, therefore, be seen as a systemic approach to corporate responsibility which requires a wide understanding of the political place of the company in national and international communities as well as the economic, social and environmental impact and performance of the company as a whole. The study of corporate citizenship must then necessarily be transdisciplinary and incorporate ideas from business, management, politics, economics, → development, anthropology, environment, ethics and other disciplines. This may mean that its study requires working outside the traditional silos of management, business and ethics.

However, this view of the company as a citizen, as a political entity, begs many questions and for some confuses the issue of what a company is for. On the other hand anyone who has either run a company or looked in any depth at how a company, or for that matter, any organisation, runs on a day-to-day basis, knows that financial performance is dependent on a range of inputs and outputs and a range of relationships with stakeholders and the use of resources – financial, environmental and social. Should this be called corporate citizenship? Perhaps not, but this has become the lingua franca and the conversation continues. What is more important is where we began in this brief discussion: that companies should be able to articulate their role, scope and purpose and understand and take responsibility for their relationships and all their impacts. But, for this to have meaning beyond the small number of companies that have risen to the challenge, there needs to be continuous ongoing public pressure as well as regulations that force enterprise in all its shapes and forms to be enterprising for the good of all, and not just the few. That is the radical heart of much of the corporate citizenship debate. Corporate citizenship can therefore be described as an aspirational metaphor for business to be part of developing a better world.

The ability of companies to articulate their role, scope and purpose in order to maintain their validity, reputation and self-worth depends on their ability to understand their place in society. The burgeoning social and environmental report industry is one sign that some businesses are addressing the challenge of telling their stories. As such this means that there is an increasing global conversation between different parties on the role that business plays in every individual's day-to-day life and in global → development issues. Businesses are beginning to understand their ripple effect and move from minimum citizenship through a discretionary phase to strategic corporate citizenship.

Malcolm McIntosh

CORPORATE COMMUNICATIONS
→ Public affairs, Reporting

CORPORATE CULTURE
→ Institute of Corporate Culture Affairs (ICCA)

Corporate culture can be defined as an organisation's unique body of knowledge that is nurtured over a long period of time resulting in commonly held assumptions, values, norms, paradigms and world views. These shape the behaviour and thinking of the people within the organisation and thus form the organisation's core identity characterising the organisation's way of doing business with qualities distinct from others.

In the organisational behaviour literature, corporate culture has been defined by E. H. Schein, a leading theorist on organisational behaviour, as a pattern of shared basic assumptions that a group learns in dealing with its problems of external adaptation and internal integration. Organisations communicate the spirit of their corporate culture in several visible and invisible manifestations which may include formal and informal management structures, statements of values and aspirations, rewards and recognition systems, staffing and selection procedures, training and development activities, company ceremonies and rituals as well as stories and physical symbols. More recently, CSR, branding and corporate culture have become entwined as a way of increasing the identification of employees with a company's values, mission and practices.

This has become increasingly important as employers now rate the corporate culture and image of a company as a key determinant in attracting, motivating and retaining key staff.

Manfred Pohl

CORPORATE ENVIRONMENTAL MANAGEMENT

→ Eco-efficiency, Environmental auditing, Environmental management systems (EMS)

Corporate environmental management (CEM) is an umbrella term that encompasses policies, tools, systems and strategies that can be put in place to enhance the environmental performance of a company. It is closely associated with the concept of → eco-efficiency that argues that a company can simultaneously improve both its environmental performance and its economic competitiveness by adopting CEM practices. This has come to be known as a win – win situation. It is now widely recognised that businesses, through environmentally sound management practices, have a major role to play in contributing to mitigating environmental problems at a local, national and global level.

Many CEM practices can save companies money. Measures to reduce energy, minimise → waste and reduce → water consumption, for example, will directly reduce costs and add to profitability. But companies are increasingly becoming aware that even where CEM becomes more expensive, it can still help a company's competitiveness by differentiating a company from its competitors and enhancing image, brands and reputation.

However, companies are also increasingly being influenced by a variety of external pressures and a company's stakeholders often expect environmentally responsible behaviour. Increasingly therefore CEM is becoming part of a company's so-called social → licence to operate.

Given the internal and external demands to improve the environmental performance of a company, those companies that achieve high standards of environmental performance will benefit in a number of ways. In order to realise this → competitive advantage, companies must seek to develop policies, management systems, strategies and assessment and communications tools which will improve their environmental performance and address the environmental demands placed upon them by their stakeholders. By incorporating the increasingly important environmental dimension into the decision-making processes of the firm, managers can seek to reduce costs and exploit the opportunities offered by increased public environmental concern within a dynamic marketplace.

Industry, particularly in the developed world, must increasingly take into account the costs of the effect of its operations on the → environment, rather than regarding the planet as a free resource. In the past, few companies counted the costs of the pollution which they discharged into the atmosphere, and the debate has now turned to legislation aimed at forcing companies to comply with certain standards and taxing firms which pollute. The so-called 'polluter-pays-principle' is now central to legislation. The implication here is clearly that prices will rise for consumers as firms experience increased costs associated with environmental improvements. Less energy consumption and more efficient use of resources are obvious targets for improvement and should not conflict with industry's aims since their attainment can actually reduce costs.

The ultimate aim of corporate environmental management must be to reach a situation where companies are operating in a way which is consistent with the concept of → sustainable development. Sustainable development stresses the interdependence between economic growth and environmental quality.

For most companies the starting point for CEM is to develop an environmental policy. This should be a statement that lays out the organisation's commitment to environmental improvements along with its intentions, overall aspirations and vision. The policy provides a framework for action and for the setting of the organisation's environmental aims, objectives and targets.

The precise style and content of the policy will be dependent on the industry the company is in and the significant environmental impacts that it has. But it is likely to include reference to issues such as energy use and efficiency, emissions to → water, emissions to air, resources and materials, noise, responsibilities of suppliers and contractors, transport and logistics, local community impacts, staff training, emergency preparedness and → sustainable development. The environmental policy will usually commit a company to compliance-plus strategies, that is, CEM practices that allow the company not only to obey the law but to go beyond it.

In addition to company-specific environmental policies, many companies also sign up to voluntary environmental initiatives at an industry, local or national level. In many industries we find common → codes of conduct on environmental issues.

Once a company has decided to embark on a concerted effort to improve its environmental performance it must build a comprehensive → environmental management system (EMS) within the organisation. The EMS aims to pull together the tools and stragegies that are used to meet the aspirations of the environmental policy and subsequent objectives and targets set.

Experience suggests that in most organisations a systems-based approach to attaining the goals of the enterprise is most likely to be successful. Failure to meet such goals is often a result of an ineffective system or, alternatively, that although there was a system in place, there were gaps in it which allowed mistakes and errors to occur. Inadequate management systems have been the cause of environmental damage and have cost firms and organisations heavily in terms of clean-up costs and damaged reputations. At the extreme we can think of disasters such as the *Exxon Valdez* oil spill and the Union Carbide Bhopal explosion, where it was the → environment which became irreparably damaged due, at least in part, to inadequacies in systems which were supposed to prevent such disasters.

At the core of the systems approach is the role of the EMS where companies put into place processes and procedures which ensure that environmental performance is improved over time and that environmental damage caused by abnormal operations does not occur. Management systems aim to pull a potentially disparate system into an integrated and organised one. To that end, the system covers not only management's responsibilities but the responsibilities and tasks of every individual in an organisation.

A fully integrated system which covers the totality of operations helps management and workers to see their place in the organisation and recognise the interdependence of all aspects of business. Through establishing clear communications, information and reporting channels it should provide a clear and understandable organisational map laying out both responsibilities and reporting arrangements. This means that functions are less likely to be overlooked and gaps in the system are less likely to occur.

An effective management system is therefore central to the avoidance of environmental degradation, in so much as it pulls together all the CEM tools and strategies for the avoidance of risks and provides a framework for a clear and focused approach to environmental improvement.

The management system must have three main attributes. First, the system needs to be comprehensive, covering all the activities of the organisation. Gaps must not occur in the coverage of the system since this is where errors and mistakes will creep in and where accidents and disasters may happen. Every part of an organisation must be involved in the implementation of the system and every person must recognise his or her responsibility for putting the system into practice.

Second, the systems and procedures need to be understandable to everybody involved. If roles and duties are not specified in an understandable way they may not be carried out. This will usually involve documenting the system, training people fully in their tasks and responsibilities and reviewing or → auditing what is actually happening periodically. It requires that the system and all its elements are monitored and if the system breaks down it must be rectified quickly.

Third, the system must be open to review and there must be a commitment to a continuous cycle of improvement in the operations of the firm and in the positive environmental attributes of products or services it will produce. This continuous cycle of improvement can also be applied to the → environment where firms should aim for an ultimate goal of zero-negative impact on the → environment.

A central aspect of any management system will revolve around decision-making. Modern management methods will highlight the need for flexibility and worker participation and this ought to mean that decisions are taken further down any hierarchy which may exist. In arriving at decisions, the calibre and personal → integrity of staff are of fundamental importance and each person in the organisation needs to understand their role in decision-making and the consequences of their actions.

The commitment of senior management to the systems-based approach and to CEM is crucial but it also must be developed creatively with the inner commitment of the entire workforce. There is a need to consider new styles of → leadership when implementing the management system and this must be informed by systems-based thinking and acting. Workers must be valued in the system and involved in decision-making through participatory styles of management.

Within the framework of the EMS there will be a need to regularly audit environmental performance and to report on that performance in some way. Many companies may consider the adoption of → environmental management system standards as both a benchmark and a sign that they are improving their performance.

Some companies opt for EMS and CEM approaches which are tailored to the individual company's requirements. Others adapt generic environmental management standards such as → ISO 14001. Many companies now use → ISO 14001 both as an internal discipline and also as a way of communicating environmental commitments externally.

The EMS approach requires a good degree of internal monitoring and → auditing. Environmental audits are now common in many companies and in some cases are required before companies can obtain finance and insurance. Auditing is a vital tool to ensure that managers get accurate information and that the external credibility of the company's environmental commitment is demonstrated.

Everything that consumers, companies and other institutions do will have some impact on the → environment. Even substances which in their final form are environmentally benign may have been unfriendly in their manufacture, especially if that manufacture was energy intensive. They may have been produced using non-renewable resources and may also pose problems after they have been used and come to be disposed of. If we take what is commonly called a '→ cradle-to-grave' view of products, where we examine their environmental impact through their life cycle from raw material usage to disposal, then there are few, if any, products that will not have some negative impact on the → environment. The key question is therefore not how we completely eliminate environmental damage, but how we reduce it over time and how we achieve a state of balance such that the amount of environmental damage done is repairable and therefore sustainable.

Therefore, many aspects of a company's performance go beyond a systems-based approach which deals primarily with the internal operations and environmental performance of the company. More and more emphasis is now being put on products themselves and impacts of all stages of the life cycle of the product. A → life cycle assessment (LCA) of many products has been undertaken by leading companies. This entails an environmental assessment of the product from '→ cradle-to-grave'. It would include an evaluation of raw materials, processing, manufacturing, transportation, use of the product and disposal. Many assessments show that it is not always the manufacturing process that is the most environmentally damaging. In the case of a car, for example, more environmental damage is caused during its use.

In order to demonstrate a company's commitment to the → environment, many organisations are now seeing great value in reporting on its performance in an open and transparent way to its stakeholders. Such reporting can be done through a periodic published report, through information on websites or by the use of ongoing interactive bulletin boards or 'blogs'. Whatever mode is chosen the aim must be to provide the public and employees with adequate, timely and reliable information on the environmental performance and future plans of the organisation. Many companies are now finding it useful to follow reporting guidelines published through the → Global Reporting Initiative (GRI). In some cases reports are independently verified or assured to add to their credibility.

Increasingly, reporting is not the end of the process for CEM. Many companies are now embarking on a process of gaining feedback on their activities, future plans and policies through a process of stakeholder dialogue. In this way the views of external stakeholders can be incorporated into a business's decision-making processes.

Richard Welford

CORPORATE FOUNDATION
→ Foundation, Philanthropy

CORPORATE GOVERNANCE
→ Business ethics, Integrity, Reporting, Risk management, Transparency

The usual definition of governance is 'the manner of directing and controlling the actions and affairs of an entity'. 'Governance' stems from the word 'gubernare', being the Latin word for 'steer'. Government is the modern word for directing and controlling the affairs of a state and has taken on the meaning of the system of governing a state.

All entities including schools, charities, clubs, sporting bodies, state-owned enterprises or business corporations need to be governed. The governance of a company carrying on a business is known as 'corporate governance'. Whatever the entity, however, the principles of quality governance apply equally to all of them. As a result of corporate scandals and the realisation of the importance of a company in modern life, the articulation of how to govern companies began in earnest in the last two decades of the 20th century. Since this articulation, the phrase 'corporate governance' has been loosely used when referring to the governance of any entity.

An informed definition of corporate governance would be processes to help directors discharge and be seen to be discharging the responsibilities created by their duties.

The various corporate governance codes which have evolved around the world have differences because each country has its own special circumstances. Most of these codes contain guidelines with the proviso that if a guideline is not followed, the user should explain what process has been adopted instead of the recommended one. This is the so-called 'comply or explain' regime of corporate governance.

In some countries the government of the day has chosen to make certain → best practices of governance compulsory by way of legislation. In short, comply or else have a sanction applied, which is usually a criminal one. The big debates at the moment are which is the better regime and can legislated → best practices create quality governance?

Certainly, around the world, governance has become a quantitative exercise in that people check, for example, whether a company has a preponderance of independent non-executive directors on its board.

Can it be good governance to comply mindlessly with the guidelines in a code or the provisions of a statute? It can never be good governance for a compliance officer to simply report to a board that a company has complied with a code or the rules promulgated in a statute. A board should apply its mind as to what is the → best practice for deciding the issue before it. When it is on a 'comply or else' basis there can be no flexibility. It is not plausible to have one size fits all when it comes to how companies are directed or steered taking into account the diversity of businesses which are owned by companies. In a 'comply or else' regime, one finds a quantitative tick box approach rather than an application of mind to process.

In the well-known case of Enron, any one of us who had been a shareholder at the time would, on applying a quantitative test, have come to the conclusion that Enron was being well governed. It had a preponderance of outside directors, an audit committee chaired by a chartered accountant, a nominations committee and a remuneration committee. Notwithstanding, it was dysfunctional. The reason for that now appears to be that certain executive directors were driven by the corporate sin of greed. There was a need to maintain or prop up the share price because of their dealing in shares and having options to exercise.

The manner of doing so was to create special purpose entities, place assets of the group in these entities and then sell them always at a profit. This profit of course would be consolidated on to the bottom line. When the group started running into liquidity problems, the thought of borrowing moneys and incurring a liability on the balance sheet was beyond contemplation. In consequence, they concluded complicated structured financial transactions from which they drew the accounting and legal conclusions that the amounts borrowed – a few billion dollars – could be kept off balance sheet.

The amount of intellectual energy that was employed by those directors becomes almost tangible when one thinks that over a period of a few years they formed these special purpose entities and entered into these complicated structured financial transactions out of greed. Was any of this energy employed in the interests of the company that they were directing? It is the harnessing of the energy that is engendered around a boardroom table honestly in the best interests of the company that is the foundation of good governance. Legislation cannot create intellectual honesty. Substance cannot be created by form. Mindless compliance with legislated governance can never be an honest application of mind acting in the best interests of the company.

There are processes on how to do things in a company and there are the business judgement calls that have to be made. None of us can get those business judgement calls right all the time. The making of the wrong business judgement call and not applying good governance practices in doing so usually results in corporate scandals and failure. There is empirical evidence to establish, however, that when directors honestly apply their minds to the best process but make the wrong business judgement call, stakeholders are quite forgiving, particularly the providers of capital, namely the shareholders. For this reason alone one should practise good governance.

The intent of Adrian Cadbury and all the others who wrote codes in the first half of the last decade of the 20th century was to improve the quality of governance. It was never intended that the codes should just give rise to a quantitative tick box exercise.

How can that intellectual energy around a table be harnessed in the best interests of the company that we are steering? Anyone of us who became a curator of an incapacitated human being would not dream of acting other than in the best interests of that unfortunate human being. Not one of us would endeavour to filch any of his or her interests for ourself. We would take great care with that person's assets, would use our practised abilities (skills) to try to enhance that person's assets. We would apply ourselves to understanding the issues concerning that person.

When a company is registered, it is a totally incapacitated person in law. It only functions and earns a reputation through the directors and senior managers appointed to act on its behalf. Why is it that the vast majority of people would not act wrongly when acting for an incapacitated human being but might contemplate doing so in acting for an incapacitated juristic person? Do people not realise that in the 21st century a company, which is an employer, a purchaser of products, a provider of products or services, plays as critical a role in society as the family unit? A company is the link that brings a myriad of stakeholders together.

Directors need to develop questions that they should silently ask themselves. For example: Do I have any conflict in this matter? Am I sure, objectively speaking, that I have all the facts as opposed to assumptions? Is the decision that I am about to make in the best interests of the company? Having made the decision, have I communicated it to all interested stakeholders in a manner which amounts to substance over form? Will I be seen to be a good steward of the company's assets on the basis of this decision? Have I applied all my practised abilities in the best interests of this incapacitated company?

We also are able to better harness that energy in the interests of the company if we are aware of corporate sins, such as: greed, sloth (more administration than enterprise), pride (having made a decision which turns out to be wrong and a board taking too long to correct it), arrogance (when a board believes that the way it is directing the business of the company in a certain industry is so superior to a competitor's way of doing things, that nothing will go wrong) and fear (when a decision in the best interests of a company is not in one's own best interests).

Also, around that decision-making table one has to constantly ask oneself, have I understood the issues? Without understanding, one can never practise good governance. If presentations are done using jargon, which managers or professional advisers tend to do, one must not be embarrassed to ask an intellectually naïve question. It is these intellectually naïve questions which make management think and sort out the wood from the trees.

A board has collective authority in making decisions but each director incurs individual liability. This alone should drive a director to practise good governance. Also, it is good, hardnosed business to do so because it is now established that those companies that practise good governance are able to raise capital more cheaply and attract a better class of employee – two very important matters in the sustainability of a business.

The major debate at the moment in the world is whether governance should be on a 'comply or else', or a 'comply or explain' basis. The probability is that a hybrid situation will develop in the sense that some governance practices will become compulsory and others remain as guidelines. For example, in most jurisdictions today companies running banks are obliged to have an audit committee, a risk committee, a directors' affairs committee and a credit committee. Terms of reference of these committees is, however, usually left to the board of directors.

The principles of good governance and the → best practices to observe these principles have virtually become universal. The world is flat in electronic communication terms. Capital flows with the click of a mouse over a borderless electronic world – and its flows to companies that practise good governance. That speaks volumes for the importance of good governance – and that connotes quality not quantity.

Mervyn King

CORPORATE HISTORY
→ Institute of Corporate Culture Affairs (ICCA)

Corporate history describes a company's past providing information about its operations, → corporate culture, mergers and acquisitions, employees and customers.

This includes everything that happens within the company as well as its external impact on societies, economies, environments and the public in general. Corporate history covers not only the company's foundation, operational business and mergers and acquisitions but also topics such as → leadership, → corporate culture, human resources, product development or the strategic directions of the company.

Corporate history is therefore one of the most important factors for understanding developments of the company – its raison d'être – and represents at the same time the basis for developing scenarios for the future, documenting past decision-making and resulting failures and successes. In this context a company's culture and its → values, for example, are not just characterised by a series of events or activities, but rather document the historic evolution of the company as an organic entity.

Corporate history remains one of the most important factors in determining the unity and identity of a company strengthening its position in the eyes of employees, competitors or the public in general. This includes, for example, the development of a company's culture and provides a basis for analysis and consequently for adaptation and change. Recently the benefit of corporate history archives has been further recognised as many companies' historical resources include a wealth of detail on national, social and indeed international history. Another development has been the increasing combination of 'corporate heritage' resources and strategies within companies' CSR operations allowing a cross-fertilisation of heritage in CSR and corporate → branding.

Manfred Pohl

CORPORATE RESPONSIBILITY
→ Corporate social responsibility

CORPORATE RESPONSIBILITY INDEX
→ Business in the Community
🖰 www.bitc.org.uk

Business in the Community's (BITC) Corporate Responsibility Index (CR Index) is one of the UK's leading benchmarks of responsible business, helping companies to integrate and improve responsible practice across their operations. It provides a systematic approach to managing, measuring and reporting their impact on society and on the → environment.

The survey covers practice in four key areas: marketplace, workplace, community and environment. Originating in → BITC's Business in the Environment Index, it is the result of a major collaborative effort by BITC member companies to articulate a comprehensive measurement tool.

From completing the survey to receiving their feedback reports, CR participants undertake a process of internal gap analysis and action planning for continuous improvement.

In addition to detaining impact performance in the four key areas, the Index can also be used as an indicator of management quality, clearly of interest to the investment community.

In terms of external verification, → BITC has commissioned global management consulting group Arthur D. Little to provide external verification of the index process.

Results of the CR Index, including full rankings, sector analysis and key trends, are published each year in May.

Results of the most recent CR Index were published in *The Sunday Times'* Companies that Count supplement on 8 May 2006.

They showed emerging themes to be:

- Integrating responsible business practice into the mainstream of the business;
- Engaging employees through company supported community investment programmes as volunteers, mentors, project teams, trustees and school governors; and
- Increasing → transparency.

A full list of participants and further data analysis are provided in the yearly executive summary produced by → Business in the

Community. A CD-ROM of key business leaders explaining the importance of integrating responsible business into core business strategy is also available.

The Index should:

- Provide a useful focus on the risks and opportunities of responsible business across a business;
- Bring different functions together to understand and manage key responsible business issues across an organisation;
- Challenge whether the business is conducting its activities in a systematic and integrated way and guide companies through the process of integration;
- Help with internal gap analysis, reinforcing ongoing good work and highlighting areas for improvement;
- Provide a practical framework for improving performance and communicating progress; and
- Provide credible, independent information to internal and external stakeholders, demonstrating a company's commitment to → transparency and continuous improvement.

By highlighting companies managing responsible business activities in an open and honest way, the Index:

- Enables more direct and focused engagement with stakeholders;
- Helps to increase stakeholder understanding of a company (its operations, the constraints it faces etc.), and a company's understanding of its stakeholders (their perceptions, issues of importance etc.); and
- Helps to build trust and long-lasting relationships.

In 2004, 53% of participants were willing to publicly disclose their feedback and share their full Index submission with investors and other Index participants; this rose to 87% in 2005.

David Halley

CORPORATE SOCIAL ENTREPRENEUR
→ Social entrepreneurship

A corporate social entrepreneur is a person who innovatively employs market forces, including new business ventures, to address or solve social or environmental problems.

A social entrepreneur may be independent or an employee of a business firm. Social entrepreneurs may be motivated by personal → values, a desire to profit from a previously unidentified market opportunity, a desire to leverage business practices to solve social problems, or some combination of these.

Independent social entrepreneurs can operate in a variety of ways. They may build traditional businesses in a socially responsible manner; create or develop new products, services, or market segments suggested by social issues; innovate in processes or technologies that are less harmful; or identify business opportunities to profit while addressing a serious social problem. An example of independent social entrepreneurship is the work of Maria Teresa Leal, founder of Coopa-Roca sewing cooperative in the slums of Rio de Janeiro.

Within large organisations, social entrepreneurs are likely to be the champions for socially responsible practices and for profit-making ventures derived from or suggested by social problems. They may develop skills at recognising and capitalising on → corporate social opportunity. An example of corporate social entrepreneurship is the spearheading of aluminium recycling by Reynolds Aluminium Co. in the early 1970s, based on both environmental concerns and a desire to stabilise raw materials sources. A more recent example from the US is the work of Ray Anderson at Interface, Inc., where process and product innovations are aimed at reducing the company's → ecological footprint to zero.

Donna Wood

CORPORATE SOCIAL INVESTMENT
→ Philanthropy

CORPORATE SOCIAL OPPORTUNITY
→ Business case, Corporate social performance

A corporate social opportunity is a potentially profitable market-oriented venture that derives from or is suggested by a company's social responsibilities or by social or environmental problems.

As the definition implies, corporate social opportunity exists at the interface between business processes and market forces, on the one hand, and social or environmental issues and problems, on the other. The concept does not assume that government is the necessary arbiter of societal problems; nor does it assume that government has no role to play. Instead, the idea of corporate social opportunity is that members of any social institution – including business – can legitimately work to solve complex, intransigent issues such as poverty, disease, illiteracy, species extinction, pollution, and more.

Cairo's privately held chain of daycare centres, The Baby Academy, is an outgrowth of its founder's identifying a corporate social opportunity to provide quality daycare for special needs children. The very successful micro-lending organisation, Grameen Bank of Bangladesh, resulted from its founder's belief that the very poor would repay the small loans needed to improve their economic situations. Ciudad Saludable, an enterprise that employs the poor to recycle → wastes that Peruvian cities cannot handle, was born of a double need for employment opportunities and → waste management.

Taking advantage of corporate social opportunities generally requires innovative perception and high tolerance for risk. The potential rewards include typical business goals such as profits, new markets, and process improvements, as well as social goals such as the alleviation of human suffering and improvements to the quality of human life.

Donna Wood

CORPORATE SOCIAL PERFORMANCE (CSP)

Corporate social performance (CSP) is defined as a business organisation's configuration of principles of social responsibility, processes of social responsiveness, and observable outcomes as they relate to the firm's human, stakeholder, and societal relationships.

The CSP concept recognises that business is a powerful social institution with responsibilities to use that power wisely on behalf of societies, stakeholders, and peoples. Every business firm exists and operates within a dense social network, and CSP provides a way of assessing every firm's inputs, processes, and outcomes with respect to that network. It does not focus narrowly on maximising shareholder wealth, but instead emphasises self-regulation.

Wood's model (*The Academy of Management Review*, 1991), on which the above definition is based, provides a systems approach to understanding CSP. The components of Wood's model are as follows:

1. Principles of → corporate social responsibility describe the structural (not normative) relationships between a firm and the business institution, the firm and its stakeholders, and the firm and the managers who act in its name. At the institutional level of analysis, the principle of legitimacy states that a firm's long-term survival depends in large part on its responsible use of power and resources. At the organisational level of analysis, the principle of public responsibility states that a firm must handle its stakeholder relationships responsibly, given its primary (mission-driven) and secondary (off-mission or unintended) involvements. At the individual level of analysis, the principle of managerial discretion states that managers are first of all moral actors, that is, their capacity to reflect ethically and to choose ethical and socially

responsible behaviours cannot be negated by other organisational demands.

2. Processes of → corporate social responsiveness are boundary-spanning behaviours that serve as the vehicles by which firms link social responsibility principles to behavioural outcomes. Primary responsive processes include (a) environmental assessment: gathering and assessing information about the firm's external environment; (b) stakeholder management: managing the organisation's relationships with those persons, groups, and organisations that can affect or are affected by the company's operations; and (c) issues management: tracking and responding to societal issues that may affect the company.

3. Outcomes of corporate operations include the → triple bottom line categories of economic, social, and natural environment impact; feedback-loop changes to the firm's policy and practices; and voluntary and involuntary harms and benefits to stakeholders and society. An important assumption of CSP is that a broad range of outcomes results from corporate behaviours regardless of the firm's intent or knowledge. Thus, CSP-relevant outcomes include traditional economic variables such as profit, return on investment/assets, share value, and market share, but also include stakeholder- and societally-relevant outcomes such as product and workplace safety, → human rights concerns, natural resource use, pollution, → corruption, and effects on local communities.

By contrast, Carroll's model (*The Academy of Management Review*, 1978) defines CSP as a firm's economic, legal, ethical, and social/philanthropic responsibilities to society. Carroll begins with the understanding that firms, as members of the business institution, have primary economic obligations, and these will naturally occupy most of managers' attention. Legal constraints follow, then ethical duties are third in magnitude, and, finally, Carroll maintains that firms have a responsibility to 'give back' through philanthropy. Carroll's model is less useful theoretically, but it appears to better reflect how managers actually perceive their companies' social responsibilities and performance.

→ Globalisation is of particular concern to both theorists and practitioners. In the absence of supranational regulatory capacity, efforts to improve corporate social performance remain largely voluntary or stakeholder driven. Nevertheless, efforts to systematise and operationalise CSP can be seen in many areas of business practice, including corporate social reporting initiatives such as those driven by AccountAbility and the → Global Reporting Initiative; development of corporate → codes of conduct guided by principles from the → UN Global Compact, → Caux Round Table, or the Organisation for Economic Cooperation and Development; socially-screened investing and venture capital; social entrepreneurship; and collaborative social problem-solving partnerships among businesses, NGOs, government agencies, and supranational organisations.

In short, CSP forms a systematic intellectual framework for grasping the structure of business and society relationships. In practice, it is a generalised template for assessing how firms identify and fulfil their responsibilities to individuals, stakeholders, and societies.

Donna Wood

CORPORATE SOCIAL RESPONSIBILITY

The concept of corporate social responsibility (CSR) refers to the general belief held by growing numbers of citizens that modern businesses have responsibilities to society that extend beyond their obligations to the stockholders or investors in the firm. The obligation to investors, of course, is to generate profits for the owners and maximise long-term wealth of shareholders. Other societal stakeholders that business would also have some responsibility to typically include consumers, employees, the community at large, government, and the natural environment. The CSR concept applies to all size organisations, but discussions tend to focus on large organisations because they tend to be more visible and have more power. And, as many have observed, with power comes responsibility.

A related concept is that of → corporate social performance (CSP). For practical purposes, CSP might be seen as an extension of the concept of CSR that focuses on actual results achieved rather than the general notion of businesses' → accountability or responsibility to society. Thus, CSP is a natural consequence or follow-on to CSR. In fact, it could well be argued that if CSR does not lead to CSP then it is vacuous or powerless. Interestingly, many advocates of CSR naturally assume that an assumption of responsibility will lead to results or outcomes. Therefore, the distinction between the two is often a matter of semantics that is of more interest to academics than to practitioners. Most of our discussion will be focused on CSR with the general assumption that CSP is a vital and logical consequence.

Evolution of the CSR concept

The definition of CSR has evolved over the decades, generally becoming more precise as to the types of activities and practices that might be subsumed under the concept. Early definitions were often general and ambiguous. Over the decades, definitions of CSR have reflected concerns such as:

- Seriously considering the impact of company actions on others;
- The obligation of managers to protect and improve the welfare of society; and
- Meeting economic and legal responsibilities and extending beyond these obligations.

A more comprehensive definition of CSR is that it encompasses the economic, legal, ethical, and discretionary or philanthropic expectations that society has of organisations at a given point in time. This definition specifies four different, but interrelated, categories of responsibilities that business has towards society. This characterisation also attempts to place the traditional economic and legal expectations of business in context by combining them with more socially oriented concerns such as ethics and philanthropy.

A brief elaboration of this definition is useful. First, and foremost, business has a responsibility which is economic in nature or kind. Before anything else, the business institution is the basic economic unit in society. As such it has a responsibility to produce goods and services that society wants and to sell them at a profit. All other business roles are predicated on this fundamental assumption. The economic element of the definition suggests that society requires business to produce goods and services and sell them at a profit. This is how the capitalistic economic system is designed and functions. Firms that do not generate economic sustainability go out of business and become irrelevant.

Just as society expects business to make a profit (as an incentive and reward) for its efficiency and effectiveness, society expects and requires business to obey the law. The law, in its most rudimentary form, depicts the basic 'rules of the game' by which business is expected to function. Society expects business to fulfil its economic mission within the framework of legal requirements set forth by the society's legal system. Law may be thought of as 'codified' ethics. Thus, the legal responsibility is the second part of this CSR definition.

The next two responsibilities attempt to specify the nature or character of the obligations that extend beyond obedience to the law. The ethical responsibility represents the kinds of behaviours and ethical norms that society expects business to follow. These ethical responsibilities extend to actions, decisions and practices which are beyond what is required by the law. Though they seem to be always expanding, they nevertheless exist as expectations 'over and beyond' legal requirements.

Finally, there are discretionary or philanthropic responsibilities. These represent voluntary roles, initiatives, and practices that business assumes but for which society does not provide as clear an expectation as in the ethical responsibility. These are left to individual managers' and corporations' judgement and choice; therefore, they are referred to as discretionary. Regardless of their voluntary nature, the expectation that business perform these is still held by society. This expectation is driven by social norms. The specific activities are guided by businesses' desire to engage in social roles not mandated, not required by law, and not expected of businesses in an ethical sense, but which are becoming increasingly strategic. Examples of these voluntary activities include making philanthropic and charitable contributions, employee volunteerism, support of non-profit organisations, and other attempts to foster improved relationships with various stakeholder groups. In short, these ethical and philanthropic activities embrace the whole range of how business attempts to do well by doing good.

Though this four part definition includes an economic responsibility, many today still think of the economic component as what the business firm does for itself and the legal, ethical and discretionary (or philanthropic) components as what business does for others. While this distinction represents the more commonly held view of CSR, it is important to think about economic performance as something business does for society as well, though society seldom looks at it in this way.

Whatever the definition used, CSR is all about business performance in a variety of social and environmental topic areas that usually embrace issues of → diversity, philanthropy, socially responsible investing (SRI), environment, → human rights, workplace issues, → business ethics, sustainability, → community development and → corporate governance.

Business's interest in CSR

Academics have had an interest in the concept of CSR for close to 50 years. But, it is important to emphasise that the business community has had a parallel development of its interest in the concepts as well, though they have not always been clearly articulated. The business community, moreover, has been less interested in academic refinements of the concept and more interested in what all this means for them, in practice. Prominent business organisations have developed specialised awards for firms' social performance. One example of this would be *Fortune* magazine's 'most admired' and 'least admired' categories of reputational performance. Among *Fortune*'s eight attributes of reputation, one will find the category of performance titled 'social responsibility'. The Conference Board is another organisation that has developed an award for corporate → leadership in the CSR realm. The Conference Board annually gives an award titled the 'Ron Brown Award for Corporate Leadership' that recognises companies for outstanding achievements in community and employee relations. Among the core principles for this award are that the company be committed to → corporate citizenship, express → corporate citizenship as a shared value visible at all levels, and it must be integrated into the company's corporate strategy.

For many years now, *Business Ethics* magazine has published its list of Annual Business Ethics and Corporate Citizenship Awards. In these awards, the magazine has highlighted companies that have made stellar achievements in CSR/CSP. One of the important criteria used by the magazine in making this award is that the companies have programmes or initiatives in social responsibility that demonstrate sincerity and ongoing vibrancy that reaches deep into the company. The award criteria also stipulate that the company honoured must be a standout in at least one area of social responsibility, though the recipients need not be exemplary in all areas.

Though one will always find individual business people who might reject or fight the idea of CSR/CSP, for the most part today, large companies all over the world have accepted the idea and internalised it. One of the best examples of this acceptance was the creation in 1992 of the association titled → Business for Social Responsibility (BSR) in the USA. BSR is a national business association that helps companies seeking to implement policies and practices that contribute to the companies' sustainability and responsible success. In its statement of purpose, → BSR describes itself as a global organisation that helps its member companies achieve success in ways that respect ethical → values, people, communities, and the → environment. A goal of BSR is to make CSR an integral part of business operations and strategies. An illustrative list of BSR's over 1000 members includes such well-known companies as ABB, Inc., AstraZeneca plc, Coca-Cola, Johnson & Johnson, Nike, Inc., Office Max, General Electric, General Motors, UPS, Procter & Gamble, Sony, Staples, Inc. and Wal-Mart. Similar organisations exist now in → Europe, such as → Business in the Community, or → Asia, such as CSR Asia.

The business case for corporate social responsibility

After weighing the pros and cons of CSR, most businesses today embrace the idea. In recent years, the '→ business case' for CSR has been unfolding. Before buying in to the idea of CSR, many business executives have insisted that the '→ business case' for it be further developed. The → business case embraces arguments or rationales as to why businesspeople believe these concepts bring distinct benefits or advantages to companies specifically, and the business community generally. Even the astute business strategy expert, Michael Porter, who for a long time has extolled the virtues of → competitive advantage, has embraced the belief that corporate and social initiatives are intertwined. Porter has argued that companies today ought to invest in CSR as part of their business strategy to become more competitive. Of course, prior to Porter, many CSR academics had been presenting this same argument.

Simon Zadek, a European, has presented four different business rationales for being a civil (socially responsible) corporation. These reasons form a composite justification for business adopting a CSR strategy. First, is the defensive approach. This approach to CSR is designed to alleviate pain. That is, companies should pursue CSR to avoid the pressures that create costs for them. Second, is the cost – benefit approach. This traditional approach holds that firms will undertake those activities that yield a greater benefit than cost. Third, is the strategic approach. In this rationale, firms will recognise the changing environment and engage in CSR as part of a deliberate corporate strategy. Finally, the innovation and → learning approach is proposed. Here, an active engagement with CSR provides new opportunities to understand the marketplace and enhance organisational → learning, which leads to → competitive advantage. Most of these rationales have been around for years, but Zadek has presented them as an excellent, composite set of business reasons for pursuing CSR.

Putting forth the → business case for CSR requires a careful and comprehensive elucidation of the reasons why companies increasingly understand that CSR is in their best interests to pursue. Two particular studies have contributed towards building this case. First, a study by PricewaterhouseCoopers, presented in their 2002 Sustainability Survey Report, identifies the following top 10 reasons why companies are deciding to be more socially responsible:

- Enhanced reputation
- Competitive advantage
- Cost savings
- Industry trends
- CEO/board commitment
- Customer demand
- SRI demand
- Top-line growth
- Shareholder demand
- Access to capital

Second, a survey conducted by The Aspen Institute, in their Business and Society Program, queried MBA student attitudes regarding the question of how companies will benefit from fulfilling their social responsibilities. Their responses, in sequence of importance, included:

- A better public image/reputation
- Greater customer loyalty
- A more satisfied/productive workforce
- Fewer regulatory or legal problems
- Long-term viability in the marketplace
- A stronger/healthier community
- Increased revenues
- Lower cost of capital
- Easier access to foreign markets

Between these two lists, a comprehensive case for business interest in CSR/CSP is documented. It can be seen how CSR/CSP not only benefits society and stakeholders, but how it provides specific, business-related benefits for business as well.

Examples of CSR in practice

There are many ways in which companies may manifest their CSR in their communities and abroad. Most of these initiatives would fall in the category of discretionary, or philanthropic activities, but some border on improving some ethical situation for the stake-holders with whom they come into contact. Common types of CSR initiatives include corporate contributions, or philanthropy, employee volunteerism, community relations, becoming an out-standing employer for specific employee groups (such as women, older workers, or minorities), making environmental improvements that exceed what is required by law, designing and using → codes of conduct, and so on.

Among the 100 Best Corporate Citizens selected in 2006 by *Business Ethics* magazine, a number of illuminating examples of CSR in practice are provided. Green Mountain Coffee Roasters of Waterbury, Vermont, was recognised for its meticulous attention to

CSR including its pioneering work in the → fair trade movement, which pays coffee growers stable, fair prices.

Another example of CSR in practice is the Chick-fil-A restaurant chain based in Atlanta, Georgia. Founder and CEO Truett Cathy has earned an outstanding reputation as a business executive deeply concerned with his employees and communities. Through the WinShape Center Foundation, funded by Chick-fil-A, the company operates foster homes for more than 120 children, sponsors a summer camp, and has hosted more than 21 000 children since 1985. Chick-fil-A has also sponsored major charity golf tournaments.

In the immediate aftermath of Hurricane Katrina in 2005, judged to be the worst and most expensive ever in terms of destruction, hundreds of companies made significant contributions to the victims and cities of New Orleans, Biloxi, Gulfport and the entire Gulf Coast of the US. These CSR efforts have been noted as one of the important ways by which business can help people and communities in need.

As seen in the examples presented, there are a multitude of ways that companies have manifested their corporate social responsibilities with respect to communities, employees, consumers, competitors, and the natural environment.

CSR in the future

What is the future for corporate social responsibility? The most optimistic perspective seems dominant and it is depicted well by Steven D. Lydenberg in his book *Corporations and the Public Interest: Guiding the Invisible Hand*. Lydenberg sees CSR as 'a major secular development, driven by a long-term reevaluation of the role of corporations in society'. Lydenberg says this re-evaluation is more evident in → Europe, where the stakeholder responsibility notion is more readily assumed, but that US business people are more sceptical of this assumption. He goes on to argue, however, that the European influence will be very hard to resist over the long run.

By contrast with the optimistic perspective, David Vogel is genuinely sceptical of CSR and he develops this argument in his book *The Market for Virtue: The Potential and Limits of Corporate Social Responsibility*, in which he critiques CSR's influence and success. Vogel is very much of the mind that CSR will not be successful until mainstream companies begin reporting some aspect of CSR as being critical to the company's past or future performance. In other words, CSR is successful only to the extent that it adds to the bottom line and can be specifically delineated as having made such an impact. In reacting to Vogel's scepticism, it must be observed that this convergence of financial and social objectives characterises the trajectory that CSR has taken in the past two decades.

It is evident by CSR practices and trends, that social responsibility has both a social component as well as a business component. In today's world of intense global competition, it is clear that CSR can be sustainable only so long as it continues to add value to corporate bottom lines. It must be observed, moreover, that it is that conglomerate of stakeholders known as society, or the public, not just business executives alone, that plays an increasing role in what constitutes business success and for that reason, CSR has an upbeat future in the global business arena. The pressures of global competition will continue to intensify, however, and this will dictate that the '→ business case' for CSR will always be at the centre of discussions.

Archie Carroll

CORPORATE SOCIAL RESPONSIVENESS

→ Corporate social responsibility

Corporate social responsiveness is a set of boundary-spanning behaviours by which firms link social responsibility principles to behavioural outcomes.

The concept of corporate social responsiveness arose in the early 1970s as an antidote to the then prevailing view of → corporate social responsibility as too vague and not action oriented. A socially responsive firm participates in monitoring and responding to social demands and problems through practices such as (a) environmental assessment: gathering and assessing information about the firm's external environment; (b) stakeholder management: managing the organisation's relationships with those persons, groups, and organisations that can affect or are affected by the company's operations; and (c) issues management: tracking and responding to societal issues that may affect the company.

A socially responsive corporation will typically have ongoing budgeted response mechanisms for those issues and stakeholders that remain relevant over time. Public affairs offices, for example, manage the firm's relationships with governments and monitor and respond to public policy issues. Corporate → foundations or local community relations offices handle much of the firm's philanthropic and voluntary involvements. Environmental assessment and issues management are now typically functions of strategic planning or the top management team. In addition, responsive companies will make sure to retain the flexibility needed to respond to emerging issues and to new stakeholder concerns.

To be fully responsible, a socially responsive firm must link its responses with its core → values as well as with its overall strategy. Such linkages help to ensure that the firm's responsive actions are logical as well as ethical.

Donna Wood

CORPORATE SUSTAINABILITY
→ Sustainability, Sustainable development, Triple bottom line

The average life expectancy of a company is relatively short. When the oil crises of the 1970s spotlighted the finite nature of fossil fuels, for example, Shell wondered whether there would be life – or at least industrial life – after oil. It investigated how other long-lived firms had addressed earlier market discontinuities, and did not particularly like the answer that it found. In most cases, companies simply died or disappeared. They merged, were taken over, or went out of business. Of the original 30 constituents of the Financial Times Ordinary Share Index, launched in 1935, just nine survived more or less intact by the late 1990s. And the US corporate death rates turned out to be even higher. Nearly 40% of the 1983 Fortune 500 had dematerialised, 60% of 1970's, and of the 12 companies making up the Dow Jones Industrial Index in 1900, General Electric (GE) was the only substantial survivor.

More positively, although the average corporate life expectancy might be in the region of 40–50 years, there may be several hundred companies around the world which have been operating for between 100 and 150 years. This imbalance between the broad mass of companies and the long-winded few is a reflection of many factors, but perhaps the most important is the fact that in a capitalist world companies that fail to deliver shareholder value are starved of capital and die. To date, sustainability factors have only very rarely affected capital availability, but understanding of such linkages is likely to grow fairly rapidly.

Corporate sustainability, then, is probably better understood not so much as the discipline by which companies ensure their own long-term survival – though that is clearly part of the equation – but as the field of thinking and practice by means of which companies and other business organisations work to extend the life expectancy of: ecosystems (and the natural resources they provide); societies (and the cultures and communities that underpin commercial activity); and economies (that provide the governance, financial and other market context for corporate competition and survival). By paying attention to such wider issues, it is often argued, companies are better placed to ensure that their own business models remain valid and adaptable.

As for the corporate sustainability agenda, recent decades have seen sustainability issues gradually being forced up through corporate hierarchies. They started very much on the fringes, being handled (if at all) by professionals in such areas as site security, public relations and legal affairs. Through the 1970s, as new techniques like environmental → impact assessment evolved, the impact was felt by new groups of people, among them project planners, process engineers and site managers. Then, during the late 1980s, the spotlight opened out to illuminate new product development, design, marketing and life cycle management. As the → triple bottom line agenda of → sustainable development spread through the 1990s, with an inevitable growth in the complexity and political impact of key issues, the agenda was driven up to top management and boards. In the next round, in addition to all those already involved, expect to see new ventures people, chief financial officers, investment bankers and venture capitalists getting involved.

Over time, the agenda has opened out profoundly, increasingly embracing challenging issues like → human rights, bribery and → corruption, and global poverty. The key text in this area has been 1987's Brundtland Commission report, *Our Common Future*. Its definition of → sustainable development is now widely accepted. It was brought into greater focus in 1994 with the introduction of the → triple bottom line concept, which has subsequently been widely adopted − for example, by the → Global Reporting Initiative (GRI).

As the agenda has morphed, several other factors have conspired to increase the challenge for business. First, business has increasingly been expected to do things that governments would once have done, if they were done at all. Second, the processes of → globalisation have enormously extended the areas and timescales over which companies are held accountable, while the processes of outsourcing and offshoring mean that corporate value chains have become increasingly extensive, complex and vulnerable to challenge. And, third, the spread of the internet and the introduction of search engines like Google have subjected business to ever-growing levels of scrutiny.

As the agenda has evolved, the calls on the time and resources of business have increased almost exponentially. In 1999, for example, UN secretary-general Kofi Annan called on business leaders 'to join the United Nations on a journey'. He commented that business was already well down the road with a journey of its own, → globalisation. At the time, → globalisation appeared like 'a force of nature', seeming to 'lead inexorably in one direction: ever-closer integration of markets, ever-larger economies of scale, ever-bigger opportunities for profits and prosperity'.

However, even 10 months before the Seattle protests against the → World Trade Organisation (WTO), the secretary-general also felt it necessary to warn that → globalisation would only be as sustainable as its social foundations. 'Global unease about poverty, equity and marginalization,' he stressed, 'is beginning to reach critical mass.' These issues are no less important today, although some focus has shifted to political and security concerns in the wake of 9/11, Iraq and Madrid − which, some would argue, are intimately connected to unresolved problems of poverty and inequity. In tackling such challenges, business is being told it must pay more attention to the need for new forms of → global governance.

'Governance' became a buzzword in the 1990s. 'Corporate' governance, although not a new concept, began its rise up the public agenda in 1992, for example with the publication of the Cadbury Report in the UK. That same year, the United Nations held its Earth Summit in Rio de Janeiro, highlighting the urgent need to shift the global economy towards more sustainable forms of → development—and the World Bank released *Governance and Development*, making the case that governance failures lay behind the poor progress of development efforts to date. A decade later the spotlight has opened out, with those seeking 'responsible → globalisation' now calling for meaningful '→ global governance'. So what are the emerging agendas for both business and governments?

There is a central paradox here – and it has two main dimensions. First, the voluntary corporate responsibility (CR) movement has evolved as a pragmatic response to pressing environmental, community or → human rights issues. Companies are being asked to address problems and even deliver public goods because governments have been unable or unwilling to do so. But, second, because of the weakness – or absence – of appropriate governance systems, CR initiatives are generally disconnected from wider frameworks. As a result, they are at risk of amounting to little more than drops in the ocean when compared to the scale of the challenges. At worst, they may even undermine long-term solutions.

But huge progress has been made. From the defensive stances adopted in the heyday of government-driven responses, we have seen companies begin to explore ways forward with an expanding range of external stakeholders. There has been:

- Acknowledgement of the legitimate – and critical – role of companies – while there are still sceptics, there is also an emerging consensus among civil society, government and business that, in principle, companies play an important role in developing and implementing solutions to pressing → sustainable development problems.
- Engagement of a significant number of leading multinationals – for example, some 180 companies are members of the → World Business Council for Sustainable Development (WBCSD). Nearly 1000 companies use part or all of the → Global Reporting Initiative (GRI) guidelines to report on their social and environmental performance. → Business in the Community, a UK business association focused on CR, has a membership accounting for one in five private sector employees in the UK and a global workforce of over 15.7 million people. Similarly, membership of Brazil's Ethos Institute accounts for more than a quarter of the

country's GNP. A key question is: How can this potential critical mass be used to drive forward → sustainable development even more powerfully?

- A clearer understanding of the → business case (and its limits) – the '→ business case' clearly has limits in driving CR 'to scale'. But the extent of the → business case for CR, and the links with investment value drivers such as reputation, risk management, → corporate governance and management quality, are increasingly recognised both by business and key stakeholder groups (e.g. government and the investment community).

While these certainly reflect accomplishments and progress, and individual companies can also claim substantial performance improvements, the fundamental question is whether the CR movement as a whole has made a real difference in addressing longer-term sustainability issues? The conclusion must be that current CR initiatives will increasingly run up against system limits. As former US President Bill Clinton argued at the 2004 → World Economic Forum summit, the scale of the challenges the world now faces is such that systematic change will not be enough. Instead, he said, we need systemic change, changes to the system itself.

We have been here before. Professor John Ruggie, responsible for Harvard's new Corporate Social Responsibility Initiative and a key architect of the → UN Global Compact, explains: 'We in the industrialised world were slow to learn the lesson that markets must be embedded in broader frameworks of social → values and shared objectives if they are to survive and thrive. Before we got to that point, we had struggled through the collapse of the Victorian era of → globalisation, a world war, the rise of the left wing revolutionary forces in Russia, right wing revolutionary forces in Germany and Italy as well as the Great Depression.' When the lesson did finally sink in, Ruggie says, 'we called the new understanding by different names: the New Deal, the social market economy and social democracy'. The basis of these social bargains was that all actors agreed to open markets – but they also agreed to 'share the social adjustment costs that open markets inevitably produce'. And governments played a central role in the process, 'moderating the volatility of transaction flows across borders and providing social investments, safety nets and adjustment assistance – but all the while pushing liberalization'.

One of the most striking recent trends has been the formation of new forms of partnerships and alliances, linking business with NGOs and other civil society actors. But if future corporate efforts and alliances are to bridge the challenge – response gap, the scaling issue will need to be addressed more seriously. And more thought needs to be given to how we scale geometrically, where the challenges are serious. One answer here is to change market conditions to favour particular outcomes, which is where governments have a key role to play.

And that is why two additional challenges that are evolving in the corporate sustainability space have to do with → lobbying and tax policy. On corporate → lobbying, there is growing concern that companies that give every surface sign of being committed to sustainability are often – directly or indirectly – → lobbying behind the scenes to slow progress. The question here is not only how to make such → lobbying more transparent, but how, over time, corporate → lobbying could be swung around to support initiatives designed to tackle major problems like → climate change. And, second, given the growing importance of government in dealing with so many of the challenges that have landed on the business agenda in recent years, there is a real question about how government can be properly funded. As a result, the ability of companies in a globalising world to manage down their tax burdens is coming under growing scrutiny.

One more sign, in short, that the corporate sustainability agenda has plenty of steam in it yet. Meanwhile GE, that sole survivor of the top 12 in the 1900 Dow Jones Industrial Index, has raised the stakes by announcing its 'Ecomagination' initiative – designed to build a series of new business around sustainability-linked opportunities. Some environmentalists remain sceptical, but the fact that GE has announced its intention to create a $20 billion business in this area by 2010 is a striking illustration of the market opportunities now emerging.

John Elkington

CORPORATE VOLUNTEERING
→ Volunteering

CORRUPTION
→ Business ethics, Corporate governance, UN Global Compact, Transparency International, UN Declaration against Corruption and Bribery in International Commercial Transactions

Corruption can be defined as the misuse of entrusted power for private gain, which is also the definition used by → Transparency International (TI). Corruption occurs where people collude to improperly benefit themselves or others with whom they are associated, by misusing the authority and trust which they have been given.

Individuals can act corruptly on their own without involving another party, but TI's definition is confined to where there are two parties to the act of corruption, namely the person who offers or provides the inducement and the party influenced by or acting on it.

Though this is a simple definition it encompasses a complex topic with many forms of corruption which include:

- → Fraud
- Bribery
- → Conflict of interest
- Defalcation
- Embezzlement

- Nepotism and favouritism
- Trading in influence
- Collusive bidding
- Extortion
- Illegal information brokering
- Insider trading

Money laundering, although not corruption in itself, is an associated activity to corruption as proceeds from corrupt activity often need to be laundered to gain a veneer of legitimacy.

The terms grand and petty corruption are often used to distinguish between corruption involving large amounts, and corruption involving small payments. A classic example of grand corruption is private sector bribery of public officials for large contracts. Correspondingly, petty corruption describes small payments, commonly known as facilitation payments, paid to secure or expedite services to which the briber is legally entitled, such as installing a telephone; or to avoid being subject to illegitimate harassment, for instance by the police. Grand and petty corruption are part of a continuum of corruption, and so tolerating or ignoring petty corruption confuses the boundaries and provides an adverse signal, thereby feeding widespread corruption.

The relevance to CSR is that corruption is widespread and damages societies, economies, enterprises and the lives of people. Enterprises can make a contribution to countering corruption through CSR. The word corruption comes from the Latin *corruptus*, meaning to destroy, and this characterises the severity of change and damage that can be caused by a corrupt act. The trust given to the individual is destroyed, and the effects can be highly damaging. Corrupt behaviour can damage the rule of law, democratic rights and → human rights. It can act as a tax on the poor, be the cause of environmental damage such as deforestation, provide funds for terrorism, facilitate smuggling, counterfeiting, money laundering and numerous other criminal activities. For enterprises it presents a risk to reputation, business success and sustainability and may also lead to civil and criminal sanctions.

Countering corruption is carried out through a range of approaches including:

- Legislation – the USA was first to introduce national legislation in 1976 with the Foreign Corrupt Practices Act. A number of international conventions have been introduced in recent years to require states to implement national legislation. These conventions include the OECD Convention on Countering Bribery of Foreign Public Officials in International Transactions, and the → United Nations Convention against Corruption.
- Building national integrity systems – this involves strengthening the key institutions which between them uphold → integrity in a country, such as the executive, judiciary or the media.
- Encouraging good governance and anti-corruption measures through international aid and → development.
- Enterprises adopting no-corruption polices and implementing → codes of conduct and systems – enterprises can also demand anti-corruption performance from key business partners such as suppliers.
- Sectoral initiatives such as the → Extractive Industries Transparency Initiative and the → Wolfsberg Principles.
- Civil society advocacy and action by organisations such as → Transparency International, the global coalition against corruption, Global Witness or local NGOs.
- Media investigating and exposing corruption.
- Socially responsible investment – anti-corruption criteria being included in SRI indices such as has been done with the → FTSE4Good Index.
- International instruments setting standards and providing implementation tools, such as the → UN Global Compact and its 10th Principle against Corruption, and the → Business Principles for Countering Bribery.

- Increased → transparency – transparent procurement and tendering processes, freedom of information legislation, use of information technology to make available information to citizens or parties to a contract tender, use of the TI Integrity Pact.
- Enhanced reporting and credibility – greater clarity and range of public reporting from all forms of organisation, and the use of independent verification.
- Greater expression of expectations and action by societies – collectively and through individual action.

Most forms of corruption are illegal in countries around the world and therefore it could be assumed that the scope is limited for CSR which is 'beyond compliance'. In fact, while laws tend to proscribe or sanction, they are often insufficiently enforced and even if so, do not usually provide for the depth and range of activity needed to implement anti-corruption policies.

The CSR opportunity for enterprises is to build a culture of no-corruption in their organisations and encourage this in their business partners and in the communities in which they operate. Most large enterprises have in place → codes of conduct but fewer have comprehensive implementation systems such as providing → leadership, communication, training, HR policies and procedures, internal controls and sanctions.

Fewer enterprises carry out activities that contribute to strengthening the anti-corruption structures in the societies in which they operate such as supporting or encouraging local business associations and NGOs.

Corruption – while behind so many of the major societal issues such as poverty, deforestation, earthquake damage, deaths from counterfeit drugs – does not yet receive the same attention on the CSR agenda as environment, → human rights, community needs or medical causes. CSR provides a framework within which enterprises can enhance their management of preventing corruption, have greater chance of competing on a level playing field for con-tracts, build greater trust among stakeholders and make a significant contribution to people in countries most vulnerable to corruption.

David Nussbaum and Peter Wilkinson

CORRUPTION PERCEPTIONS INDEX

→ Corruption, Transparency International

🖰 www.transparency.org

→ Transparency International's annual → Corruption Perceptions Index (CPI) ranks countries according to perceived levels of → corruption among public officials and politicians. The CPI is a composite index drawing on → corruption-related data in multi-ple expert surveys carried out by a variety of reputable institutions. The CPI reflects the views of businesspeople and analysts from around the world, including experts who are resident in the coun-tries evaluated. The CPI focuses on → corruption in the public sector and defines → corruption as the misuse of public office for private gain. The surveys used in compiling the CPI ask questions that relate to → corruption, with a focus, for example, on bribe-taking by public officials in public procurement. The sources do not distinguish between administrative and political → corruption or between petty and grand → corruption.

David Nussbaum and Peter Wilkinson

CRADLE-TO-GRAVE

→ Life cycle assessment

In a cradle-to-grave approach all the pollution from the stage of dig-ging or harvesting raw materials to the → waste that remains after using a product is taken into account. The aim is to minimise the environmental burden throughout the complete production chain rather than optimising individual production processes within that chain. Not only is the latter approach less efficient, it may also be counterproductive. For instance, when a printing company starts using water-based inks to minimise the emissions of volatile organic solvents, recycling of the paper → waste may become much more difficult if the paper producing companies cannot handle paper pulp containing these new inks. In a cradle-to-grave approach the optimum is sought in water-based inks that can also be easily extracted from paper pulp. An important instrument in the cradle-to-grave approach is → life cycle assessment. Such an analysis also enables the comparison of the environmental performance of products and services in order to choose the least burdening one.

Theo de Bruijn

CSR ACADEMY
→ CSR Competency Framework

CSR ASIA
→ Asia
⌐ www.csr-asia.com

CSR Asia is a social enterprise that is the leading provider of information about → corporate social responsibility in the → Asia-Pacific region. Through its offices in Hong Kong, Singapore, Shenzhen and Bangkok, CSR Asia builds capacity in companies and their supply chains to promote awareness of CSR in order to advance → sustainable development across the region. Founded by Richard Welford and Stephen Frost in 2004, it provides training, organises conferences, and offers consultancy services through strategic partnerships with the private sector. As a social enterprise is does not aim to make profits, but instead to reinvest in environmental and community-based initiatives. The organisation has a website, updated on a daily basis and a free weekly newsletter covering CSR issues in → Asia and from an Asian perspective. It also conducts structured stakeholder dialogues for clients and undertakes contract research.

Richard Welford

CSR COMPETENCY FRAMEWORK
→ Business in the Community (BITC)
⬚ www.bitc.org.uk

The CSR Competency Framework is a manual used by the CSR Academy in the UK between 2004 and 2007 to help around 5000 UK companies to implement CSR in their operations. It is a basic, practitioner-oriented template of how CSR can be implemented in an organisation. It provides an understanding of the background of CSR, the role of stakeholder relations, the strategic role CSR can play and overall has a slight focus on human resources issues. The CSR Academy was set up in 2004 by the Department of Trade and Industry in the UK and has been taken over by → Business in the Community in 2007. The framework will continue to be used to support companies in developing the skills and competencies to implement CSR into their daily operations.

CSR EUROPE
→ Europe
⬚ www.csreurope.org

CSR Europe is a European business network for → corporate social responsibility with over 70 leading multinational corporations and 22 National Partner Organisations as members. Since its inception in 1995, the mission of CSR Europe has been to help companies integrate corporate social responsibility (CSR) into the way they do business.

Today, the companies that make up CSR Europe are at the forefront of CSR globally and setting the agenda for responsible and competitive business in → Europe. CSR Europe has become an inspiring network of business people throughout → Europe, willing to exchange business → best practices and solutions in an innovative and enriching environment.

CSR Europe engages with member companies and the wider business community in various ways. In 2005, the organisation launched a European Roadmap for a sustainable and competitive enterprise. This Roadmap serves as a set of goals and strategies to integrate corporate social responsibility into daily business practices. CSR Europe also provides helpdesk services and engages with its members through the organisation of business exchanges and seminars as well as the provision of CSR information. Stakeholder engagement is another important activity of CSR Europe. CSR Europe has a strong network through partnerships with global, regional and national players as well as thematic CSR experts.

Catherine Rubbens

CULTURAL ISSUES

Cultural issues related to CSR are many and complex. As described by Geert Hofstede, culture is 'the collective programming of the mind which distinguishes one group or category of people from another'.

It is hard to build a culture-free understanding of CSR as the concepts that underlie CSR themselves have developed within a particular cultural context of → values, beliefs, patterns of thinking, behavioural norms, practices, customs, and traditions about the role of business in society and the relation of business to its stakeholders. Cultural differences in understanding CSR are all pervasive. Cultural issues arise largely out of the differences among these diverse ways of thinking and → values.

The differences in the understanding of CSR across the US, the UK, among the European countries, and Japan are commonly discussed. Differences in CSR across → Africa, South and → Latin

America, China, or Russia remain less discussed but have gained more attention recently.

Cultural issues in CSR also relate to religion, i.e. the religious beliefs that underlie and guide the conduct of business and characterise business responsibilities towards society, vary across, for example, Islam, Christianity, or Hinduism.

Issues across the Eastern and Western cultures of capitalism have been commonly contrasted. Western capitalism being described as inherently individualistic derived from an exclusivist nature of private property and Eastern capitalism as inclusive of stakeholders, inherently predisposed to seeking harmony and consensus, as well as being based on trust, reciprocity, and family → values. However, this may not be altogether tenable as many continental European countries also demonstrate fairly stable long-term trust-based relationships between business and its stakeholders and a consensus-based style of decision-making.

Thus, cultural issues may vary based on how societies are organized, e.g. these may be monistic (US, UK), dualistic (France, Germany), or pluralistic (Japan, → Africa); and individualist (US, UK); or collectivist (France, Germany). Societies characterised by individualism value the short-term success of the individual; while those based on communitarianism value the long-term flourishing of the community.

Diversity in how the societal, political, legal and economic institutions in a country interact also leads to cultural issues for CSR. Institutional traditions have influenced patterns of industrial development in a country. These influence types of → corporate governance structures, organisational characteristics, behaviour, and strategies that business adopts for CSR.

Contrasting institutional differences are evident across developing countries and developed countries leading to many differences in CSR in each of these contexts.

In addition to geographical or societal contexts, cultural differences also exist across industry sectors and across organisations, and even within an organisation. These different cultures determine what CSR issues are addressed and how to 'walk the talk'. So, for example, the chemical industry is marked by a dominant '→ health and safety culture'.

Cultures of CSR may vary across corporations within an industry. Corporations identify their concepts of CSR based on their analysis of risks, bottom line, and according to its → corporate culture and the → values of its leaders. For example, on the issue of global warming, Exxon-Mobil or Texaco, on the one hand, and TotalFinaElf and BP, on the other, have adopted CSR in very different ways.

These cultural issues are around the different strategic postures and actions that companies adopt for CSR, and how they manage priorities among stakeholders or handle conflicts of interest.

Challenging cultural issues arise for joint ventures, mergers or takeovers when CSR cultures of companies that are coming together conflict even within the same industry.

Within an organisation, there are cultural issues based on diverse thinking on CSR at different levels of the company, e.g. the top management, or the HQ culture of CSR may differ from that of the subsidiary's CSR culture. Similarly, there tends to be different thinking across board, executive, or operations levels. Thereby, within the company, what is deemed important, and how it is practised differs across these different levels.

The understanding and approach to CSR also varies across the functional areas within a business, e.g. among the 'more boundary spanning' functions (human resources, marketing, public affairs, community affairs, environment affairs) and the 'less boundary spanning' functions (finance, legal, R&D, engineering).

Cultural issues also arise among communities of stakeholders as the vested interests, → values and expectations differ across the different stakeholder groups. For example, investors, employees, suppliers, and neighbouring communities may relate to CSR differently.

There also are ideological differences among members of different sectors, i.e. between government, civil society and business. These ideological differences influence what CSR issues are prioritised, the expectations from business and what gets accepted or practised as CSR.

Conflictual issues arise from the diversity of these different CSR perspectives and the tensions between value systems and practices, and/or any prevalent stereotypes, misconceptions and prejudices.

Cultural issues in CSR pose challenges for achieving a universal understanding of CSR or for the convergence of practices across these diverse geographical, socio-political or ideological cultures. These issues are also challenging when trying to change from one type of culture to another, or in getting cultural fit for the multinational companies that have to work in and with different cultures of CSR.

Anupama Mohan

DEVELOPING COUNTRIES
→ Development, Poverty

CSR in developing countries incorporates the formal and informal ways in which business makes a contribution to improving the governance, social, ethical, labour and environmental conditions of the developing countries in which they operate, while remaining sensitive to prevailing religious, historical and cultural contexts.

The category of 'developing countries' is used broadly to include countries that have relatively lower per capita incomes and are less industrialised. For a listing of countries that might fall into this grouping, see the World Bank's classification of lower and middle income countries.

Far from being a unified field, debate on CSR in developing countries is extremely diverse, ranging from optimistic views about the role of business in society to highly critical perspectives. However, there seems to be an emerging consensus that developing countries provide a socio-economic and cultural context for CSR which is, in many ways, different from developed countries.

In particular, CSR in developing countries has the following distinctive characteristics:

- CSR tends to be less formalised or institutionalised in terms of the CSR benchmarks commonly used in developed countries, i.e. CSR codes, standards, management systems and reports.
- Where formal CSR is practised, this is usually by large, high profile national and multinational companies, especially those with recognised international brands or those aspiring to global status.
- Formal CSR codes, standards and guidelines that are most applicable to developing countries tend to be issue specific (e.g. → fair trade, supply chain, → HIV/AIDS) or sector led (e.g. agriculture, textiles, mining).
- In developing countries, CSR is most commonly associated with philanthropy or charity, i.e. through corporate social investment in education, health, sports development, the → environment and other community services.
- Making an economic contribution is often seen as the most important and effective way for business to make a social impact, i.e. through investment, job creation, taxes, and → technology transfer.
- Business often finds itself engaged in the provision of social services that would be seen as government's responsibility in developed countries, e.g. investment in → infrastructure, schools, hospitals and housing.
- The issues being prioritised under the CSR banner are often different in developing countries, e.g. tackling → HIV/AIDS, improving working conditions, provision of basic services, supply chain integrity and poverty alleviation.

- Many of the CSR issues in developing countries present themselves as dilemmas or trade-offs, e.g. → development versus environment, job creation versus higher labour standards, strategic philanthropy versus political governance.
- The spirit and practice of CSR is often strongly resonant with traditional communitarian → values and religious concepts in developing countries, e.g. African humanism (*ubuntu*) in South Africa, coexistence (*kyosei*) in Japan and harmonious society (*xiaokang*) in China.

The drivers for CSR in developing countries include:

- Cultural tradition – drawing strongly on deep-rooted indigenous cultural traditions of philanthropy, → business ethics and community embeddedness.
- Political reform – including democratisation, → globalisation and liberalisation, which can drive business behaviour towards integrating social and ethical issues.
- Socio-economic priorities – including poverty alleviation, healthcare provision, → infrastructure development, education and empowerment of marginalised groups.
- Governance gaps – where CSR is seen as a way to plug the 'governance gaps' left by weak, corrupt or under-resourced governments that fail to adequately provide various social services.
- Crisis response – including philanthropic responses to economic, social, environmental, health-related or industrial crises, catastrophes or accidents.
- Market access – seeing unfulfilled human needs as an untapped market, including the now burgeoning literature on '→ Base of the Pyramid' strategies.
- International standardisation – including the adoption of global CSR codes and standards by the subsidiaries of multinationals or national companies wishing to export.

- Investment incentives – including investments in developing countries being screened for CSR performance through the trend of socially responsible investment (SRI).
- Stakeholder → activism – in the absence of strong governmental controls over the social, ethical and environmental performance of companies.
- Supply chain – including the social and environmental requirements that are being imposed by multinationals on their supply chains, especially among small and medium-sized companies.

The focus on CSR in developing countries can also be a catalyst for identifying, designing and testing new CSR frameworks and business models, e.g. Visser's CSR Pyramid for Developing Countries and the C.K. Prahalad's Bottom of the Pyramid model.

Research into CSR in developing countries is still relatively underdeveloped and tends to be ad hoc with a heavy reliance on convenience-based case studies. The focus is often on high profile incidents or branded companies and a few select countries (e.g. Brazil, China, India, South Africa), rather than being comprehensive national or regional surveys that produce comparable → benchmarking data. Hence, a massive opportunity exists to improve our knowledge about CSR in developing countries by expanding the scope and coverage of CSR research. For a more comprehensive review of CSR in developing countries, see the chapter by Visser in the *Oxford Handbook of CSR*.

Wayne Visser

DEVELOPMENT
→ Base of the pyramid model, Developing countries, Poverty

At its broadest, the term 'development' denotes the progression, evolution or maturation of an individual or society. Despite the wide usage – and crucial importance – of terms such as international development, → sustainable development, → community development, and economic development, there remains widespread debate and disagreement on the precise definition of these terms, let alone their most appropriate and effective forms of implementation, and the positive and negative linkages between them.

Despite the lack of precise and universally accepted definitions, there has been growing consensus during the past decade that poverty reduction, at both the household level and national level, lies at the heart of the concept of development. Linked to this, there is growing consensus that an effective process of development requires:

- Improving people's access to products and services to meet their basic needs;
- Improving opportunity and access to markets to enable people to build income and assets, including both economic and human capital;
- Giving people a political voice and enabling them to participate in and influence the policy-making, decision-making and resource allocation processes that directly affect the quality of their lives; and
- Ensuring people have sufficient financial and physical security or social insurance to enable them to better survive natural and economic crises or conflict.

In short, development involves a multi-faceted, multi-disciplinary and multi-sector set of actions, mechanisms and institutions aimed at improving the quality of people's lives. Sustainable development adds the further dimension – in short, the need to sustain or build environmental capital, in addition to economic, social, human and political capital, over the long term as well as in the short term.

For the first time in over 50 years of international development efforts, an increasingly clear and widely accepted framework is emerging on the roles and responsibilities of different development actors and the key types of intervention that are most likely to make a difference. Since 2002, the → UN Millennium Development Goals (MDGs) have become broadly accepted by, if not yet fully integrated into the policies and practices of, most donor and developing country governments and major multilateral institutions in the UN system, the World Bank Group, the IMF, and OECD. Leading international non-governmental organisations and corporations are also increasingly using the MDGs as a frame of reference when they address development challenges and opportunities.

These goals have become the defining framework for international development, calling for action by a more diverse group of actors than ever before, ranging from donor and developing governments to non-governmental organisations, trade unions and community-based groups, to large multinational corporations and small-scale entrepreneurs and farmers. The Millennium Project's 2005 report to the UN Secretary-General, Investing in Development, described them as, 'the most broadly supported, comprehensive, and specific poverty reduction targets the world has ever established, so their importance is manifold'. A results-oriented emphasis on measurable indicators is one of the MDGs' key advantages and innovations. In devising the MDGs, the United Nations Development Programme worked with the World Bank, the IMF, the OECD, and other UN departments, funds and programmes, to agree on a set of concise goals, backed by numerical targets, quantifiable indicators, and an annual reporting framework to monitor progress. The eight MDGs are backed up by 18 targets and over 40 indicators.

The growing acceptance of the MDGs has been supplemented and endorsed by a series of recent global commissions and reports which reflect similar fundamental changes and growing consensus in the thinking and practice of international development. Most of them emphasise the following five critical components that are likely to be of growing importance in achieving more equitable and sustainable patterns of development and tackling global poverty in the 21st century:

1. The centrality of pro-poor and environmentally sustainable economic growth;
2. The foundation of good governance and effective institutions;
3. The shared responsibility of developed and developing country governments as development partners;
4. The active participation of the poor themselves; and
5. The importance of private sector development, ranging from foreign direct investment by large corporations to small and micro-enterprise development.

It is reasonable to argue that on a collective basis the international community already has the necessary technologies, financial resources, entrepreneurial acumen and human ingenuity to create the wealth and technical solutions that are required to achieve the → UN Millennium Development Goals. What is needed are more effective institutions, more efficient market mechanisms and more accountable approaches to mobilising and allocating resources. To achieve this, new types of market-driven partnerships, new funding instruments and new governance structures are required in order to harness the competencies and resources of all sectors − public, private and civil society.

Achievement of the MDGs creates new challenges and opportunities for business and for → corporate social responsibility. There is obviously wide variation in the specific contributions that different companies can make to development. Their contribution depends not only on the type of development intervention needed − such as increasing access to jobs, income, education, health, energy, → water, → technology and markets, or improving governance and public capacity − but also on factors such as the industry sector, the individual company's business model, ownership structure, and size, and its ability to act collectively with other companies and in partnership with government and non-governmental organisations.

Despite these differences, almost all companies regardless of industry sector and other variables have the potential to make a contribution to development and poverty alleviation through the following three spheres of business impact and influence:

1. Core business operations and investments – including the company's activities and relationships in the workplace, the marketplace, and along the supply chain. The greatest and most sustainable contribution that any company can make to development is through carrying out its core business activities in a profitable, productive and responsible manner. The key goal should be to minimise any negative impacts on development that may arise from these activities, and to increase and leverage positive impacts.
2. Strategic philanthropy and community investment – aimed at mobilising not only money, but also the company's people, products and premises to help support and strengthen local communities and non-profit partners.
3. Public policy dialogue, advocacy and institution building – efforts by companies, either individually or collectively, to participate in relevant public policy dialogues and advocacy platforms with both developing country governments and donor governments, and to help governments build public capacity and strengthen institutions in order to better serve their citizens.

While achievement of the MDGs should remain primarily the responsibility of governments, the private sector can play an important role – and do so in a manner that not only helps to build a more secure and stable operating environment, and to manage direct business risks and costs, but also in a manner that harnesses new business opportunities.

Jane Nelson

DIGITAL DIVIDE

→ Base of the pyramid (BOP) model, Personal and household goods sector, Poverty, Telecommunications sector

The term digital divide describes the asymmetric distribution of access to information technology between social groups. It is most commonly applied to people living in the industrialised global north (who have good access to TV, telecommunication, computers and the internet) and those in the global south (who have only limited or no access to these commodities). It is, however, also possible to think of the digital divide along socio-economic (rich/poor), racial (white/minority), or geographical (urban/rural) lines which can then even be applied to developed countries. Corporations play a crucial role in overcoming the digital divide and it is increasingly seen as an issue on their CSR agenda, in particular the global digital divide between north and south. The digital divide, for instance, plays a role in corporations addressing poverty or in the → base of the pyramid (BOP) approaches. The digital divide can be addressed either by corporate philanthropy in providing access to electronic communication through provision of goods and services below market prices or by deployment of innovative business models which allow economically viable use of → technology through new patterns of use.

Dirk Matten

DISCRIMINATION

→ Diversity, Employee rights

The ILO Convention No. 111 defines discrimination as including 'any distinction, exclusion or preference made on the basis of race, colour, sex, religion, political opinion, national extraction or social origin, which has the effect of nullifying or impairing equality of opportunity or treatment' (Article 1a). This definition is applicable in the context of any difference/distinction in society and has been applied to a range of other issues, such as age and disability, for example.

As well as direct discrimination (as above), the issue of indirect discrimination is also acknowledged in international law. Indirect discrimination involves setting a condition or requirement which effectively excludes certain groups without reasonable justification. For example, insisting that a job can only be done on a full time basis excludes many women in the workforce who are unable to work full-time due to caring commitments. The Convention covers this by referring to 'such other distinction, exclusion or preference which has the effect of nullifying or impairing equality of opportunity or treatment' (Article 1b).

The UN Declaration of Human Rights also outlaws discrimination with regard to protection under the law (Article 7), and with regard to pay (Article 23).

Many CSR instruments incorporate freedom from discrimination. For example, company → codes of conduct for supply chain workers normally include non-discrimination, as recommended by the OECD Guidelines for Multinational Enterprises, the Ethical Trading Initiative and others. Companies also include non-discrimination in equal opportunity in the workplace policies and programmes. However, as non-discrimination is a legal obligation and CSR is often defined as actions beyond the law, corporate programmes for equal opportunity need to extend beyond non-discrimination. Such programmes that address disadvantage extend to positive treatment to help those in disadvantaged groups, loosely applying Aristotle's idea that 'nothing is so unequal as the equal treatment of unequals'.

Kate Grosser

DIVERSITY
→ Discrimination, Employee rights

Diversity as a CSR issue has come on to the agenda due to → globalisation, increasing population movements and changing demographics, which means that companies have to relate to an increasingly diverse group of stakeholders. Many businesses now acknowledge that there are enormous benefits to be gained from actively engaging with this diversity among employees, customers, suppliers, and in communities. The risks of ignoring diversity are also growing.

In an increasing global and diverse marketplace, companies must ensure that their workforces and marketing strategies reflect their changing customer base. Local expertise around the globe can provide invaluable information, helping to open up new markets, provide improved customer service, and build relationships with local communities, for example. Having a workforce that is representative of the changing demographic context in any country, such as an aging population, or growing minority communities, can have similar benefits.

Diversity among employees is the most common focus for CSR work on diversity. Workplace diversity involves building and maintaining a diverse workforce and trying to ensure that all employees are able to fully contribute their ideas to company development, at all levels, and across all functions. Most broadly workplace diversity can be defined as the protection, respect and inclusion of the entire package of attributes that each employee brings to the workplace. An effective workplace diversity strategy therefore requires a workplace environment that is free from → discrimination, hostility and harassment with respect to race, → gender, colour, national origin, religion, age, disability, and sexual orientation, for example, as well as other differences. Thus 'diversity' builds upon non-discrimination and equal opportunities, and develops an approach that fosters inclusion. Diversity management positively values difference, using it strategically for business benefits.

Workplace diversity strategies originally focused on traditionally recognised minority groups and visible differences; however, the term has been broadened in recognition of the fact that effective utilisation of different skills, experiences, backgrounds, and working styles can also drive business innovation and success. The benefit of viewing all individual differences as part of diversity is that the term becomes relevant to all employees, not just those in so-called minority groups. The drawback has been that difference based on group disadvantages, and inequalities of power, can be downplayed. CSR, with its focus on social impacts and the value of social justice, as well as stakeholder voice means that the inclusion of diversity within CSR initiatives can put equality issues back on the agenda.

The → business case for workplace diversity extends to: better utilisation of talent; improved employee satisfaction which links to improved customer satisfaction; enhanced creativity and innovation; better decision-making; enhanced corporate reputation and attraction of talent; and more likelihood of meeting varied stakeholder needs, all of which can lead to better performance. Investors are increasingly interested in how companies are effectively using their human capital, including the extent to which they are addressing workplace diversity. There is growing acknowledgement of the risks of not managing workplace diversity. For example, diversity strategies have been viewed as essential in gaining a global → licence to operate, and diverse workplace groups can have a negative impact on communications unless effective training and diversity programmes are put in place.

Workplace diversity programmes involve many elements; however, measurement, monitoring and → accountability are key issues which are especially useful at business unit as well as company level. Improved diversity at management level is one indicator of successful diversity integration. One of the most effective actions has been to include diversity in management appraisal systems. While workforce monitoring and employee surveys provide the basis for action in many companies, in some countries such monitoring is illegal in relation to sensitive issues such as race or sexual orientation, for example. Despite this, diversity is now included within many CSR tools, such as reporting guidelines and SRI indexes, and there are numerous specific diversity-related benchmarks and awards sponsored by business and government.

Companies that value difference and diversity strategically are building consideration of diversity well beyond HR and integrating it in all functions, especially marketing, product design and development (e.g. diverse R&D teams), and supplier diversity programmes. Some recognise the importance of diversity by including it in governance structures, monitoring diverse representation on their boards, for example. Others are integrating diversity into community affairs work. Some firms have moved the entire diversity function out of HR and into CSR to give it more breadth in the organisation. Others require that diversity is on all business unit agendas.

Key diversity issues will vary enormously depending on context. For this reason the consideration of diversity within stakeholder engagement is critical to both companies and their stakeholders. As yet many stakeholder engagement programmes have not effectively addressed diversity. Consideration of diversity would seem to be an essential element of inclusive and complete stakeholder dialogue.

Kate Grosser

DOMINI 400 SOCIAL INDEX

→ Socially responsible investment (SRI)

✍ www.kld.com

In 1990, the SRI firm Kinder-Lydenberg-Domini (KLD) created the Domini 400 Social Index – the first socially responsible investment benchmark – to measure how social and environmental screens affect investment performance. The DSI has generated the most complete data available on the risk, return and financial characteristics of SRI portfolios. Over the years, KLD has created a family of indexes to provide investors with a variety of ways to integrate environmental, social and governance factors into their investment decisions. The KLD Index also creates custom indexes to meet specific client requirements. KLD can be considered as one of the pioneers in the global SRI industry.

DONATIONS
→ Philanthropy

DONORS
→ Philanthropy

DOW JONES SUSTAINABILITY INDEXES
→ Socially responsible investment (SRI)
⌨ www.sustainability-indexes.com

Launched in 1999 the Dow Jones Sustainability Index (DJSI), and its sub-indexes, has become one of the leading indexes that rate corporations according to their performance towards the broader goal of sustainability. The DJSI follows a 'best-in-class approach' comprising those identified as the sustainability leaders in each industry. Companies are assessed in line with general and industry-specific criteria, which means that they are compared against their peers and ranked accordingly. The companies accepted into the index are chosen along the following criteria:

- Environmental sustainability, e.g. environmental reporting, eco-design, → environmental management systems, executive commitment to environmental issues;
- Economic sustainability, e.g. strategic planning, quality and knowledge management, supply-chain management, → corporate governance mechanisms; and
- Social sustainability, e.g. employment policies, management development, stakeholder dialogue, affirmative action and → human rights policies, anti-corruption policies.

In 2004, the index included 318 companies out of 10 economic sectors in 24 countries. Since its inception in 1999, the DJSI has slightly outperformed the mainstream Dow Jones Index, although it should be noted that financial robustness also forms an important part of the DJSI. It has also attracted significant interest from the investment community. In 2006, 56 DJSI licences were held by asset managers in 14 countries to manage a variety of financial products representing some US$5 bn in total.

DOWNSIZING

→ Labour issues

Downsizing is the reduction of workforce due to rationalisation, closure of operations or, more common, relocation of operations to lower wage environments. From a CSR perspective corporations normally face the dilemma that economic responsibilities to shareholders have to be aligned with ethical responsibilities to employees and local communities, both at the current location as well as at a future location. While many European countries have detailed legislation with regard to downsizing most parts of the world leave a responsible approach to the voluntary discretion of the employer. Ethical considerations would suggest that employees have a right to know well ahead of the actual point of redundancy that their job is on the line. A second important consideration is the compensation package employees receive when laid off, typically including enough money to bridge the time s/he needs for finding a new job.

Dirk Matten

DRUG AND ALCOHOL TESTING

→ Health and safety

Drug and alcohol testing is an instrument by which employers aim at verifying that potential and present employees are not using or are not addicted to substances which might impede their performance on the job. It is a highly contentious issue in CSR. It appears legitimate in cases where a job has the potential to do harm and where drugs can directly be causes of employees' underperformance or dysfunction. Critics though argue that these tests normally provide an employer with far more information about her/his employee then s/he actually needs, and thus represents a breach of → privacy. The latter applies particularly in cases where the use of recreational drugs has only limited influence on employees' performance.

Dirk Matten

DUE DILIGENCE
→ Risk management

In terms of CSR, due diligence refers to the process of investigating, identifying and quantifying material (financially significant) social, environmental and ethical risks and liabilities associated with an organisation's activities prior to carrying out a major financial transaction, most notably a corporate merger, acquisition, valuation or stock market listing.

Typical material issues which may be identified during a CSR due diligence study include:

- Environmental risks or liabilities, e.g. the existence of contaminated land and hence the potential costs of clean-up obligations;
- Health risks or liabilities, e.g. the economic impact of high levels of → HIV/AIDS or tuberculosis among employees;
- Community risks or liabilities, e.g. reputational damage or litigation costs due to conflict with local communities or health and pollution impacts; and
- Ethical risks or liabilities, e.g. inflated transaction costs and economic inefficiencies due to the prevalence of → corruption in the sector or country.

Among the most widely accepted CSR guidance for conducting due diligence investigations is ISO 14015:2001 on Environmental Assessment of Sites and Organisations. This international standard provides guidance on how to conduct an environmental due diligence investigation through a systematic process of identifying environmental aspects and environmental issues and determining, if appropriate, their business consequences. ISO 14015 also covers the roles and responsibilities of the parties to the assessment (the client, the assessor and the representative of the assessee), and the stages of the assessment process (planning, information gathering and validation, evaluation and reporting).

Wayne Visser

DUE PROCESS
→ Employee rights, Labour relations

EARTH CHARTER
✍ www.earthcharter.org

The Earth Charter is a widely recognised, global consensus statement on ethics and → values for a sustainable future. It has been formally endorsed by over 2400 organisations, including global institutions such as UNESCO and the World Conservation Union (IUCN). The Charter is a declaration of fundamental principles for building a just, sustainable, and peaceful global society for the 21st century.

Created by the largest global consultation process ever associated with an international declaration, endorsed by thousands of organisations representing millions of individuals, the Earth Charter seeks to inspire in all peoples a sense of global interdependence and shared responsibility for the well-being of the human family and the larger living world. The Earth Charter is an expression of hope and a call to help create a global partnership at a critical juncture in history.

The 16 principles of the Charter are grouped under the following themes:

- Respect and care for the community of life;
- Ecological integrity;
- Social and economic justice; and
- Democracy, non-violence, and peace.

EARTH SUMMIT
→ Rio Declaration on Environment and Development

ECO-EFFICIENCY
→ Factor 4/10

Eco-efficiency means using fewer resources to achieve the same or improved services while reducing negative environmental and social impacts. The term was introduced in the 1970s by the work of Walter Stahel, who developed many of the concepts of modern sustainability. His concept of a cradle-to-cradle economy was the first description of what is now called eco-efficiency. It includes:

- Greater durability;
- Minimum materials design and manufacturing;
- Recovery of scrap;
- Repair, reuse, and remanufacturing;
- Recycling; and
- Downcycling.

Other early developers of the concept included Hunter and Amory Lovins who demonstrated in the late 1970s that using energy and other resources more efficiently was a better way to meet human needs than focusing on increased supply. The books *Factor Four* and *Natural Capitalism* describe how eco-efficiency is the first principle of doing business in a way that solves most environmental problems while enhancing profits.

Critics such as McDonough and Braungart in their 2002 book *Cradle to Cradle* allege that by being only less bad, eco-efficiency is still bad.

The term was popularized by the → World Business Council for Sustainable Development (WBCSD) in its 1992 book *Changing Course*, and endorsed by the 1992 Earth Summit at Rio. WBCSD defines eco-efficiency as: the delivery of competitively priced goods and services that satisfy human needs and bring quality of life while progressively reducing environmental impacts of goods and resource intensity throughout the entire life cycle to a level at least in line with the earth's estimated carrying capacity.

This requires:

- A reduction in the material intensity of goods or services;
- A reduction in the energy intensity of goods or services;
- Reduced dispersion of toxic materials;
- Improved recyclability;
- Maximum use of renewable resources;
- Greater durability of products; and
- Increased service intensity of goods and services.

It is promoted by such organisations as the Wuppertal Institute in Germany, founded by Ernst von Weizsacker, another proponent of eco-efficiency. To calculate eco-efficiency Wuppertal developed the MIPS analysis (Materials Intensity per Service Unit). Other common eco-efficiency tools include pollution prevention (P^2), design for the environment (DfE), and → life cycle assessments (LCA).

Eco-efficiency is the basis for the Factor 10 Club, leading international advocates of → waste reduction as the basis for increasing human welfare. The Club called for an efficiency revolution in its Carnoules Declaration in 1994. Such countries as Austria, Holland and others have subsequently made factor 10 increases in efficiency as the basis for their → sustainable development programmes. UNEP and WBCSD call for factor 20 increases in efficiency. Most

OECD countries have also embodied some form of eco-efficiency in their basic environmental protection legislation.

L. Hunter Lovins

ECO-FRIENDLY PRODUCTS AND SERVICES
→ Green marketing, Labelling

ECO-LABELLING
→ Green marketing, Labelling

ECOLOGICAL FOOTPRINT
The term ecological footprint was first coined in 1992 by Canadian ecologist, William Rees. It refers to the total quantity of productive land and → water needed by the human population to provide the resources (such as energy, → water and raw materials) necessary to support itself and harmlessly recycle its → wastes. It is estimated that the ecological footprint of the current global human population has exceeded the biocapacity of the planet by around 25%.

Footprinting is now widely used as an indicator of environmental sustainability. Increasingly, it is used in the context of carbon footprints, which measure the sustainability and environmental impact of our day-to-day actions on → climate change, from an individual to a global level. As such, it can also be a useful method of measuring and managing resources throughout the national and global economy.

Rebecca Collins

ECO-MANAGEMENT AND AUDITING SCHEME (EMAS)
→ Auditing, Corporate environmental management (CEM)
🖰 ec.europa.eu/environment/emas

EMAS – the EU Eco-Management and Audit Scheme – is a voluntary initiative designed to improve the environmental performance of organisations. It was initially established by European Regulation 1836/93, and has subsequently been replaced by Council Regulation 761/01.

The aim of EMAS is to recognise and reward organisations that go beyond minimum environmental legal requirements and continuously improve their environmental performance. In addition, it is a requirement of EMAS that participating organisations regularly produce environmental reports, available to the public and interested parties that provide information on their environmental performance and initiatives.

EMAS is a management tool for companies and other organisations to evaluate, report on and improve their environmental performance. Organisations participating in EMAS are also required to implement an → environmental management system in accordance with the requirements of → ISO 14001:2004.

The scheme has been available for participation by companies since 1995 and has been open to all economic sectors including public and private services since 2001.

Participation is voluntary and extends to public or private organisations operating in the European Union and the European Economic Area – Iceland, Liechtenstein, and Norway. An increasing number of candidate countries are also implementing the scheme in preparation for their accession to the EU.

Organisations that wish to obtain registration to EMAS are evaluated during a process comprising the following stages:

- An environmental review considering all environmental aspects of the organisation's activities, products and services, methods to assess these, its legal and regulatory framework and existing environmental management practices and procedures.
- Following on the results of the review, organisations need to establish an effective → environmental management system

aimed at achieving the organisation's environmental policy defined by the top management. The management system needs to set responsibilities, objectives, means, operational procedures, training needs, monitoring and communication systems.

- The organisation also needs to conduct an environmental audit, assessing in particular the management system in place and conformity with the organisation's policy and programme, as well as compliance with relevant environmental regulatory requirements.
- The organisation then needs to provide a statement of its environmental performance which indicates the results achieved against the environmental objectives and the future steps to be undertaken in order to continuously improve the organisation's environmental performance.

The environmental review, EMS, audit procedure and the environmental statement must be approved by an accredited EMAS verifier and the validated statement needs to be sent to the EMAS Competent Body for registration and made publicly available before an organisation can use the EMAS logo.

Johann Möller

ECONOMICALLY TARGETED INVESTMENT
→ Community investing

An economically targeted investment (ETI) is one intended to produce both a competitive, risk-adjusted rate of return to the investor and collateral economic benefits to the broader community. These benefits may include the creation or preservation of jobs offering → living wages, building of affordable housing, → infrastructure development, and/or other investments resulting in increased economic development of the targeted region.

Generally undertaken by institutional investors (e.g. public pension funds), ETIs are subject to policies established by the investors' governance structure. ETIs frequently fall within the fixed income, private equity or real estate asset classes, but can appear in other asset categories as well.

There has been some controversy over whether ETIs represent a violation of fiduciary duty, by considering factors other than the traditional measure of maximising financial return. The US Department of Labor (which has oversight of the Employee Retirement Income Security Act of 1974) has issued several interpretive bulletins on the issue.

These note that the fiduciary standard for ETIs is no different than that for any other investment, and as long as the investment decision process for an ETI is comparable to that for other investments, ETIs represent no violation of fiduciary duty. Decisions in state and federal courts have reached similar conclusions.

Betsy Zeidman

ECO-SUBSIDIES
→ Eco-taxes, Externalities

Eco-subsidies refer to the use of fiscal measures by governments to support sectors, technologies, products or services that have environmental benefits or help to reduce environmental impacts. In economics terms, eco-subsidies are a way to internalise the → externalities that the market fails to take account of. Typical examples include the provision of subsidies for renewable energy, bio-fuels, organic farming and low carbon technologies like carbon-capture and storage. By contrast, many government subsidies currently support ecologically harmful and unsustainable practices, such as monocropping agriculture and fossil fuels.

Wayne Visser

ECOSYSTEM DEGRADATION

Ecosystem degradation is the depletion of the components of an ecosystem to such an extent that the system is no longer able to deliver its normal flow of benefits. An ecosystem is a community of organisms and their physical environment interacting as an ecological unit. Ecosystems provide numerous services to people, including:

- Provisioning services – goods produced or provided by ecosystems, such as → food, fresh → water, and timber;
- Regulating services – the benefits from regulating climate, diseases, extreme natural events, and the flow of nutrients;
- Cultural services – the non-material benefits from ecosystems, including spiritual, recreational, aesthetic, inspiration, and education benefits; and
- Supporting services – those necessary for the production of the other ecosystem services, including soil formation, nutrient cycling, primary production, and carbon sequestration.

Examples of ecological degradation include deforestation, pollution, desertification and soil erosion. Ecological degradation can lead to increasing floods and droughts, lowered productivity and fewer resources available to local people. As companies, including their suppliers and customers, depend on ecosystems and their services, it makes business sense to minimise activities that lead to ecological degradation and identify possible opportunities associated with the risks.

Valli Moosa

ECO-TAXATION
→ Carbon tax, Eco-subsidies

Eco-taxation refers to the use of fiscal measures by governments to discourage certain sectors, technologies, products or services that have significant negative environmental impacts. In economics terms, eco-taxation is a way to internalise the → externalities that the market fails to take account of. Typical examples include the taxation of fossil fuels, energy inefficient houses, aviation, → waste and pollution. Among the most common ecological taxes include fuel taxes, landfill taxes, → water quality charges and airport taxes.

Wayne Visser

ECO-TOURISM
→ Travel and leisure sector

Eco-tourism is responsible → travel to natural areas that conserves the → environment and sustains the well-being of local people. The intention is to enjoy an area's natural resources while minimising any ecological and social impact from the visitor. Tourism is the fastest growing industry in the world, with eco-tourism representing its fastest growing segment. Eco-tourism can contribute to → sustainable development, but the term can also be misunderstood and abused through → greenwash. → Certification schemes have been introduced that recognise ecotourism businesses that incorporate the true values of → conservation of biological and cultural diversity, sharing of economic benefits with local communities, and informing tourists about the natural values of the area they are visiting. Much eco-tourism involves visits to protected areas, which are areas that have been legally designated to achieve → conservation objectives, on both land and → water. For many protected areas, tourism is both a major source of funding and a serious management challenge; this calls for considerable investments in visitor management, both to ensure that the eco-tourist receives the expected experience and to ensure that the → environment, including the wild species people come to see, is not unduly disturbed.

Valli Moosa

E-LEARNING
→ Learning

E-learning is a cost-effective way of training that can be used to good effect in a variety of contexts, including awareness-raising about the complex challenges and dilemmas surrounding CSR and → sustainable development. E-learning allows users to work at their own pace and at times that are convenient to the individual. In order to be effective, it should cater for a range of different → learning styles and should offer users opportunities for interaction. There are relatively few e-learning tutorials that tackle the wider issues of CSR and → sustainable development from a business perspective. Examples include Sustainability: Step by Natural Step from → The Natural Step, and Chronos, developed jointly by the University of Cambridge Programme for Industry and the → World Business Council for Sustainable Development. Various organisations are also now developing e-learning solutions to tackle specific issues such as → climate change.

Sheila von Rimscha

EMERGING MARKETS
→ Developing countries

EMISSION TRADING
→ Climate change, Kyoto Protocol

Emission trading is a regulatory instrument which governments may use to cap the level of emissions. This involves a four stage process. First, policy-makers set a cap on the emissions allowed from a given group of emitters. Second, emitters are issued 'allowances' or 'emission permits' which can be traded. Allowances can be issued in auctions, or distributed for free to emitters or any other party. Third, market participants trade allowances in the market. This allows them to use the cheapest reduction opportunities to achieve the required emission reduction target. Finally, installations report their monitored or verified emissions and submit allowances to the state to cover these emissions.

It is debated whether emission trading or eco-taxes are better suited to achieve emission reductions. If damages from emissions rise rapidly when emissions exceed the target, then emission trading with a fixed cap can avoid excess emissions. In contrast, if costs of emission reductions are predicted to rise rapidly with tighter emission limits, then a fixed tax avoids excessively expensive emission reductions. In reality all schemes are hybrids, not least because future emission targets or tax levels can always be adjusted.

Emission trading creates new assets, which are allowances to emit pollutants within the limits of the cap. The state often owns these assets and thus has the flexibility to use them at their discretion. Usually in the first years of emission trading schemes some allowances are allocated for free to emitters to compensate them for direct costs of the environmental regulation and to gain their political support. This has facilitated the implementation of the → EU Greenhouse Gas Emission Trading Scheme, after CO_2 taxation failed. After the initial compensation the free allocation of allowances to emitters can be phased out.

Trading of allowances ensures that the initial distribution of allowances does not affect economic efficiency of the scheme. Market participants can trade the allowances to make emission reductions wherever this involves the lowest costs. With emission trading emitters also face incentives to find innovative ways to reduce their emissions and thus sell excess allowances or reduce their need to buy allowances. Environmental taxation is equally efficient and has the same incentives for innovation. Traditional regulation, which sets emission limits for installations based on existing → technology, has neither of these properties.

One basic requirement for the economic efficiency of emission trading is that market participants are confident that their operational, investment and closure decisions will not affect any future allocation decisions. The US SO_X and NO_X trading scheme on the Chicago Securities Exchange ensures this by using one historic baseline to determine the volume of free allocation. Even closed plants continue to receive allowances while new plants do not. The iterative climate negotiation and policy process as well as the significantly higher value at stake prevents such long-term allocation for CO_2 allowances, e.g. under the → EU Greenhouse Gas Emission Trading Scheme. The scheme will be economically efficient as soon as entrants do not receive allowances and the market expects future allowance allocation not to be free.

Emission trading is a political as much as an economic instrument. With initial free allowance allocation emitters can be compensated for the extra cost of the environmental regulation. As allowances can be traded, all emitters face real costs of buying or opportunity costs of not selling allowances when using them. They will reflect the allowance price in their product price, like the cost of any other input factor. This allows for a rapid shift from free allocation for the initial compensation towards auctioning of allowances to ensure long-term economic efficiency.

Karsten Neuhoff

EMPLOYEE RIGHTS

→ Discrimination

Employee rights are enforceable legal entitlements for employees on the basis of a contract of employment, collective agreements or statutory rights. Individual statutory rights based on laws can include the right to a minimum wage, notice of dismissal, minimum holiday pay, parental leave, equal opportunities and minimal health and safety protection. Collective statutory rights include the rights to join a union, to engage in collective bargaining, to participate in firm decision-making, and receive work-related information from employers (e.g. through works councils).

Employee rights are often a product of political struggles about legitimate procedures at the workplace. Employee rights can also be seen as concessions from employers and a means to legitimate their use of labour power to increase profitability and improve public relations regarding recruitment and marketing. Judicial decisions related to employment disputes tend to see the employee as the weaker contractual partner in relation to the employer. Employment contracts and collective agreements can give greater rights than the law but they cannot take away statutory rights, which are a basic minimum.

The extent of employee rights and the degree of codification differs between countries. In continental → Europe rights tend to be legally codified, the Anglo-Saxon common law tradition (e.g. US, UK) includes non-statutory law derived from repeated practices that have been acknowledged by the courts as a right. Countries with a common law tradition tend to be liberal market economies that leave more discretion to the employer and emphasise the freedom of employers and employees to individually negotiate the terms and conditions of their exchange relationship. In contrast, other European countries restrict employers' rights to freedom of contract and grant core employees more far-reaching codified rights.

Rights can also vary between workers in the same country, as well as in the same firm. This is because employers can offer workers different contractual arrangements. Agency workers, freelance workers, casual workers, trainees or the self-employed are usually entitled to fewer rights than firms' core employees.

The enforcement of employee rights and sanctioning of employers when they violate these rights vary. In some countries codified employee rights exist but are not enforced. Globally, → child labour, modern forms of slavery, and exploitative working conditions (→ sweatshops) are still widespread phenomena. This is one reason why supranational actors such as the International Labour Organisation (ILO) or the UN and UNICEF have sought to develop worldwide standards and principles concerning rights at work (see → ILO Declaration on Fundamental Principles and Rights at Work). The enforceability of such standards is limited, but becoming an issue on international agendas.

Corporate social responsibility (CSR) stresses firms' voluntary engagement in environmental, social and → labour issues. Employers are meant to improve employee well-being and participation. In particular multinational corporations (MNCs) currently put employee rights on their CSR agenda. By respecting employee rights in business environments, where these rights do not exist, or are commonly neglected or violated, they can be seen as good, socially responsible (global and national) corporate citizens. This respect for employee rights can be a reaction to societal pressures, but it can also be used proactively as part of → fair trade policies aiming at attracting conscientious customers. However, some see CSR as an augmentation to employee rights whereas others are more sceptical that it is little more than a public relations exercise.

In countries with strongly enforced rights CSR is often seen as unnecessary. This is because it is in conflict with existing corporatist systems that give power to different societal actors (e.g. trade unions) representing their members. Weaker unions thus tend to see CSR as a threat to their role in achieving and maintaining employee rights. The lack of enforceability and the unilateral character of CSR are also seen sceptically by stronger unions and works councils, for example in continental → Europe.

Employee rights are an important and established part of firms' CSR policies. CSR can be particularly beneficial for employees in countries where employee rights are not codified or not respected and enforced. But there is also scepticism about this idea coming from the US and imposed by employers in countries with very different industrial relations and employee rights traditions.

Axel Haunschild

EMPLOYEE VOLUNTEERING
→ Volunteering

EMPOWERMENT
→ Diversity

Under empowerment in a CSR context we can understand a set of policies, strategies and programmes to allow disadvantaged, marginalised, often discriminated groups of society a fair share of participation in the economic activities and benefits in a society. The most striking current example is South Africa: since democratic elections in 1994, South Africa has pursued a policy of black economic empowerment (BEE). It is an explicit political intervention to ensure that black South Africans can participate equitably in the economic activities of the country, both from the perspective of income sharing and decision-making.

The focus is on all but very small enterprises – and in particular the mainstream corporate sector, which the government believes has an obligation to change its white character to become more representative of society at large.

There are a number of component parts to BEE policy, notably the promotion of black corporate ownership, black employment (particularly at managerial and executive levels), training and skills development, procurement from black owned and controlled companies, as well as small enterprise development. The approach of government is to ensure that the benefits of empowerment are felt across a broad base of society. This is in contrast to the initial focus, where BEE ownership dominated and attracted criticism for promoting the enrichment of the emerging black elite.

The initial policy drivers were political suasion and the buying power of the state (which insisted that companies meet BEE obligations in order to qualify as a supplier to the state). Today, the drivers are underpinned by legislation (e.g. the → mining sector) and regulations (e.g. → telecommunications), with an extensive

BEE Code of Good Practice being finalised (October 2006). There are more than 25 legislative, regulatory and policy measures in place to promote BEE. As such, BEE has effectively become a matter of compliance rather than voluntary initiative reflecting political imperatives of the South African government.

Jenny Cargill

ENERGY MANAGEMENT
→ Renewable resources

Energy management is the monitoring, control and optimisation of the use of energy. Energy is one of the major concerns of the environmental performance of companies. The use of energy is inextricably linked to → climate change through the emissions of carbon dioxide. In order to reduce the effects of → climate change those emissions (and by implication the use of fossil fuels) will have to be cut substantially. The goal of energy management is to minimise the use of energy and to use renewable sources of energy, such as solar, wind and biomass, as much as possible. Energy management involves using different technologies and equipment but is also about creating a system of tasks, responsibilities and procedures through which the focus on energy is ensured throughout the organisation. Through such a system a company can work on the continuous improvement of its energy efficiency.

Theo de Bruijn

ENGAGEMENT
→ Shareholder activism, Stakeholder engagement

ENVIRONMENT
In the CSR context, the environment is seen in terms of both responsibility and opportunity. Corporate responsibility towards the environment (also framed as corporate → accountability)

encompasses → waste management, pollution, ecological degradation, → energy management, → conservation and sustainable
management of natural resources. Business opportunities include
→ green marketing, green/ethical consumerism, ethical investment
and → eco-efficiency. However, what may be an opportunity for a
large multinational company may be an obstacle to development for
a small or medium-sized enterprise, particularly in → developing
countries.

The environment can be defined as 'the surroundings or conditions in which a person, animal or plant lives or operates; the
natural world, especially as affected by human activity' (*Concise
Oxford Dictionary*).

The baseline for corporate environmental responsibility is compliance with environmental legislation, which is now relatively
well developed in most parts of the industrialised world. However,
business implementation and public enforcement of environmental
legislation remain significant challenges in many countries. Proponents of corporate → accountability advocate further reform of the
legal framework.

Environmental priorities differ, particularly between OECD countries and → developing countries. Global convergence on a core
set of environmental principles for business is consequently unlikely
for the foreseeable future. There is no environmental equivalent
of the → UN Universal Declaration on Human Rights or the →
ILO Declaration on Fundamental Principles and Rights at Work.

The environment is well established within voluntary CSR
instruments. Three out of the 10 → UN Global Compact principles (launched in 2000) relate to the environment, focusing on:
'a precautionary approach to environmental challenges'; greater
environmental responsibility; and environmentally friendly technologies. The OECD Guidelines for Multinational Enterprises
(adopted in 1976 and revised in 2002) include recommendations
relating to: → environmental management systems; disclosure; life
cycle assessment; precaution; contingency planning; continuous

improvement of environmental performance; staff training; and contribution to public policy development.

Several environmental reporting initiatives also exist. The → Global Reporting Initiative's Sustainability Reporting Guidelines require disclosure on nine environmental areas: materials, energy, → water, → biodiversity, emissions/effluents/→ waste, products and services, compliance, transport and environmental protection spending. Europe's → Eco-Management and Audit Scheme (EMAS) also includes environmental reporting and there are now legal requirements for environmental disclosure in Norway, Sweden, Denmark, the Netherlands and France.

Environmental impact assessment (EIA), which was introduced in the USA in 1969, is another environmental tool and is required by law in many countries. Increasingly experts and activists are also calling for the application of strategic environmental assessment (SEA) to policies, plans and programmes relating to industrial development. SEA is receiving rapidly increasing attention among governments and donors (with the EU SEA Directive, UNECE SEA Protocol, and recent SEA Guidance from the OECD). Together with sustainability appraisal, SEA is seen as offering a tangible way to integrate environment into decision-making. These are also seen as major tools to help deliver → UN Millennium Development Goals (MDGs).

A company may seek project finance from international financial institutions that require compliance with their own environmental standards and/or the safeguard policies of the World Bank Group/International Finance Corporation (IFC). Increasingly, private banks are also signing up to the → Equator Principles, which have an environmental element, as do many ethical investment funds.

A strong corporate commitment to the environment can lead to better relations with civil society and other stakeholders, thus reducing the costs of stakeholder management, and enhancing a company's reputation in the eyes of consumers. The environment is also an area prioritised by many pressure groups and other NGOs.

Good environmental performance can provide a competitive edge in the marketplace (e.g. in the case of eco-labelling). However, private-sector environmental standards can work against smaller producers and suppliers in → developing countries, as the costs of → certification and compliance are proportionately higher for small-scale enterprises. Manufacturers and retailers tend to limit their suppliers to a select few who can comply with stricter environmental standards. Furthermore, these standards may be poorly adapted for local realities and priorities of developing country producers, and comprise a barrier to market access.

Climate change is emerging as the dominant environmental agenda in many countries. This has catalysed commitment and action in the public and private sectors, and has resulted in heightened public awareness. While this may benefit the planet by reducing carbon emissions, it may also exacerbate existing tensions between the 'environment' and other CSR agendas, notably on '→ development'. This requires more sophisticated consumer education to help people overcome their confusion about conflicting aspects of ethical consumerism (e.g. '→ fair trade' vs '→ food miles').

This is symptomatic of a growing disconnect between the environmental agenda and the parts of CSR concerned with economic and social → development, such as the → base of the pyramid, 'business and poverty' and 'business and the → UN Millennium Development Goals'.

Emma Wilson

ENVIRONMENTAL ACCOUNTING
→ Social and environmental accounting

ENVIRONMENTAL AUDITING
→ Auditing

Environmental auditing encompasses different types of audit which are used to measure and report on an organisation's environmental impacts, policies, management systems or performance.

It is an objective, systematic and documented process of collecting and evaluating evidence against predetermined criteria to establish the environmental status of the organisation or confirm assertions regarding the organisation's environmental performance. The audit criteria may be determined by: the organisation's internal policies, practices or controls; statutory standards, conventions, laws or regulations or codes of practice (environmental compliance auditing); the requirements of a formal recognised → environmental management system such as → ISO 14001 (EMS audit); or internal or external environmental reporting guidelines. The most common goal of environmental auditing is ultimately to improve the organisation's environmental performance.

Environmental auditing may form part of an independent environmental → due diligence investigation which assesses and quantifies the financial consequences of a company's environmental status and performance.

Environmental auditing may be undertaken by the organisation itself (self assessment). In relation to → certification, compliance or report verification, the audit is undertaken by an independent (external) team of environmental specialists.

Jennifer Iansen-Rogers and George Molenkamp

ENVIRONMENTAL CHAMPIONS
→ Corporate social entrepreneurs, Environmental entrepreneurship

An environmental champion is someone who uses their power, knowledge and influence in an organisational or social context to promote an environmental agenda. They tend to imbue a combination of characteristics, including being a catalyst, champion, sponsor, facilitator and demonstrator.

Successful environmental champions have the ability not only to identify the most pressing environmental issues, but also to communicate them in a way that is compelling to top management and non-threatening to their colleagues.

Not surprisingly, environmental champions are often characterised as entrepreneurs – or as some call them 'intrapreneurs' and 'ecopreneurs'.

The research on environmental champions suggests that they are critical to efforts of organisational greening and environmental performance improvement.

Championing is not confined purely to the environmental dimension of sustainability – there are equally social and ethical champions in organisations, who promote these causes based on their → values and beliefs, despite the personal and professional risks that this may entail.

Wayne Visser

ENVIRONMENTAL DUE DILIGENCE
→ Due diligence

ENVIRONMENTAL ENTREPRENEURSHIP
→ Corporate social entrepreneurs, Environmental champions

The first use of the term environmental entrepreneur came in the mid-1980s, when it was applied in the UK by the Groundwork Trusts, which were highly entrepreneurial organisations, working with government, local communities and businesses to regenerate rundown urban and industrial areas, particularly in the north of the country. The term was designed to counter the widespread perception that environmentalists were conservative and known for opposing development. But the term has since enjoyed wider currency – alongside social entrepreneur – as people have come to acknowledge the need to move beyond basic forms of → corporate citizenship to innovation and the pursuit of entrepreneurial solutions to sustainability challenges. The USA now leads in this area, with growing numbers of entrepreneurs developing new technologies and business models linked to areas such as biofuels, environmental clean-up, new materials and solar energy. The Cleantech Venture Network estimates that since 1999 over $8.3 billion has been invested in 'Cleantech' venture deals in North America alone, with demand for capital between 2006 and 2009 estimated as likely to run as high as $3.9 billion.

John Elkington

ENVIRONMENTAL EXCELLENCE

Environmental excellence was first used at the United Nations Environment Programme's World Industry Conference on Environmental Management, held in Versailles, France, in November 1984. It was conceived as an enlargement of the then current management bestseller *In Search of Excellence*, by Tom Peters and Robert Waterman, which contained no references to health, safety or environment. The term was designed to encourage engineers, executives and directors to see environmental performance as an area in which they could – should – excel. It subsequently became popular, especially in the USA, where it was adopted by many of the relevant professional associations, leading companies and even by the US Air Force, with its Center for Environmental Excellence to train future USAF leaders.

John Elkington

ENVIRONMENTAL IMPACT ASSESSMENT (EIA)
→ Impact assessment

ENVIRONMENTAL LIABILITIES
→ Due diligence, US Superfund Legislation

Environmental liabilities consist of actual, or potential, financial obligations imposed on an organisation as a result of the impacts of its operations on the → environment. Such liabilities most typically arise in the context of cleaning up contaminated land, toxic spills and other accidents involving hazardous products, and failures to comply with environmental legislation.

The advent of the 'polluter pays' principle as a driving force behind environmental legislation (most notably in the United States under the provisions of the Superfund regulations) has resulted in the issue of such liabilities becoming a financially material one for many companies, particularly those operating in environmentally sensitive sectors. This has led to accounting regulators on an international scale, following a lead set by the USA and Canada, issuing specific requirements relating to the disclosure of environmental liabilities within published corporate financial statements. The general procedure is for financial provisions to be disclosed in the accounts when future expenditure is probable and costs can be estimated within a reasonable range of possible outcomes. In cases of uncertainty over the nature and financial amount of future claims to be made on the company's resources, normal practice is to provide a non-financially quantified description of the 'contingent liability' in the notes accompanying the financial statements.

David Owen

ENVIRONMENTALLY FRIENDLY PRODUCTS AND SERVICES
→ Green consumerism, Green marketing, Labelling

ENVIRONMENTAL MANAGEMENT
→ Corporate environmental management

ENVIRONMENTAL MANAGEMENT SYSTEM (EMS)

→ Continual improvement, Eco-Management and Auditing Scheme (EMAS), ISO 14000 Series on Environmental Management

Before considering the definition of an environmental management system (EMS), it is important to consider the sub-terms 'environment', 'management' and 'system' which all add meaning to the term.

The 'environment' in the context of this discussion can best be defined by looking at the definition contained within → ISO 14001:2004, which defines it as the surroundings in which an organisation operates, including air, → water, land, natural resources, flora, fauna, humans, and their interrelation.

'Management' refers to all activities related to development, implementation and operation of the EMS, including coordination, issue of directives, assessment of activities and various types of monitoring.

'System' refers to a systematic way of work established prior to activities required by the EMS actually being operational (implemented).

In general an EMS is considered as the part of a management system of an organisation (enterprise, authority etc.), in which specific competencies, behaviours, procedures and demands for the implementation of the operational environmental policy of the organisation are defined. An EMS can also be seen as a set of interrelated elements used to establish policy and objectives and to achieve those objectives.

The EMS thus provides the organisation's management with a structured framework for identifying, evaluating, managing and improving its environmental performance. It also helps to ensure that the organisation's overall environmental goals, as set out in its environmental policy, are implemented throughout the organisation and that employees, contractors and suppliers know their roles and responsibilities in helping the organisation to achieve them with the ultimate aim to systematically manage the environmental matters of the organisation.

Regular monitoring and → auditing of the organisation's environmental performance and the system that is put in place to improve it, provide management with a basis for evaluating the effectiveness of the EMS. The EMS also provides a system for collecting and managing data on environmental performance which is used in environmental reporting and can also be used to make validated product claims.

The most popular kind of EMS is one which is developed in accordance with → ISO 14001:2004, an international standard published for the first time in 1996 by the International Organisation for Standardisation (ISO) and which was reviewed and published again in 2004.

From an operational point of view, an EMS can be viewed as a continual cycle of planning, implementing, reviewing and improving the processes and actions that an organisation undertakes to meet its business and environmental goals.

To achieve a clear understanding of → continual improvement and where it applies, it is also necessary to consider terms used in the definition of → continual improvement. The terms are:

- Environmental performance, which relates to measurable results of the environmental management system, related to an organisation's control of its environmental aspects, based on its environmental policy, objectives and targets.
- Environmental policy, which is a statement by the organisation of its intentions and principles in relation to its overall environmental performance, and which provides a framework for action and for the setting of its environmental objectives.
- Environmental aspect can be described as an element of an organisation's activities, products or services that can interact with the → environment. A significant environmental aspect has or can

have a significant environmental impact, while an environmental impact can be described as any change to the → environment, whether adverse or beneficial, wholly or partially resulting from an organisation's environmental aspects.

- Environmental objectives and targets are described as overall environmental goals, consistent with the environmental policy, that an organisation sets itself to achieve, while an environmental target is a detailed performance requirement, applicable to the organisation or parts thereof, that arises from the environmental objectives, and that needs to be set and met in order to achieve those objectives.

An EMS can result in both business and environmental benefits. Business benefits are usually the main driving forces behind the development and implementation of an EMS. Examples of such benefits include:

- Improved environmental performance;
- Enhanced compliance with legal and other requirements;
- Prevention of pollution and → conservation of resources;
- Reduction and mitigation of risk;
- Market access and enhanced credentials for marketing purposes;
- Increased efficiency;
- Cost reduction;
- Enhanced employee morale;
- Enhanced reputation with the public, regulators, lenders and investors; and
- Qualification for recognition/incentive programmes and reduction on insurance premiums.

Johann Möller

ENVIRONMENTAL MOVEMENT
→ Corporate environmental management, Environment, Sustainable development

In retrospect, the environmental movement was one of the most powerful social and political forces of the 20th century. The intellectual foundations were laid by people like Rachel Carson (with her 1962 book *Silent Spring*) and Jane Jacobs (in 1961's *The Death and Life of Great American Cities*). Much of the early concern focused on single issues like the disruption of animal reproduction by synthetic → chemicals, the impact on wildlife and fisheries of giant oil spills, and the near-extinction of marine mammals like the blue whale. Photographs of distant earth brought back by the Apollo astronauts played a critical role in crystallising concerns around the future of the planet, leading among other things to several books with the title *Spaceship Earth*.

The roots of environmentalism go way back, to the preservation and → conservation movements of the 19th and 20th centuries. But the first great wave of modern environmentalism really began to build from the early 1960s – with WWF founded in 1961 – culminating in 1970's Earth Day in the USA. Earth Day helped spur a major push to green government, with the US Environmental Protection Agency also founded in 1970. The peak period of the first pressure wave ran from 1969 to 1973, with the first UN conference on the human environment held in Stockholm in 1972. The first downwave, running from 1974 through 1987, saw a secondary wave of environmental ministries and agencies established across the OECD region, resulting in a proliferation of new environmental laws and regulations. Business and industry were pushed onto the defensive, at best trying to achieve compliance with the new requirements.

The first wave peak saw the launch of several key new environmental organisations, among them Friends of the Earth and Greenpeace. Unlike WWF, which had been founded by conservationists who were largely pro-business, the new generation of environmentalists were largely anti-capitalist, anti-growth, anti-business and anti-profit. So the 1970s and 1980s were marked by energetic disputes with business, punctuated – and aggravated – by a series of major industrial disasters, culminating in India's Bhopal chemical disaster of 1984 and the Ukraine's Chernobyl nuclear disaster in 1986. The net result: major international politicians began to make green speeches, including President Mikhail Gorbachev, Prime Minister Margaret Thatcher and President George Bush, Snr.

By the late 1980s, issues like ozone depletion had brought the environmental challenge home to growing numbers of ordinary people. One result was rapid growth in the green consumer movement, with intense pressure brought to bear on a growing spectrum of industries – making products as diverse as aerosols, batteries, nappies and cars. There was much discussion at this period about 'dark green' versus 'light green' strategies for saving the world, with the 'Deep Ecology' movement being counterposed, in the dark green corner, to → green consumerism in the light green corner.

Key books in this area include Anna Bramwell's *Ecology in the 20th Century* (1989) and *Something New Under the Sun: An Environmental History of the Twentieth-Century World* by J.R. McNeill (2000). For a sense of where all this is headed, see SustainAbility's report, *The 21st Century NGO* (2003).

As momentum built towards the 1992 UN Earth Summit in Rio de Janeiro, competitive and citizenship pressures increased. Environmentalism spread to business. In 1991, DuPont's CEO announced that, in his case, CEO meant 'chief environmental officer,' while Swiss billionaire Stephan Schmideiny founded the precursor of the → World Business Council for Sustainable Development, to help leading companies address environmental issues more positively and imaginatively.

The concept of → sustainable development, introduced in 1987's Brundtland Commission report, *Our Common Future*, helped bring environmental thinking into the business mainstream, as did concepts like → eco-efficiency and the → triple bottom line. But in the process the focus on environment tended to blur, as new issues like → human rights and bribery and → corruption took centre stage. In 2004, partly as a result, Michael Shellenberger and Ted Nordhaus threw a cat among the pigeons with their provocatively titled paper *The Death of Environmentalism*. A useful caution, perhaps, but subsequently environmentalism has got a new burst of energy with the growing concerns around → climate change, particularly as articulated by former US Vice President Al Gore in his film *An Inconvenient Truth*. In parallel, demographic trends and the issues faced by emerging economies like Brazil, China and India seem set to ensure environmentalism new legs in the 21st century.

John Elkington

ENVIRONMENTAL REPORTING
→ Non-financial reporting

ENVIRONMENT, HEALTH AND SAFETY (EHS)
→ Corporate environmental management, Health and safety

EQUAL OPPORTUNITIES
→ Discrimination, Diversity

EQUATOR PRINCIPLES
→ Banking sector
⌐ www.equator-principles.com

The Equator Principles were established in 2003 between a small group of the largest investment banks and the IFC in order to improve the environmental performance of project finance. They were revised in 2006 and presently more than 40 financial institutions have signed on to them.

The signatories agree to categorise all capital investments in industrial projects above US$10 million capital costs in identified countries according to the definitions of the IFC and to apply the social and environmental Performance Standards of the IFC to these projects, or provide a justification for not complying with them. Annual reporting on compliance is required.

The Principles intend to ensure that projects are developed in a manner that is socially responsible and reflect sound environmental management practices. They specifically commit to not lending to borrowers who are unable to comply with the social and environmental policies and procedures of the Principles. Among the most important features of the Equator Principles are the following. Participating banks must:

- Ensure a social and environmental assessment is carried out by the borrower that identifies relevant social and environmental impacts, and the appropriate measures to be taken to mitigate and manage them.
- Guarantee compliance with all local laws.
- Commit to a process of free, prior and informed consultation with affected communities for projects with significant adverse impacts, including demonstrating how those communities' concerns have been adequately addressed.
- Ensure an independent social or environmental review of the project and the consultation process by an expert not directly associated with the borrower to ensure Equator Principles compliance.
- Appointment of an independent environmental and/or social expert to verify the monitoring information of the borrower.

Matt Jeschke

EQUITY
→ Intergenerational equity, Intragenerational equity

ERGONOMICS
→ Health and safety

Ergonomics is the study of efficiency of individuals in their working environment. In an age when people spend increasing amounts of time in front of computer screens employers assume increasingly the duty of care to their employees to ensure that their equipment, furniture and work environment meets their requirements and to reduce the risk of conditions such as upper limb disorders, back pain, stress, headaches or visual fatigue.

Simple steps that an employer can take to reduce risk include making eye and eyesight tests available, providing ergonomic chairs which are fully adjustable incorporating features such as lumber support, access to ergonomic mice and keyboards and plans for breaks or changes of activity. The introduction of software which prompts users to take short pauses, regular breaks and exercises and stretches, can prevent computer fatigue, discomfort and eyestrain thus ensuring greater comfort for employees.

Self-assessment workstation checklists can be used to identify concerns but their findings need to be followed up by skilled personnel who can advise on posture, equipment settings and use of ergonomic peripherals. Responsible employers also need to address concerns raised about environmental factors such as humidity, temperature, light and space in the working environment to ensure that employees can work healthily and effectively.

Jane Batten

ETHICAL CONSUMPTION
→ Green consumerism, Fair trade

Ethical consumption refers to retail customers' opting for goods that are perceived to create more preferable social, economic or environmental impacts and outcomes than competing equivalents. By definition, since ethical consumption requires consumers who have both above average levels of disposable income and high levels of education, political awareness and motivation, it is a particularly noticeable phenomenon among well-off groups in post-industrialised countries.

Within these broad boundaries ethical consumption's precise outline blurs. An emphasis on retail customers rightly distinguishes ethical consumption from the similar decisions companies make regarding their supply chain, even though these decisions may be concerned with the same issues as individual customers are. Further, because ethical consumption is essentially a product of consumer groups' awareness-raising, the issues or impacts that have been the object of ethical consumption campaigns have varied widely and have little coherence as a group. We have as it were a discipline of '→ business ethics' but not one of 'consumption ethics'. Attempts to consume ethically may therefore appear to have been applied haphazardly: from banks, to cosmetic companies, supermarkets to apparel and footwear companies. In this sense the issues 'covered' by ethical consumption are defined more by attractiveness to campaigners seeking to galvanise consumers to action, than by any inherent commonality of impact. This is a key distinction with → sustainable consumption, where emphasis is placed on an outcome, rather than the role that individual consumers alone play.

Our primary definition also implies that consumers independently apply value-based preferences to the products and services they consume, hence creating 'ethical consumption'. This may be true in some contexts. As already noted, however, what ethical consumption can mean to a given society has been highly conditioned by the advocacy of particular groups, especially religious and consumer advisory groups, and NGOs of different stripes and outlooks. These have played crucial roles in selecting products and targeting consumers. In some cases such groups have even gone so far as to set up companies (e.g. offering 'ethical' chocolate when no such products were available). It is for this reason that the products to which ethical consumption has been historically applied are such an odd hotch-potch of goods as, say, coffee, toiletries, washing up liquid, chocolate and bananas (→ fair trade and → labelling).

In principle, however, ethical consumption can be applied to any product or service, assuming that there are 'more' or 'less' ethical ways of providing this service. Indeed, more recently, the range of products and services where avowedly 'ethical' versions are on offer has broadened immensely. These would include retail → banking, energy suppliers or car manufacturers. Within foodstuffs, arguably the most established area of ethical consumption, the issue of ethical consumption has raised complex (and ultimately incomparable) trade-offs for concerned shoppers to navigate. 'Should I buy this foreign organic banana, this foreign → fair trade banana or this locally grown banana which has not created any of the transport costs or impacts associated with the organic or → fair trade banana and which supports my local economy?' might be the question one very confused shopper asks.

Such a question brings out an important and perhaps obvious aspect of ethical consumption. Since we are talking about ethical consumption rather than ethical non-consumption, the operative question is 'Which types of product/service Y can be bought ethically?', rather than the more fundamental 'Should any type of product/service Y be consumed at all?' This is well brought out by the phenomenon of boycotts, a key aspect of ethical consumption. Those who boycotted apartheid-era South African goods were not boycotting the principle of, say, drinking red wine, they were boycotting the conditions under which it was produced. The boycott is also the most extreme political form that ethical consumption takes, since normally it is limited to exercising a preference for one type of good over another in the marketplace. Nevertheless the wider question 'Should any type of product/service Y be consumed at all?' is becoming more discussed in some areas of ethical consumption, such as, say, cars or air → travel. This is partly because the contrast between more or less 'ethical' alternatives here is weak. By contrast, in other areas, ethical consumption has become a brand in and of itself, as when global financial companies sell highly branded credit cards such as 'Red' on the basis of their socio-economic benefits. The tension between these two approaches (buying more with a cleaner conscience vs questioning the need to buy) is likely to increase, particularly as global environmental problems deepen. Just as the range of products and services in which ethical consumption can occur expands, so will the tensions implicit in the idea itself.

John Sabapathy

ETHICAL DECISION-MAKING

→ Business ethics

Ethical decision-making refers to the psychological processes that allow an individual facing an ethical situation to assess decision alternatives as ethically right or wrong and to select a course of action.

Most work on ethical decision-making has been normative in nature. Through the centuries, numerous scholars (i.e. philosophers) have proposed a wide variety of criteria, frameworks, principles and ideals (e.g. utilitarianism, rights) as guides prescribing how individuals ought to make ethical decisions. More recently, there has been a growing interest in a descriptive approach to ethical decision-making. Using principles of social science, scholars have sought to describe how individuals make ethical decisions and to identify factors that help or limit the ethical decision-making process. Though quite different in nature, normative and descriptive approaches to ethical decision-making are both motivated by a general interest in improving individual ethical decision-making.

The most popular descriptive model of ethical decision-making depicts the ethical decision-making as a cognitive process involving four stages. First, the individual recognises and identifies the situation as an ethical issue. This stage is referred to as ethical or moral awareness. Second, the individual assesses the alternatives and makes an ethical judgement about what is ethically right and wrong. Third, the individual establishes an intention to act ethically. Finally, the individual commits the ethical act.

Historically, the second stage, ethical judgement, has been considered the most important – individuals are unlikely to act ethically if they do not know which behaviours are ethical. For this reason, researchers have focused a great deal of attention on ethical judgements. Empirical findings have demonstrated that numerous individual characteristics, personality traits, and psychological conditions can influence ethical judgements, as can peers, bosses, organisational policies, organisational and national cultures, and even industry and market practices.

Though comparatively less attention has been paid to the other stages of ethical decision-making, research findings in these areas are equally interesting and informative. Generally speaking, research has demonstrated that moral awareness is critical to the process of ethical decision-making – if an issue is not identified as an ethical issue then the individual does not subject it to ethical judgements and thus ethical behaviour is less likely to occur. Other research has demonstrated that one's identity, the roles one plays and the extent to which the individual thinks of him-/herself as an ethical individual, affects the individual's motivation to follow through on his or her ethical judgements. Finally, research has shown that the nature of the ethical issue shapes this entire process. Issues can vary in their moral intensity, and thus individuals treat situations of low moral intensity (e.g. a white lie) very differently than they do situations of high moral intensity (e.g. murder).

To date, philosophers and social scientists have focused primarily on cognitive processes in ethical decision-making, but many scholars are currently looking at other factors that influence the ethical decision-making process, such as emotions and intuition.

Both theory and empirical research indicates that ethical decisions are often the result of many different internal processes that are each subject to many different external forces. As one might imagine, ethical decision-making is a very complicated activity, but as philosophers and social scientists continue to work together our understanding of this activity grows and we become increasingly capable of predicting and promoting ethical behaviour.

With regards to CSR, many consider CSR to revolve around what are fundamentally ethical decisions. Any CSR decision involves a variety of alternatives, and leaders, managers and employees of the organisation must assess those alternatives on relevant criteria to make a judgement and act. To the extent that CSR-related actions contain an ethical element, ethical decision-making is the process by which individuals make CSR a reality.

Scott J. Reynolds

ETHICAL INVESTMENT
→ Socially responsible investment

ETHICAL SOURCING
→ Ethical consumption, Fair trade, Supply chain

ETHICAL TRADING INITIATIVE (ETI)
→ ETI Base Code

ETHICS
→ Business ethics

ETHICS AND COMPLIANCE OFFICER ASSOCIATION (ECOA)
→ Business ethics, Ethics officer
⌨ www.theecoa.org

The Ethics and Compliance Officer Association (ECOA) was founded in the USA in 1991. The ECOA was set up against the backdrop of → corruption and ethical infractions in the 1980s in particular in the US defence industry and was triggered by the promulgation of the US-Sentencing Guidelines for Organisations. The latter offer the opportunity to reduce fines for white collar crimes if an organisation has in place an effective programme of preventing these crimes. The ECOA was set up as an organisation of ethics professionals to share → best practice. It has the mission of being the leading provider of ethics, compliance, and → corporate governance resources to ethics and compliance professionals worldwide and to provide members with access to an unparalleled network of ethics and compliance professionals and a global forum for the exchange of ideas and strategies.

ETHICS OFFICER
→ US Federal Sentencing Guidelines

CSR needs to be established within an organisation's governance structure. The function of an ethics officer is to establish such structures, next to the board of directors, board committees or individual working groups on CSR issues.

The ethics officer is an organisational function that holds formal responsibility for ethical issues of CSR, in particular the prevention and detection of criminal conduct and the compliance of employees, company representatives and business partners with the law and the organisation's → values and → codes of conduct.

In practical terms, the chief responsibility of an ethics officer comprises the integration of an organisation's → values, → codes of conduct and compliance initiatives into the decision-making process at all levels of the organisation. To achieve such integration, the ethics officer may implement, monitor and enforce company-specific ethics and compliance programmes, recommend corrective action in the case of criminal conduct and report on the company's progress to the top management and the board of directors.

In the US, the content and scope of an ethics officer's responsibilities have been largely defined by the Federal Sentencing Guidelines, the Sarbanes-Oxley Act and the → Ethics and Compliance Officer Association (ECOA).

Katharina Schmitt

ETI BASE CODE

→ Fair trade

↪ www.ethicaltrade.org

The ETI Base Code is a code of conduct launched by the Ethical Trading Initiative (ETI) in 1998. The ETI was founded by companies, NGOs and trade unions in the UK to share experience and promote → learning about implementing international labour standards in international supply chains. The ETI Base Code is closely modelled on the conventions of the ILO and is accompanied by implementation principles for member companies. It focuses on retailers and suppliers of → food, clothing and other products in UK markets. It includes monitoring, verification and reporting of the company's performance with regard to monitoring practice and implementation of codes on an annual basis.

EU DIRECTIVE ON WASTE ELECTRICAL AND ELECTRONIC EQUIPMENT (WEEE)

→ Waste management, Personal and household goods sector

↪ www.ec.europa.eu

Directives 2002/95/EC on the restriction of the use of certain hazardous substances in electrical and electronic equipment and 2002/96/EC on waste electrical and electronic equipment (WEEE) are designed to tackle the fast increasing → waste stream of electrical and electronic equipment and complements European

Union measures on landfill and incineration of → waste. Increased recycling of electrical and electronic equipment limits the total quantity of → waste going to final disposal. Under this legislation, producers are responsible for taking back and recycling electrical and electronic equipment. This provides incentives to design electrical and electronic equipment in an environmentally more efficient way, which takes → waste management aspects fully into account. Consumers are able to return their equipment free of charge. In order to prevent the generation of hazardous waste, Directive 2002/95/EC also requires the substitution of various heavy metals (lead, mercury, cadmium, and hexavalent chromium) and brominated flame retardants (polybrominated biphenyls (PBB) or polybrominated diphenyl ethers (PBDE)) in electrical and electronic equipment put on the market from 1 July 2006.

EU GREEN AND WHITE PAPERS ON CORPORATE SOCIAL RESPONSIBILITY

→ Corporate social responsibility, Europe, Regulation

⌁ ec.europa.eu/employment_social

In 2001 the European Commission issued a Green Paper on CSR, which provided all interested parties with a platform for further discussion with the goal of policy generation in the CSR area in → Europe. After a year's consultation, the White Paper entitled 'CSR – A business contribution to → sustainable development' was released in 2002, which represents the official policy intention of the Commission in the field of CSR. Both papers represent a broad consensus and have been debated in the course of a multi-stakeholder process including companies, business associations, governments, NGOs and trade unions. This consensus-based approach represents a typical European element of policy-making as well as the focus on environmental issues, as the subtitle of the White Paper suggests.

Dirk Matten

EU GREENHOUSE GAS EMISSION TRADING SCHEME (EU ETS)

→ Climate change, Emissions trading

⌐ ec.europa.eu/environment/climat/emission.htm

The European Union Greenhouse Gas Emission Trading Scheme (EU ETS) is the largest multi-country, multi-sector greenhouse gas → emission trading scheme worldwide and commenced operation in January 2005 with the aim of helping EU Member States achieve compliance with their commitments under the → Kyoto Protocol. The Scheme is based on Directive 2003/87/EC, which entered into force on 25 October 2003.

The EU ETS is considered to be a crucial mechanism in the fight against → climate change. It is the first international trading system for CO_2 emissions in the world. It covers over 11 500 energy-intensive installations across the EU, which represent close to half of → Europe's emissions of CO_2. These installations include combustion plants, oil refineries, coke ovens, iron and steel plants, and factories making cement, glass, lime, brick, ceramics, pulp and paper.

In terms of the EU ETS, → emission trading does not imply new environmental targets, but allows for cheaper compliance with existing targets under the → Kyoto Protocol. Letting participating companies buy or sell emission allowances means that the targets can be achieved at the least cost. According to the EU ETS, if the Scheme had not been adopted, other – more costly – measures would have had to be implemented.

EU MULTI-STAKEHOLDER FORUM ON CSR

→ Corporate social responsibility, Europe, EU Green and White Papers on Corporate Social Responsibility

⌐ www.forum.europa.eu.int

The European Multi-Stakeholder Forum on Corporate Social Responsibility (CSR EMS Forum), chaired by the Commission, brings together European representative organisations of employers, business networks, trade unions and NGOs, to promote innovation, convergence and → transparency in existing CSR practices and tools. The Forum's mandate was approved at the launch on 16 October 2002. The CSR EMS Forum thematic round tables exchanged good practices and assessed the appropriateness of establishing common guiding principles for CSR practices and instruments. Various meetings took place in 2003 and 2004 to take stock of progress, and findings and conclusions were presented to the Commission on 29 June 2004. The CSR EMS Forum is the centrepiece of the Commission's strategy for promoting CSR and → sustainable development, as set out in the 2002 White Paper on CSR.

EUROPE

→ CSR Europe, EU Green and White Papers on Corporate Social Responsibility, EU Multi-stakeholder Forum on CSR, European Academy of Business in Society (EABIS)

According to the European Commission, CSR is a concept whereby companies integrate social and environmental concerns in their business operations and in their interaction with stakeholders on a voluntary basis. The business community in Europe subscribes to the voluntary nature of CSR.

In Europe, companies' CSR goals and strategies are aligned with the 2010 strategic goal for Europe that was defined at the Lisbon summit: to turn Europe into the most competitive and dynamic knowledge-based economy in the world by 2010.

Due to the wide variety of CSR practices across business sectors and countries a formally recognised approach towards CSR in Europe has not been established. However, the 'European

Roadmap for businesses – 2010', launched in 2005 as an initiative led by → CSR Europe together with its National Partner Organisations around Europe, includes elements that describe companies' CSR commitments and activities as a contribution to the Lisbon strategy:

- A clear vision for a European contribution towards a sustainable and competitive enterprise in Europe.
- Commitments to a sustainable and competitive European Enterprise.
- A business appeal to the European Union, governments and stakeholders to get strongly involved, together with business in the achievement of → sustainable development in Europe. The stakeholders that are explicitly mentioned are employees and their representatives, consumer organisations and non-governmental organisations, investors, academia, deans and teachers.

The Roadmap includes five goals:

- Innovation and entrepreneurship;
- Skills and competence building;
- Equal opportunities and → diversity;
- → Health and safety; and
- Environmental protection.

It also includes five strategies to achieve these goals:

- Corporate responsibility in the mainstream of business;
- Stakeholder engagement;
- → Leadership and governance;
- Communication and → transparency; and
- Business-to-business cooperation and alliances.

CSR in Europe has the following characteristics:

1. Strong business → leadership and involvement in the field of CSR.

After having launched the above European Declaration of Businesses against social exclusion and the European Roadmap on CSR, businesses display a great enthusiasm to participate in the European Alliance on CSR, launched in March 2006. This is an open alliance of European enterprises, launched by the European Commission in 2006 to further promote and encourage CSR. The alliance is a political umbrella for CSR initiatives by large companies, small and medium-sized enterprises, and their stakeholders.

At a more practical level, European CSR business networks like → CSR Europe and its 20 National Partner Organisations work with around 1400 companies in Europe in areas such as sharing of → best practice, information and the provision of research and individual services.

2. Diversity in terms of thematic CSR focus of businesses across European countries, depending on their political and economic contexts.

Key factors that determine these different approaches towards CSR are:

- Contextual factors such as socio-political, demographic, institutional and technological considerations;
- Proactive strategies adopted by businesses, including considerations related to reputation, trust, and operational efficiency;
- Stakeholder-based factors, whereby businesses respond to external pressures of stakeholders such as investors and NGOs.

Some evidence of the diversity in CSR approaches across Europe has been collected in the 2006 'European Cartography on CSR Innovations, Gaps and Future Trends' based on 545 business solutions and 140 networking activities. Countries covered in this analysis are the 19 European Union countries where → CSR Europe has National Partner Organisations. EU countries not covered are: Cyprus, Denmark, Estonia, Hungary, Latvia, Lithuania, Luxembourg, Malta and Slovenia. The analysis does include Norway and Switzerland.

This research suggests that mainstreaming CSR, innovation and entrepreneurship and equal opportunity and → diversity are expected to be key priorities in Europe in the next five years.

3. The European Commission and European national governments play different and complementary roles in the promotion of CSR.

In 2001, the European Commission unveiled a Green Paper to launch the European debate about the concept of CSR and how to promote it. The outcome, published in a Communication in July 2002, was a new CSR strategy that sought to provide greater support for voluntary efforts, research and awareness raising. In October 2002 – in line with its new strategy – the European Commission established the European Multi-stakeholder Forum on CSR, which produced a final report to promote innovation, convergence and → transparency in existing CSR practices and tools. In its 2006 communication on CSR, the Commission launched the above-mentioned European Alliance on CSR.

At the national level, policy approaches towards CSR differ from one country to another, depending on factors such as the traditional role of the government, and economic, social and demographic priorities.

Jan Noterdaeme and Catherine Rubbens

EUROPEAN ACADEMY OF BUSINESS IN SOCIETY (EABIS)

→ Europe

🖰 www.eabis.org

The European Academy of Business in Society (EABIS) is an alliance of companies, business schools and academic institutions, with the support of the European Commission, committed to integrating business in society issues into the heart of business research, teaching and practice in → Europe. EABIS was established in 2002 after CEOs and deans across → Europe agreed on the urgent need for more and better knowledge and skills on CSR issues. EABIS aims to equip current and future business leaders with the mindset and capacity to put CSR at the heart of the way companies are run by integrating the changing role of business in society into the mainstream of business research, education and training. EABIS sponsors various collaborative research projects across → Europe and brings academics, business practitioners, policy-makers, other key stakeholders as well as smaller workshops all across → Europe together at an annual conference.

Peter Lacy

EUROPEAN ALLIANCE FOR CSR

→ EU Green and White Paper, Europe, European Multi-Stakeholder Forum on CSR

🖰 ec.europa.eu/enterprise/csr/policy

In March 2006, EU Commissioners for enterprise and industry as well as for employment, social affairs and equal opportunities, together with the CEOs of major European companies, launched the European Alliance for CSR. The key novelty of the Alliance is its focus on voluntary initiatives for business and an explicit dismissal of further regulatory or mandatory initiatives to foster socially responsible business behaviour. This initiative took place with a particular eye on the accession countries in Eastern Europe where business is expected to take a much more central role in addressing social needs. Some see the European Alliance as a distinct break in the EU Commission's approach to CSR which hitherto was characterised by a multi-stakeholder approach. The European Alliance is therefore hotly contested by some NGOs and trade unions who denounced the shift in EU policies for being excessively driven by business interests.

Dirk Matten

EUROPEAN BUSINESS ETHICS NETWORK (EBEN)

→ Business ethics, Europe

🖰 www.eben-net.org

The European Business Ethics Network is a network of academics interested in → business ethics in → Europe. It was one of the first organisations of its kind when it was set up in the early 1990s at a time when CSR and related issues were still fairly exotic topics in European business schools. EBEN also encourages the formation of national chapters, which exist meanwhile in Germany, Spain, the UK, the Netherlands, the Czech Republic and Poland. While the general nature of EBEN is more focused on the academic community, some of the national chapters, most notably the German, have been able to attract a large community of practitioners. EBEN organises an annual conference which attracts scholars from all over the world as well as a number of smaller research workshops across Europe.

EXECUTIVE PAY

→ Corporate governance

EXTERNALITIES

→ Ecological economics, Eco-taxation

Externality refers to the practice, intended or not, of excluding from the producer of a product some of the costs of its production, thus externalising part of the input cost. If, for instance, producing a product or service entails using an input for which the producer does not pay – say, by using ocean or forest products without replacing them – or by creating an expense that the producer does not cover – say, by polluting air, → water or soil which others must rectify – then externalities have been created.

If a producer creates no externalities, then the product internalises the full cost into the product, as reflected in its price.

CSR requires that companies take responsibility for the full cost – including the cost to society – of what they produce and sell. Obvious examples include the accepted practice that mining companies make good the damage they do to the landscape when mining an area is complete. Such acceptance is far from universal: recent examples include failure of oil companies to restore national or individual property after oil spills; the uncorrected effect of toxic air emissions around factories; and → water pollution as rivers are used as sinks to save the cost of → waste disposal.

Such practices are increasingly subject to state regulation and punitive measures. Socially responsible companies support ordered processes for internalising externalities, such as carbon trading, and paying the pollution costs of air → travel for people and goods.

Margaret Legum

EXTRACTIVE INDUSTRIES REVIEW
→ Mining sector
⌐ www.worldbank.org

From 2002 to 2004, the World Bank carried out a comprehensive review of its activities in the extractive industries sector – the Extractive Industries Review – in response to concerns expressed by a variety of stakeholders, primarily environmental and → human rights organisations. The Review included multiple in-depth, independent technical reviews, project site visits, and a series of conferences around the globe to solicit the views of stakeholders in government, industry, civil society and local communities. It lasted approximately two years.

The central message of the reviews was that while extractive industries investments, and the World Bank's efforts in funding them, can contribute to → sustainable development, the World Bank should further enhance its efforts in several areas: more explicitly identifying and tracking poverty reduction associated with its projects, the overall quality of governance in host countries, broader inclusion of local stakeholders, → transparency of revenue management and project documents and the promotion of renewable energy. It was also noted that the World Bank's capital and expertise can help ensure that such projects meet high environmental, social, and governance standards, and that revenue from the projects is used transparently and effectively.

Matt Jeschke

EXTRACTIVE INDUSTRIES TRANSPARENCY INITIATIVE (EITI)

→ Mining sector, Transparency

⌐ www.eitransparency.org

The Extractive Industries Transparency Initiative (EITI) aims to ensure that the revenues from extractive industries contribute to → sustainable development and poverty reduction. At the core of the initiative is a set of Principles and Criteria that establish how EITI should be implemented through the full publication and verification of company payments and government revenues from oil, gas and mining. It was launched in 2002 at the World Summit on Sustainable Development in South Africa by UK Prime Minister Tony Blair.

Many countries are rich in oil, gas, and minerals and studies have shown that when governance is good, these can generate large revenues to foster economic growth and reduce poverty. However, when governance is weak, they may instead cause poverty, → corruption, and conflict – the so-called 'resource curse'. The

EITI aims to defeat this 'curse' by improving → transparency and → accountability.

The EITI Secretariat, located in the UK's Department for International Development, has developed a Source Book to provide guidance for companies and countries implementing the initiative. The Secretariat works closely with the World Bank and the IMF in implementation efforts. As of late 2006, 20 countries had endorsed EITI, with a number also implementing it. Many of the largest oil and gas companies have also signed on, as well as the International Council on Mining and Metals (ICMM). From civil society, the Publish What You Pay Coalition and the Revenue Watch Institute also actively participate.

Matt Jeschke

FACTOR 4/FACTOR 10
→ Eco-efficiency

The 'Factor 4' concept was first introduced by Ernst Ulrich von Weizsäcker, Amory B. Lovins and L. Hunter Lovins of the Rocky Mountain Institute in a 1997 report to the → Club of Rome, a global think-tank and centre of innovation and initiative. The concept was subsequently developed into a book in 1998 by the same authors entitled Factor 4.

Factor 4 describes a hypothetical fourfold (factor of four) increase in 'resource productivity', brought about by simultaneously doubling wealth and halving resource consumption. The concept is often summed up as 'doing more with less'.

'Factor 10' is a similar concept, suggesting a hypothetical 10-fold (factor of 10) increase in 'resource productivity'. The term was used to describe the onus on OECD countries to reduce their per capita consumption of energy and materials by a factor of 10.

To achieve Factor 4 globally, consumption of energy and materials would need to be reduced by 50%, but because OECD countries are responsible for per capita consumption of energy and materials five times as high as → developing countries, the OECD countries would need to reduce per capita consumption by 90%.

Dermot Egan

FAIR LABOUR ASSOCIATION (FLA)

→ FLA Workplace Code of Conduct

FAIRTRADE

→ Ethical consumption, Supply chain

Fairtrade is a trading partnership, based on dialogue, → transparency and respect, that seeks greater equity in international trade. It contributes to → sustainable development by offering better trading conditions to, and securing the rights of, marginalised producers and workers – especially in the south. Fairtrade organisations (backed by consumers) are engaged actively in supporting producers, awareness raising and in campaigning for changes in the rules and practice of conventional international trade.

This is the definition produced by FINE, a network that involves the → Fairtrade Labelling Organisations International (FLO) as well as the International Federation for Alternative Trade (IFAT), the Network of European Worldshops (NEWS!), and the European Fair Trade Association (EFTA).

Fairtrade is a partnership giving poor producers in poor countries a direct opportunity to trade on better terms to boost their economic development, and consumers in rich countries to use their spending power to support this. The system provides a series of guarantees to groups of organised producers: a stable, minimum price to cover the costs of sustainable production and provide a sustainable livelihood (even if market prices fall below this); an additional premium to invest in → development projects democratically selected by the producers, such as building schools or clinics, and schemes to improve or diversify their incomes.

Most → Fairtrade producers are smallholder farmers working together in organised groups, but there are also criteria for workers on large estates and for industrial workers in football factories, for example. These standards insist on adherence to key employment standards, in particular those enshrined in the key International Labour Organisation (ILO) conventions. Freedom of association and collective bargaining are vital with trades unions clearly recognised as the means for workers to organise and be represented. In addition, there are environmental requirements including outlawing the use of the internationally recognised most harmful pesticides.

An international network of independent, non–profit national organisations in 22 countries around the world, the → Fairtrade Labelling Organisations International (FLO), sets rigorous standards for producers and traders in all these areas. It then inspects and certifies producers against the standards, and audits the flow of goods between producers and importers. The → Fairtrade system is also dynamic – in that it does not simply verify compliance with minimum standards but also establishes a process of → continual improvement.

Producer groups (usually cooperatives or associations of smallholder farmers) who meet these standards are then certified as Fairtrade producers. Traders register with FLO and can produce under Fairtrade terms. Products certified as meeting these standards can then be sold under licence displaying a Fairtrade label, known in the UK as the → Fairtrade Mark. The consumer can then buy a Fairtrade product in confidence that it meets robust, independent criteria that deliver significant, long-term benefits to poor producers.

This approach helps prevent the value of the concept from being debased by businesses making unsubstantiated claims. This also distinguishes Fairtrade from the → codes of conduct that many companies now work to as part of their purchasing policies, but which are not subject to independent external → certification. While all this entails significant commitment and engagement from the businesses wishing to market Fairtrade products, the credibility provided by the system and the → Fairtrade Mark also brings strong and sustained consumer confidence, commitment and sales.

This has helped contribute to the huge growth of Fairtrade in recent years. From the introduction of the first Fairtrade coffee in the Netherlands in 1988 and the establishment of the Fairtrade Foundation in Britain in 1992, it has spread to an international movement covering 22 consumer countries and over 60 producer countries. In 2006, there were over 2000 products in the UK alone. Market penetration of Fairtrade products in some markets is also becoming significant – with, for example, over 20% of UK roast and ground coffee sales.

Today both dedicated Fairtrade companies and major global companies are responding to demand from a public eager to buy Fairtrade products. For example, in Britain all the major supermarket chains now offer Fairtrade products – while both Marks & Spencer and the Co-op have switched all their own-brand coffee to Fairtrade. Major out-of-home → food suppliers such as Starbucks and Costa have also taken up offering Fairtrade lines.

The growth of Fairtrade sales developed and continues to expand with the support of a diverse set of constituencies including schools, women's organisations, churches, → development groups and local councils. The success of campaigns to get workplaces, public bodies and catering outlets to switch to Fairtrade has further boosted sales. The pace of growth in sales, demand and brand awareness of Fairtrade shows no signs of abating. All this is delivering benefits back to the producers who through Fairtrade gain access to markets, receive a fair price that enables them to stay on their land and invest in the future of their communities, develop long-term relations with traders and participate more fully in the trade.

While the bulk of current Fairtrade products are traditional developing-country → food and beverage products like bananas, coffee, tea and cocoa, this is changing with the growth of non-food products like cotton. Development work is now being focused on future new categories which may in the end give reality to the vision of a Fairtrade lifestyle.

Harriet Lamb

FAIRTRADE LABELLING ORGANISATIONS INTERNATIONAL (FLO)
→ International Fairtrade Standards
↗ www.fairtrade.net

Fairtrade Labelling Organisations International (FLO) is the leading → fair trade standard setting and → certification body. Established in 1997 and located in Bonn, Germany, FLO is the umbrella organisation for a worldwide network of → fair trade organisations actively involved in supporting producers in → developing countries, raising awareness of → fair trade, and campaigning for changes in the rules and practices of conventional international trade.

FLO's 20 members, known as Labelling Initiatives, promote and market the International Fairtrade Certification Mark in their own country. The Mark is a consumer guarantee that appears on products that meet → fair trade standards, including a fair price and additional premium to invest in → community development. Companies that are licensed to carry the Mark on a Fairtrade certified product pay a fee that contributes to the funding of the international Fairtrade system. FLO members currently operate in 15 European countries as well as → Australia and New Zealand, Canada, Japan, Mexico (associate member) and the United States.

Harriet Lamb

FAIRTRADE MARK

→ Fairtrade, Fairtrade Labelling Organisations International (FLO)

✍ www.fairtrade.net

The Fairtrade Mark is a label carried on a product as a consumer guarantee that it meets the → fair trade standards set and verified by the international network of independent, not-for-profit organisations, → Fairtrade Labelling Organisations International (FLO). These producer and trader standards provide guarantees of better prices and conditions to the producers growing or making them. The label is issued under licence from the FLO partner organisation in the country where the product is sold (such as the Fairtrade Foundation in Britain) which requires an auditable supply chain and quarterly reports on transactions from licensees as part of the trade audit process. The Mark is awarded to specific products – not to companies or brands as a whole. The brand awareness of the Mark is now high – and is a key part of the process of enabling consumers to use their purchasing power to support → fair trade and the better deal it delivers for producers in → developing countries.

Harriet Lamb

FINANCIAL SERVICES SECTOR

→ Banking

FINE

→ Fair trade

✍ www.bafts.org.uk

FINE was created in 1998 and is an informal association of the four main Fairtrade networks:

- F Fairtrade Labelling Organisations International (FLO);
- I International Fair Trade Association (IFAT);
- N Network of European Worldshops (NEWS!); and
- E European Fair Trade Association (EFTA)

The aim of FINE is to enable these networks and their members to cooperate on:

- The development of harmonised core standards and guidelines for Fairtrade;
- harmonisation, and increase in the quality and efficiency of Fairtrade monitoring systems;
- advocacy and campaigning work; and
- harmonisation of their information and communication systems.

FINE is an informal working group. It has no formal structure and no decision-making power. Meetings are held as required. Preparation, hosting and facilitation of the meetings rotates between members. Decisions are taken by the boards of the FINE members.

FIVE CAPITALS FRAMEWORK

→ Corporate sustainability, Ecological economics, New economics
⊕ www.forumforthefuture.org.uk

The Five Capitals Framework (or Five Capitals Model) provides a theoretical context in which to understand what a completely integrated approach to → sustainable development looks like in practice.

Building on the earlier concept of the → triple bottom line, the Five Capitals Framework expands the idea of the economic bottom line into Manufactured and Financial Capital, the social bottom line into Human and Social Capital, and interprets the environmental bottom line as Natural Capital.

As such, the Framework represents a conscious attempt to locate → sustainable development more explicitly within the discourse of capitalism. On the assumption that capitalism is likely to remain the dominant macro-economic system for the foreseeable future, those promoting → sustainable development must seek out an intellectually rigorous alignment with the tenets of capitalism if it is ever to get the necessary traction.

At the heart of capitalism is the concept of capital, defined as 'a stock of anything that has the capacity to generate a flow of benefits which are of value to humankind'.

The five different stocks of capital in the Framework are defined as follows:

- Natural Capital is any stock of matter or energy that yields valuable resources and services; it is the basis not only of production but of life itself.
- Human Capital consists of health, knowledge, skills and motivation, as well as an individual's emotional and spiritual capacities.
- Social Capital takes the form of structures, institutions, networks and relationships which enable individuals to maintain and develop their human capital in partnership with others.
- Manufactured Capital comprises material goods (tools, machines, buildings and other forms of → infrastructure) which contribute to the production process but do not become embodied in its output.
- Financial Capital reflects the productive power of all other types of capital, enabling them to be owned and traded.

The Framework was initially developed by Forum for the Future in the UK, heavily influenced by the earlier work of Herman Daly and Paul Ekins, and has since been taken up by the Prince of Wales's Business and the Environment Programme, and by a number of individual companies and other organisations.

Jonathon Porritt

FLA WORKPLACE CODE OF CONDUCT
→ Labour issues
🖰 www.fairlabour.org

The New York-based Fair Labor Association (FLA) is a multi-stakeholder coalition of companies, NGOs and university to promote ethical labour practices in particular in the global apparel industry. Launched in 1997 it has set up a Workplace Code of Conduct which commits member organisations to implement and monitor workplace conditions according to ILO conventions. A particular speciality of the FLA is that next to its 20 corporate brands it counts nearly 200 universities among its members. This reflects considerable campaign activities from students throughout the 1990s against goods sold on campus which were of questionable origin with regard to labour conditions. By joining the FLA a university commits itself to make sure that the products sold on campus are sourced from suppliers who comply with the FLA Workplace Code of Conducts.

FOOD AND BEVERAGE SECTOR

Companies in the food and beverage sector are obviously faced with many of the same generic questions of → accountability, responsibility and sustainability as companies elsewhere. There are two issues, however, which are central to food and beverage companies' wider societal impacts: first, health-related impacts, and second, → globalisation-related impacts. The former relate largely to users of the products, the latter chiefly to those who are affected by its production methods.

Health-related impacts

These impacts are of concern by and large to consumers of food and beverage products and the principle of such concern is not new. However, given widespread media coverage and increasing concern with health-related issues, companies are under renewed scrutiny in this area. Health concerns are far broader today and are likely to arise from increased nutritional awareness, changes in global eating patterns or innovative science. To exemplify: in the first case, alcoholic drink manufacturers have for a long time been scrutinised about links between their products and alcoholism. In the second case, given increasing levels of diabetes and child obesity in post-industrial societies food and drink companies are drawn into public health debates which are relatively novel to them. → Genetically modified organisms (GMOs) exemplify health concerns around scientific innovation. Here public concern about food products' potential health and environmental impacts seriously forestalled concerted attempts to introduce GMOs into the European food chain in the early 21st century and damaged a number of companies seeking to do so. Questions of health-related impacts can quickly adapt wider political dimensions, especially if food and drink manufacturers are perceived to be providing quasi-public goods of some sort such as food to schools or hospitals. Ultimately corporate liability may become an issue, as in the US where food manufacturers' liability for consumers' obesity has been explored in the courts.

Advertising and → labelling are key tools in such health-related debates. In 2006, for instance, a serious EU-level campaign was under way to restrict the advertising of 'unhealthy foods' to children. The rise and fall of the children's drink Sunny Delight between 1998 and 2003 is a case in point. What had been perceived (and marketed) as a healthy 'orange' drink was punished at the cash tills after questions were raised about how healthy it was when cases of children 'turning orange' were documented. Often the actual nutritional science implied in media stories is fiercely contested, as with the documentary *Super Size Me* (2005) which charted the month-long effects of a McDonald's-only diet. By contrast, organic, → Fairtrade, or free-range labels have become increasingly important to affluent consumers.

Globalisation-related impacts

In contrast with health-related impacts, → globalisation-related impacts can directly affect individuals who may not be consumers of the products at all. They may be involved in its production or simply caught up in the wider effects of these production processes. They are usefully bracketed as relating to → globalisation insofar as they relate either to the global effects of complex extensive supply chains or the global scale of these sectors' production impacts (often again within complex supply chains). Both of these are characteristic of problems associated with → globalisation.

The global food and beverage sector's supply chain is immense, complicated and includes agricultural machinery, fertilisers and pesticides, fishing fleets, food processing and distribution. Associated CSR issues can only be illustrated here. Pesticides needless to say have been linked to both human illness and the disruption of food chains and ecosystems. In Brazil, deforestation and conversion of land is linked with everything from soy bean production to demand for beef and the consequent need for pasture. And, given the projected economic growth of → Asia, demand for meat and hence land is likely only to increase. In the oceans, scientists estimate that global fish stocks might, at current levels of depletion, last until ca. 2050. And in relation to transport global 'food miles' (the distance from 'plough to plate') has become a particular concern. While the impact of air transport here is often exaggerated, food and drink production's energy and climate, → water and → waste impacts remain significant.

For companies, the challenge is how to reduce such negative impacts, inefficient resource use and ultimately to find ways of identifying solutions that increase 'resource productivity'. In specific areas organisations have been established to help companies work out how to do so (e.g. the → Marine Stewardship Council or the Roundtable on Sustainable Palm Oil). These initiatives are also partly intended to reduce the first mover disadvantages of addressing these (often initially costly issues) while your competitors look on. Given complex supply chains and/or commodity markets this is crucial.

A particular problem of intervening in specific production processes or supply chains is unwanted side effects. Providing British consumers with organic asparagus all year round may seem 'green', but what are the aggregate transport costs of shipping it from Peru? An interesting attempt to address this is seen in life cycle analyses which attempt to evaluate the overall impacts of products and processes. Some use this to develop 'closed loop production', i.e. managing all aspects of production from → cradle-to-grave sustainability and hence minimising negative impacts. The role of governments in enabling these approaches is crucial. The complexity of such techniques reflects the extremely difficult nature of achieving more sustainable outcomes in food and drink production – and consequently the scale of the challenge for meaningful CSR in this sector.

John Sabapathy

FORENSIC ACCOUNTING
→ Corruption, fraud

The forensic concept is derived from the Latin *forensis* (referring to the forum where law courts were held in ancient Rome). The intention of any forensic activity is to determine facts or to provide evidence that would be suitable for use in a court of law or other dispute resolution forum. There are different modern applications that all relate to the scientific side of legal investigations, such as forensic medicine, forensic linguistics and forensic accounting.

Forensic accounting is a specialised area of the accounting industry, and often involves the detailed analysis of complex financial information to investigate → fraud and misconduct, recover assets and reduce exposure to white collar crime and other irregularities. Forensic accountants also often appear as expert witnesses in civil and criminal trials or other dispute resolution forums.

Petrus Marais and Daniel Malan

FOREST STEWARDSHIP COUNCIL (FSC)

→ Labelling

⌐ www.fsc.org

The Forest Stewardship Council (FSC) is a non-governmental organisation that sets international standards for responsible forest management, for accreditation of independent → certification bodies who certify forest management units to the standards, and for → labelling forest products originating from certified forest management units.

Established in 1993, the FSC is a stakeholder-owned and open-membership organisation, incorporating organisational and individual members and a number of national FSC initiatives within its global network.

To promote environmentally appropriate, socially beneficial, and economically viable management of the world's forests, the FSC has developed global principles and criteria which cover issues like: tenure and use rights and responsibilities; → indigenous peoples' and workers' rights; maintenance of forests with high → conservation value; environmental impact; monitoring and assessment; and planning and management of plantations. These principles and criteria are tailored to meet conditions in different regions through a process in which ecological, social, and economic stakeholders collaborate on a level playing field.

Forest management units can apply to be independently assessed against the regionally adapted principles and criteria by accredited → certification bodies. The assessment process requires extensive stakeholder consultation. Forest management units that meet the principles and criteria are certified and subjected to annual → auditing of practices.

Using the FSC label requires chain-of-custody tracking, which involves tracking the origin of the forest products through every stage of the supply chain.

Lars H. Gulbrandsen

FORUM EMPRESA

→ Latin America

🖰 www.empresa.org

Forum EMPRESA is the hemispheric alliance of CSR-based business organisations that promotes → corporate social responsibility (CSR) throughout the Americas. Today Forum EMPRESA gathers 22 organisations in the region and more than 2000 companies through its member organisations. These companies associated through member business organisations account for more than 20% of the GDP of the region.

Since 1997, Forum EMPRESA has brought together CSR-based organisations and associated companies that share the same vision of promoting CSR in the Americas. Likewise, it provides support in order to encourage CSR practices within other American companies. The network strengthens national and regional organisations committed to CSR and encourages the establishment of new CSR-based business organisations in → Latin American countries where Forum Empresa is not currently active.

Forum EMPRESA's vision is for 'a more equitable and sustainable society based on Corporate Social Responsibility', and the mission is to 'promote and reinforce Corporate Social Responsibility of member organisations in their respective countries, and promote exchange and cooperation among them'.

The value of integrating a regional network devoted to these matters lies in its role as articulator and promoter of convergences and synergies between all its members, strengthening them in their mission of promoting CSR development in their countries.

Hugo Vergara

FOUNDATION

→ Philanthropy

A foundation is a non-profit institution established with self-sustaining funding to serve a charitable or philanthropic purpose. Independent non-profit foundations exist to support a myriad of issues and causes. Corporations establish private, non-profit foundations with funding from profits to promote their brands and to positively impact the communities in which they operate. Corporations and their namesake foundations tend to have close relationships. Corporate foundations operate grant giving programmes to beneficiaries.

The company-sponsored foundation often maintains close ties with the donor company, but it is a separate, legal organisation, sometimes with its own endowment, and is subject to the same rules and regulations as other private foundations.

According to the Council on Foundations, as of 2005 more than 2000 corporate foundations in the United States exist with holdings of some $11 billion in assets.

Independent foundations also exist with a mission to impact → corporate social responsibility, whether through the creation of such businesses, setting CSR standards or campaigning against socially irresponsible corporations.

Jonathan Cohen

FRAUD
→ Corruption, Forensic accounting

Fraud can be defined as a deliberate act of deception with the intention of inducing another person to act in a way which enables the deceiver to gain unfair or unlawful gain. As a broad legal concept it is often used in conjunction with the term 'misconduct', referring to violations of laws, regulations, internal policies and general market expectations of ethical business conduct, but always includes an element of knowing or intentional dishonesty. Examples of fraudulent behaviour include the following: improper revenue recognition, understatement of liabilities, embezzlement, payroll fraud, theft, procurement fraud, counterfeiting and the falsification of compliance data provided to regulators.

As a rough guideline to determine whether an act is fraudulent or not, the answers to both the following questions have to be positive:

1. Was the act deliberate? The difference between fraud and error is whether the act was deliberate or not – if there was no deliberate act of deception there cannot be fraud; and
2. Was the intention to gain unfair or unlawful gain? Unlawfulness is much easier to prove than unfairness. Within a specific jurisdiction, relevant legislation can be applied by a court of law to determine if a gain was lawful. Unfairness, however, relies far more heavily on interpretations that will be influenced by the specific context and cultural differences.

Most countries have detailed legislation, accompanied by well-developed common law or criminal codes in place to combat fraud. Examples are the UK Proceeds of Crime Act of 2002, the US Sarbanes-Oxley Act of 2002, the Australian Commonwealth Criminal Code Act of 1995 and the South African Prevention and Combating of Corrupt Activities Act of 2003. There are also many international treaties and conventions aimed at combating fraud, → corruption and misconduct, and most multinational companies have sophisticated anti-fraud programmes in place. In broad terms, a successful programme should focus on three objectives:

- Prevention – controls designed to reduce the risk of fraud from occurring in the first place – elements include a fraud risk assessment, development of a code of conduct or a code of ethics, → due diligence processes, communication and training and process-specific fraud risk controls;

- Detection – controls to discover fraud when it occurs – elements include the introduction of whistleblower mechanisms, the proactive analysis of data (e.g. comparing the names that appear on supplier and employee lists) and regular → auditing and monitoring activities; and
- Response – controls to take corrective action and remedy the harm caused by fraud – elements include internal investigations and enforcement (e.g. disciplinary procedures) and corrective action (e.g. disclosing information and investigating the causes of fraud).

Petrus Marais and Daniel Malan

FTSE4GOOD INDEX

→ Socially responsible investment (SRI)

✍ www.ftse.com

The FTSE4Good Index Series has been designed to measure the performance of companies that meet globally recognised corporate responsibility standards, and to facilitate investment in those companies. Transparent management and criteria alongside the FTSE brand make FTSE4Good useful for the creation of socially responsible investment products. Unlike the → Dow Jones Sustainability Index, the FTSE4Good uses well-defined positive and negative criteria in assessing the CSR performance of companies and bases its decision for inclusion on these criteria. For inclusion, eligible companies must meet criteria requirements in five areas:

- Working towards environmental sustainability;
- Developing positive relationships with stakeholders;
- Upholding and supporting universal → human rights;
- Ensuring good supply chain labour standards; and
- Countering bribery.

Companies that have been identified as having business interests in the following industries are excluded from the FTSE4Good Index Series:

- Tobacco producers;
- Companies manufacturing either whole, strategic parts, or platforms for nuclear weapon systems;
- Companies manufacturing whole weapons systems;
- Owners or operators of nuclear power stations; and
- Companies involved in the extraction or processing of uranium.

GAIA HYPOTHESIS

James Lovelock's Gaia Hypothesis states that the earth functions as a single, self-regulating organism which ensures the conditions required for its own survival through positive and negative feedback between constituent systems. Life on the planet – the biosphere – responds to changes caused by external or internal disturbances through changing its patterns of growth and metabolism and thus regulating the → environment.

For example, a 30% rise in solar energy over the last 3.5 billion years, which would naturally result in a massive temperature increase, has been offset by a higher rate of conversion of carbon dioxide, ensuring that surface temperatures remain fairly constant.

Lovelock developed the hypothesis – named after the Greek goddess of the earth – during the 1960s while working as a research scientist for NASA. It was largely ignored until the 1970s, when publication of Lovelock's *Gaia: A new look at life on Earth* began to cause controversy. The concept is now widely accepted as an aspect of earth system science – an approach that treats the entire planet as a system comprised of numerous complex sub-systems and interrelationships.

The importance of the hypothesis for → sustainable development, and for consideration in CSR policies, is that the complex interrelationships that comprise this self-regulating system are delicate, and can be altered by human activity to the point where they can no longer recover. The theory implies that humans, for their own survival, must reduce their pressure on ecosystems to enable them to continue maintaining the conditions necessary for life.

Ruth Findlay-Brooks

GENDER ISSUES
→ Discrimination, Diversity

Gender issues in CSR comprise the multiple ways that companies impact on the lives of women as well as men, as employees, consumers, supply chain workers, investors, and community/society members. Gender equality is a key social justice issue. Gender inequalities are deeply entrenched in all societies, and are reproduced through a variety of practices and institutions, including corporations. Gender issues in CSR cover the extent to which companies advance gender equality, rather than perpetuating or increasing existing inequalities.

The Council of Europe defines gender equality as '... an equal visibility, → empowerment and participation of both sexes in all spheres of public and private life...'. This is not about making women the same as men, but valuing equally the diverse roles they play in society.

The growing role of business in societal governance means that the → accountability of corporations for their gender impacts is increasingly important. The right to live and work free from → discrimination based on gender is recognised in the Universal Declaration of Human Rights, ILO conventions and the Convention on the Elimination of All Forms of Discrimination against Women (CEDAW). The latter requires states 'to take all appropriate measures to eliminate → discrimination against women by any person, organisation or enterprise'.

Many women work in the field of CSR; however, most CSR and SRI organisations and instruments have not yet effectively incorporated gender issues. Where these are included, for example in reporting tools, they are often optional elements, limited in scope, submerged in the category of → diversity (leaving gender invisible), or confined to human resource issues. Exceptions can be found, e.g. The Calvert Women's Principles.

In CSR gender has been addressed primarily in relation to the workplace and → employee rights, including: women's representation at different levels of the organisation; equality in all aspects of employment from recruitment to redundancy; equal pay; job segregation; non-discrimination during pregnancy; harassment; part-time working and → work–life balance. Monitoring and → benchmarking on these issues has proved immensely useful in driving progress and → accountability in a number of countries, but there remains much room for improvement in the majority of companies. Focusing on individual rights to equal opportunities is important. Additional strategies involve programmes for positive or affirmative action to address women's group disadvantage, and attempts to mainstream gender and transform the workplace so that it is fairer for those (mostly women) who combine paid employment and domestic labour.

Significant benefits may accrue to businesses that address gender equality, including reduced risks associated with litigation, impaired reputation, and high turnover. Increased participation of women in the workplace worldwide, and the need to recruit and retain the best motivated, skilled and committed workers, especially in service and high-tech sectors, underpins the → business case for equality for women employees. Connection with the customer base can also be improved.

Non-discrimination based on gender is included in many CSR supply chain → codes of conduct; however, cases of

→ discrimination and harassment remain commonplace. Women often still are concentrated in insecure, poorer paid, lower skilled, dead-end jobs. They are also especially likely to work in informal, particularly precarious, employment involving sub-contracted and home-based work. Poor conditions in such jobs contribute to perpetuating women's poverty and lie beyond the reach of most → codes of conduct. The ETI has begun to address these issues. While companies often provide new sources of employment for women, they need to ensure that their supply chain CSR practices develop improved monitoring of gender impacts.

Other key gender issues in CSR include:

- Gender representation on governance bodies/boards of directors;
- Incorporating gender → impact assessments when evaluating company community impacts;
- Gender analysis of philanthropic donations;
- Product development for, and marketing to, women consumers;
- Gender representation in advertising;
- Opportunities for women owned businesses as suppliers; and
- Analysis of the gender impacts of core business activities, e.g. the gender implications of environmental impacts, community relocation programmes, and financial inclusion (women are disproportionately represented among the poor).

Gender issues in CSR will vary according to business and sector. Increased gender disaggregated information is needed, and another high priority is to ensure that women's voices are routinely heard in stakeholder relations and consultations. The latter is particularly important if women's → diversity is to be represented in CSR.

Women's civil society organisations have been slow to participate in CSR multi-stakeholder initiatives, except those relating to supply chains (e.g. ETI). Their greater participation will help to develop CSR as a means to advance gender equality.

Gender equality needs to be addressed in CSR analysis, action and evaluation if it is to be comprehensive and complete.

Kate Grosser

GENERAL AGREEMENT ON TRADE AND TARIFFS (GATT)
→ World Trade Organisation

GENETICALLY MODIFIED ORGANISMS (GMOs)
→ Food and beverage sector

A genetically modified organism is a plant or an animal that is a result of applying recombinant DNA technology. Particularly associated with the genetic alteration of commercial plants in order to make them (e.g.) hardier, bigger or more colourful, the term increasingly applies to the modification of animal genomes, generally for commercial or medical reasons.

GMOs raise sustainability related and ethical issues, the former often in relation to vegetable modification, the latter often in relation to animal modification.

Sustainability issues may arise when altered species' resistance to disease disrupts ecosystems, causing some species (animal or plant) to die out and others to thrive. Ethical issues may relate to the appropriateness of using human DNA material in medicine; the appropriateness of different types of animal experimentation; or concern about the effects of intertwining different species' genetic material. In all cases the effects of such technology are contested in the public sphere where the novelty, complexity (and sometimes) intimacy of the technology makes discussion difficult.

Distinct ethical issues arise specifically in relation to the commercial patenting of (altered) vegetable matter when this is thought to be either inappropriate in principle and/or a means of imposing financial dependence on users (e.g. in the sale of non-self-pollinating seed which needs to be repurchased annually by farmers). The latter example indicates how sustainable and ethical concerns can conflict since, from a sustainability perspective, such 'terminator' seeds ought to restrict the undesirable emergence of 'natural' GMO hybrids in the wild which would alter ecosystems.

John Sabapathy

GEOGRAPHICAL INFORMATION SYSTEMS (GIS)

A geographical information system (GIS) is a system for managing data that is spatially referenced. Modern GIS systems use digital information to manage and analyse spatial data (such as maps). Data can be sourced from aerial and satellite photography, land surveying and 'human'-based surveys (such as a government census). GIS systems allow the user to analyse this data in a simple way to get information relating to geographically specific data. Uses range from flood plain risk analysis and 'Where's my nearest?' applications on mobile phones, to planning → travel routes, military planning and in the development of oil fields. In a CSR context, the use of GIS is particularly related to conducting environmental and social → impact assessments and modelling climate impacts.

Aled Jones

GLOBAL BUSINESS COALITION ON HIV/AIDS

→ HIV/AIDS

🖰 www.businessfightsaids.org

Founded in 2001 after UN Secretary General Kofi Annan asked Ambassador Richard Holbrooke to lead the private sector response to → HIV/AIDS, the Global Business Coalition on HIV/AIDS (GBC) is the pre-eminent organisation mobilising international business in the fight against → HIV/AIDS. With more than 200 leading international member companies, the organisation maintains offices in Beijing, Geneva, Johannesburg, Nairobi, New York, and Paris and is the official focal point for the private sector delegation to the Global Fund to Fight AIDS, Tuberculosis, and Malaria (GFATM). Its Business AIDS Methodology (BAM)™ enables companies to develop tailor-made → HIV/AIDS programmes that suit their individual needs.

Since its inception, GBC has encouraged businesses to respond to → HIV/AIDS in four main ways:

- Implement prevention, testing and care programmes and policies for employees and immediate communities – in many countries, company programmes are the only source of accurate HIV information.
- Bring business core strengths of innovation and efficiency to improve the reach and efficacy of AIDS programmes – businesses' marketing, communication, and logistics skills significantly strengthen the impact of global AIDS programmes.
- Leverage products and services in unique ways to benefit the fight against → HIV/AIDS.
- Lead and advocate for greater action on → HIV/AIDS and participation with governments and civil society.

GBC is currently undergoing a process to join organisations with Transatlantic Partners Against AIDS (TPAA) and incorporate tuberculosis and malaria in its mandate.

John E. Tedstrom

GLOBAL COMMONS
→ Externalities, Tragedy of the commons

The global commons comprise natural resources which cross national boundaries, such as rivers, and those which have no boundaries, such as oceans, the atmosphere and the ozone layer. They could also be seen to include resources which benefit all, even when confined within national boundaries, such as rain forests or threatened species.

The problems of identifying and protecting the global commons are even greater than for other public goods. As demonstrated by the → tragedy of the commons, there are great difficulties in preventing overexploitation of commonly held resources and public goods. These problems are greatly magnified when these resources cross national boundaries, and governments may not agree on regulation or control. A current example of this is the problem of → climate change, where effective action depends on multilateral agreement to tackling the problem, and negotiations can drag on for years or decades.

Ruth Findlay-Brooks

GLOBAL COMPACT
→ UN Global Compact

GLOBAL CORRUPTION BAROMETER
→ Corruption, Transparency International
⌐ www.transparency.org

→ Transparency International's (TI) Global Corruption Barometer (the Barometer) presents the results of a public opinion survey carried out in many low, middle, and high income countries. The Barometer seeks to understand how and in what ways → corruption affects ordinary people's lives, providing an indication of the form and extent of → corruption from the view of citizens around the world. The Barometer asks people about their opinions on which sectors of society are the most corrupt, which spheres of life are most affected, whether → corruption has increased or decreased in relation to the past, and whether it is likely to be more or less prevalent in future. Furthermore, the Barometer explores bribery in depth, and presents information on: how frequently individuals or families pay bribes; how these payments take place; whether they are paid to gain access to public services; and how much they pay. The Global Corruption Barometer is one of TI's tools for measuring → corruption internationally. Through its focus on public opinion, the Barometer complements the → Corruption Perceptions Index and the → Bribe Payers Index, which are based on the opinions of experts and business leaders.

David Nussbaum and Peter Wilkinson

GLOBAL GOVERNANCE
→ UN Global Compact, Globalisation

The term 'governance' denotes rule systems that structure human interaction and help achieve joint goals. At global level, governance takes place among others through United Nations (UN) Security Council decisions, the trade regime of the → World Trade Organisation (WTO), and rules of public–private or private organisations like ISO norms or the → Forest Stewardship Council (FSC) standard. The challenge of international governance is that states, to solve transboundary conflicts and sustain global public goods, rely on voluntary cooperation.

Global governance is a normative concept according to which the system of international institutions should be more tightly knit and better coordinated in order to re-embed politics in objectives such as international solidarity and ecological responsibility. The global governance debate is fairly sceptical of laissez-faire liberalism. A global governance 'architecture' is often conceptualised on the basis of the existing web of international organisations and policy-field specific rule systems ('regimes'), with the goal of extending from global to local level. An important role is allotted to the private sector and civil society to help define and implement policy goals. Against the backdrop of rapid global change and transformations in national sovereignty there is an emphasis on resourcing, empowering and legitimising private stakeholders, such as companies and NGOs, in order to tackle transnational challenges such as pollution, currency crises, terrorism, AIDS, or → food security. CSR is one way for businesses to engage in global governance.

The global governance concept emerged in the 1990s, when the Cold War had ended and economic → globalisation started to intensify. Critics consider the concept as idealistic or technocratic, and some warn against a 'capture' of international politics by private, especially business, actors.

Franziska Wolf

GLOBALISATION
→ Anti-globalisation

Globalisation refers to a trend or process whereby economies and societies become more connected across national and geographic boundaries. With globalisation questions of production, trade, finance, ecology, health, communications, regulation and conflict all increasingly play themselves out on a planetary scale. Much of contemporary CSR relates to companies that operate globally. Indeed, concerns to develop socially and environmentally sustainable forms of globalisation have arguably been one of the main drivers behind the recent rise of CSR.

Contemporary society has become a more global society. The collective life of human beings in the 21st century has substantial and growing planetary dimensions. All manner of flows connect people with one another wherever on earth they might be located. Global links (forged through merchandise, messages, microbes, migrants, money, organisations, pollutants, → technology, weapons, and more) have today acquired unprecedented scale, range, frequency, intensity and impact. Concurrently, people in general have developed greater global consciousness, that is, heightened awareness of planetary realms as a significant aspect of their lives. We 'think globally' far more than earlier generations.

Global connections are of course not completely new to contemporary history. The tellingly named 'world religions' have existed as long as two and a half millennia. The East India Companies plied trade between continents 400 years ago. Transoceanic telegraph cables were laid in the mid–19th century. World spanning peace movements, labour movements, black solidarity movements, and women's movements were active at the turn of the 20th century.

However, globalisation has unfolded at historically unprecedented rates and to historically unprecedented extents since the middle of the 20th century. Recent decades have been the main period of growing global → telecommunications, the internet, global mass media, global tourism, global ecological challenges, intercontinental missiles, and so much more that was not known in earlier times. The most comprehensive measure currently available, the CSGR Globalisation Index, suggests that the overall level of global links in the world rose (on a scale 0–1) from 0.18 in 1982 to 0.46 in 2001.

This is not to say that all human lives today are equally globalised. Certain countries and regions have more global connections than others. Cities tend to be more globally oriented than rural areas. Wealthier circles generally have more global links than poorer circles. In cultural terms → indigenous peoples are on the whole less globalised than populations steeped in modernity. In spite of such variations, however, all people everywhere in the world today are to some degree influenced by global circumstances.

With particular regard to CSR, it is important to note that recent globalisation has seen massive growth in firms that operate on a transnational basis. For example, thousands of companies now engage in global production, meaning that they conduct different phases of their production processes in widely separated locations across the world. Even greater numbers of corporations operate in global markets, meaning that they sell their outputs to clients spread across multiple continents, often through globally coordinated strategies. In addition, global finance today provides much of the credit lines on which business depends, and global accounting (through operations such as offshore centres and transfer pricing) enables companies greatly to enhance their bottom lines.

Many observers have raised concerns about the economic, social, environmental and political implications of this globalisation of firms. The more globalised corporations are often very large, with capacities to make far-reaching impacts on society, negative as well as positive. Moreover, globalisation has given companies much enhanced mobility, enabling them to move more easily to the most attractive regulatory environments. In principle this flexibility could allow companies to locate at sites which generate large financial profits at the cost of considerable social and environment damage. National governments might be wary of requiring higher legal standards for fear that the companies might migrate to countries with less demanding legislation.

In this situation it would be helpful to have some kind of framework of principles that could be applied to corporate behaviour anywhere and everywhere on earth. Some might argue that official → global governance mechanisms are required to meet this need, for example through a global competition agency and a global corporate taxation regime. In effect this would entail the construction of some kind of global investment authority alongside the → World Trade Organisation and the International Monetary Fund. However, critics might counter that legally binding → global governance arrangements of this kind are impracticable and/or undesirable.

Alternatively, companies could be held to global baselines of conduct through various CSR tools, most notably → codes of conduct. CSR then lays down global principles of corporate behaviour in respect of labour standards, ecological sustainability, → human rights etc. without, however, giving these rules the force of international law. CSR takes a self-regulatory approach, whereby companies voluntarily submit to what is in effect a form of private or market-based → global governance. It is an open question whether the voluntary CSR approach will succeed, or whether pressures will grow for forms of more global mandatory corporate regulation.

Jan Aart Scholte

GLOBAL REPORTING INITIATIVE (GRI)

→ Non-financial reporting

🖰 www.globalreporting.org

The Global Reporting Initiative's (GRI) vision is that reporting on economic, environmental, and social performance by all organisations becomes as routine and comparable as financial reporting. The GRI network accomplishes this vision by developing, continuously improving and building capacity around the use of a Sustainability Reporting Framework, the core of which are the Sustainability Reporting Guidelines.

The Sustainability Reporting Guidelines consist of:

- Reporting Principles – including materiality, stakeholder inclusiveness, sustainability context, completeness, balance, comparability, accuracy, timeliness, reliability, and clarity, along with a brief set of tests for each Principle;
- Reporting Guidance – on how to define the range of entities represented by the report (also called the 'Report Boundary'); and
- Standard disclosures – including the organisation profile, management approach and performance indicators (economic, environmental and social).

Other components in the Reporting Framework are:

- Sector Supplements – for → automotive, financial sevices, logistics and transportation, mining and metals, public agency, tour operators, → telecommunications; and
- Protocols, the 'recipe' behind each indicator in the Guidelines, including definitions for key terms in the indicator, compilation methodologies, intended scope of the indicator, and other technical references.

There are also topic-specific resource documents on reporting on → HIV/AIDS, → climate change, → biodiversity, supply chain and small enterprises.

To ensure the highest degree of technical quality, credibility, and relevance, the GRI Reporting Framework is developed and continuously improved through intensive multi-stakeholder engagement that involves reporting organisations and information seekers, who together develop and review content for the Reporting Framework.

To date, nearly 1000 organisations in over 60 countries have declared their use of the GRI Reporting Framework.

GLOBAL SULLIVAN PRINCIPLES OF SOCIAL RESPONSIBILITY

⌒ www.thesullivanfoundation.org

The Global Sullivan Principles of Social Responsibility is a voluntary code of conduct instigated and drafted by the late Reverend Leon H. Sullivan from the USA. The overreaching objective of the Global Sullivan Principles is to encourage companies and organisations of all sizes, in widely disparate industries and cultures, to work toward the common goals of economic, social and political justice including respect for → human rights and equal work opportunities for all peoples. The principles are inclusive in that they embrace businesses' existing → codes of conduct and work in conjunction with them.

The original Sullivan Principles were launched in 1977 and were designed to assist US companies operating in South Africa in an effort to address apartheid policies. The Sullivan Principles called US companies with investments in South Africa to treat their Black African employees the same as they would their American employees.

These same principles were then relaunched in November 1999 as the Global Sullivan Principles for Corporate Social Responsibility.

Companies wishing to be associated with the Principles are expected to provide information which publicly demonstrates their commitment to the principles and to apply them while they pursue their business objectives around the world. The principles have been endorsed and implemented by a number of business councils, campaigning NGOs, local authorities, companies and representative organisations.

Aron Ghebremariam and Nick Tolhurst

GLOBAL WARMING
→ Climate change

GOVERNANCE
→ Corporate governance, Global governance

GREEN CONSUMERISM
→ Ethical consumerism

In consumerist cultures, the use of consumer-related language can be powerful. The term green consumer was first used at a UK Design Centre exhibition in 1986, and was then introduced to a wider world by the 1988 bestseller, *The Green Consumer Guide* – written by John Elkington and Julia Hailes. The Guide sold a million copies and went into more than 20 overseas editions, signalling – and helping to fuel – growing consumer appetite for greener products and services. The idea was to introduce an additional form of influence for environmentally aware citizens, alongside voting, joining NGOs and protesting. Some environmentalists protested the use of the term green alongside the word consumer, arguing that they were mutually exclusive, but the early impact of the movement blunted most such concerns.

The earliest impacts were felt in retail, with supermarkets caught off balance – and then passing the pressure on to suppliers. In some cases, they also launched their own green product lines. Among the achievements were that manufacturers removed CFCs from aerosols, heavy metals from products like batteries, and chlorine from paper production processes. There were intense debates about whether product X (e.g. a disposable nappy or diaper) was better than product Y (e.g. a cotton nappy). Such controversies, in turn, drove growing interest in business in environmental → auditing and life cycle management and design. As consumer confusion grew, a number of eco-labelling schemes were introduced, including an EU-wide scheme. Most of these had limited success, but some – like the Soil Association's organic label – went on to powerfully shape relevant markets.

John Elkington

GREENHOUSE GASES

→ Climate change, Emissions trading, Kyoto Protocol

Greenhouse gases (GHGs) are the gases in the atmosphere that contribute to the greenhouse effect. Sunlight passes through the atmosphere and warms up the earth's surface. The warm surface then radiates part of this energy away as infrared radiation and the greenhouse effect is the process of absorption of this re-radiated infrared radiation by the gases, thereby trapping the heat. Due to the greenhouse effect, the earth's climate is about 30 degrees Celsius warmer than it would otherwise be.

Naturally occurring GHGs include water vapour, carbon dioxide, methane, nitrous oxide and ozone. GHGs that are not naturally occurring include sulphur hexafluoride, hydrofluorocarbons and chlorofluorocarbons. The relative contribution to the greenhouse effect is measured by the radiative forcing of each gas. The radiative forcing is a measure of the extra energy trapped by the GHGs – a positive forcing implies warming and a negative forcing implies cooling.

The concentration of GHGs has varied over time and is closely correlated with changes in the earth's average global temperature. Human activity, such as burning fossil fuels or livestock farming, has dramatically increased the concentration of certain GHGs. This has led to an increase in the average global temperature, often referred to as anthropogenic → climate change. For example, the concentration of carbon dioxide (the main GHG increase from human activity) has increased in concentration by over a third since the beginning of the industrial revolution.

Aled Jones

GREENHOUSE GAS PROTOCOL
→ Climate change, World Business Council for Sustainable Development (WBCSD)
↪ www.ghgprotocol.org

A greenhouse gas protocol is a protocol for identifying, quantifying, aggregating and reporting emissions of → greenhouse gases from organisations, facilities or particular projects.

Concern about → climate change has driven the need for more reliable information on emissions of → greenhouse gases to the atmosphere, which in turn has created a need for standardised protocols for reporting on greenhouse gas emissions. Protocols have been developed for reporting both emissions from existing activities, and emissions (or emissions reductions) from new projects, particularly projects designed to generate → carbon credits. Greenhouse gas protocols have been produced by companies, governments and other organisations. For example, companies (especially in the oil and gas sector) have produced internal protocols to create inventories of emissions from their operations, and governments have also created protocols to support regulatory schemes designed to reduce emission.

The Greenhouse Gas Protocol is one specific protocol produced by the → World Business Council for Sustainable Development (WBCSD) and the World Resources Institute (WRI). This is a multi-stakeholder partnership of businesses, non-governmental organisations, governments, academics, and others with the mission to develop internationally accepted greenhouse gas accounting and reporting protocols, and to promote their broad adoption.

Stirling Habbitts

GREEN MARKETING
→ Labelling, Marketing ethics

Green marketing is an effort on the part of organisations to develop products and services that either help or at least do not hurt the sustainability of the natural environment. It would describe efforts by automakers to make cars that consume less fuel and create fewer pollutants; by large appliance manufacturers to produce appliances operating with lower power consumption; and by chemical companies to produce → chemicals in a way that cause fewer noxious effects on the quality of the air, → water, or soil.

Philip Kotler

GREEN MOVEMENT
→ Environmental movement

GREENWASH
→ Bluewash, Green marketing, Public affairs

Greenwash is the use of marketing or public relations practices to create a misleading impression of an organisation's environmental performance. Greenwash often exaggerates good practices while downplaying or ignoring harmful activities. Broadly, greenwash aims to deflect criticism and build reputational capital while allowing an organisation to conduct business in ways that might be viewed as unacceptable if people knew about them. Specifically, companies use greenwash in the hope of alluring eco-conscious consumers, allaying protests of activist stakeholders, enhancing their corporate reputation, increasing shareholder value, and circumventing government regulation through pre-emptive, voluntary campaigns.

Greenwash has broadly negative consequences. It creates cynicism among stakeholders, reducing credibility and trust in all corporate communications, making it more difficult for well-meaning corporations to communicate their real CSR achievements. Greenwash distorts markets by depriving consumers of the ability to make informed purchasing decisions, and it damages → corporate governance, because shareholders cannot make informed investment and voting decisions.

For all its many ills, greenwash has had some positive reaction effects on CSR – it has created an increase in the demand for independent → certification bodies, increased the knowledge and sophistication of consumers, and increased the expectation of → transparency and candor concerning corporate communications and behaviour. One way this manifests is in the rising number of companies that publish annual CSR or sustainability reports, which aim to communicate a full picture of a corporation's social and environmental performance. As more information on all aspects of corporate behaviour becomes available, greenwash will become riskier and less effective.

Paula Ivey

HAZARDOUS WASTE
→ Waste management

HEALTH
→ Health and safety, Pharmaceutical sector

HEALTH AND SAFETY
→ HIV/AIDS, ILO-OSH 2001, OHSAS 18001, Pharmaceutical sector

Health and safety in the workplace addresses two basic concepts: promoting the well-being of workers and safeguarding against accidents and injuries. Health and safety issues must be seen in the context of the sector in which they occur, as each sector poses different types of conditions and risks. Despite the sector-specific nature of the issues, there are internationally recognised standards on health and safety.

The ILO has formulated labour standards through conventions and recommendations that set minimum standards. The ILO has a tri-partite structure, which ensures that the conventions are developed through consultation between governments, trade unions, and employers' organisations. ILO conventions are ratified by countries, which commit to ensuring that their domestic legislation conforms to their obligations under the conventions.

The ILO has defined a very wide range of conventions on health and safety, including:

- No. 148: concerning the Protection of Workers against Occupational Hazards in the Working Environment (1977)
- No. 155: concerning Occupational Safety and Health and the Working Environment (1981)
- No. 16: concerning Occupational Health Services (1985)
- No. 162: concerning Safety in the Use of Asbestos (1986)
- No. 170: concerning Safety in the use of Chemicals at Work (1990)

- No. 174: concerning the Prevention of Major Industrial Accidents (1993)

The ILO has also developed sector-based conventions, including:

- No. 167: concerning Safety and Health in Construction (1988)
- No. 176: concerning Safety and Health in Mines (1995)

The → ILO Tripartite Declaration of Principles Concerning Multinational Enterprises and Social Policy is also a key document in the promotion of labour rights, including health and safety. The Declaration refers to a wide range of ILO conventions and recommendations and contains mechanisms for dispute settlement.

The OECD Guidelines for Multinational Enterprises also contain significant sections on health and safety provisions. The OECD Guidelines encourage multinational enterprises (MNEs) to observe standards that are 'not less favourable than those observed by comparable employers in the host country', a point of departure from many other guidelines and codes that promote universal standards. According to the OECD Guidelines for MNEs, companies should refrain from seeking or accepting exemptions not contemplated in the statutory or regulatory framework related to a wide range of issues including health and safety issues.

While the ILO conventions and OECD Guidelines provide an overall framework for health and safety issues, the Occupational Health and Safety Assessment Series (OHSAS 18001) defines management systems that help organisations to prevent accidents and manage risks related to health and safety.

One of the most important changes in the past two decades is the evolution of management systems to address health and safety issues. These management systems include the use of policies and practices, as well as training and records to embed health and safety issues into the workplace. By developing and implementing management systems, companies can track progress over time in their adherence to health and safety legislation and good practices. The development of management systems seeks to foster awareness in the workplace so as to make employees more responsible for their own well-being.

One of the key elements of prevention is the use of personal protective equipment including, for example, goggles to protect the eyes or safety guards on sewing machines. Employees need to receive training on the use of protective equipment, and this equipment should be provided free of charge.

The rise of computers in the workplace has caused the notion of health and safety concerns to evolve in new directions. One of the growing issues is the rise in repetitive strain injuries (RSI). RSI involves a wide range of health problems associated with prolonged computer use or other types of repetitive tasks and machinery. People suffering from RSI have different types of complaints, including muscle pain. One of the most common types of RSI is carpal tunnel syndrome, a progressive condition caused by the compression of a key nerve in the wrist. While estimates vary, there are in the region of 100 million people worldwide who suffer from RSI or other types of computer-related health problems. The cost of RSI is estimated at hundreds of billions of dollars, factoring in absence from work, worker compensation, rehabilitation, surgical costs, and preventive measures.

→ Globalisation has brought with it a concern about global pandemics. Concern about such pandemics has changed the landscape of health and safety concerns. → HIV/AIDS has emerged as a major health and safety issue in the workplace. According to the ILO, an estimated 40 million people live with → HIV/AIDS. Nine out of every 10 cases occur in adults, making → HIV/AIDS a workplace issue. The ILO has developed a Code of Practice on HIV/AIDS that provides a framework for addressing → HIV/AIDS in the workplace. The key issues covered include: the prevention of → HIV/AIDS, care and support for infected workers, and eliminating the stigma and → discrimination of people infected with the disease. Companies are offering workers information on how to prevent → HIV/AIDS, including providing condoms free of charge. Voluntary workplace testing is a growing trend. Some companies provide medicines to workers and their families who are infected with → HIV/AIDS.

Workers in hospitals, laboratories, and nursing homes who come into direct contact with blood are at high risk of becoming infected with → HIV/AIDS. To avoid this risk, and the spread of hepatitis B, the US Occupational Safety and Health Administration has developed a standard on blood-borne pathogens.

Avian bird flu is considered such a risk to normal business functions that many multinational companies have developed scenario planning to address this potential threat. In the case of high rates of infections, one of the most pressing concerns will be access to vaccines.

Stress-related ailments are also increasing. With companies under pressure to reduce their workforce, many employees are struggling with growing workloads and increasing demands. Some of the stress-related problems in the workplace include: cardiovascular problems, depression, alcoholism, and increased susceptibility to infectious diseases. Some companies are taking a proactive approach and offering wellness programmes to their employees, including fitness initiatives in an effort to mitigate stress in the workplace.

Workplace violence is seen as a growing problem, with a rise in violence by workers and consumers, which may also be stress related. Many airlines have developed policies on how to deal with violent passengers. According to the US Bureau of Labor Statistics 70% of US employers do not have a formal policy or programme in place to deal with workplace violence, despite the fact that 5% of these employers have reported incidents of violence.

Increasingly, the issue of domestic violence is viewed as a workplace issue, as victims of domestic violence may be at risk from violent acts committed by their partners in the workplace. Moreover, these employees may suffer higher rates of absenteeism due to health problems.

Mobbing in the workplace has also become a serious health and safety issue. Mobbing involves hostile communication or persistent bullying on a systematic basis over a long period of time. Like sexual harassment, mobbing can lead to serious mental and physical problems in people victimised by these practices.

The ILO has taken a wide range of measures to address violence in the workplace. In 2004, the ILO published the Code of Practice: Workplace Violence in Services Sectors and Measures to Combat this Phenomenon.

The last few decades have witnessed an unprecedented flow of women into the workforce. Despite this trend, workplaces have not fully evolved to address the needs of women workers. Many health and safety issues have a → gender-based component. Pregnant women in the workplace need to work under conditions that are safe for them and for their offspring. For example, exposure to pesticides, solvents, and organic pollutants is especially harmful to pregnant women and can lead to premature births and malformed babies. Breast milk can also be contaminated through exposure to → chemicals. Greater research is needed to understand the impact of → chemicals on the reproductive health of both women and men.

With → globalisation has come the advent of the global assembly line, with products assembled in low wage countries. The assembly of garments, toys, and electronics has come under increased media scrutiny, as working conditions are precarious in many parts of → Asia, → Latin America, and → Africa. Since the 1990s, US and European companies have developed → codes of conduct for suppliers to ensure they address issues of health and safety.

Health and safety issues are among the more visible and therefore measurable issues within → codes of conduct. Hence, health and safety issues are more likely to be addressed than some of the more deeply rooted social problems, such as → child labour or lack of democratic structures within a workplace. It is easier to place a protective shield on sewing machines than to erase centuries of discriminatory practices.

Health and safety issues are inherently linked with other issues within → codes of conduct. For example, health and safety is often linked with → discrimination, with migrant or disadvantaged workers exposed to more dangerous working conditions or given limited access to protective equipment. Health and safety issues also relate to → child labour, as special care must be taken to protect the health of children in the workplace. For example, children must not come into direct contact with pesticides. Moreover, protective equipment must be available in the correct size for young apprentices and other workers. Machinery and equipment must be located at the right level for all workers so as to avoid injury. Health and safety issues are inherently linked with excessive working hours, as there are more accidents when workers suffer from fatigue.

Another important linkage is between health and safety and trade union rights. The presence of effective trade unions can promote healthy and safe conditions in the workplace.

As more and more companies began to adopt their own → codes of conduct, there was growing concern that companies were excluding the more difficult social issues from their codes, such as → living wages, freedom of association, and the right to collective bargaining. The multiplicity of codes led to a significant duplication of audits. To combat this duplication, several standards and joint initiatives were developed, among them:

- SA 8000 (SA 8000)
- The Ethical Trading Initiative (→ ETI Base Code)
- Fair Labour Association (FLA)

These initiatives are based on conventions of the International Labour Organisation and address health and safety issues. SA 8000 introduced management systems into the → human rights arena, with the goal of preventing problems. By introducing health and safety training, manuals, and safety procedures, management systems can prevent accidents in the workplace. SA 8000 is a → certification standard, and over 1000 companies certified.

SA 8000, the ETI and the FLA have developed codes and guidance materials for companies concerned with making their supply chains more socially responsible and safe.

Since the development of SA 8000 and the ETI, there has been an increase in sector-based CSR initiatives, many of which have made in-roads into health and safety issues, including the:

- Business for Social Compliance Initiative;
- Electronics Industry Code of Conduct;
- Ethical Tea Partnership;
- International Cocoa Initiative; and
- International Council of Toy Industries, CARE Process, among others.

As sector-based → codes of conduct and partnerships develop further, health and safety issues will be better understood within a sector-based framework.

Deborah Leipziger

HIV/AIDS
→ CSR in the health care sector, Health and safety

Nearly 40 million people are currently living with HIV. In the 25 years since the Centers for Disease Control (CDC) released the first clinical definition of what was eventually called Acquired Immune Deficiency Syndrome (AIDS), the disease has wreaked enormous and unprecedented havoc, killing more than 25 million people worldwide, who have been infected through unsafe sex, contaminated blood transfusions and needles, or mother-to-child transmission (MTCT). The disease continues to vex scientists who have yet to discover a cure or vaccine and remain puzzled by the disease's genetic diversity in specific geographic regions, inconsistent progress rates in infected individuals, and other equally puzzling questions.

Initially misinterpreted as a disease limited to homosexual men, AIDS was given an erroneous early name – Gay-Related Immune Deficiency (GRID) – before being accurately labelled as an equal-opportunity affliction resulting in a collection of symptoms and infections that are caused by the human immunodeficiency virus (HIV). Today, the majority of HIV infections are acquired through unprotected sexual relations between partners. Indiscriminate with regard to age, → gender, class, race, geographic location, or sexual orientation, HIV is an extraordinarily complicated pandemic. Its transmission is facilitated by certain social behaviours (injection drug use, unprotected sex) that may be mitigated through harm reduction strategies. At the same time, prevention efforts are complicated by the fact that the disease thrives in conditions that are difficult if not impossible to control (e.g. poverty) and thus warrant holistic measures that acknowledge and address socio-economic disparities. Atypical of other diseases, which tend to affect the very young or the very old, AIDS targets individuals aged 15–45, who comprise the most economically productive demographic.

In the mid-1990s, the advent of highly active antiretroviral therapies (HAART) transformed treatment possibilities, changing the disease from a death sentence to a chronic condition that could be controlled and maintained through medication. Following the United Nations' Declaration of Commitment on HIV/AIDS in 2001, funding to fight AIDS has significantly increased and prevention education reaches more people than ever before. Massive research campaigns are uncovering the disease's etiology, paving the way for a future vaccine and other prevention techniques, including microbicides, which would enable women to protect themselves even when their male partners do not wear condoms. Still, harsh facts continue to characterise HIV/AIDS: 9 out of 10 people living with the disease do not know they have it; the disease will create 20 million AIDS orphans by 2010; many → developing countries lack the resources to protect their citizens from the disease or the deadly stigma that frequently surrounds it; the epidemic threatens to derail progress in emerging economies, including Brazil, India, China, and Ukraine; and there is no cure. Also exacerbating the situation is the controversy surrounding condom promotion, the resistance to needle exchange programmes, AIDS denialism, and grossly inaccurate disease myths, which purport that AIDS can be spread through casual contact, HIV can only infect homosexual men and drug users, and sexual intercourse with a virgin will cure AIDS.

If HIV/AIDS is ever to be eradicated, the private sector must facilitate disease prevention, treatment and care efforts. Companies operating in the hardest hit regions have a financial incentive to become active stakeholders – AIDS is significantly correlated with gross national product declines in many African countries with prevalence rates over 10% – but even those with no bottom-line stake in HIV/AIDS prevention display invaluable resources and core competencies that must be tapped. This view prompted the 2001 creation of the → Global Business Coalition on HIV/AIDS (GBC), which advocates that HIV/AIDS always be included as a key component of → corporate social responsibility efforts, regardless of the industry rubric – consumer products, → pharmaceutical, media, → mining, → banking etc. – in which businesses are defined. At the bare minimum, companies must have firm policies that elucidate zero-tolerance for stigma and → discrimination. Because companies are often the only source for accurate disease information in resource-limited settings with poor public health infrastructure, they are strongly encouraged to create workplace programmes equipped with testing facilities to ensure that all employees can comfortably determine their disease status in a safe, supportive environment. A particular expectation has been placed on the → pharmaceutical sector to engage in the fight against HIV/AIDS as patent protection (→ TRIPS) has led to a pricing of drugs that makes them unaffordable for many of the hardest hit countries in the developing world.

John E. Tedstrom

HUMAN RIGHTS
→ Business and Human Rights Resource Centre, UN Universal
   Declaration on Human Rights

Human rights are the basic rights of each human being, independent
of race, sex, religion, political opinion, social status, or any other
characteristic. The Universal Declaration of Human Rights, the
International Covenant on Civil and Political Rights, and the International Covenant on Economic, Social and Cultural Rights, are
the three fundamental United Nations agreements on human rights.
Through international human rights conventions, governments
commit to respect, protect, promote and fulfil the human rights of
their citizens and other individuals within and beyond their borders.

Today there is broad agreement that the private sector should
do its part to help ensure respect for human rights around the
world. More and more business leaders from the global north and
south are showing that they are ready to take on their appropriate
role in promoting and protecting human rights. A growing number of leading companies are committed to using a human rights
framework to help shape more principled and profitable corporate
behaviour. They understand that corporate equal opportunity and
anti-discrimination programmes are in fact addressing human rights
issues: non-discrimination is a fundamental human right. The same
with labour and 'health and safety' policies: labour rights and the
right to highest attainable standard of health are basic rights spelled
out in international human rights instruments.

Many are making these connections for clear business reasons.
These range from protecting company reputation and attracting
the best employees to reducing cost burdens and meeting new
investor expectations. These leaders recognise that the activities of
business can provide an enabling environment for the enjoyment of
human rights. They also know that company operations can have
serious negative impacts on the protection of human rights when
not carried out in a responsible manner.

Yet despite the growing consensus that companies do have human rights responsibilities, and despite the business and moral arguments for companies to take these responsibilities seriously, difficult questions remain. For example, many business leaders remain concerned that by expressing their commitment to international standards such as the Universal Declaration of Human Rights, they might be going beyond their proper role into the realm of government responsibilities. They point out that international human rights are addressed primarily to states, and oblige them to take necessary actions to ensure enjoyment of the various rights they protect, including by responding to abuses committed by non-state actors. It is clear that there is still a need for greater clarity about the precise nature and scope of business responsibilities for the promotion and protection of human rights.

Fortunately, governments working within the UN system have recognised this need as well. In 2005 they established a mandate of Special Representative of the UN Secretary-General to make progress on these issues. The Special Representative, John Ruggie of Harvard University, submitted his first report in early 2006. It provides a valuable perspective on where we stand today in coming to grips with a rapidly evolving subject which will only be furthered in a constructive direction by more dialogue and careful analysis. He stresses that one of the most significant challenges in the years ahead is 'to make the promotion and protection of human rights a more standard and uniform corporate practice'.

In developing a shared understanding of business responsibility, many factors must be considered, including the nature of the product or service a company produces, the type and location of the consumers, the size and power of the company, the prevailing human rights situation in the countries where the company operates, and the proximity to potential violations. It will also be important to consider how a regulatory framework could be helpful in more clearly defining the human rights responsibilities of the private sector. Companies have always recognised the importance of the rule of law in the context of their investments and operations around the world. They are the first to stress the importance of a transparent, well-functioning and just legal system as a critical part of an enabling environment for investment and economic growth. Human rights advocates similarly seek respect for the rule of law.

What is clear is that human rights offer a common framework for businesses to understand societies' expectations and deliver value to stakeholders in a more sustainable way. In a business context, advancing human rights is about realising new opportunities and managing risk as well as about meeting essential global standards.

Mary Robinson

HUMAN SECURITY
→ Health and safety

Human security has three primary components: the sanctity of the individual; the relationship of the individual to the community; and the preservation of people and communities in the face of national, international and global interventions. In 2003 the UN Commission on Human Security, chaired by Sadako Ogata and Amartya Sen, reported that the world needed 'a new security framework that centres directly on people'. Human security, they argued, 'focuses on shielding people from critical and pervasive threats and empowering them to take charge of their lives'. The necessity of paradigm shift is because there is 'a consensus that the meaning of security is eroding; existing institutions and policies (are) unable to cope with weakening multilateralism and global responsibilities. The state has the primary responsibility for security, but the security challenge is complex and various new actors attempt to play a role.' The Commission sought to develop a global framework focused on 'survival, dignity and livelihood; freedom from fear; and freedom from want'. Of particular concern were the most vulnerable individuals who need protection from violent conflict, those people who are on the move and those people who are economically insecure due to the global economic system having failed to enrich them or whose lives have been destabilised by forces far beyond their control.

Traditional approaches to security issues tend to focus on military security and are concerned with territorial issues. Economic → globalisation and open global social networks mean that the professional worlds of humanitarianism, → development, → human rights, conflict and business must find space to meet and integrate. Human security has become a CSR issue in a number of ways. Corporations often are the promoters and economic beneficiaries of technological developments which can threaten human civilisation, such as → genetically modified organisms (GMOs) or nuclear power and nuclear weapons. Furthermore, corporations often are the locus of a number of risks and hazards to health, life and well-being of employees and other stakeholders, as the example of the chemical industry shows. Finally, corporations are increasingly seen in a role − often for better, sometimes for worse − in conflict regions where they can actively contribute to stabilise a region and disincentivise armed conflicts.

Human security therefore calls on all partners (business, government, civil society and individuals) to find ways to develop a new paradigm of sustainable human development. The concept of security has until now tended to be shaped by the potential for conflict between states and this has often meant that security has been equated with the threats to a country's borders. And, for too long nations have sought arms to protect their security.

As the 1994 UNDP Report said: 'For most people today a feeling of insecurity arises more from worries about daily life than the dread of a cataclysmic world event. Job security, income security, health security, environmental security, and security from crime − these are emerging concerns of human security all over the world.

Malcolm McIntosh

HYDROGEN ECONOMY
→ Climate change

Hydrogen economy is the term used to describe a future economy in which the energy is stored and transported as hydrogen. Hydrogen can be used in similar applications as hydrocarbons such as fossil fuels which are currently dominant (e.g. energy generation and transportation). The by-product of using hydrogen in this way is water rather than → greenhouse gases and therefore a hydrogen economy is often used to refer to a 'greener' way of using energy. However, hydrogen is not naturally abundant on the earth and therefore needs to be manufactured by using some other primary source of energy. If this primary source of energy is low carbon then a hydrogen economy can be low carbon. From a CSR perspective, this mainly affects the research and development efforts of the → automotive, oil and gas and transportation sectors.

Aled Jones

ICC BUSINESS CHARTER FOR SUSTAINABLE DEVELOPMENT
→ Corporate sustainability
✍ www.iccwbo.org

The Business Charter for Sustainable Development, developed by the International Chamber of Commerce in response to the → World Commission on Environment and Development 1987 report on → sustainable development, sets out 16 principles for environmental management, covering environmentally relevant aspects of health, safety and product stewardship. Its objective is 'that the widest range of enterprises commit themselves to improving their environmental performance in accordance with the principles, to having in place management practices to effect such improvement, to measuring their progress, and to reporting this progress as appropriate, internally and externally'.

The 16 principles set out in the charter cover the following areas: corporate priority; integrated management; the process of improvement; employee education; prior assessment; products and services; customer advice; facilities and operations; research; the precautionary approach; contractors and suppliers; emergency preparedness; transfer of → technology; contributing to the common effort; openness to concerns; and compliance and reporting.

To date, more than 2300 companies have signed up to the Charter. In addition, several industry associations use it as the basis for their sustainability programmes. Endorsement of the Charter is voluntary. By signing it, companies commit themselves to respecting its 16 principles for environmental management. The ICC claims to be currently assessing how companies that have endorsed the Charter are applying the principles, and what their experiences were with implementation.

ICFTU CODE OF LABOUR PRACTICE
→ Labour issues, Labour relations
⌨ www.icftu.org

The International Confederation of Free Trade Unions (ICFTU) was set up in 1949 and is a confederation of national trade unions of 156 countries (with a membership of 155 million), each of which links together the trade unions of that particular country. Membership is open to bona fide trade union organisations, which are independent of outside influence, and have a democratic structure.

At its 1997 meeting the ICFTU Executive Board adopted a text for a 'Basic Code of Conduct covering Labour Practices'. The text of this code was developed by the ICFTU/ITS Working Party on Multinational Companies in a process that involved extensive consultations with various trade union organisations and other interested stakeholders. It aims to establish a minimum list of standards that ought to be included in → codes of conduct covering labour practices.

The purpose of this basic code is to promote the primacy of international labour standards and the inclusion of trade union rights in → codes of conduct. A central idea of this code is that labour exploitation and abuse cannot be separated from the repression of workers and that therefore → codes of conduct must incorporate freedom of association and the right to collective bargaining. The basic code is meant to assist any trade union organisation in negotiations with companies and in working with NGOs in campaigns involving → codes of conduct. It can also be used as a benchmark for evaluating any unilaterally adopted codes of labour practice.

IFC SOCIAL AND ENVIRONMENTAL PERFORMANCE STANDARDS
→ Banking sector
🖰 www.ifc.org

These are standards created by the IFC to ensure that large industrial projects, including mining, do not socially or environmentally damage affected communities. They are applied to all industrial projects in which the IFC participates.

The most important standard is the first one, Social and Environmental Assessment and Management System, as it determines the application of all of the rest. This requires the carrying out of an integrated Social and Environmental Impact Assessment that identifies all positive and negative impacts of the project. The free, prior and informed participation of affected communities regarding these identified impacts is then required to ensure the development of an adequate mitigation management plan that incorporates community concerns. The demonstration of broad community support for the project is required for IFC approval.

The other seven standards are:

- Labour and Working Conditions;
- Pollution Prevention and Abatement;
- Community Health, Safety and Security;
- Land Acquisition and Involuntary Resettlement;
- Biodiversity Conservation and Sustainable Natural Resource Management;
- → Indigenous Peoples; and
- Cultural Heritage.

Matt Jeschke

ILO DECLARATION ON FUNDAMENTAL PRINCIPLES AND RIGHTS AT WORK

→ Diversity, Labour issues, Labour relations

⌐ www.ilo.org

Adopted in 1998, the 'Declaration on Fundamental Principles and Rights at Work' by the International Labour Organisation (ILO) is an expression of commitment by governments, employers' and workers' organisations to uphold basic human → values – → values that are vital to social and economic life. The Declaration covers four areas:

- Freedom of association and the right to collective bargaining;
- The elimination of forced and compulsory labour;
- The abolition of → child labour; and
- The elimination of → discrimination in the workplace.

The commitment to the declaration is supported by a follow-up procedure. Member states that have not ratified one or more of the core Conventions are asked each year to report on the status of the relevant rights and principles within their borders, noting impediments to ratification, and areas where assistance may be required. The Declaration and its follow-up provides three ways to help countries, employers and workers achieve the full realisation of the Declaration's objective.

- An Annual Review composed of reports from countries that have not yet ratified one or more of the ILO Conventions that directly relate to the specific principles and rights stated in the Declaration. This reporting process provides governments with an opportunity to state what measures they have taken towards achieving respect for the Declaration. It also gives organisations of employers and workers a chance to voice their views on progress made and actions taken.
- A Global Report each year provides a dynamic global picture of the current situation of the principles and rights expressed in the Declaration. It serves as a basis for determining priorities for technical cooperation.
- Technical cooperation projects are designed to address identifiable needs in relation to the Declaration and to strengthen local capacities thereby translating principles into practice.

ILO-OSH 2001 GUIDELINES ON OCCUPATIONAL SAFETY AND HEALTH MANAGEMENT SYSTEMS

→ Health and safety

⌁ www.ilo.org

These guidelines on OSH management systems were issued by the International Labour Organisation (ILO) in 2001 according to internationally agreed principles defined by the ILO's tripartite constituents. They are voluntary guidelines on OSH management systems which reflect ILO values and instruments relevant to the protection of workers' safety and health.

At national level, the guidelines are intended to be used to establish a national framework for OSH management systems, and to provide guidance for the development of voluntary arrangements.

At the level of the organisation, the guidelines are intended to provide guidance regarding the integration of OSH management system elements in the organisation as a component of policy and management arrangements. They are also intended to motivate all members of the organisation, particularly employers, owners, managerial staff, workers and their representatives, in applying appropriate OSH management principles and methods to continually improve OSH performance.

ILO TRIPARTITE DECLARATION OF PRINCIPLES CONCERNING MULTINATIONAL ENTERPRISES AND SOCIAL POLICY

Adopted in 1977, the ILO Tripartite Declaration is a tool that addresses employment promotion, equality of opportunity, security of employment, training, wages, benefits, and conditions of work, as well as minimum age, and → health and safety, freedom of association, the right to organise, and collective bargaining. The Tripartite Declaration of Principles describes the roles and responsibilities of governments, workers' organisations, and business. The Principles are applicable to multinational enterprises as well as local businesses.

Together with the ILO's conventions, the Tripartite Declaration provides an international legal framework and policy consensus on → labour issues.

The Declaration refers to a wide range of ILO conventions and recommendations and contains mechanisms for dispute settlement. The Tripartite Declaration was amended in 2006.

Deborah Leipziger

IMPACT ASSESSMENT

Impact assessment is a process for ensuring that the possible future effects of a particular intervention (e.g. a project, plan, programme or policy) on the → environment, society or the economy are understood and taken into account in decisions concerning the progression and implementation of that intervention (e.g. a project consent decision).

The most commonly practised form of impact assessment is environmental impact assessment (EIA) which is a process for ensuring that the potential environmental effects of a major project (e.g. a new airport development or a wind farm) are taken into account at the development or funding stages. EIAs are generally a regulatory requirement of development control regimes in many countries or a requirement set by international donor organisations, such as the World Bank, when funding major projects in → developing countries.

Put into practice, EIAs should be embedded into the process of developing project design, evaluating project alternatives, developing mitigation, consultation, decision-making and project implementation.

EIAs have a close relative in strategic environmental assessment (SEA), which is a process for ensuring that the potential environmental effects of a plan, programme or policy are taken into account in their formulation and approval. SEA tends to be driven by regulatory requirements and in Europe is driven by a specific directive transposed in member state law.

There are many other forms of impact assessment, including social impact assessment (SIA), health impact assessment (HIA), integrated environmental, social and health impact assessment (ESHIA), equality impact assessment (EqIA) and life cycle (impact) assessment. These types of impact assessment are not necessarily required by regulation, but are increasingly undertaken by developers with a strong focus on the → environment and CSR.

The key characteristics of impact assessment comprise:

- A robust evidence base – i.e. clear understanding of the baseline situation, that is, the current and future environment which would exist in the absence of an intervention.

- Prediction of how the intervention, and realistic alternatives to it, would change the baseline situation and evaluation of the significance of this change.
- Identification of mitigation measures to avoid, reduce or remedy significant impacts and subsequent evaluation of residual impacts (i.e. the impacts which remain after mitigation).
- Reporting of the predictions, evaluation and significant residual impacts in documents accessible to the public.
- Consultation with relevant statutory bodies (e.g. government agencies for environmental protection), non-government organisations and the public.
- Decision-making that makes explicit how significant impacts arising from the intervention have been taken into account in progressing/implementing the intervention.

Impact assessment places a strong emphasis on engaging stakeholders through consultation and on decision-making which is transparent. It provides a robust tool for helping to ensure that interventions are implemented only where they support relevant environmental, social and economic goals and therefore the principles of → sustainable development.

Bruce Davidson

INDIGENOUS PEOPLE

→ Diversity

Indigenous communities especially in → Africa, the Americas, → Asia and Australasia/Oceania have become an increasingly important part of → corporate social responsibility (CSR) thinking for many companies seeking to operate on the land, and within the communities, of specific indigenous groups of people.

The nature of these groups differs dramatically worldwide, and there is no single CSR approach a business, let alone an entire industry, can, or should, take. Often very company-specific, and even site-specific CSR approaches have to be taken, though most, if not all, of the larger companies involved with indigenous peoples, have now developed highly defined, though often generic, terms of references and codes of CSR conduct, → human rights and guidelines for working with indigenous people.

It is not easy. There is no single universal CSR approach because there is no single universal definition of 'indigenous people', because there is no single universal indigenous group. This is the first, often very difficult, CSR lesson that has had to be learnt by business worldwide. However, the term 'indigenous' generally identifies people who are descendents of the original inhabitants of a particular area of land and who have long-standing cultural roots in that land which is now, more often than not, controlled by a dominant non-indigenous power base. As such, indigenous people are generally a rural, highly marginalised, disempowered and disadvantaged people. This presents business with a quite different set of CSR challenges to those it may face in densely populated urban and metropolitan areas of its operations, especially if access to indigenous land is a necessity for a company to continue trading.

We have seen a dramatic change of thinking in the last 10 years – from an earlier business refusal to engage with any indigenous issues at all, through a growing resentment of the ever increasing compliance requirements needed to secure access to indigenous land, to a more developed CSR approach which has gone well beyond paternalistic 'well-meaning' welfare, grant-making, sponsorship deals and philanthropy arrangements, to a much more sophisticated, though not necessarily complicated, involvement designed to help build robust regional economies. Coupled with this is a growing awareness of (and call for) both business and governments, worldwide, to better understand the still massive consequences of colonisation and its subsequent effects on the cultural and social disruption of indigenous people and the enormous disadvantages many continue to face.

This growing awareness has been led by, and in turn has led to, a much greater business knowledge, and sensitivity to, indigenous cultures, needs, problems and potential, resulting in a much wider range of programmes, policies and protocols designed to help build local economies. These include microfinancing, microlending, community capacity building, housing, education, small business development, health, work skills, training and apprenticeship schemes, technical assistance, management expertise, and employee → volunteering, as well as help in the rebuilding, and/or preserving of lost indigenous culture and heritage which may or may not have occurred as a result of past company policies and operations.

Self-help and self-sufficiency hand-ups rather than passive welfare hand-outs are at the heart of such CSR approaches. This has been led by an increasingly vocal group of indigenous leaders worldwide who have had increased access to relevant business in ways which would have been considered unthinkable several years ago.

Consequently, probably the most significant development in CSR with respect to indigenous people has not simply been the value and benefit of specific local programmes and partnerships, but dialogue and engagement between business and indigenous leaders. To consider indigenous leaders and communities as stakeholders of business, as is increasingly the case worldwide now, is a dramatic turn around in thinking and practice. It cannot be emphasised enough how dramatic this change has been in the last 10 years or so − and it is far more dramatic a change than the developments that have taken place worldwide in non-indigenous communities through CSR policies and programmes.

This does not imply that effective CSR solutions are in place all over the world, or that business is (or should be) responsible for solving all the world's indigenous social, economic and cultural problems through CSR, or that it has yet actually reduced many of the dominant indigenous inequities which still exist, but relevant business and indigenous leaders are increasingly seeing each other as mutual stakeholders, and this is, and will be, by far, the most effective long-term form of CSR for indigenous peoples worldwide.

David Birch

INDUSTRIAL ECOLOGY
→ Eco-efficiency, Life cycle assessment

The term industrial ecology was first introduced by Harry Zvi Evan at a seminar of the Economic Commission of Europe in Warsaw (Poland) in 1973. But it is Robert Frosch and Nicholas E. Gallopoulos who are responsible for popularising the term through their 1989 article in *Scientific America*. They focused on using the metaphor of metabolism to analyse production and consumption by industry. Their vision centred around the question: why could our industrial system not behave like an ecosystem, where the wastes of a species may be a resource to another species? Why could the outputs of an industry not be the inputs of another, thus reducing use of raw materials, pollution, and saving on → waste treatment?

In industrial ecology the industrial system is not viewed in isolation from its surrounding systems; it is seen inherently as part of the same system linked through transactions, activities and impacts. Often this involves a coordinated effort among individual businesses up and down the supply chain.

Industrial ecology rejects the concept of → waste, defined as useless material. As a natural system, industry should have the capacity to efficiently use materials left over from one process as inputs for another. This requires the shifting of industrial process from linear (open loop) systems, in which resource and capital investments move through the system to become → waste, to a closed loop system where wastes become inputs for new processes.

Dermot Egan

INFRASTRUCTURE SECTOR

'Civil infrastructure' refers to all the components of the built environment that society uses to enable a modern life in, mainly, urban areas – housing, commercial and public buildings, and transport and utility systems. It is an important sector, because of its large proportion of overall social and environmental impacts.

In this context, CSR refers to all the formal (e.g. complying with planning and noise regulations) and informal (e.g. community relations campaigns) ways in which the complex ownership and supply chains in this sector can improve the social, environmental and economic outcomes – the overall public benefit – delivered by their activities.

The typical sequence of stages in providing a civil infrastructure project will include:

- Planning and scoping – framing the need or problem;
- Feasibility – choosing the best solution;
- Design – fixing the detail;
- Procurement – buying the construction services and materials needed;
- Construction – building the project; and
- Operation – handover to the end-user, and long-term operation and maintenance.

Each of these involves different supply chain members. In general one could argue for the rule that the earlier the stage in the process, the greater the opportunity for a bigger 'CSR value' contribution.

The best way to illustrate the potential impact of CSR is by example, at each stage of the project. For instance:

- At the planning and scoping stage, the owner/planner team might find that they can redefine the problem so that the social need being addressed can be met with no new project at all – no extra materials or energy use, and no local disruption from construction.

- At the feasibility stage, the planner/designer team may introduce specific environmental and social criteria into the choice of the best' solution, and find a 'Best Practice Sustainable Solution'. They may also incorporate non-technical components into outline designs, such as 'social capital' principles which assist safe street and building layouts, as well as technical safety components such as CCTV; or incorporate the use of renewable energy, or find a '→ carbon neutral' solution.
- At the design stage, the design team can look to optimise the use of low embodied energy or reused materials; plan excavation and filling to avoid the need for off-site transport and disposal; and plan for low energy input during operation.
- At the procurement stage, the owner can specify high CSR standards as criteria for supplier and contractor choice; can include requirements for employing maximum numbers of local labour and suppliers; and define 'lowest cost' for selection as 'whole life cost', including long-term operation, not just 'initial construction cost'.
- At the construction stage, the constructor can make → health and safety and environmental permitting and compliance a very high priority; can adopt 'considerate contractor' principles involving minimising noise, dirt, dust and transport; can use the most energy efficient construction machinery possible; and can make a priority of local community engagement and communication.
- At the operation stage, the end-user can 'fine-tune' the facility, both to utilise the absolute minimum energy, → chemicals, materials and other inputs, and to maximise its public service outputs.

Improving the CSR performance of the whole civil infrastructure sector is difficult, because of the large number of players in the complex supply chains – many of them very local and small. Also, the average life of a typical project is long – say 20 to 100 years – so very large improvements are needed in new projects, to raise the average rate of change across all infrastructure assets. On the other hand, the largest owners – including particularly government – and players in each stage can have a major impact for improvement, through the specifications and choice criteria built into their procurement systems.

There are a large number of current actions for improvement in the sector:

- Government, e.g. the UK's Sustainable Procurement initiative, 'Sustainable Communities' specifications for new building and a commitment to require all new houses to be → carbon neutral in the future.
- Professional engineering institutions, nearly all have 'sustainability' and/or 'ethical principles and → codes of conduct' which apply to all individual engineers.
- Industry initiatives, e.g. 'Sustainable Construction', BREEAM efficiency standards for buildings, and CEQUAL standards for other civil projects.
- Major client or planning control initiatives, of various kinds, e.g. the sustainability plan for the 2012 Olympics and the Mayor of London's planning requirement for a minimum percentage of renewable energy supply on all new buildings.

Charles Ainger

INSTITUTE FOR CORPORATE CULTURE AFFAIRS (ICCA)

→ Corporate culture

✍ www.cca-institute.org

The Institute for Corporate Culture Affairs (ICCA) is an independent not-for-profit think-tank founded by Professor Manfred Pohl in 2003 and based in Frankfurt am Main, Germany. ICCA is dedicated to the mainstreaming of CSR within international corporations. In addition to CSR, ICCA focuses on issues in the world today of particular interest and importance to the international business community – such as the future of → globalisation, business history and → corporate culture.

ICCA links up the most important business executives, organisations, academics and opinion formers in the world today in a quest to coordinate and align profit-based goals with the good of society. ICCA believes that international business has the key role to play in ensuring that the world reaps the positive benefits of → globalisation with the consequent raising of standards for all, whether this be in the economic, social or environmental spheres.

ICCA's main activities include primary research (including book publications such as the *ICCA Handbook of CSR* or the web-based *CSR Globe* directory), as well as facilitating the global exchange through its networks of corporate → best practices through conferences, workshops and in-house trainings covering topics such as sustainability, pre-merger and acquisitions cultural → due diligence, CSR or business archive management.

Nick Tolhurst

INSTITUTE OF ENVIRONMENTAL MANAGEMENT AND ASSESSMENT (IEMA)
→ Environmental auditing
√ð www.iema.net

The Institute of Environmental Management and Assessment (IEMA) is a not-for-profit organisation established to promote → best practice standards in environmental management, → auditing and assessment. Its origins lie in the merger in 1999 of the Institute of Environmental Management, the Institute of Environmental Assessment, and the Environmental Auditors Registration Association.

With over 11 000 individual and corporate members, the IEMA is now a leading international membership-based organisation dedicated to the promotion of → sustainable development, and to the professional development of individuals involved in the environmental profession, whether they be in the public, private or non-governmental sectors.

The Institute maintains an internationally acknowledged auditor registration scheme with over 2000 members from 60 countries around the world. The Auditors Register provides an efficient and effective means of demonstrating to interested parties that an individual is adequately qualified, trained and experienced to perform a range of → environmental auditing tasks. Membership of the IEMA Environmental Auditor Register is often stated as a requirement in pre-qualification tenders.

The EIA Practitioner Register scheme was developed between 1999 and 2002 and launched at the IEMA's Annual Conference in April 2002. The scheme is the result of extensive international consultation and a pilot exercise in which all the major elements in the scheme were tested. The scheme is aimed at all those currently involved in EIA activities from consultants and developers to environmental regulators, both in the UK and internationally. The scheme is likely to grow rapidly in terms of membership numbers and significance over the next five years.

INSTITUTE OF SOCIAL AND ETHICAL ACCOUNTABILITY
→ AA 1000 Series of Standards

INTEGRATED POLLUTION CONTROL
→ Pollution

INTEGRITY
→ Values

The concept of integrity has been derived from the Latin *integritas* (wholeness). It is defined as consistency between beliefs, decisions and actions, and continued adherence to → values and principles.

When someone is described as a person of integrity, the suggestion is that such a person is not corruptible as a result of the 'wholeness' and 'connectedness' of the → values and principles that such a person subscribes to. Integrity is often used in conjunction with ethics, suggesting that the → values and principles that are adhered to should be ethical → values. Some of the → values that are often mentioned in this regard are honesty, openness, → accountability and trustworthiness.

Organisational integrity refers to the ability of individual organisations to develop and implement an integrity management framework, and for employees to act in accordance with the → values of the organisation. This framework usually comprises a combination of integrity measurement activities, policies (e.g. codes of ethics or → codes of conduct), training programmes and ongoing support (e.g. help lines or hotlines). Once again, the emphasis is on the integration of all these activities – if they are not integrated, the integrity (wholeness) of the organisation will be compromised.

Daniel Malan

INTELLECTUAL PROPERTY RIGHTS (IPRs)
→ TRIPS

Intellectual Property Rights (IPRS) comprise all rights created by law to protect creative ideas and inventions, such as copyrights, patents, trademarks or logos, in order to achieve two goals: the individual benefit of public identification of the author or inventor, entailing his or her exclusive right to an economical exploitation of his or her work, and – as a consequence – the societal benefit of encouraging creativity and innovation. Intellectual property rights are of essential value to knowledge-based economies and to all their market participants. Their use by companies has a number of CSR-related implications.

Intellectual property rights are granted for a certain period of time vis-à-vis artistic and literary achievements as well as scientific and industrial inventions in exchange for their publication. After expiry of that period they may be exploited by anyone. Trade or business secrets on the other hand are not covered. IPRs are protected by national laws and international conventions such as the → TRIPS Agreement.

In recent years consumer groups, researchers and competitors have severely criticised the use of IPRs, especially by big companies. Their behaviour has been perceived as perverting the original aim of IPRS by obstructing follow-on innovation and progress rather than fostering it. This can lead to conflicts with competition policy. Examples include pharmaceutical companies' rigorous enforcement of IPRS allegedly hindering the allocation of vital drugs to poorer countries and Microsoft's refusal to disclose information on its operating systems, which competitors would need to develop innovative compatible software programs. One solution to this problem can be licensing out of inventions.

Satish Sule

INTERESTED AND AFFECTED PARTIES
→ Stakeholders

INTERFAITH DECLARATION: A CODE OF ETHICS ON INTERNATIONAL BUSINESS FOR CHRISTIANS, MUSLIMS AND JEWS
🖰 astro.ocis.temple.edu/~dialogue/Codes/cmj_codes

This Declaration came about as a consequence of a series of interfaith consultations, beginning in 1984 and concluding in 1993, between distinguished members of the three monotheistic faiths

(Christianity, Islam and Judaism) under the patronage of HRH Prince Philip, the Duke of Edinburgh and HRH Crown Prince El Hassan Bin Talal of Jordan. The Declaration offers an ethical base and framework to the international business community, drawing on the shared moral, ethical and spiritual → values inherent in the common Abrahamic traditions, transcending what is often seen or portrayed as divergence or conflict between different cultures and belief systems.

The Declaration lays down four key principles common to the religious and moral teachings and scriptures of Christianity, Islam and Judaism:

- Justice – just conduct, fairness and the exercise of authority in the maintenance of right;
- Mutual respect – reciprocal regard, love or consideration for others
- Stewardship – trusteeship of God's creation and all that is in it; and
- Honesty – truthfulness, reliability and → integrity in all aspects of human relationships, thought, word and action.

The Declaration also conveys a series of guidelines which aim to facilitate the implementation of the principles by addressing the:

- Morality of the economic system in which business operates;
- Strategy and policies of individual organisations; and
- Behaviour of individuals in the context of their work.

While the Declaration is no substitute for individual or corporate → values, the aspiration is that it would contribute to maintaining high standards of business behaviour by allowing business leaders to draw on the essence of the principles and guidelines it advocates by weaving them into corporate 'statements of purpose' and '→ codes of conduct'. It is recommended to followers of each of the three faiths and commended to leaders and educators of international business, whether or not they adhere to these religious traditions.

Kelly Lavelle

INTERGENERATIONAL EQUITY

→ Intragenerational equity

'Intergenerational equity' reflects the concept that future generations have the right to inherit a planet which can meet their needs, with at least the same levels of → biodiversity, natural resources and clean air and → water as the current generation enjoys. Most would agree that our children and grandchildren should not have to inherit a world impoverished by the greed or short-sightedness of the current generation.

However, in a market-driven world, groups with no purchasing power are marginalised, and the interests of people not yet born cannot be taken into account. Thus the drive to maximise profits now frequently shifts negative → externalities into the future – for example, the impacts of CO_2 emissions now will only be felt in around 40 years' time, while current changes were triggered 40 years ago.

Governments and businesses inevitably tend to place short-term considerations above long term, whether driven by the need to please current voters, or by the imperatives of quarterly reporting and obligations to shareholders. CSR, therefore, needs to balance the short-term imperatives of capital markets with a long-term perspective which emphasises investment in human capital and resource efficiency, and the minimisation of lasting environmental damage and depletion.

Ruth Findlay-Brooks

INTERNATIONAL ACCREDITATION FORUM (IAF)

→ Certification

⌐ www.iaf.nu

The International Accreditation Forum (IAF) is the world association of Conformity Assessment Accreditation Bodies and other bodies interested in conformity assessment in the fields of management systems, products, services, personnel and other similar programmes of conformity assessment. Its primary function is to develop a single worldwide programme of conformity assessment which reduces risk for business and its customers by assuring them that accredited certificates may be relied upon. Accreditation assures users of the competence and impartiality of the body accredited. IAF members accredit Certification Bodies that issue certificates (e.g. → ISO 14001) attesting that an organisation's management, products or personnel comply with a specified standard (called conformity assessment).

The primary purpose of IAF is two-fold. First, to ensure that its Accreditation Body members only accredit Certification Bodies that are competent to do the work they undertake and are not subject to conflicts of interest. Second, to establish mutual recognition arrangements, known as the Multilateral Recognition Arrangements (MLA), between its Accreditation Body members which reduces risk to business and its customers by ensuring that an accredited certificate may be relied upon anywhere in the world.

John Owen

INTERNATIONAL ASSOCIATION FOR BUSINESS AND SOCIETY (IABS)

⌐ www.iabs.net

The International Association for Business and Society (IABS) is a learned society devoted to research and teaching about the relationships between business, government and society. Founded in 1990, today it has over 300 members worldwide from over 100 universities in more than 20 countries as well as members from various corporations and not-for-profit organisations. IABS is a multidisciplinary association which attracts scholars and executives from all the disciplines of management. Its research domain covers the various aspects of the interface between management and the social political dynamics of the surrounding society. It includes, among others, research on → corporate social responsibility and performance, emerging social issues for business, → business ethics, environmental affairs as well as business and government relations. IABS sponsors a journal, *Business & Society*, published by SAGE. IABS also organises annual conferences, which take place in countries around the globe.

INTERNATIONAL ASSOCIATION FOR IMPACT ASSESSMENT (IAIA)

→ Impact assessment

⌐ www.iaia.org

The International Association for Impact Assessment (IAIA) was organised in 1980 to bring together researchers, practitioners, and users of various types of → impact assessment from all parts of the world. IAIA involves people from many disciplines and professions and members now number more than 2500 and represent more than 100 countries. Training programmes are held regularly in conjunction with IAIA international conferences.

IAIA activities seek to:

- Develop approaches and practices for comprehensive and integrated → impact assessment;
- Improve assessment procedures and methods for practical application;
- Promote training of → impact assessment and public understanding of the field;

- Provide professional quality → assurance by peer review and other means; and
- Share information networks, timely publications, and professional meetings.

The quarterly journal *Impact Assessment and Project Appraisal* contains a variety of peer-reviewed research articles, professional practice ideas, and book reviews of recently published titles.

INTERNATIONAL AUDITING AND ASSURANCE STANDARDS BOARD (IAASB)
→ ISAE 3000

INTERNATIONAL BUSINESS LEADERS FORUM (IBLF)
🖰 www.iblf.org

The IBLF is an international not-for-profit organisation based in the UK. It was set up in 1990 by the Prince of Wales and a group of chief executives of international companies, in response to the emerging challenges of economic growth and change in the global economy. It promotes responsible business practices internationally that benefit both business and society, and which help to achieve social, economic and environmentally → sustainable development, particularly in new and emerging market economies. IBLF encourages continuous improvement in responsible business practices in all aspects of company operations; develops geographic and issue-based partnerships to take effective action on social, economic and environmental issues; and helps to create an 'enabling environment' to provide the conditions in which such partnerships can flourish. IBLF retains its distinctive character by combining its understanding of the social dimensions of business; its leading edge championing of cross-sector partnering and development of generic partnership-building methods together with practical action in more than 30 countries undergoing political and/or economic transition.

INTERNATIONAL FAIR TRADE ASSOCIATION (IFAT)

→ Fair trade

🖰 www.ifat.org

IFAT, created in 1989, is the International Fair Trade Association, the global network of Fairtrade organisations. IFAT's mission is to improve the livelihoods and well-being of disadvantaged producers by linking and promoting Fairtrade organisations, and speaking out for greater justice in world trade.

Almost 300 Fairtrade organisations in 70 countries form the basis of the network and approximately 65% of members are based in the South (Asia, the Middle East, Africa and South America) with the rest coming from North America and the Pacific Rim and Europe.

Members have the concept of fair trade at the heart of their mission and at the core of what they do. They come in many shapes and sizes and represent the fair trade chain from production to sale. Members are producer cooperatives and associations, export marketing companies, importers, retailers, national and regional Fairtrade networks and financial institutions, dedicated to fair trade principles.

INTERNATIONAL FEDERATION FOR ALTERNATIVE TRADE (IFAT)

→ International Fair Trade Association (IFAT)

INTERNATIONAL ORGANIC ACCREDITATION SERVICE (IOAS)

→ Food and beverage sector, Labelling

🖰 www.ioas.org

The International Organic Accreditation Service (IOAS) is a non-profit independent organisation, which offers international oversight of organic → certification, through a voluntary accreditation process for → certification bodies active in the field of organic agriculture.

The IOAS implements the International Federation of Organic Agricultural Movements' (IFOAM) Accreditation Programme which is an industry-based global guarantee of organic integrity, unburdened by national barriers and implemented by one body which has no other interests.

INTRAGENERATIONAL EQUITY
→ Intergenerational equity

Intragenerational equity refers to the concept of justice and equal access to basic needs and → human rights for all of the current population – whether within or between countries.

The early → environmental movement emphasised the protection of nature from the impacts of economic development, overlooking the urgent need for basic → development among the world's poor. The 1987 report of the → World Commission on Environment and Development, Our Common Future, linked environment and → development for the first time by recognising that poverty and social injustice inevitably undermine → sustainable development. The consequences of environmental damage caused by unsustainable consumption among the wealthy affect the poor disproportionately, while the poor and landless in turn put pressure on fragile natural resources in their struggle to survive. In a world where over 2 billion live on less than $2 a day and a similar number lack civil and political freedoms, the drive to meet immediate needs undermines attempts to plan for a sustainable future or to consider → intergenerational equity.

Inequity, however, is difficult to address – be it social exclusion within wealthy societies, or the extremes of the north–south divide. CSR policies can contribute, both through proactive measures such as → fair trade initiatives, and through consideration of the uneven impacts of economic transactions and resource consumption.

Ruth Findlay-Brooks

ISAE 3000 STANDARD FOR ASSURANCE ENGAGEMENTS

→ Assurance, Report verification

✑ www.ifac.org

ISAE 3000, issued by the International Auditing and Assurance Standards Board (IAASB) of the International Federation of Accountants (IFAC), stands for the International Standard on Assurance Engagements 3000: Assurance Engagements other than Audits of Reviews of Historical (financial) Information. It is a generic standard which is used for → assurance engagements relating to CSR reports. It excludes audits or reviews of financial statements.

ISAE 3000 is one of the standards issued by the IFAC which are designed to ensure a standardised, thorough methodology for carrying out independent → assurance engagements. The → assurance provider must also comply with the IFAC Code of Ethics for Professional Accountants, including independence.

As part of this standard, the International Framework for Assurance Engagements provides a frame of reference for the → assurance provider, the reporter and the users of the → assurance report. It includes:

- Definition and objective of an → assurance engagement;
- Requirements for accepting an engagement; and
- Engagement elements – three parties, subject matter (e.g. a CSR report), criteria (e.g. GRI), evidence and an → assurance report with conclusion(s).

ISAE 3000 covers basic principles and the essential procedures for the engagement from acceptance through to issuing the → assurance report. It covers two types of → assurance engagement – reasonable and limited (or a combination) and gives some guidance on the differences. It also determines the wording of the conclusions in the → assurance report, to ensure that users do not place more reliance on the conclusions than can be warranted by the amount of work undertaken.

Jennifer Iansen-Rogers

ISEAL ALLIANCE

→ Certification, Labelling

🖰 www.isealalliance.org

The International Social and Environmental Accreditation and Labelling (ISEAL) Alliance is an association of leading voluntary international standard-setting and conformity assessment organisations that focus on social and environmental issues.

ISEAL members represent standards and conformity assessment systems in sectors ranging from forestry and agriculture to fisheries, manufacturing and textiles. ISEAL members are committed to the highest standards for credibility in their work including the ISEAL Code of Good Practice for Setting Social and Environmental Standards and relevant ISO standards.

ISO 9000 SERIES OF STANDARDS ON QUALITY MANAGEMENT

→ Quality management

🖰 www.iso.org

The ISO 9000 family is primarily concerned with 'quality management'. This means what the organisation does to fulfil the customer's quality requirements, and applicable regulatory requirements, while aiming to enhance customer satisfaction and achieve → continual improvement of its performance in pursuit of these objectives.

More specifically, → ISO 9001:2000 is used if an organisation is seeking to establish a management system that provides confidence in the conformance of their product to established or specified requirements. It is now the only standard in the ISO 9000 family against whose requirements a quality system can be certified by an external agency.

There are five sections in the standard that specify activities that need to be considered when implementing the system, namely:

- Product realisation;
- Quality management system;
- Management responsibility;
- Resource management; and
- Measurement, analysis and improvement.

ISO 9004:2000 is used to extend the benefits obtained from → ISO 9001:2000 to all parties that are interested in or affected by business operations. Interested parties include employees, owners, suppliers and society in general.

The eight Quality Management Principles stated in ISO 9000:2000 and ISO 9004:2000 provide the basis for the performance improvement and include:

- Customer focus;
- → Leadership;
- Involvement of people;
- Process approach;
- System approach to management;
- → Continual improvement;
- Factual approach to decision-making; and
- Mutually beneficial supplier relationships.

The → ISO 14001 standard for → environmental management systems is based on a similar approach and is designed to be compatible with → ISO 9001.

ISO 14000 SERIES OF STANDARDS ON ENVIRONMENTAL MANAGEMENT

→ Corporate environmental management, Environmental management systems

⌕ www.iso.org

The most popular kind of → environmental management system (EMS) is an EMS which is developed in accordance with → ISO 14001:2004, an international standard which was published for the first time in 1996 as → ISO 14001:1996 by the International Organisation for Standardisation (ISO) and which was reviewed and published again in 2004.

→ ISO 14001:2004 defines an → environmental management system as that part of the overall management system of an organisation that includes organisational structure, planning activities, responsibilities, practices, procedures, processes and resources for developing, implementing, achieving, reviewing and maintaining the environmental policy.

It is generally agreed that the implementation of a robust EMS, which may incorporate → ISO 14001, should lead to improved environmental performance, including better and more consistent → legal compliance which should ultimately lead to enhanced efficiency of the organisation.

The ISO 14000 series of standards reflect different aspects of environmental management. The following list outlines the broad coverage of each:

- Environmental Management Systems: 14001, 14002, 14004
- Environmental Auditing: 19011
- Environmental Labelling: 14020, 14021, 14022, 14023, 14024, 14025
- → Life Cycle Assessment: 14040, 14041, 14042, 14043
- Evaluation of Environmental Performance: 14031

Johann Möller

ISO 26000 STANDARD ON CORPORATE SOCIAL RESPONSIBILITY

→ Corporate social responsibility

⌐🖑 www.iso.org

ISO 26000, expected to be finalised in 2008, is currently the result of a still ongoing international and multi-stakeholder process based on the consensus and consolidated results of science, → technology, and → best practice to assist an organisation in addressing its social responsibilities. The document is intended to be an International Standard providing guidance related to:

- Operationalising social responsibility;
- Identifying and engaging with stakeholders;
- Enhancing credibility of reports and claims made about social responsibility;
- Emphasising performance results and improvements;
- Promoting common terminology in the SR field; and
- Promoting → sustainable development.

The standard is not to be intended for third-party → certification, is not a management system standard and also will not conflict with existing documents, treaties, conventions and other ISO standards.

Jorge E. Reis Cajazeira

JOHANNESBURG DECLARATION ON SUSTAINABLE DEVELOPMENT

→ Sustainable development

⌐🖑 www.johannesburgsummit.org

The Johannesburg Declaration on Sustainable Development was issued by the World Summit on Sustainable Development which took place in South Africa in 2002. Convened by the UN 10 years after the Rio 'Earth Summit', the meeting brought together political, business and NGO leaders. It aimed to build on the Stockholm

Declaration of 1972 and the Rio Declaration of 1992. The Declaration covered areas such as improved sanitation, → biodiversity and fish stocks, and placed considerable emphasis on the self-regulation of businesses through working in partnership.

Among critics and many in the NGO community, there was disappointment in the outcomes of the Johannesburg Summit, which were viewed as a stark contrast to the optimism and urgency of the Rio Summit. The non-participation of George W. Bush, and the USA's blocking of key targets, was seen as compounding the reluctance of political leaders to commit to regulation or financial support. Instead, the UN Secretary General Kofi Annan called on the private sector, NGOs and governments to work in partnership to address the complex issues of → sustainable development. In place of external regulation, the pressure shifted to businesses to take responsibility for their own environmental impacts through CSR policies which would ensure → accountability to all stakeholders.

Ruth Findlay-Brooks

JOINT IMPLEMENTATION
→ Kyoto Protocol
⌐ www.unfccc.int

Joint Implementation (JI) is one of the mechanisms of the → Kyoto Protocol, under which projects to reduce, avoid or sequester emissions of → greenhouse gases in countries categorised as Annex I under the → Kyoto Protocol generate → carbon credits that can be used in other Annex I countries to assist these countries to meet their greenhouse gas emissions targets.

Under the → Kyoto Protocol, countries are divided into two categories, Annex I (industrialised countries and countries with economies in transition) and non-Annex I countries (typically, → developing countries). Annex I countries have targets to reduce greenhouse gas emissions, and non-Annex I countries do not. To meet their greenhouse gas emissions targets, Annex I countries may use → carbon credits obtained from projects developed in other Annex I countries, referred to as Joint Implementation.

Joint Implementation is overseen by the Joint Implementation Supervisory Committee (JISC), appointed under the United Nations Framework Convention on Climate Change (UNFCCC). JI projects will be required to obtain third party → assurance on compliance with the rules for JI and on the emissions reductions generated. Although the rules are not finalised, JI projects are currently being developed based on expectations of what the rules will be. Countries with economies in transition (from the former Soviet Union) are particularly attractive for JI projects because they are Annex I countries, and because emissions reductions can generally be made in these countries at lower cost than in other Annex I countries.

Stirling Habbitts

KING REPORT ON CORPORATE GOVERNANCE IN SOUTH AFRICA

→ Corporate governance

✐ www.iodsa.co.za

The Institute of Directors in Southern Africa (IOD) established the King Committee on Corporate Governance in July 1993. The committee is chaired by Judge Mervyn King, past president of the Commonwealth Association of Corporate Governance and director of numerous companies.

The Second King Report on Corporate Governance 2002 (King II) represents a formal review of South African → corporate governance arrangements, similar to the Combined Code in the UK. The report comprises main sections that focus on the board and directors, risk management, internal audit, integrated sustainability reporting (→ non-financial reporting) (including a section on organisational integrity), accounting and → auditing, relations with shareowners and communication.

From a CSR perspective, the section on integrated sustainability reporting (→ non-financial reporting) is of particular importance. This section states that 'every company should report at least annually on the nature and extent of its social, transformation, ethical, safety, health and environmental management policies and practices'. Specific matters that require particular consideration are:

- → Health and safety practices (including → HIV/AIDS);
- Environmental governance, including use of Best Practice Environmental Option Standard;
- Social investment and black economic → empowerment;
- Human capital development and equal opportunity; and
- The development and implementation of a company code of ethics, and disclosure of adherence to that code. Whereas King I only required companies to have a code of ethics, King II requires companies to demonstrate a commitment to organisational integrity.

Compliance with certain aspects of the King Report has been made compulsory for listed companies (such as the separation of the chairperson of the board and chief executive officer positions), while compliance with other aspects such as → non-financial reporting is not compulsory. In all cases, listed companies have to report on whether they comply with the recommendations of the King Report and, if not, why not.

Daniel Malan

KYOTO PROTOCOL
→ Climate change
🖰 www.unfccc.int

The Kyoto Protocol is an international legally binding agreement between most of the world's countries created in 1997 under the United Nations Framework Convention on Climate Change (UNFCCC) to address the accumulation of greenhouse gas emissions in the atmosphere and associated → climate change through a combination of country-specific greenhouse gas emission reduction targets and → emission trading mechanisms.

The objective of this Convention is to stabilise concentrations of → greenhouse gases in the atmosphere at levels that would prevent dangerous anthropogenic (human-induced) changes to the world's climate. It is based on the recognition that the atmosphere is a shared resource, and that countries have 'common but differentiated responsibilities' to take action to address → climate change. In practice, this means that all countries have a responsibility to take action, but industrialised countries have a responsibility to take the lead, given their dominant role in creating the problem. The Convention has been ratified by most of the world's countries (including the USA and → Australia, which ratified the Convention but not the Kyoto Protocol) and entered into force in 1994.

After adoption of the Convention, at the first Conference of Parties (COP) to the convention in 1995, a second round of international negotiations was launched to agree on specific greenhouse gas emission reduction targets for countries. This was concluded at the third Conference of Parties in Kyoto, Japan, in 1997, with the adoption of the Kyoto Protocol.

The Kyoto Protocol shares the Convention's objective, principles and institutions, but goes further by committing certain countries to individual, legally binding targets to limit or reduce greenhouse gas emissions. For the first commitment period of the Kyoto Protocol (from 2008 to 2012), countries with targets are required to reduce their greenhouse gas emissions to an average of 5% below their emissions in 1990. A total of 35 industrialised countries have targets under the Kyoto Protocol, which vary from country to country depending on what was negotiated at Kyoto in 1997. Examples of targets are an 8% reduction (below 1990 levels) for most countries across → Europe, a 7% reduction for the USA, a 6% reduction for Canada and Japan and an 8% increase for → Australia.

Countries with targets are referred to as Annex I Parties, and countries that do not have targets during the first commitment period (most of the world's → developing countries) are referred to as non-Annex I countries. Encouragement to take action to reduce emission in non-Annex I countries is provided through the Kyoto Mechanisms, in particular the → Clean Development Mechanism (CDM), which allows → carbon credits generated from emissions reduction projects in non-Annex I countries to be used by Annex I countries to assist in meeting their targets.

Two additional mechanisms are also included in the Kyoto Protocol, → Joint Implementation (JI) which allows → carbon credits from specific emissions reduction projects in one Annex I country to be used in another Annex I country, and international → emission trading which allows → carbon credits from one country to be transferred to another country on national level rather than on a project basis. Through the CDM, JI and international → emission trading the Kyoto Protocol has established a new global framework and market for trading → carbon credits.

The threshold for the Kyoto Protocol to come into force (determined by the number of countries that ratified it and their emission levels) was passed in February 2005 when the Russian Federation ratified. Only countries that ratify both the Convention and the Kyoto Protocol become legally bound by the Kyoto Protocol's commitments. To date 164 countries have ratified the Kyoto Protocol. The only two countries with major economies that have not ratified the Kyoto Protocol are the USA and → Australia. The decision by the USA not to ratify the Kyoto Protocol, taken in 2001, is particularly significant, as the USA is the largest emitter of greenhouse gas emissions (accounting for approximately 25% of global emissions) and has the highest per capita emissions of any country. The decision by the USA not to ratify the Kyoto Protocol significantly reduces the overall effectiveness of the Kyoto Protocol by reducing the total projected emissions reductions that will be achieved.

The Kyoto Protocol's targets only apply until 2012, the end of the first commitment period. International negotiations of targets for the second commitment period have commenced, but many countries remain reluctant to commit to further targets, particularly without clear commitment and leadership from the USA.

Stirling Habbitts

LABELLING

→ Ethical consumption, Green marketing

Labelling is the practice of marking products and services with a distinctive label to show consumers that they conform to recognised environmental, ethical and social standards.

Labels offer information on the characteristics or impact of particular production methods, products or services and are increasingly used to help consumers make informed choices. There are a number of different types of labels. Life cycle labels are based on a → life cycle assessment (also referred to as → cradle-to-grave) of a product's environmental impact. They entail an examination of a product's life, comprising its raw material use, production, distribution, use, and disposal. This kind of labelling compares similar products within a product category and authorises producers to label the most environmentally preferable in terms of the products' whole life cycle. Well-known examples are government-sponsored programmes such as the German Blue Angel, the Nordic Swan, and the European Union Flower.

Single issue labels describe one or several specific traits in a product's life cycle, but do not provide an overall assessment of the product's whole life cycle. Examples include labels on aerosol cans reading 'CFC-free' or 'ozone-friendly', labels on tuna cans reading 'dolphin safe', labels on electrical appliances signalling energy efficiency, and various recycling symbols. Other labels signal that an independent → certification body assures that a product originates from a natural resource managed in compliance with standards set by non-governmental organisations like the → Forest Stewardship Council or the → Marine Stewardship Council.

Some → fair trade and → ethical consumption labels, such as the 'Fairtrade' mark by the FLO, guarantee consumers that farmers receive a minimum price for their products, for example coffee and cocoa beans. Other labels signal that → food products are produced in conformance with organic or sustainable agriculture standards or that they do not contain genetically modified (GM) material. A new area still under development is carbon labelling on retail products, signifying how carbon-intensive production and transportation has been. Labelling is also increasingly used to show consumers that certain services, like sustainable tourism schemes, meet recognised standards.

The award of a label usually requires third-party → auditing to provide independent → assurance that the manufacture of products conforms to the recognised standards. According to ISO, life cycle labels awarded on the basis of independent → auditing are 'Type I' labels. Third-party → auditing has been shown to generate benefits to the producer, including enhanced environmental and social awareness in the organisation and improved internal monitoring and capacity to continually enhance performance.

During the last few years there has been a significant growth in labels based on environmental claims about products or services made by their manufacturers, distributors, or providers. These self-declaratory labels are 'Type II' labels according to ISO definitions. A third type of label, called 'Type III' but not yet recognised by ISO, quantifies the environmental impact of a product according to preset categories. Unlike 'Type I' labelling schemes, this scheme does not approve or reject products, leaving it up to the consumer to make informed choices based on the information provided on the product.

While most environmental, ethical, and social labels are voluntary, meaning that producers are not required by law to use them, some labels are mandatory. Sometimes referred to as 'negative labels', these labels identify dangers to human, animal or plant life or health associated with a product's use or disposal. Other mandatory labelling requirements pertaining to the manufacture of products ('process and production methods') could be in breach of → World Trade Organisation (WTO) rules. However, the WTO generally accepts voluntary and non-discriminatory labelling, as witnessed in several dispute panel rulings in recent years.

Labelling consumer items and → food products is meant to increase consumers' choices and to motivate producers to adopt environmentally friendly, socially responsible and ethical business practices by rewarding them with a lucrative brand. Being a market-based instrument, labelling relies mainly on the moral persuasion of consumers and strategic market changes by producers and professional purchasers along the supply chain, but it also allows producers to make ethically motivated choices.

Critics claim that eco-labelling is a way to '→ greenwash' questionable practices or to justify certain product requirements and trade restrictions. Developing countries increasingly see eco-labelling as a barrier to trade and have voiced their concerns in the WTO Committee on Trade and Environment. Some labelling schemes, on the other hand, such as those for → fair trade and → ethical consumption, are beneficial to producers in → developing countries. Other schemes have taken steps to facilitate participation from → developing countries. However, challenges for most labelling schemes are to increase participation from developing country producers and to enhance consumer awareness.

Lars H. Gulbrandsen

LABOUR ISSUES

→ Diversity, ILO Declaration on Fundamental Principles and Rights at Work, ILO-OSH 2001 Guidelines on Occupational Safety and Health Management Systems, ILO Tripartite

....

> Declaration of Principles Concerning Multinational Enterprises
> and Social Policy, Labour relations, SA 8000, Supply chain

Labour is the stock of productive skills and technical knowledge held by humans and sold through the labour market. Labour and capital traditionally have been the two essential elements of the capitalist system. Labour issues essentially arise out of the tension between labour and capital, and the competing interests of different participants in the labour market.

Capitalism as described by liberal economists requires that labour is free (i.e. that workers can sell their labour for the optimum price) as anything else would be a market distortion leading to inefficient use of material capital. Therefore, any kind of forced labour (irrespective of moral concerns) is in theory damaging to the free enterprise model because it is the individual rather than the product of his or her labour that is being sold. However, forced labour in its various forms (e.g. slavery, debt bondage, servitude) remains a worldwide phenomenon, and some of the earliest attempts at ethical sourcing arose because of allegations that forced labour was being used in the manufacture of goods for global brands (e.g. Levi Strauss in 1992).

The tension between labour and capital occurs over the distribution of the surplus value resulting from the production of goods and services. Most renowned are negotiations between workers and management (as representatives of investors) about remuneration, and the allocation of surplus. Since the earliest days of capitalism, workers (including of course managers) have sought to increase their bargaining power by collective organisation. The free trade union movement with its championing of freedom of association and collective bargaining is the most well-known example of collective action, and in many respects has defined what we think of as labour issues today. For example, Australian construction workers organised to win the first eight hour working day in 1856, British unions combined to organise the 1926 General Strike in response to cuts in miners' wages and longer hours, and unions are today behind legal action against Wal-Mart for → discrimination against women.

The right to organise has long been a major labour issue, and economic → globalisation has weakened the position of trade unions in the private sector because it is now easy for capital to take advantage of the global competition for investment and employment. Alternatives and supplements to unions have emerged such as workers' committees and labour NGOs, and arbitration and legal action have become alternative to strike action in some countries. CSR can in some ways be seen as part of this alternative approach to tackling labour issues, and progress has been made in protecting some of the most fundamental rights of workers in global supply chains through codes of labour conduct and ethical sourcing. Although enforcement has been problematic, many major companies now accept the principle that excessive and compulsory overtime, workplace → discrimination and harassment, remuneration below the minimum wage or → living wage, → child labour, forced labour, and unsafe and harmful working conditions are unacceptable.

However, outside of supply chains, business credibility in relation to labour issues has been harmed by its failure until relatively recently to consider employees as stakeholders, and the range of labour issues that are still barely discussed in a CSR context. For example, labour issues that are high on workers' agendas in developed economies such as pensions, health care, security of employment, the outsourcing and off shoring of jobs, and wage stagnation often are not part of mainstream CSR. → Work–life balance has achieved some attention, but companies with strong CSR reputations have not shown to be any less likely to engage in → downsizing, labour-displacing technologies, attempts to increase working hours, or any other means of enhancing efficiency regardless of the consequences for labour.

This is not to say working conditions are worsening worldwide. Although there are many examples of neglect and abuse, workplace

→ health and safety in industries from construction to mining to → chemicals has probably improved, and more importantly it has been shown that such improvements do not undermine competitiveness. Equality in the workplace, not least for the disabled, ethnic minorities, and for women, has been embodied in law in some of the most successful economies.

Flexible labour markets – which for some is shorthand for less security and protection – have worked to the advantage of some workers, especially those with transferable and in-demand skills who feel free to pursue the best job opportunities. Increasingly, economic migration is becoming a major political issue as not only the best-educated workers shop their intellectual property on a global market, but unskilled and semi-skilled workers move from rural areas to urban ones, and from poor countries to richer ones in pursuit of better opportunities. In particular in → developing countries, urban slums, → sweatshops and smoke-bilging factories remain some of the most vivid reminders of the importance of addressing labour issues in a just society, but there are also some more subtle issues faced by the rural poor, home workers and → indigenous populations.

Mick Blowfield

LABOUR RELATIONS

→ Diversity, ILO Declaration on Fundamental Principles and Rights at Work, ILO Tripartite Declaration of Principles Concerning Multinational Enterprises and Social Policy, Labour issues, SA 8000, Supply chain

Labour relations (or industrial relations) concern the relationship between management and workers, in particular organised labour as represented by trade unions or other kinds of professional bodies.

Labour relations can be managed at company level, or at regional, national or even international levels. Typically the relations' environment is determined by national labour and employment law, and government may also control tribunals, councils, arbitration boards, and other labour-related bodies. But that environment is itself the result of concerted efforts by investor, management and worker representatives in having their interests adopted as national policy.

Although normally discussed in terms of trade union structures, collective bargaining, industrial harmony, dispute resolution, employment security and management of redundancies, labour relations also include employee participation in company management, and how management addresses the consequences for workers of → globalisation and flexible labour markets.

Mick Blowfield

LAND CONTAMINATION
→ Environmental liabilities

LATIN AMERICA
→ Forum EMPRESA

CSR is a new way of doing business, in which the company manages its operations in a sustainable way in economic, social and environmental matters, recognising the interests of its different stakeholders – such as shareholders, employees, the community, suppliers, clients – and considering the → environment and → sustainable development of future generations.

When examining CSR in Latin America and the Caribbean we have to acknowledge that the 35 countries in this region show an enormously diverse degree of socio-economic development. While available evidence on the progress in CSR in the region is mixed, a general notion is that CSR is a growing movement, but still in its infancy. Likewise, there is a need to improve the institutional capacity of governments and the investment climate, and also to adapt the CSR agenda to the specific characteristics of each country.

In general, we can say that there is a significant gap between the most developed countries of the Americas (Canada and the US) and the rest of the region. Also, a similar gap exists between the most advanced → developing countries of the region and the rest. Overall, it is possible to say that there are four different levels of CSR activity in the Americas, in declining order of activity:

- Running (Canada and US);
- Catching up (the most developed Latin American countries, such as Brazil, Argentina, Chile and Mexico);
- Walking (the rest of South America); and
- Crawling (Central America and the Caribbean).

In Latin America, CSR is still strongly associated with philanthropy, which was the initial stage of socially responsible practices. There is a long tradition of corporate philanthropy in Latin America and the Caribbean, where the private sector has had a paternalistic view of its role in society. Increasingly, however, this is being complemented by more evolved conceptions of → corporate citizenship and CSR in the region.

In this respect, three overall trends can be identified in the Americas:

- Private sector CSR activity is relatively weak, and much of the work being done to promote CSR is conducted by industry associations or independent business and professional associations (business/industry NGOs or B/INGOs);
- Government involvement and promotion of CSR is also relatively weak and not integrated at the policy level; and
- Public awareness about CSR across the region leads the other categories, with media coverage fairly widespread (especially in business reviews) in the more industrialised economies.

Many CSR courses are included in business school programming (probably reflecting the North Americanisation of business schools across the hemisphere – a phenomenon which is particularly strong in Mexico). In addition, independent NGOs working to advance the CSR agenda exist, but are less numerous and active than business friendly B/INGOs.

Hence, the reality is that the private businesses that choose to adopt and implement CSR codes are in the centre of a system of pressures, incentives, and advocacy that involves many other actors. The system of CSR promotion and advocacy is therefore a set of interactions that occur between three different 'systems': the national system (where the firm is located), the home country system (if the firm has links to foreign or multinational enterprises), and the international system.

The point that distinguishes the way the CSR system works in Latin America from developed countries is the influence of international actors. In Latin America, CSR is supported financially by external agents such as the OECD, IDB, OAS, private → foundations, international NGOs, and the home offices of multinational enterprises. It is also run through a network of local civil society organisations, government offices, academic institutions and of course private companies.

Consumer demand for good → corporate citizenship does exist, but remains weak in Latin America – in general, while consumers identify socially responsible activities as being important to their opinion of companies, in the end, brand remains the most important determinant of opinion.

Ultimately, the key weakness of the CSR system in Latin America is that it is not suited to either monitoring or promoting compliance. Recognising how CSR works in Latin America is key to understanding how to promote the adoption of CSR codes and to increase the seriousness of that commitment. Turning CSR commitments into CSR results is therefore a matter of:

- Having structured methodologies to introduce CSR in management processes;
- Promoting the adoption of CSR codes that meet 'specificity' criteria and which can be evaluated by independent third party audits;
- Strengthening watchdog agencies and truly independent NGOs capable of evaluating company compliance with CSR codes; and
- Funding research and building a common methodology for evaluating CSR effects that can be applied across sectors and countries, thus permitting the generation of aggregate and comparable data that can support policy-making in this area.

Although there are some signs of increasing CSR interest, there is still much to do in promoting real implementation and in disseminating the social and economic benefits of CSR practices. Responsible companies can make a significant difference in the social and economic development of the region.

Hugo Vergara

LEADERSHIP

In a CSR context, leadership is the conscious and sustained commitment of those with power and influence to understand and respond courageously and constructively to the world's most critical social, ecological and economic challenges. In responding to these challenges, CSR leadership incorporates a distinctive mix of knowledge, skills, vision, passion, action and impact.

Knowledge and skills

CSR leaders:

- Appreciate the global and local context in which they are operating, and the issues and drivers for change, both now and in the long term.

- Understand their organisation's impact on social and ecological systems, respect environmental limits and build human, social and natural capital.
- Steer their organisations to create and compete in evolving markets for goods and services that address sustainability challenges and provide solutions.
- Seek out the perspectives of others, with an openness to question accepted wisdom, to be challenged about their assumptions and to learn from others.
- Use their leadership skills to motivate and catalyse individual, organisational and societal change towards sustainability.

Vision and passion
CSR leaders:

- Help to craft a compelling and credible vision of the role of business in a more sustainable world.
- Support the leadership potential of others to effect transformational change towards a more sustainable world.
- Challenge and inspire others to join in mainstreaming CSR and scaling up sustainability solutions.
- Encourage open and transparent dialogue about the connection between business practice and personal → values.
- Lead by example, being consistent and willing to both 'talk the talk' and 'walk the walk' of sustainable business practices.
- Engage with opinion leaders to raise the debate to new levels and act as trailblazers of new standards of CSR and sustainability.

Action and impact
CSR leaders:

- Are aware of and accountable for the social and ecological impacts of their organisations at both local and global levels.

- Communicate the ways in which sustainability creates both short- and long-term investment opportunities and financial returns.
- Make visible and credible commitments to sustainability principles which are integrated into mainstream → corporate governance and management systems.
- Encourage innovative change within their organisations by providing adequate levels of resources and leadership support for entrepreneurial action.
- Invite collaboration and partnerships to develop and implement integrated solutions to the complex challenges of sustainability.
- Prepare bold strategies and policies that would be resilient in the face of abrupt and non-linear change and multiple future scenarios.

The emerging cadre of leaders that embody these critical competencies will be those that society will increasingly look to in order to confront and respond to the complex global dilemmas that we face. After all, the challenge of CSR and → sustainable development is one of the greatest leadership challenges of our time.

Polly Courtice

LEARNING

Learning is a lifelong process that goes beyond any individual training programme or educational initiative. In a CSR context, learning is the process by which individuals develop new competencies (skills, knowledge and capabilities) that enable them to continually deepen their understanding of the social, ecological and economic context, and to identify the most effective responses to the challenges which arise for them and their organisation.

The complexity of CSR issues – in particular in an era of → globalisation where the pace of social change is rapid, where stakeholder relationships are both local and global, and where actions have environmental, social and economic impacts – means that effective learning is a vital element in embedding good CSR practice within an organisation. Many companies, however, have experienced difficulties in addressing the CSR learning needs of their people. Learning has a low profile in many CSR management models and systems, and while published CSR reports typically include information on 'people' aspects of performance, there is often precious little information available on personal learning and its relationship to the company's objectives. This absence is partly connected to the complexity of the CSR learning process, but is also caused by the difficulty in accurately communicating what it is that people have learnt and what they are doing differently because of this learning.

Some preliminary efforts have been made to clarify the competencies that individuals require in order to effectively address CSR issues. The Sustainability Competency Framework produced by the Cambridge Programme for Industry identifies three main themes: strategy (sense-making and planning); stakeholders (managing relationships); and → leadership (creating change). The UK Government's CSR Academy has, somewhat similarly, picked on five elements: understanding society; building capacity; questioning business as usual; stakeholder relations; and harnessing → diversity.

These competency models parallel the emergence in recent years of formal training programmes on CSR issues. Many companies have developed their own in-house initiatives for senior executives, CSR specialists and staff across the organisation. Higher education insitutions have also entered the market, with the *Beyond Grey Pinstripes* report produced by the Aspen Institute and the WRI indicating that the number of business schools requiring students to take courses in CSR or related subjects has risen from a third in 2001 to just over a half in 2005. A 2003 survey by → EABIS and Nottingham Business School found that two-thirds of European schools provided some form of CSR education. These CSR programmes cover a range of topics including → business ethics, → corporate citizenship, sustainability, → corporate environmental management, governance, → globalisation and stakeholder management.

Formal training is only one of a range of possible responses that an organisation can undertake to support individuals' learning. It tends to be most effective where the training is seen as part of a broader process of personal development, and where it builds the capacity to adapt and respond to new challenges as well as building specific technical skills. Effective models of CSR learning therefore pay particular attention to supporting the learner on an ongoing basis. This can involve the use of: further courses and seminars; → e-learning and blended learning options; peer networking events and opportunities; exposure to thought leaders; and updates on CSR research and trends. It will also be critical for the success of any CSR learning initiative that its outcomes are placed at the centre of the organisation's incentive systems, performance measurement frameworks and personal development processes.

In summary, critical success factors of CSR learning include:

- Challenging worldviews;
- Triggering personal reflection;
- Creating a positive vision; and
- Inspiring action.

Mike Peirce

LEGAL COMPLIANCE

→ Corporate social responsibility, Ethics and Compliance Officer Association, Global Sullivan Principles, Regulation, Tax avoidance

Legal compliance refers to organisational behaviour which respects the letter and the spirit of the laws under whose jurisdiction the organisation falls. Legal compliance is a somewhat contested issue in CSR as many would argue that CSR is only about voluntary action. However, Archie Carroll's seminal definition of CSR includes legal responsibilities as a key component, suggesting that complying with the law – even if it is only to avoid sanctions – is a voluntary activity. The voluntary nature of compliance becomes an even more pronounced topic for CSR in situations where infringements are difficult to discover (as in some cases of pollution) or in contexts of poor governance where laws are insufficiently enforced (as with → human rights in some countries). Conspicuously, the 'US → Ethics and Compliance Officer Association' closely associates itself with compliance as a first step in developing ethical organisational practices. Legal compliance is also a CSR issue in respect of compliance with voluntary → codes of conducts and other self-regulatory instruments which – once voluntarily adopted – demand compliance as a mandatory element.

There are also specific situations where legal compliance may become a problem from a CSR perspective: when US multinationals adopted the (→ Global) Sullivan Principles as part of their CSR in the 1980s, it committed them to break compliance with the apartheid laws of South Africa as the host country of their subsidiaries. Therefore, if the legal standards of a host country are ethically inferior to the laws of the home country of a multinational corporation, CSR might actually suggest avoiding legal compliance.

Dirk Matten

LEGISLATION
→ Regulation

LICENCE TO OPERATE
Licence to operate' carries two meanings – the formal access granted by national authorities to operate within their jurisdiction and society's seal of general approval on corporate behaviour. In the realm of CSR, the term generally refers to a company's 'social licence to operate' – the acceptance, express or implied, of a corporation's impact on people, society and the → environment by their

stakeholders or the public at large. As → globalisation continues, responsible companies consider cultivating their 'licence to operate' as a prerequisite to market entry, seemingly as an international business visa.

Society grants companies' licence to operate and make profits. In turn, companies earn society's approval and trust through living up to society's expectations, in other words, practising CSR. What constitutes good CSR in this context? The answer varies from industry to industry and organisation to organisation; however, → transparency, CSR/sustainability reporting (→ non-financial reporting), consistency, and stakeholder and community engagement are vital to every company's interpretation of CSR.

Placing importance on the licence to operate improves relations with regulators, investors, consumers, and local communities. Failing to obtain local community and municipal support can lead to lengthy and costly hindrances in approvals and operations. There are strong grounds to argue that companies gain and maintain their licence to operate through a serious commitment to CSR.

Paula Ivey

LIFE CYCLE ASSESSMENT
→ Corporate environmental management

Life cycle assessment is the assessment of the environmental impact of a product in a → cradle-to-grave approach. It is also known as life cycle analysis, material flow analysis or life cycle inventory. Through life cycle analysis all the pollution from the stage of digging or harvesting raw materials to the waste that remains after using a product is taken into account. The aim is to minimise the environmental burden throughout the complete production chain rather than optimising individual production processes within that chain. Through life cycle assessment a comparison can be made of the environmental performance of products and services in order to choose the least harmful one.

Although in principle it is a powerful way of dealing with different products, its use in practice is highly complicated. Establishing, for instance, what emissions occur during the complete life cycle of a product can hardly be done without many assumptions. Next, evaluating the impacts of different emissions and material use often involves qualitative and normative judgements. Companies often do not carry out a complete life cycle assessment but look more closely at specific elements or processes. Software, for instance the widely used SIMAPRO, is available to ease the use of life cycle assessment in practice, as are guidelines like ISO 14040-43.

Theo de Bruijn

LIVING WAGE
→ Human rights, Labour issues

A living wage refers to the minimum level of remuneration a person should earn during a reasonable working week (e.g. 40 hours) so that without any additional income they can achieve an acceptable quality and quantity of housing, → food, → utilities, transport, health care, education and recreation for themselves and their dependants.

Different formulae and criteria have been developed to decide the living wage. These might, for instance, take into account the size of household, number of earners, cost of basic needs plus the need for savings and investment. In the US, some cities have established Living Wage Ordinances that determine and oversee the application of the living wage. In most cases, a living wage is significantly higher than the legally prescribed minimum wages.

What constitutes a living wage varies significantly from place to place, and cannot be divorced from the norms, needs and aspirations of a given society. For example, a living wage in a rural area may have to include the cost of running a car, not because the rural worker deserves a car, but because there is no other way poor people can get to work in areas that lack adequate public transport.

Some believe that given the variables at play, no formula can accurately determine what a living wage actually is, and that the most important determinant is a fair system of negotiation that will allow workers to bargain collectively.

Mick Blowfield

LOBBYING

Lobbying is the practice of using paid professionals (i.e. lobbyists) to influence legislation, administrative regulations, or other governmental decision-making. In western-style democracies like the United States, lobbying is a legitimate process used openly by corporations, non-profits, trade organisations and others to advance their interests. In other countries, lobbying is often covert. A good deal of controversy exists about whether lobbyists' activities are sufficiently transparent, and whether lobbyists allow special interests to exert an undue influence over government that may not be in the broader interests of all citizens.

Most corporations conduct lobbying to a greater or lesser degree. There are two emerging trends in the CSR community concerning the use of lobbying – one leaning toward abstinence, the other toward → activism. For instance, Timberland's policy states that they 'do not make contributions, directly or indirectly, to any political party or candidate, in any country, even if such contributions are legal in that country'. Conversely, Whole Foods Market takes the more common activist approach by actively lobbying for legislation that is in harmony with their → values, such as protecting our waters and the humane treatment of animals.

Whether or not a company chooses to engage in lobbying is a complex decision that may change depending upon the issue or circumstances. If a company does enter the sphere of politics – including lobbying – stakeholders expect those efforts to align with the company's stated → values and CSR goals. → Best practices for responsible lobbying and political donations revolve around → transparency.

Paula Ivey

LOCAL ECONOMIC DEVELOPMENT
→ Community development, New economics

The term local economic development (LED) theoretically distinguishes economic activity at a local level from that at national level. It is significant that the term LED has achieved prominence largely in the past three decades. Before then, although nations' prosperity was unevenly spread, there was a positive relationship between national and local economic development.

But since the 1970s – when the → globalisation of finance and trade came to dominate economic theory and practice – wealth and economic activity have increasingly concentrated in capital cities, richer countries and developed economic zones. The result is clearly marginalised areas, communities without effective demand patterns, increasingly impoverished individuals and zones apparently without development potential. Hence the perceived need for a new theory and practice to achieve economic development at the local level, since it no longer reflects national economic development.

The obvious poverty, deprivation and marginalisation of some areas even in rich nations attract the concern of CSR. Ethics and compassion apart, enlightened self-interest suggests that economic development in poor areas will enlarge the market for goods and services, increase the pool of healthy and educated employees and enrich the soil for enterprise.

CSR-initiated LED generally takes the form of funded projects designed to raise skills, productivise land, improve health, build markets and enhance physical infrastructure. CSR projects, in other words, follow the pattern of national and international LED strategies to alleviate poverty, on which literally billions of funds have been spent in the past decades.

CSR funded infrastructure apart, few projects have succeeded in diminishing poverty, let alone in creating a pattern of sustained economic development. Successes stand out for their rarity: the exceptions have proved the rule. The key reason for failure is the chronic and systemic lack of effective demand in poorer areas, which means there is no market for the fruits of economic activity. Funding projects puts cash into these areas, but they quickly flow to more prosperous markets for both labour and goods.

The reason is that the → globalisation of economic activity has the effect of a vortex rather than a centrifuge. It draws resources from poorer areas to richer, from the margins to the centre. People who live in poor areas must work outside their communities to earn money; and they tend to spend their earnings outside as well, where choice is wider and prices lower because of the economics of scale. Poor areas have been likened in that respect to a leaking bucket. The circulation of each unit of currency in a poor area is typically, according to the research, between a fifth and a tenth of that in a prosperous city.

LED programmes that show promise, therefore, incorporate the principle of preventing purchasing power leaving the area. That cannot be done without circumventing normal market forces. Three examples are:

- Where small towns and villages have become ghost towns as enterprise leaves, a local authority can deliberately use its procurement powers to create and build local enterprise, instead of buying where the price is lowest. In that way they give efficiency a longer-term perspective.
- Similarly in very poor areas local buying policies of civic society, donors and NGOs can enhance local capacity. This may include

→ food for school meals, making school uniforms and labour recruitment. It is essential that such localisation of sourcing – to keep buying power local – is prioritised over cheapness. That is counter-culture in terms of strict market-based policies.

- Local currencies may also be introduced to encourage local economic activity, activate skills and meet local needs. These require funding in the early stages. When they have taken hold they have the effect of anchoring local economic activity, especially if reinforced by the other two examples.

Margaret Legum

LONDON BENCHMARKING GROUP MODEL

→ Best practice, Reporting

⌐ www.lbg-online.net

The London Benchmarking Group (LBG) is a group of over 100 companies working together to measure corporate community investment (CCI). It is a member-driven organisation where companies have been working collectively since 1994 to:

- Continue development of a global measurement standard – the LBG Model;
- Benchmark and share → best practice;
- Develop and refine measurement tools;
- Improve management and implementation of CCI projects; and
- Better communicate CCI results to stakeholders with LBG centres.

The Model is used by hundreds of leading businesses around the world and LBG has centres in a number of key world markets including → Australia, Canada, the Czech Republic, Germany and the US. Members include multinationals such as HSBC, Vodafone and Unilever, as well as major UK companies such as Marks and Spencer and BSkyB.

The LBG model provides a comprehensive and consistent set of measures for CCI professionals to determine their company's contribution to the community, including cash, time and in-kind donations, as well as management costs. The model also captures the outputs and longer-term impacts of CCI projects on society and the business itself.

LONDON PRINCIPLES

→ Banking sector

🖰 www.cityoflondon.gov.uk

The London Principles Project, commissioned by the City of London from Forum for the Future's 'Centre for Sustainable Investment' and launched in 2002 at the Johannesburg Earth Summit, examines the role of the UK financial services sector in promoting → sustainable development. The report contains a compendium of → best practice, draws out lessons for future innovation and proposes mechanisms to ensure continual progress. With respect to the last point, one of the mechanisms explored is the following set of seven London Principles, which propose conditions under which financial market mechanisms can best promote the financing of → sustainable development:

- Provide access to finance and risk management products for investment, innovation and the most efficient use of existing assets;
- Promote → transparency and high standards of → corporate governance in themselves and in the activities being financed;
- Reflect the cost of environmental and social risks in the pricing of financial and risk management products;
- Exercise equity ownership to promote efficient and sustainable asset use and risk management;
- Provide access to finance for the development of environmentally beneficial technologies;

- Exercise equity ownership to promote high standards of → corporate social responsibility by the activities being financed; and
- Provide access to market finance and risk management products to businesses in disadvantaged communities and developing economies.

MAQUILADORAS STANDARDS OF CONDUCT
→ Latin America

The Maquiladoras Standards of Conduct were issued in 1991 by the Coalition for Justice in the Maquiladoras, a Texas-based tri-national coalition of religious, environmental, labour, Latino and women's organisations. 'Maquiladoras' are approximately 2300 foreign-owned assembly plants in Mexico employing around 650 000 workers. The maquiladoras are often owned by US companies and criticised for → sweatshop working conditions.

The Maquiladoras Standards of Conduct aim to pressure US transnational corporations to adopt socially responsible practices within the maquiladora industry, to ensure a safe environment along the US/Mexico border, safe work conditions inside the maquila plants and a fair standard of living for the industries' workers. The Standards are drawn from existing Mexican and US laws and labour standards of the ILO and the UN and focus on:

- Environmental contamination;
- → Health and safety practice;
- Fair employment practices and standards of living; and
- Community economic development and improvements in the quality of life of local communities.

The impact of the Standards beyond their effective use as a campaign tool remains difficult to assess.

Dirk Matten

MARINE STEWARDSHIP COUNCIL (MSC)

→ Food and beverage sector, Labelling

🖰 www.msc.org

The Marine Stewardship Council (MSC) is a non-governmental organisation that sets international standards for sustainable fisheries management, for accreditation of independent → certification bodies who certify fisheries to the standards, and for → labelling fish and fish products originating from certified fisheries.

The MSC was established by the World Wide Fund for Nature (WWF) and the transnational corporation Unilever, a major buyer of seafood, in 1997. Since 1999 the MSC has operated as an independent, non-profit organisation, incorporating a number of stakeholders within its global network.

The MSC has developed a set of principles and criteria for sustainable fishing, based on the Code of Conduct for Responsible Fisheries by the Food and Agriculture Organisation (FAO) of the United Nations. Fisheries around the world can apply to be independently assessed against the principles and criteria by accredited → certification bodies. The assessment process requires extensive stakeholder consultation. Fisheries that meet the principles and criteria are certified and subjected to annual → auditing of practices.

Using the MSC label requires chain-of-custody tracking, which involves tracking the origin of fish and fish products through every stage of the supply chain.

Lars H. Gulbrandsen

MARKET-BASED INSTRUMENTS

→ Carbon tax, Carbon trading, Eco-taxes, Eco-subsidies, Externalities

In a CSR context, market-based instruments are the use of fiscal measures, trading mechanisms or voluntary agreements to incentivise market behaviours that support responsible and sustainable technologies, products and services. In economic terms, market-based instruments are used to internalise the → externalities of business, i.e. to allocate the cost (or benefit) of negative (or positive) social and environmental impacts to the companies which are responsible for these effects.

The rationale of market-based instruments is that, by incorporating social and environmental costs in market prices, the market is able to work efficiently to bring about sustainable outcomes without resorting to command-and-control type government regulation. One of the best current examples of market-based instruments applied to CSR is the three flexible mechanisms under the → Kyoto Protocol to encourage reductions in greenhouse gas emissions, namely → emission trading, → Joint Implementation, and the → Clean Development Mechanism.

Wayne Visser

MARKETING ETHICS
→ Consumerism, Consumer rights, Greenwash

Marketing ethics involve conducting marketing efforts such as product development, pricing, marketing communications and promotions, sales efforts, and other marketing activities in a way that is transparent, honest, and operating in the interests of the buyers. Violations of marketing ethics occur when products or services are described dishonestly or with a high level of exaggeration of the expected outcomes for the buyer. Marketing ethics are also violated when companies fix prices or availability in an artificial way.

Philip Kotler

MEDIA SECTOR
There are several different ways of defining companies in the media sector. Two useful frames are to differentiate between

content creators vs content distributors. Companies that produce information for broadcast, digital, or print consumption would fall in the first category. The second category is a much more mixed bag as very few, if any, companies would now fit into only one of these multiple categories. While companies like Time Warner and Viacom digitise their content, → technology companies such as Google (with its YouTube acquisition) and Yahoo! have become major content providers.

Current CSR issues in the media sector include, but are not limited to:

- Social impact of content – do media companies have a responsibility to promote content that is generally accepted as more 'socially responsible'? Who dictates these standards and how are they implemented? What level of violence is acceptable for children to watch?
- Fairness and objectivity – is the information we receive as content consumers fairly reported? How is the news reported? When should content distributors take a stand on issues and how is this communicated?
- Advertising – what products are being advertised to consumers of media and how?
- Accessibility – accessibility can be interpreted on many levels. What content is accessible to children? Is digital content accessible by people with disabilities? Do people in deprived communities have the same access to information as those in more resource-rich environments?
- Cultural diversity – are all of the cultures in our society represented fairly in our media? Is there a balance with regard to race, ethnicity, sexual orientation, and socio-economic factors on television? How are these different groups portrayed?
- Freedom of expression and privacy.

- Environment – what are the environmental impacts of the business? How much paper is a magazine or newspaper publisher using? Are publishers investigating alternative sources of paper or using recycled goods? What is the environmental impact of setting up movie sets and other large, semi-permanent structures?
- Supply chain – are products manufactured for the media industry created responsibly? This is an issue beyond the social impact of content. This area of the supply chain looks at the impact of promotional items associated with industry content (movies, cable and TV shows etc.) and the relationships companies have with their suppliers and licensees.

Two current trends in the industry are convergence and user-generated media. In 2006, *Time* magazine named 'You' as person of the year. In a departure from previous years, the editors felt that the 'story about community and collaboration' is being experienced 'on a scale never seen before... It's about the many wresting power from the few and helping one another for nothing and how that will not only change the world, but also change the way the world changes.' The editors astutely observed that the 'tool that makes this possible is the World Wide Web.' As consumers of media also assume the role of media creators, the lines between corporate and personal responsibility are inextricably linked, and very blurred. Who holds the responsibility for racist, hateful content on a blog? The user who wrote and published it or the company that enabled the publishing with their software and which hosts the site?

Of course, these questions about responsibility are not new – as far back as 1999 Amazon and eBay were grappling with a precursor to the user-generated content issues we see today through a debate over 'policing' user-posted items such as Nazi memorabilia. Nonetheless, user-generated content and convergence are, today, generating so many sizable changes so rapidly that it will stretch the creativity and adaptability of every stakeholder involved in the process – in particular, the private and public sectors.

Kara Hartnett Hurst

MICROFINANCE
→ Banking sector, Community investing

Microfinance is defined as a range of financial products (loans, savings/checking accounts, insurance etc.) that focus on low income people who have generally been overlooked by traditional financial service providers. They have been neglected by or denied access to mainstream financial institutions because of perceived risk or the relatively low balances/high transaction accounts these types of customers tend to maintain.

The concept of specifically targeting low income and/or poor people with financial products tailored to their needs was largely established over the past 30 years. Initially, microfinance referred to providing very small loans (also known as microcredit) to an individual or a collective of individuals who could not afford to offer collateral for the loan, but microfinance has grown to encompass a wider range of products as the sector realised that low wealth people have needs beyond basic lack of access to credit.

Microfinance customers are typically self-employed, may live in either urban or rural areas, but due to their economic straits do not have bank accounts and/or have relied on informal financial product purveyors such as storefront currency exchanges.

In the United States, financial institutions that focus on servicing low wealth people are called Community Development Financial Institutions (CDFIs), which consist of regulated, for profit banks and credit unions, as well as non-profit financial intermediaries. In the developing world, microfinance has increasingly gained momentum through changing business models, such as that of the Bangladeshi Grameen Bank, founded by Nobel prize winning economist Mohammad Yunus.

Debbie Kobak

MICROLENDING
→ Microfinance

MILLENNIUM DEVELOPMENT GOALS (MDGs)
→ UN Millennium Development Goals (MDGs)

MINING AND MINERALS FOR SUSTAINABLE DEVELOPMENT (MMSD)
→ Mining sector
🖰 www.iied.org/mmsd

In the 1990s, the mining and minerals industry was under pressure to improve its social, developmental, and environmental performance. There were significant concerns about the social and environmental costs of mining operations, their economic impacts, and the association of mining with corrupt governments or alleged → human rights abuses.

Nine of the largest mining companies decided to carry out the Global Mining Initiative to examine a programme of internal reforms, a review of industry associations they belonged to, and a rigorous study of the societal issues they had to face. Through the World Business Council for Sustainable Development (WBCSD), they commissioned the International Institute for Environment and Development (IIED) to undertake a global, two-year process of participatory analysis to explore the role of the sector in the transition to → sustainable development. This became known as Mining and Minerals for Sustainable Development (MMSD). From April 2000 to February 2002, multiple studies were commissioned, hundreds of meetings, workshops and conferences were held, and thousands of stakeholders were consulted on all continents.

The MMSD made recommendations in the following areas:

Economic

- Ensuring efficient use of all resources;
- Internalising environmental and social costs;

Social

- Reinforcing → human rights, cultural autonomy, and personal security;

Environmental

- Responsible stewardship of natural resources;
- Protection of critical natural capital;

Governance

- Support for participatory decision-making; and
- Ensuring → transparency of information to all stakeholders.

Matt Jeschke

MINING SECTOR

Socially responsible mining refers to mining that takes into account the social, environmental and economic impacts of its activities in all phases of its operations and attempts to minimise, or mitigate, the negative consequences of those activities, while maximising the positive benefits from them in order to contribute to a process of long-term → sustainable development from mining.

Mining can potentially have a large social, environmental and economic impact in the area in which it operates. At the end of the 1990s, fuelled by a number of high profile cases, mining was criticised for its lack of responsible conduct by a variety of stakeholder groups on issues such as open pit mining, 'social diseases' (e.g. alcohol and drug use, prostitution) associated with new mining developments, the impacts of mining on → indigenous communities, and the economic impact on communities of mine closure.

The response of large mining companies and other actors from the sector was to undertake a worldwide review under the auspices of the World Business Council for Sustainable Development (WBCSD) from 2000 to 2002 called → Mining and Minerals for Sustainable Development (MMSD). Following this process, the World Bank also conducted their → Extractive Industries Review (EIR) in order to determine how mining could contribute to → sustainable development and what the role of the World Bank should be in supporting such aspirations.

The conclusion of both exercises, while not unanimous, was that mining did have a role to play in contributing to → sustainable development if certain conditions could be met. Generally, these included:

- Proactive engagement with stakeholders to ensure local concerns (social, environmental, cultural and economic) are addressed in the early planning for a mining project;
- A more integral involvement of local communities in designing and carrying out → development programmes, with a strong emphasis on developing human capital;
- A holistic approach to addressing the ecosystem impacts of mining, including how to manage → biodiversity, ecologically sensitive areas, → water quality, greenhouse gas emissions and promoting a life cycle approach to minerals production; and
- A recognition that in order to have positive impacts, mining needs to occur within a strong governance environment.

In recognition of the latter point, numerous mining companies, as well as the International Council on Mining and Metals (ICMM), have signed up to the → Extractive Industries Transparency Initiative (EITI), committing them to greater → transparency on revenue flows to government authorities.

The International Finance Corporation (IFC) has also developed social and environmental Performance Standards which are increasingly seen as the international benchmark applied to mining projects. For example, large investment banks worked with the IFC to develop the → Equator Principles which, among other things, commit supporting banks to review all investments over US$10 million according to the IFC's Performance Standards.

Another key CSR issue for the mining industry is the challenge of closing mines in an environmentally responsible way. Increasingly, this includes planning and providing financially for land rehabilitation and closure from an early stage of a mining operation.

A number of high profile legal cases under the Alien Tort Claims Act alleging mining complicity in → human rights violations by local security forces also pushed the industry to adopt the → Voluntary Principles on Security and Human Rights formulated in 2000 which attempts to ensure that → human rights risk for companies and surrounding civil populations is reduced.

Taken together, all of these initiatives have had an impact on improving the performance of the mining sector in the areas indicated, although criticisms continue, particularly regarding performance of individual companies.

Matt Jeschke

MONTREAL PROTOCOL

→ Ozone depletion
🖰 www.unep.ch/ozone

The Montreal Protocol on Substances that Deplete the Ozone Layer is viewed by many as the most successful international environmental agreement to date. Adopted in 1989 in response to recognition of the seriousness of ozone depletion and its implications for human, plant and animal health, it has since been revised and strengthened a number of times.

The treaty covers the reduction in production and use of a number of ozone-depleting substances, in particular chlorofluorocarbons (CFCs), which are used in foam extrusion, cleaning, refrigeration and fumigation. A multilateral fund provides support for → developing countries to help them comply with the treaty.

Problems with the Protocol include the smuggling of CFCs back into signatory nations, and the discovery that hydrochlorofluorocarbons and hydrofluorocarbons (HCFCs and HFCs) used to replace CFCs, are powerful → greenhouse gases. However, overall it has been successful, with a levelling off of CFC concentrations in the atmosphere, and it is viewed as an encouraging indicator that, with support from corporations, multilateral environmental agreements can be effective.

Ruth Findlay-Brooks

MORAL CASE
→ Business case, Moral responsibilities, Values

The moral case for CSR or → sustainable development prescribes action by drawing directly on fundamental → values and methods of moral reasoning. The moral case applying to a business, an NGO, a government, or a particular person, will vary according to their roles. A civil servant has different → moral responsibilities from an NGO activist. Nevertheless, certain fundamental principles apply to them all.

The moral case treats these principles and → values as intrinsic − as opposed to instrumental − → values. Instrumental approaches are concerned to promote certain consequences. In this view, if an action is not likely to be effective, there is no moral case for it. If an individual's motivation for cutting CO_2 emissions is only dependent on collective action, then the expectation that collective action is unlikely to happen will automatically result in the individual's lack of action. In contrast, an intrinsic view of → values is concerned with honouring those → values even if they may not be fully realised by everyone. If protecting the planet has intrinsic value for an individual, s/he will cut emissions regardless of what everybody else is doing. Paradoxically, an intrinsic moral case may actually be more effective in the long run, because it may inspire others to act while also drawing on a sustaining and deep source of motivation.

The term 'moral case' was coined to parallel the '→ business case', which it either complements, or challenges. In complementing a particular → business case, the moral case may provide a deeper source of motivation and a higher level of awareness. For example, while an ordinary → business case concerned with the bottom line is enough to prescribe → eco-efficiency measures, a moral case for the same measures – rooted in a religious, spiritual or philosophical imperative to protect the earth – is likely to be more motivating for employees and may help them identify entirely new areas of possible action. Sometimes, however, the moral case will prescribe options different from ordinary business reasoning. Using an overseas supplier whose labour practices violate international standards, even though they may meet the supplier's domestic regulations, could be challenged on a moral case, while its status on the → business case would depend on whether the firm's brand or its employees' morale would be harmed by this or not. Here, the moral case challenges the conclusions of the → business case in determining what should be done.

Two major debates have arisen about the moral case. First, is it possible for businesses, in particular, to pursue a moral case; and second, if possible, is it right for them to do so? Critics addressing the first question would argue that corporations are more like soulless machines, or even 'psychopaths' (as the film *The Corporation* puts it), than like moral agents. They are simply automats for using assets to generate profit. But corporations consist of human beings and are represented by people who are moral agents, and they, like other human beings, are concerned with their reputation and their relationships. Corporations, like people, may have mixed motives for engaging with ethics and morality. But this does not prove that they are not capable of doing so at all.

Addressing the second question, even if businesses are capable of pursuing the moral case, is it right for them to do so? Opponents of the moral case say that 'the [only] social responsibility of business is to increase its profits' (Milton Friedman, article of that name, *New York Times*, 13 September 1970); business should obey the law and not try to pursue any further moral obligations. But this view collapses at both extremes. On the one hand, the best way to increase profits might be to break the law and pay the penalty for doing so, if the rewards are rich enough. This example shows that the moral case does not presuppose voluntary in place of legally required action, as some critics contend. Obeying the law when one could afford to flout it, and doing so wholeheartedly rather than tactically and evasively, is itself a moral choice. On the other hand, it is hard to argue that business should obey a law mandating forced labour. Law, the product of an always imperfect political process, may go too far in the direction of immorality, or not far enough or fast enough to enjoin what morality or sustainability require. Thus even in a society well governed by law, there will be a place for the moral case.

Melissa Lane

MORAL RESPONSIBILITIES
→ Business case, Business ethics, Moral case, Values

Moral responsibilities are a subcategory of responsibilities. They refer to responsibilities that arise from considerations of moral relationships rather than legal obligations set and enforced by the state. Moral responsibilities (or ethical responsibilities, as Carroll would say) would have us go beyond the letter of the law in our conduct out of concern for others. Thus, there are no penal consequences for failing to meet moral responsibilities, only the risk of having our esteem lowered in the eyes of others and of having to think less of ourselves.

Moral responsibilities arise only out of relationships with others. They are the building blocks of community, keeping individuals within expected actions and aspirations felt to be beneficial to that community. And, more responsibilities are defined by cultural and social codes that vary with cultures, religions, and family patterns. Moral relationships constitute patterns of established conduct with respect to the dignity and status of others. They also imply self-restraint and self-control as selfishness and indulgence are placed under constraint out of regard for others.

Moral responsibilities exist where we are held accountable for our actions according to some social standard. We are expected to think reasonably about that standard and apply it to our actions. In being morally responsible we make ourselves more trustworthy and reliable, attracting thereby the support and goodwill of others to our endeavours.

Stephen B. Young

NATIONAL CORPORATE RESPONSIBILITY INDEX

→ Responsible competitiveness

⌐ www.accountability21.net

The National Corporate Responsibility Index (NCRI) assesses the degree of CSR activities in different nations worldwide. The index assesses over 80 countries on criteria including → corruption, civic freedom, → corporate governance and environmental management to establish a global ranking. The 2005 NCRI suggested the following results:

- Nordic countries score well alongside Canada, Austria and Belgium.

- South Africa is the highest ranking emerging economy (excluding Eastern Europe), followed closely by Korea, Chile, Malaysia, Costa Rica and Thailand.
- Eastern Europe seems to be pursuing a sustainable path. Estonia and Slovenia in particular are well ranked.
- There were some good performers in → Africa including South Africa and Mauritius, but other countries like Zimbabwe and Algeria are among the lowest scoring overall.
- In → Latin America the positive examples are Chile and Costa Rica. → Latin America scores poorly on the internal dimension of corporate responsibility.

The NCRI is published by the NGO/think-tank AccountAbility and has so far been conducted on a bi-annual basis.

NATURAL CAPITALISM
→ Five Capitals Framework

Natural capitalism is a sustainability framework that describes how to do business more profitably in ways that protect the → environment and enhance human and natural capital. Described in *Natural Capitalism: Creating the Next Industrial Revolution*, by Paul Hawken, Amory Lovins and L. Hunter Lovins, it has three principles:

- Buy time using radical resource efficiency – radically increase the productivity with which all resources are used. The growing number of profitable efficiency solutions to environmental challenges can buy the time needed to implement measures that will attain true sustainability.
- Redesign each product and process in society using nature's wisdom – such innovative design processes as biomimicry and other forms of green design enable businesses to drive innovation and eliminate → waste and toxics while delivering superior products and services.
- Manage systems and institutions for prosperity and sustainability – employ the emerging practice of sustainable management

to restore, enhance and sustain the natural and human capital needed for continuing financial prosperity. Effective sustainable management enables companies and communities to enhance core business value and reinforce → competitive advantage by treating people fairly and protecting the → environment.

Such organisations as Natural Capitalism Solutions use the approach to help companies and communities identify opportunities to enhance well-being, cut operating costs and generate opportunities for market leadership.

L. Hunter Lovins

NATURAL STEP FRAMEWORK
→ Sustainability
🖰 www.naturalstep.org

Founded by Karl-Henrik Robèrt, a cancer researcher and physician, The Natural Step (TNS) is a strategic framework to describe sustainability based on scientific fundamentals. TNS has four sustainability 'systems conditions':

- Substances from the earth's crust must not systematically increase in nature – this is because these substances (e.g. heavy metals) in sufficient concentrations are harmful to organic life. And since everything disperses and nothing disappears, sooner or later harmful concentrations will be reached if substances are mined more quickly than they can break down in nature.

- Substances produced by society must not systematically increase in nature – this is because, once again, these substances (e.g. persistent → chemicals) in sufficient concentrations are harmful to organic life. In many cases, nature cannot break these substances down into harmless components; or it cannot do this faster than they are being produced.

- The physical basis for the productivity and diversity of nature must not be systematically degraded – this is because life is sustained by a complex web of interdependent species and ecosystems which provide a wide array of 'free ecological services' (e.g. → water purification, weather regulation and → waste assimilation). Most of these services are either too complex or too expensive to replicate.
- We must be efficient enough to meet basic human needs – this is because humans are part of the → environment and a key aspect of sustainability. Resource inefficiency, including inequities in resource distribution, not only obstructs a social system from becoming sustainable but also tends to compromise other systems.

Today, The Natural Step has more than 70 people in 11 countries working with an international network of sustainability experts, scientists, universities and businesses to create solutions, innovative models and tools that will lead the transition to a sustainable future.

Wayne Visser

NEW ECONOMICS
→ Ecological economics

New economics comprises an as yet disparate body of thought about an alternative political economy, based on an ethical intention to create an equitable, humane and sustainable dispensation. It claims that neither capitalism nor communism as previously conceived and practised have succeeded in these aims. New economics cannot yet be closely defined, but its proponents offer a paradigm that includes some or all of the following:

- Independent livelihoods predominating over large-scale employment; local production for local consumption replacing the global emphasis; sustainable organic food production for more self-sufficient communities of varying sizes.

- Replacement of the current monetary system, in which new money is created through commercial banks making loans, by one in which central banks give the required new money to governments to spend into the economy without debt.

- A taxation system that collects, for public revenue, the value of assets such as land, which is created by society as a whole and is a non-renewable or limited resource. Thus tax would be levied on the extra value to property created by new public → infrastructure like roads, or on extra value deriving from discovery of useful minerals.

- Replacement of all taxes based on value added by levies on value subtracted, such as pollution, toxic emissions and despoiling of land, → water or air.

- Local or regional currencies that tend to localise production and consumption, used in conjunction with time banks and community banks.

- A citizens' income given to all citizens as of right throughout their lives to enable them to live at a basic level of decency. This is a distributive mechanism made necessary by the fact that modern → technology inevitably creates jobless growth; thus employment must give way to independent livelihoods as a means of getting income.

- Other related concepts, including well-being, new sustainability indices, social auditing and ethical trading.

New economics will probably be accurately defined only with some degree of hindsight: it is a movement in progress.

Margaret Legum

NON-FINANCIAL ASSURANCE
→ Auditing, Report verification

NON-FINANCIAL REPORTING

→ Greenwash, Public affairs, Report verification

Non-financial reporting is a generic term used to describe various types of external reporting by organisations to their stakeholders, covering aspects of the organisation's performance other than historical financial performance.

This usually means reporting environmental, social and/or economic performance in a printed report (either a separate report or integrated into an annual (financial) report) or through web-based reporting or a combination of these. Corporate non-financial reports are the most common type of report but some companies report at country and/or site level and this type of reporting by public sector and NGOs also appears to be on the increase.

The content of non-financial reporting and reports varies considerably. A report may cover all aspects of non-financial performance or be limited to specific topics. The title of the report generally reflects its content (scope):

- Sustainability report
- Corporate (social) responsibility report
- Environmental report
- Social report
- Triple bottom line report
- Corporate citizenship report
- Health, safety and environment report
- Community report

Non-financial reporting has undergone a rapid development process since 1990. In the early years reporting was largely dominated by environmental concerns. However, the trend toward sustainable business practice, against a backdrop of → corporate governance scandals over the last few years, has increased company awareness of the need to be accountable to a wider audience for all aspects of performance. While quantitative performance results are still more often reported for environmental, → health and safety issues, the extension of reporting on, for example, economic issues, labour standards, working conditions, → human rights, community investment and philanthropy reflects this change.

In addition to the rising strategic importance of corporate responsibility and non-financial performance at board level, increasing standardisation and new regulations, not least in the field of → corporate governance, are now also influencing non-financial reporting. Although separate reports are still the most common way for organisations to report their non-financial performance, they are increasingly integrating non-financial reporting with financial reporting to provide all stakeholders with a comprehensive picture of overall performance. New legislation such as the EU Accounts Modernisation Directive, requiring the incorporation of non-financial performance indicators (social and environmental) in the annual financial review, may push companies further in this direction.

As corporate responsibility increasingly becomes integrated into core business → values and strategy, the reporting of non-financial performance is starting to move away from the blanket reporting of as many quantitative indicators as possible (compliance-related disclosure which leads to information overload) to the reporting of information that is relevant and material to the organisation's key stakeholders and decision-makers. Stakeholder dialogue is playing a role in this transition and is encouraging the reporting of CSR dilemmas and future challenges and plans to deal with these alongside historical performance data. The value of non-financial reporting should therefore be considered from two perspectives: that of management and that of the users of the information – the external or internal stakeholders. Reporting is an important medium for companies to communicate their responsibility to their stakeholders, thereby improving → transparency and public trust. To do so effectively means recognising and understanding the information needs of the target audience based on stakeholder analysis and consultation. In addition, when it is properly structured, non-financial reporting can be used as an internal → learning process to improve internal business value and good management practices.

Although there is no formal reporting standard for non-financial reporting, the Sustainability Reporting Guidelines of the GRI, together with the supporting range of technical and sector protocols, is now well established as a basis for this type of reporting by all types of organisations. The guidelines are designed to fulfil the need for consistency and comparability of reporting on non-financial performance which is essential to stakeholder decision-making. The financial community in particular is taking a greater interest in how companies are managing their non-financial risks, especially where these may have short- or medium-term financial consequences. Companies are increasingly being asked to report on non-financial performance in a standardised manner by identifying and prioritising key challenges, and to report this, where relevant, as part of the annual (financial) report.

One other difference between financial and non-financial reporting is verification, i.e. confirming the reliability of the reported information on non-financial performance. This is still voluntary and not standardised as it is for the → auditing of annual financial accounts, although standards are emerging (e.g. → ISAE 3000 and AA 1000 AS). A range of organisations from accountants to consultants and → certification bodies currently offer this type of → assurance.

Jennifer Iansen-Rogers and George Molenkamp

NON-GOVERNMENTAL ORGANISATIONS (NGOs)

→ Stakeholders

NGOs include a whole plethora of pressure groups, civil society organisations, charities, religious groups and other actors that are neither business nor government organisations, but which are involved in the promotion of certain interests, causes and/or goals. NGOs can be described as having five characteristics:

- They are organisations.
- They are private, in that they operate outside the boundaries of the state.
- They do not distribute profits to their members, and therefore are different from a typical private business organisation.
- They are self-governing.
- They are voluntary.

NGOs are known by many names – civil society, private voluntary organisations (PVOs), non-profits, third sector, charitable, voluntary, or independent sector, grassroots organisations (GROs), community-based organisations (CBOs), civil society organisations (CSOs), international NGOs (INGOs), business/industry driven NGOs (BINGOs), northern NGOs (NNGOs), southern NGO (SNGO), government organized NGO (GONGO), and government run and inspired NGOs (GRINGOs).

A harbinger of NGO strength is growth. According to a 1995 report by the Commission on Global Governance 176 international NGOs existed in 1909. That number grew to about 800 in 1930, over 2000 in 1960, and nearly 4000 in 1980, according to John Boli and George Thomas in 1999's *Constructing World Culture*. By 1993, that number had grown to 28 900 and by 2004 to 51 509 (Union of International Associations, *Yearbook of International Organisations*, 2004).

Spikes in growth occurred, respectively, after the end of WWI, WWII, and the cold war. The opening up of societies after conflicts that were won by democratic forces contributed greatly to global NGO growth, dubbed by some as a 'global associational revolution'.

NGOs work on every broad scope of issues, such as religion, environment, → human rights, women, population, labour, aging, children, cultural, educational, → volunteering, economic development, health, hospitals, humanitarian relief, professional development, social service, social well-being, disarmament and peace – just to name a few.

NGOs are different from government and business in their very reason to be. Their purpose is not to carry out a social contract, as with government. It is not to manufacture products or services for profit. Rather, the purpose of NGOs is to achieve certain social, ethical or political goals.

They are also a powerful presence on the global scene. NGOs dictate agendas, raise awareness of important issues, move citizens, governments, and businesses to act in ways they would not have if it were not for the mobilisation of concerned citizens and the articulation of concerted messages advocating distinct strategies.

In the post-cold war context, a dramatic global expansion of markets and an increase in foreign direct investment and capital flows have taken place. At the same time a decline in governmental investment in the form of overseas development assistance has also occurred. The rise and spread of the internet has democratised and spawned the worldwide decentralisation of information, levelling the playing field for NGOs, who tend to wield information on the issues of the day more effectively than governments. The growth and impact of NGOs has paralleled that of business. While NGOs, business and the flow of capital and information have become global, governments have remained national, losing ground as a result.

NGOs are prominent at the international, regional, national, local, and community-based levels. They are, as it were, in the streets and in the boardrooms. They are driven by paid professionals and unpaid volunteers.

While global NGO activity existed before the past century and the prominence of the post-cold war era in particular, as with religious movements for example, the current global movement of empowered citizens making a difference tends not to be top down and centralized. Rather, it tends to emanate from individuals, the grassroots (or grasstops, as NGO leaders sometimes are referred to) at the local level, and is diffuse.

What is behind the NGO movement and all of its diversity? In a word, → values. The movement has a moral underpinning based in the 'solidarity and compassion for the fate and well-being of others, including unknown, distant others: a sense of personal responsibility and reliance on one's own initiative to do the right thing; the impulse toward altruistic giving and sharing; the refusal of inequality, violence, and oppression', as cited in the 1994 book *Citizens Strengthening Global Civil Society.*

NGOs currently face major challenges with regard to their → accountability and → transparency. In most cases, there is only a rather vague 'mandate' from those constituencies whose interests NGOs claim to represent. Like corporations, NGOs increasingly think about their → accountability to their stakeholders and, certainly the larger ones, are developing mechanisms and tools to enhance → accountability and → transparency towards their larger constituents in civil society.

Jonathan Cohen

NORTH AMERICA
→ Business for Social Responsibility (BSR)

In the aftermath of World War II, a group of companies in the American state of Minnesota, including Honeywell, 3M, Dayton-Hudson Corp., agreed to dedicate a percentage of their profits to community investments. This initiative is widely considered to constitute the birth of CSR in the sense of good citizenship in North America. Over the past 25 years, North American companies have steadily moved away from CSR as philanthropy to a more holistic definition that addresses the full range of a company's social, environmental and governance impacts. Indeed, CSR in North America has moved through four distinct phases since its emergence in the late 1940s.

- Beginning in the 1950s, some American companies sought explicitly to integrate their workforces, signalling business engagement in the desegregation and civil rights movements that culminated in fair employment and voting rights legislation in the 1960s. Companies such as Levi Strauss & Co. played a significant role in demonstrating the possibility of integrating workforces in the southern United States, where such practices were then widely rejected.
- The first major shift began in the late 1960s, when rising opposition to American involvement in the Vietnam War elicited calls to protest companies involved in supplying arms and → chemicals used in that conflict. Out of that movement grew the first stirrings of shareholder activism, as socially minded investors called for disinvestment in companies involved in the war effort. This development is viewed by many as the birth of socially responsible investment (SRI). In the mid-1980s, opposition to the apartheid regime in South Africa revived such efforts, which shifted attention to massive divestment campaigns, especially on university campuses.
- These developments also gave rise to the first generation of business standards on social issues developed by growing civil society. The Sullivan Principles were established in 1977 to provide a framework for companies choosing to continue doing business in South Africa during the apartheid era, following on the MacBride Principles for companies engaging in business in Northern Ireland during the civil conflict there.
- In the late 1980s and early 1990s, a new generation of business leaders founded new companies designed to operate in a more sustainable manner. Companies such as Stonyfield Farms, Ben & Jerry's, and Patagonia sought to place CSR at the very centre of

their practices, which included caps on executive compensation, rejection of toxic materials, and embraced consumer education on these matters.

- In the mid- to late 1990s, ideas of environmental sustainability moved into the mainstream of American business. Motivated both by business opportunities and growing concerns about → globalisation, companies ranging from Ford Motor Co. to Nike to General Electric came to embrace sustainability as the modern CSR movement accelerated.

CSR in this current stage of its development is characterised by senior management attention, board governance, and increasing efforts to measure outputs and impacts. While North American CSR in its first stages reflected truly American concerns and social developments, the more modern understanding of CSR generally reflects global questions.

American multinationals embracing CSR address the same fundamental questions considered by multinationals elsewhere. Such companies have steadily developed business principles, → human rights policies and practices, approaches to → climate change, and systems for engaging with an ever more diverse set of stakeholders. The number of CSR reports emanating from American companies, while once lagging behind European and Japanese counterparts, is now increasing quickly.

In the middle of the first decade of the 21st century, American companies are increasingly considering how they can integrate CSR into core business functions ranging from product development to marketing to procurement. Like companies elsewhere in the world, American companies are seeking to come to grips with potentially significant resource costs and scarcity, particularly on resources such as → water and carbon. Companies in the United States will in particular face an increasing need to address the country's disproportionately high energy use if global warming continues to advance. American companies have also, in the view of many, faced particular challenges as general favourability ratings for American institutions have declined in recent years.

CSR in the United States will undoubtedly continue to evolve, and be marked by the yet unforeseen social and technological innovations that have marked its history since it was born a half-century ago.

Aron Cramer

NORTH–SOUTH DIVIDE

→ Developing countries, Development

The north–south divide is often used as 'shorthand' for the gap in income, wealth, → development prospects and political power that exists between so-called developed, high income countries and developing, low income countries and/or regions. While not always geographically accurate, in the sense that there are wealthy countries in the southern hemisphere and low income countries in the northern hemisphere, the majority of the world's wealthiest and most powerful countries are in the north and vice versa for the world's poorest.

In today's globalising economy, however, this relatively simple distinction is increasingly challenged, not only by geographic anomalies, but also by the fact that a number of previously low income, → developing countries are rapidly becoming economic, political and military 'powerhouses' with large and growing middle classes – the emerging geo-strategic and economic importance of China and India being obvious examples. At the same time, others are transitioning to middle income status creating a growing 'south–south divide', especially between → Africa and the rest. Equally, growing inequality between resource-rich and resource-poor regions within both developed and → developing countries is creating a more complex set of economic and political

divisions – America's own north–south divide being vividly illustrated, for example, in the aftermath of Hurricane Katrina.

Jane Nelson

NOT IN MY BACK YARD (NIMBY)

NIMBY is an acronym for 'Not in my back yard', and is a term
used to describe people who oppose a development locally even
when they agree to the need for such development in general.
The term first came to prominence in the United States during the
late 1970s in the wake of the mounting frictions between organised
communities on the one hand and the consequences of rapid growth
and suburban sprawl on the other.

Typical examples of developments opposed by NIMBYs include
affordable housing, land refill sites, superstores, chemical plants or
prisons. While NIMBYs justify their stance by arguing for the
need to protect the local environment and local communities, their
arguments are often perceived in terms of social versus private
costs/risks and benefits, or the friction between individual rights
and social responsibility. The ethics of NIMBYs are also often
called into question as a NIMBY community may well directly
benefit from developments whose costs or disadvantages they wish
to externalise by locating them somewhere else.

Often accompanying criticisms of the concept of NIMBYs
(and 'NIMBYism') are accusations of elitism, parochialism or a
'drawbridge mentality'. That is, those well-organised communities
that are homogeneous and/or successfully act under the cover of
environmental reasons to protect their communities against the
perceived dangers of increased diversity.

Nick Tolhurst

OCCUPATIONAL HEALTH AND SAFETY (OHS)

→ Health and safety

OECD CONVENTION ON COMBATING BRIBERY OF FOREIGN PUBLIC OFFICIALS IN INTERNATIONAL BUSINESS TRANSACTIONS

→ Corruption, Fraud

⌖ www.oecd.org

The OECD Convention on Combating Bribery of Foreign Public Officials in International Business Transactions is an internationalinstrument in the fight against the bribery of foreign public officials. The Convention has been ratified by all 30 OECD countries as well as six non–OECD countries (Argentina, Brazil, Bulgaria, Chile, Estonia and Slovenia). In these countries it is a crime to bribe a foreign public official. The Convention defines the bribery of foreign public officials as 'the voluntary giving (promising or offering) of something of value to a foreign public official in order to obtain or retain business or other improper advantage in the conduct of international business'.

Petrus Marais and Daniel Malan

OECD GUIDELINES FOR MULTINATIONAL ENTERPRISES

⌖ www.oecd.org

The OECD Guidelines for Multinational Enterprises constitute a set of voluntary recommendations to multinationals in all the major areas of → business ethics, including employment and industrial relations, → human rights, environment, information disclosure, combating bribery, consumer interests, science and → technology, competition, and taxation. Adhering governments have committed to promote them among multinationals operating in or from their territories. The distinctive implementation mechanisms include National Contact Points (NCP), which are government offices charged with promoting the Guidelines and handling enquiries in the national context. In addition, the

Guidelines are complemented by commentaries which provide information and explanations of the Guidelines text and implementation procedures. Adhering countries comprise all 30 OECD member countries, and nine non-member countries (Argentina, Brazil, Chile, Estonia, Israel, Latvia, Lithuania, Romania and Slovenia).

OECD PRINCIPLES OF CORPORATE GOVERNANCE

→ Corporate governance

↗ www.oecd.org

The Organisation for Economic Cooperation and Development (OECD) describes itself as a 'unique forum where the governments of 30 market democracies work together to address the economic, social and governance challenges of → globalisation as well as to exploit its opportunities'.

The OECD Principles of Corporate Governance were endorsed by OECD Ministers in 1999 and revised in 2004. They aim to advance the → corporate governance agenda and to provide specific guidance for legislative and regulatory initiatives in both OECD and non-OECD countries. There are six principles which describe that an effective → corporate governance framework should:

- Promote transparent and efficient markets, be consistent with the rule of law and clearly articulate the division of responsibilities among different supervisory, regulatory and enforcement authorities;
- Protect and facilitate the exercise of shareholders' rights;
- Ensure the equitable treatment of all shareholders, including minority and foreign shareholders. All shareholders should have the opportunity to obtain effective redress for violation of their rights;
- Recognise the rights of stakeholders established by law or through mutual agreements and encourage active cooperation between

corporations and stakeholders in creating wealth, jobs, and the sustainability of financially sound enterprises;

- Ensure that timely and accurate disclosure is made on all material matters regarding the corporation, including the financial situation, performance, ownership, and governance of the company; and
- Ensure the strategic guidance of the company, the effective monitoring of management by the board, and the board's → accountability to the company and the shareholders.

Daniel Malan

OFF-SHORING
→ Labour issues, Supply chain

Off shoring is defined as the movement of a business process previously undertaken by a company in one country to another, different country – either by itself or through associated business. The main motivation for such relocation is to reap the benefit of the lower costs of operations in the new country. Off-shoring is sometimes contrasted with outsourcing. Outsourcing is primarily the movement of internal business processes to an external company either abroad or domestically.

The main arguments in favour of off-shoring are that the process is another means of comparative advantage at play. That is, this process allows production or economic activity to be undertaken in areas where it is most efficient. Allied to this is the fact that the recipient country can utilise off-shoring to build up its industrial base and benefit from knowledge and educational transfer. In recent years, however, there has been increased debate about the disadvantages of such activity particularly with regard to supply chains. By off-shoring whole productive processes to low cost areas companies have sometimes been able to reap the benefits, not just of lower costs, but, also of far lower standards such as labour and human rights or environmental regulations. This has particularly been the case where operations are further distanced from the mother company through various levels of supply chains.

Nick Tolhurst

OHSAS 18001 STANDARD ON OCCUPATIONAL HEALTH AND SAFETY
→ Health and safety
🖰 www.bsi-global.com

Many organisations are implementing an Occupational Health and Safety Management System (OHSMS) as part of their risk management strategy to address changing legislation and protect their workforce.

An OHSMS promotes a safe and healthy working environment by providing a framework that allows an organisation to consistently identify and control its → health and safety risks, reduce the potential for accidents, aid legislative compliance and improve overall performance.

OHSAS 18001 is the internationally recognised assessment specification for occupational → health and safety management systems. It was developed by a selection of leading trade bodies, international standards and → certification bodies to address a gap where no third party certifiable international standard exists.

OHSAS 18001 has been designed to be compatible with → ISO 9001 and → ISO 14001, to help an organisation meet their → health and safety obligations in an efficient manner.

The following key areas are addressed by OHSAS 18001:

- Planning for hazard identification, risk assessment and risk control;
- OHSAS management programme;
- Structure and responsibility;
- Training, awareness and competence;

- Consultation and communication;
- Operational control;
- Emergency preparedness and response; and
- Performance measuring, monitoring and improvement.

OHSAS 18001 can be adopted by any organisation wishing to implement a formal procedure to reduce the risks associated with → health and safety in the working environment for employees, customers and the general public.

Deborah Leipziger

OIL AND GAS SECTOR
→ Responsible Care Programme

The oil and gas industry, comprising between 5 and 10% of the global stock market and including some of the world's biggest companies, is deeply embedded in our lives − most of us drive cars, benefit from oil fuelled machines and use plastic every-day. However, CSR in the oil and gas industry tends to be a somewhat polarised debate, with companies claiming that they conduct themselves responsibly and governments often courting their investments and tax revenues, while NGO activists remain highly critical and some ethical funds exclude the whole sector from their portfolios.

Among the critics, oil is frequently vilified for causing pollution, including CO_2 emissions and associated → climate change effects, while the social benefits of the product (from fuelling mobility to the ingredients of Disprin) and the economic contribution of the sector (through investment, taxes, jobs and philanthropy), often areas of high poverty, are seldom acknowledged. Many social and environmental risks are associated with the production process, including oil tanker spills or on-the-ground gas flaring practices. Relations with communities surrounding oil and gas operations are also especially challenging, as are disparities in the flow of economic benefits, accusations of exacerbating → corruption (the so-called 'resource curse'), associating with authoritarian regimes (e.g. Burma) and land claims of → indigenous peoples' organisations.

In response, many oil and gas companies are:

- Continuing their commitment to the principles and practices of the sector-led Responsible Care programme;
- Making efforts to develop new, cleaner products, including low pollution fuels and renewable energy technologies (e.g. Global Climate and Energy Project);
- Engaging with → conservation NGOs to enable the protection of → biodiversity (e.g. Energy & Biodiversity Initiative); and
- Moving towards transparent disclosure of oil revenues, especially payments to government in taxes and political donations (e.g. the → Extractive Industries Transparency Initiative, the NGO-led Publish What You Pay campaign).

Oil and gas is one of the closely monitored industries in the ethical field. Given its significant social and environmental impacts (positive and negative), it is likely to remain in the CSR spotlight, especially among NGO activists, the media, and increasingly financial investors. The sector is in the position of being at the heart of society's most pressing global challenges (like → climate change and poverty) and also potentially being a profound source of solutions.

Antoine Mach

OPERATING AND FINANCIAL REVIEW (OFR)

→ Corporate governance, Reporting, Social and environmental accounting

The basic aim of an Operating and Financial Review (OFR), which UK businesses have been encouraged to voluntarily produce since the early 1990s, is to provide a framework within which directors can discuss the main factors influencing the company's current and future financial performance and position. One outcome of the company law review process undertaken by the Blair government soon after assuming office was a recommendation that publication of an OFR should become mandatory, and that it might provide a suitable vehicle for the disclosure of social and environmental information. These recommendations were supported by the government, and after a prolonged consultation process enacted into legislation to be applied to all quoted companies in March 2005.

As far as social and environmental disclosure is concerned, companies were to be required to provide information on policies and performance relating to environmental matters, employees and social and community issues 'to the extent necessary' for shareholders to evaluate past performance and future prospects of the company. An Accounting Standard issued by the UK Accounting Standards Board in May 2005 provided guidance on disclosure issues, including the specification of possible key performance indicators (KPIs). Somewhat surprisingly, in view of the extended consultation process undertaken, Chancellor Gordon Brown, in a speech to the CBI in November 2005, announced the abolition of the mandatory OFR requirement as part of a drive to reduce the regulatory burden on business. Further consultation resulted in a requirement to produce a slimmed down version of the OFR in the form of a business review having no statutory disclosure requirements.

David Owen

ORGANIC FOOD
→ Food and beverage sector, International Organic Accreditation Service (IOAS)

ORGANISATIONAL CULTURE
→ Corporate culture

OZONE DEPLETION
→ Montreal Protocol

The ozone layer in the stratosphere is a delicate but vital component of the earth's atmosphere. Comprised of one of the rarest of the atmospheric gases, it absorbs ultraviolet radiation, protecting plants, animals and humans from its harmful effects. Concentrations of ozone vary through the seasons and around the planet, normally being most dense at the poles.

In the 1970s scientists realised that chlorofluorocarbons (CFCs), then common in aerosols, refrigeration and the production of foam, were destroying atmospheric ozone. The seriousness of ozone depletion was realised in the 1980s, with the discovery that the particular wind and light patterns over Antarctica were causing a vast 'hole' in the ozone layer each spring, in addition to the more general degradation of the ozone layer elsewhere.

The resulting increase in UV-B radiation reaching the earth's surface is likely to result in an increase in skin cancers, weakening of immune systems, damage to plant growth, and a decrease in plankton which form the base of the → food chain and help to reduce levels of carbon dioxide.

The → Montreal Protocol has helped to limit the production of CFCs, but the persistence of chlorine atoms in the stratosphere and existing CFCs still to be released mean that they are likely to continue depleting the ozone layer for decades to come.

Ruth Findlay-Brooks

PARTNERSHIPS
'The state of being a partner' is how the *Cambridge Dictionary* defines 'partnership', where 'partner' is defined as 'a person you are closely involved with in some way'. The dictionary also notes that a partner can be 'one of the owners of a company', and traditionally in the

context of organisations, 'partnership' describes a particular form of incorporation involving shared ownership and liability.

Since the late 1980s the term partnership has become more widely used in describing both relations between organisations (often from different sectors) and new forms of organisation beyond the traditional business partnership model. Therefore a useful distinction can be made between an inter-organisational partnership and a partnership organisation.

An inter-organisational partnership is an arrangement between two or more separate organisations to pursue a common activity or interest, where risks and benefits are shared. Such partnerships may or may not involve formal agreements or financial exchange; they can be based on legally binding contracts or purely voluntary arrangements. Activities of the partners can differ, yet serve a common interest, or the partners may agree to work together on a set of activities that are undertaken for different interests.

Examples of inter-organisational partnerships include Benetton and the United Nations Volunteers Programme, for the 2001 International Year of Volunteers, and the World Bank-initiated Business as Partners for Development and the Public–Private Partnership 2000 for national disaster reduction (USA). For the most part, inter-organisational partnerships are time limited and yet some of them may evolve into a longer-term strategic alliance or partnership organisation (see below).

A related form of inter-organisational collaboration is that of a strategic alliance, which is a mutually beneficial long-term formal relationship formed between two or more parties to pursue a set of agreed upon goals or to meet a critical business need while remaining independent organisations.

A partnership organisation describes an institutionalised collaboration between organisations, whereby a new organisation is created with its own board and secretariat. Examples include the Star Alliance of airlines, the → Forest Stewardship Council, and the Global Alliance to Improve Nutrition.

Many partnerships seek to serve broader public goals as well as meeting the interests of their participating organisations. Some companies are increasingly using partnership approaches to implement their CSR strategies and activities.

Partnerships can be single sector, such as strategic alliances between companies, and cross-sectoral, involving government agencies, civil society organisations and private sector businesses. The latter are sometimes referred to as public–private partnerships (PPPs); however, many PPPs are essentially service-delivery contracts where public sector bodies contract out the delivery of certain services (e.g. → waste management).

Since the late 1980s, there has been considerable scholarship on single sector partnerships and strategic alliances in the fields of business, management and organisational studies and in the → development studies' literature.

Cross-sectoral partnerships have become more common in recent years, particularly in relation to the challenges of → globalisation and the imperative of → sustainable development. Such partnerships have been particularly prominent among large global corporations and various international NGOs working on environment, → development and → human rights. Given that cross-sector partnerships involve the meeting of different organisational and personal interests in business, civil society and government, they give rise to a range of complex and contentious issues.

By bringing together their respective competencies and resources for the greater good, governments, business, civil society and multilateral agencies have the potential to develop innovative partnerships to respond to many of the key → development challenges of our time: the impact of → climate change; → human security; the prevention, care and treatment of → HIV/AIDS and other major diseases; the generation of new investment, entrepreneurship and employment; and financing for → development. Cross-sector partnerships offer considerable promise as a means of contributing to the realisation of targets such as the → UN Millennium Development

Goals (MDGs), the effective implementation of national poverty reduction strategies, among other → development, environment and → human rights' initiatives.

Although cross-sector partnerships hold considerable hope as a new organisational form for promoting → sustainable development and other societal aims, all partners from the different sectors recognise that there are considerable inherent risks. NGOs and UN agencies are concerned that partnerships (particularly with business) could threaten their → integrity and independence. Businesses fear that too much time and money spent on cross-sector partnerships (particularly with not-for-profit partners) might divert them from their ultimate aim of producing goods and services as profit-making enterprises in order to benefit their owners and workers. Governments often raise important questions about the legitimacy, governance, and → accountability of cross-sector partnerships (particularly those that exclude or undermine public sector interests).

Given that cross-sector partnerships first began to emerge only some 20 years ago, debates between partnership advocates and critics remain. Greater practitioner experience and wider academic analysis about this new organisational form and delivery mechanism are clearly needed. This in turn will help to ensure more effective and accountable partnerships between strong and capable states, private sector businesses, civil society organisations and the UN system

Ross Tennyson in *The Brokering Guidebook* makes the point that the missing link may be the development of partnering and brokering skills and competencies. Despite more than 20 years of cross-sector partnership experience, international efforts to develop capacity to broker, build and sustain cross-sector partnerships for → sustainable development remain limited. Building professional partnering and brokering capacity and making the necessary adaptations to management practice within all sectors remain key challenges for cross-sector partnerships everywhere.

Jem Bendell and David F. Murphy

PERSISTENT ORGANIC POLLUTANTS (POPs)

→ Chemicals sector, Pollution, Stockholm Convention

⌐ www.chem.unep.ch

Persistent organic pollutants (POPs) are chemical substances that persist in the → environment, bioaccumulate through the → food web, and pose a risk of causing adverse effects to human health and the → environment. With the evidence of long-range transport of these substances to regions where they have never been used or produced and the consequent threats they pose to the → environment of the whole globe, the international community has now, at several occasions, called for urgent global actions to reduce and eliminate release of these → chemicals. This is monitored globally under Article 16 of the Stockholm Convention on POPs, focusing on 12 POPs subject of the Stockholm Convention – the so-called 'dirty dozen' (DDT, Aldrin, Dieldrin, Endrin, Chlordane, Heptachlor, Hexachlorobenzene, Mirex, Toxaphene, Polychlorinated Biphenyls, Dioxins, and Furans).

PERSONAL AND HOUSEHOLD GOODS SECTOR

CSR in the personal and household goods sector incorporates the economic, social and environmental effects that come from the purchase, usage and disposal of personal products (such as soaps, shampoos, toothpastes, cosmetics) and household goods (such as cookers, refrigerators, and other household appliances).

Eighty per cent of the environmental impact that results from the normal day-to-day life of a UK individual comes from the way we run our homes, what we eat, how we → travel and holiday. The key aspect of the way we run our homes is the use of personal and household products. Twenty-seven per cent of our UK carbon emissions come from the way we use lights, heating and appliances.

Consumption of these goods is driven by the move towards a convenience lifestyle where labour saving devices free up time for other aspects of life and can have a beneficial effect on → work–life balance. Personal products play a primary role in hygiene, reducing disease and in enhancing self-esteem. The category, therefore, plays a critical role in people's well-being and quality of life.

Consumption is directly related to economic circumstances. China is expected to be the second largest market for household consumption by 2014, so consumption of these goods will rise significantly as the emerging world adopts the lifestyle enjoyed by the West.

Soap and other personal hygiene products, together with cleaning products, play a key role in the health and well-being of people through promoting better personal hygiene and the reduction of hygiene-related diseases such as *E. coli*. → Base of the pyramid products are widely available.

However, their usage involves some significant environmental impacts through the use of copious amounts of → water and power. Additionally, detergents and many similar products can cause environmental damage to rivers and waterways. The recent innovation of detergent tablets has had a beneficial effect through reduced dosing. Personal and household product packaging contribute to the significant problem of household → waste.

Household appliances provide important employment opportunities through the relocation of manufacture to emerging countries.

However, their manufacture uses valuable materials – plastics, metals, electronics etc. – and lead to serious problems of disposal and recycling.

In the case of refrigeration and freezers a great deal of work has been done, prompted by the big users, to replace ozone depleting refrigerants. Disposal of old machines, in a manner where the gases can be captured, is a particular problem across the world.

Many personal products, such as perfumes, are luxuries and are driven by fashion and aspiration. As such they meet a want but not necessarily a need. Branding, advertising and promotion are important elements of the marketing mix in the sector.

Animal testing is still used in personal product development by some manufacturers.

The success of energy efficient freezers and fridges where demand has moved to 'A' rated machines has led to the virtual eradication of energy inefficient machines in → Europe. This came about due to product policy measures (stating the energy consumption at point of sale), industry action and choice editing by retailers. This may provide a model for other product sectors.

In addition to energy consumption, → water consumption is an issue for these products. World Resources Institute data suggests that water consumption is closely related to wealth (expressed as GDP per capita at purchasing power parity with the US dollar). Water usage growth tends to level off when incomes exceed $10 000 per capita; probably because consumers have attained 'developed' world levels of facilities and appliances. If the → UN Millennium Development Goals (e.g. 7% growth p.a. for → Africa) are achieved then → water consumption will increase significantly. While the resultant availability of clean water will become a serious problem in many regions, it does provide innovation opportunities for the sector with products that do not need copious amounts of water or more widely use cold water or grey water. Unilever, one of the world's largest manufacturers of personal and household care products, states that 94% of the water imprint of a detergent is due to consumer usage.

Aerosols, one of the major packaging formats for personal products, have had a big environmental impact due to the use of CFCs. Pressure may grow from the environment lobby for reduction of aerosol usage and replacement with another format (e.g. pump sprays).

Chris Pomfret

PHARMACEUTICAL SECTOR
→ Health and safety, HIV/AIDS

At the beginning of this decade, major pharmaceutical companies had to face heavy pressure from civil society organisations regarding access to → HIV/AIDS drugs in → developing countries. This issue became the industry's greatest global CSR challenge. Companies have been confronted on their drug pricing and intellectual propriety rights policies. They have engineered a massive response by launching initiatives including drug donations, differential pricing, partnerships with the United Nations and patent agreements with southern generics producers.

As the → HIV/AIDS case illustrates, pharmaceutical companies' major CSR issues and challenges relate to their products. The human value of certain pharmaceuticals is widely recognised: 'life-saving drugs' are a great ethical strength for the pharmaceutical industry. However, these same valuable and essential drugs also generate a set of grievances and expectations regarding beneficiaries and access inequalities.

The question of access to drugs in poor countries should remain very high on the pharmaceutical industry's CSR agenda. The more the north increases its therapeutic capacity, the more people are shocked by the lack of access to drugs in the south. Globally, risks of negative side-effects caused by pharmaceuticals, along with information practices regarding such risks, garner increased attention from stakeholders and the media. A particular thorny CSR issue here is the pharmaceutical industry's approach to the → TRIPS Agreement and to the protection of → intellectual property rights.

The high end value of products generates high expectations regarding the entire production process. Pharmaceutical companies face demands to pay particular attention to clinical trials operated in → developing countries. This subject highlights economic and social differences between developing and developed countries, and is a metaphor of → globalisation.

Society is divided in its perception of the pharmaceutical industry. The industry is generally seen as good when considering the final use of products, and it is often described as bad when examining the circumstances of production (clinical trials, marketing, patenting, → lobbying). People often forget that both sides are inextricably linked: the capacity of the pharmaceutical industry to offer cures for diseases only exists because these companies expect to make a profit with their products. If the public demands free access to the drug every time it could also help people who initially cannot afford the drug; the long-term effect might be that pharmaceutical companies only concentrate on products for the 'diseases of the rich'. Global health issues are more complex than many campaigners argue and we see that the → global governance of health issues increasingly involves public–private partnerships between private companies, governmental actors and civil society.

Across industries, companies are increasingly integrating products and services into CSR strategies. Initiatives aiding impoverished peoples and the → environment garner more and more coverage. The pharmaceutical industry has long been at the forefront of product social utility. If pharmaceutical companies want to maintain their ethical profile, they need to further align their products with CSR.

The gap between developed and → developing countries in terms of access to drugs remains an important challenge to the health sector. Access to existing products and the research and development of new drugs needed in poor countries are at stake. Initiatives regarding neglected diseases could expand in the future and enable some companies to reinforce their CSR profile. Innovative → branding, pricing and patenting mechanisms are to be found to address the 10/90 gap (10% of pharmaceutical research and development investments tackle diseases mainly hurting 90% of the world's population). Considering the overwhelming consensus that places → Africa as the first priority on the international development agenda, health issues on this continent will command greater attention from pharmaceutical companies.

Next to the strife for a responsible governance of global health issues the pharmaceutical industry has traditionally faced a number of other issues. Most notably pharmaceutical research has often wrestled with the difficult ethical question whether, how and to what degree research and testing of drugs on animals should be included in the process. In particular in the UK and → Europe the industry is the ongoing target of – often violent – campaigns. In a similar vein the pharmaceutical industry is also at the forefront of the debate on (potentially) using → genetically modified organisms (GMOs) and, more recently, stem cell research. While governments have been slow and reluctant to regulate these issues a major CSR issue for the industry has to address the difficult ethical implications of these technologies and to balance them with legitimate concerns about long-term profitability.

Antoine Mach

PHILANTHROPY
→ Foundation

Philanthropy is an altruistic action designed to promote the good of society. In the context of CSR, philanthropy falls into the social sphere, but outside of a company's core operations. While philanthropy by corporations is very important and contributes to society's well-being, its core operations are CSR's primary focus, and have the potential for greater impact. In Carroll's model of CSR philanthropy is the last step which has all the other, more operational, aspects of CSR as a prerequisite.

Philanthropy can connect a corporation with the communities in which it operates and create an internal culture that improves recruiting and retention; employees can develop greater pride in their employer, → leadership skills and stronger relationships with colleagues; customers can feel that a corporation cares about more than simply fulfilling its legal obligations and making as much profit as possible; suppliers can serve as more than simply a contractually bound provider of a product; and stakeholders, such as the media, may take philanthropy into account when reporting in general and in times of potentially negative news, and NGOs can potentially partner to leverage the impact of philanthropy. When large corporations can potentially have thousands of facilities in multiple countries the need and difficulty to feel rooted in a particular location, rather than being subservient to a distant headquarter, can impact brand reputation and the intangible trust issues related to a → licence to operate.

Trust can mean the absence of fear or, in a much stronger sense, the foundation of community and self-fulfilment. In an age when corporations can and do pick up and move from one location to another based on the vagaries of the market, with consequences for the jilted community, trust generated by genuine philanthropy can overcome a sceptical public. Without trust, a corporation whose profits repatriate outside of a community or country can be seen as an 'other' instead of a potential ally or partner.

Moses Maimonides, a 12th century Jewish philosopher, created a ladder of philanthropic giving. Each step represents a higher degree of virtue, with one being the lowest and eight being the highest:

1. The lowest: Giving begrudgingly.
2. Giving cheerfully but giving minimally.
3. Giving cheerfully and adequately but only after being asked.
4. Giving before being asked.
5. Giving without knowing who the individual beneficiary is, but the recipient knows the donor's identity.
6. Giving when knowing who the individual beneficiary is, but the recipient does not know the donor's identity.
7. Giving when neither the donor nor the recipient is aware of the other's identity.
8. The highest: Giving money, a loan, time or whatever is necessary to enable an individual to be self-reliant.

Philanthropy in a CSR context can take the form of corporate volunteer programmes, lending staff and technical expertise to

NGOs, or monetary contributions. It can be measured and analysed, formalised and professionalised to achieve maximum effectiveness like any other corporate activity. Corporations with strategic philanthropic programmes view them as being fundamentally good for business, rather than an added expense. Maimonides' eight levels of philanthropy offer a guide for corporations and their stakeholders to promote the good of society.

Jonathan Cohen

POLICIES
→ Codes of conduct

Policy is the stated description, usually in writing, of how an organisation will act, respond, treat or define a given set of facts and circumstances. Aligning corporate → values and guiding principles with policies, decision-making processes and overall strategy creates consistency and strengthens → corporate culture. An integrated CSR policy affects every department and dictates how a company behaves towards their employees, suppliers, customers, shareholders, communities and the → environment.

For example, policies are often used to define the various aspects of the employment relationship between a company and a worker and are embodied in an 'employee handbook'. Strong CSR policies can also be used to positively influence or shape behaviour when an employee or organisation is faced with a choice about how to act. When employees are supported by a responsible framework and culture, they feel more confident about making responsible decisions and will do so more often. Integrated, strong CSR policies can manifest into sustainable behaviour and operations with the necessary support from company leaders and organisational culture. CSR policies are particularly important for a credible CSR approach in larger organisations while small and medium size enterprises tend to implement their CSR policy on a more informal basis.

Paula Ivey

POLITICAL ACTION COMMITTEES
→ Lobbying

POLLUTER PAYS PRINCIPLE
→ Pollution

POLLUTION
→ Eco-efficiency, Environmental liabilities, Life cycle assessment, Waste management

Pollution can be defined as the release of unwanted by-products of industrial production that degrade the quality of the natural or social environment. This release can be to air, → water and soil, but noise pollution, light pollution, visual pollution and radioactivity can also be distinguished. Pollution can harm flora, fauna, and human health to such an extent that extinction occurs. Substances, often non-existent in the natural environment, are added in such quantities that balances in the biosphere are disturbed. Although the proof is never easy to deliver, pollution is widely acknowledged to be responsible for negatively affecting quality of life and even mortality rates. Pollution can cause cancer, allergies and all forms of asthma, among other things.

Pollution as a problem came to the forefront mainly in the late 19th and 20th centuries. Pollution is as old as humanity though. Human activity will always have resulted in some kind of → waste that was left behind or dumped in rivers and other → water resources. Increasing populations and the industrial revolution with its large-scale industrial processes resulted in much more intensified impacts. Initially, pollution was seen mainly in the context of hindrance, i.e. odour, dust and litter. However, during the 1960s the effects of pollution on the biosphere and ecosystems became the centre of attention. An important publication in this respect is Rachel Carson's book '*Silent Spring*' in 1962 that focused attention on the environmental consequences of the use of pesticides.

The realisation of the immense and often irreversible effects of pollution has led to an enormous growth in environmental regulations. Already in the 19th century several countries issued Clean Air Acts and Hindrance Acts. Since the second half of the 20th century, specific legislation has also been developed for → water pollution, soil protection, noise control, → waste management and other environmental impacts.

Most of the legislation is based on direct regulation, i.e. permits. These media-specific regulations have serious shortcomings, such as shifting pollution from one media to another rather than eliminating it, constraining innovation, expensive enforcement and high transaction costs. Hence, governments have tried to develop more regulations aiming for integrated pollution control. Since the early 1990s, governments worldwide have also developed new approaches to overcome the shortcomings of direct regulation. These include market-based approaches (economic incentives) and programmes aiming at dialogue, collaboration and information exchange, rather than the adversarial policy style that often accompanies direct regulation.

A central principle underlying regulations is the polluter pays principle: the polluter should bear the corresponding expenses. Industry is, therefore, heavily involved in pollution control. Approaches to fight pollution range from simple end-of-pipe measures to pollution prevention. Initially, pollution control mainly meant trying to stop the release of pollution, for instance by installing a filter that captures the harmful substances. As such approaches often end up in new pollution, for instances dirty filters, and regulations have become more stringent over the years, companies have started to work on cleaner production, i.e. production that causes less pollution. Companies are thus striving towards more → eco-efficiency: producing less → waste per unit of raw material.

One of the first and most well-known pollution prevention approaches is the Pollution Prevention Pays (3P) programme that 3M developed as early as 1975. This and other approaches focus on the economic value of pollution and → waste: since pollution absorbs valuable raw materials there is a clear financial incentive to reduce pollution.

Since the 1980s industry has followed the example of forerunners such as 3M and become much more active in pollution prevention, often with government incentives. The focus of these programmes has shifted from the production processes of individual companies to the integral → life cycle assessment of products, in a → cradle-to-grave approach. In such an approach all the pollution from the stage of digging or harvesting raw materials to the → waste that remains after using a product is taken into account.

Theo de Bruijn

POVERTY
→ Base of the Pyramid model, Developing countries, Development, Millennium Development Goals

Within a CSR context, the dominant conception of poverty is that of a deficiency or lack of economic means, particularly money, to achieve a desired level of well-being. Poverty, however, is a hotly disputed notion whose meaning, causes, effects, and cures differ widely across disciplines and fields of interest. Differing perspectives make poverty a complex social, political, and economic concept. While many think of poverty as solely an objective matter, it also has a subjective side. There is much contention over what the word 'poverty' means, who gets labelled as 'poor', who determines the 'solutions' to poverty, and the extent to which all of these terms are victimising, patronising, or condescending.

Poverty can be framed as a process to be understood or a problem to be solved. These issues are critical as the definition and operationalization of poverty determines the flow and direction of significant amounts of resources among → development agencies and others trying to address it through aid, assistance and other forms of intervention. A better understanding of poverty can be achieved by considering three key dimensions: the attributes of poverty itself, the role of the poor in poverty alleviation, and the nature of interventions to address poverty.

Poverty has both tangible and intangible aspects. Poverty may be determined by tangible factors such as lack of health care, nutrition, shelter, education, → technology, or environmental resources. Poverty may also be distinguished by availability of communication, transportation, → waste services, and financial infrastructure. Material or consumption-based definitions of poverty – particularly those that rely on a single metric such as per-capita income – have been criticised as overlaying a Western economic understanding of → development that is inconsistent with actual lived experience. The use of money or income to define poverty is problematic for cultures where materiality has not been considered a social goal and self-perceptions of poverty do not exist until imposed from the outside.

Intangible factors include such concepts as power, social exclusion, social mobility, influence, access, and knowledge. Poverty in this case is viewed as an outcome of social relationships that subordinate individuals and groups by caste, → gender, race, ethnicity, religion, and age as a basis for depriving freedoms, opportunities, dignity, social integration, or the availability of choice. Poverty is also expressed by a lack of empathy, the presence of callousness, or the loss of spirit or ethics among those with significant means. Accounting for intangible factors of poverty yields a more holistic understanding but also leads to controversy because such factors are, by definition, difficult to measure.

Further complicating the nature of poverty is the fact that it can be applied at multiple levels of analysis – individual, community, region, country, continent, and global. Because poverty manifests itself in localised ways, relying heavily on a subset of tangible or intangible indicators tends to render generalisations about poverty inaccurate. Urban poverty differs significantly from rural poverty. Poverty in highly industrialised nations differs significantly from poverty in agrarian societies.

Tangible metrics feel precise, but mask the fine-grained nature of poverty's causes, effects and resolutions. For example, gross domestic product (GDP), life expectancy, child mortality, calories, and income distribution have all been used to determine whether a country is poor or not. But the aggregate basis for many of these indicators masks the diversity of experiences and conditions and ignores more intangible metrics such as perceived quality of life. Similarly, poverty lines set by specific income levels (e.g. $1, $2, or $3 per day) suggest definitive levels at which poverty does and does not occur. Yet such figures conceal the variety of circumstances and intangible elements affecting the human condition.

A deeper understanding of poverty occurs by taking into account the relationship between tangible and intangible elements which vary within and between geographies over time. Poverty finds its roots in power and influence, exacerbated by → corruption, illness and disease, natural disasters, political exploitation, overpopulation and geographic resources. It is intangible factors such as knowledge, power, and choice that affect tangible metrics such as income. The relationship between tangible and intangible factors determines the nature of poverty and the choice of appropriate interventions used to address it.

The role of the poor themselves in poverty alleviation is a second important dimension. Interventions often treat the poor as either passive recipients to be 'worked on' and rehabilitated or as capable individuals and communities critical to any change process. When depicted as passive recipients, the poor are assumed to be victims in need of rehabilitation and aid. Characterised as having few resources, the poor are portrayed as being in a state where they must be 'saved' through external intervention by those willing and able to dedicate the necessary time and expertise. Strong criticisms exist regarding the extent to which this view is patronising, and creates deeper dependencies and disempowerment among the poor.

An opposing view characterises the poor as creative, resourceful people who possess valuable capabilities, skills, and knowledge to pursue their own best interests. Within this paradigm of choice and empowerment, the poor are viewed as being inherently entrepreneurial and able to leverage available scarce resources to improve their own lives. The poor are seen as catalysts for robust informal economies driven by ingenuity and creativity. Active engagement with the poor in poverty alleviation efforts focused on self-directed change becomes the pre-condition for long-term effectiveness and impact. Criticisms of this perspective claim it does not acknowledge obvious and easily addressed material deprivations (e.g. starvation, curable diseases) and that efforts cannot be scaled or replicated in a timely manner. Whether the poor are classified as active participants or passive recipients, however, affects not only the conception of poverty, but also the interventions used to alleviate it.

Hence, the third dimension for understanding poverty is the nature of the interventions used to address it. These can be classified into two categories. First, there are interventions intended to directly alleviate deprivation. Such interventions usually come in the form of solutions imposed from the outside by experts who themselves are not likely to be classified as poor. These interventions can be seen in the more traditional approaches to poverty alleviation exhibited by most multilateral agencies and government assistance programmes. Corporate efforts to deal with poverty through aid and philanthropy often also mimic these approaches.

Most such interventions assume that the cure for poverty is to raise living standards and consumption to levels more in line with those in OECD countries. Many of these poverty alleviation efforts are large in scale and focus on 'one-size-fits-all' solutions. Poverty reduction goals, then, focus on single metrics such as material consumption, medical treatment or nutrition which may or may not be appropriate or desired in a specific social, cultural, political or religious context.

Business itself has been viewed as an important instrument of poverty alleviation through large-scale investment in factories and facilities, thereby creating jobs and income. Critics of this perspective, however, contend that the poor are reduced to mere factors of production with wages that do not allow them access to adequate goods and services. They argue that the constant search for cheap labour and raw material inputs compels industry to engage in a 'race to the bottom' where the exploitation of people and natural resources drives the very poverty and inequality they are presumed to be alleviating. Rapid urbanisation forces rural migrants into squalid conditions where they lack legal standing and become captive to the system from which they seek to benefit.

A second type of intervention is meant to develop capacity within the ranks of the poor themselves. Such interventions view the poor not as factors of production, but as engines for innovation and entrepreneurship that drive economic growth. These approaches seek to build capacity to mitigate the effects of poverty through private sector, market-based mechanisms. They typically begin with the conception of the poor as capable, productive people.

Capacity-building interventions have led to an increased number of hybrid organisational forms that operate as for-profit entities, but determine success based on social objectives. Such organisations – referred to as for-benefit, third sector, social entrepreneurship, or → Base of the Pyramid (BOP) ventures – depend on micro-enterprises that leverage local resources to meet culturally appropriate goals. This private sector, profit-based approach treats poverty as a potential source of business growth with the causes of poverty providing the foundation for new product and service development. By understanding and meeting the unmet needs of individuals and communities, these interventions depend on complex networks of entrepreneurs, NGOs and community leaders to facilitate innovations meant to generate mutual benefit for both the communities and the firms.

Critics of capacity-building approaches question whether the typical small scale and the high failure rate of many such enterprises embody the scale and scope necessary to deal with poverty on a global basis. These approaches are also criticised for depending on the ability of firms to convince the poor to aspire to and pay for products and services they do not need. There can be risk that such initiatives become just another way of removing what little wealth exists among the poor as local informal economies become more formalised and institutionalised.

Yet, compared to large-scale aid-based activities, these revenue-based interventions hold promise for connecting business to poverty in a way that can recognise its many forms and the important role of the poor themselves. Widespread experimentation and innovation with this approach enables the competitive process of the marketplace to reduce poverty in a way that is sensitive to local interests and needs; success can then be replicated and diffused, and positively impact the tangible and intangible factors of poverty over the long run.

Mark B. Milstein, Erik Simanis, Duncan Duke and Stuart Hart

PRECAUTIONARY PRINCIPLE
→ Pollution, Risk management

In case there is scientific evidence that a human activity poses a threat to human, animal or plant health or the → environment, measures to prevent the danger are clearly indicated (e.g. ban on the use of dangerous substances). However, if the scientific data is insufficient, inconclusive or uncertain but a threat can reasonably be detected, the precautionary principle shall be applied.

The principle is laid down in international and national regulations as well as in many voluntary standards or policies of companies.

There is no universally accepted definition of the precautionary principle but commonly used elements can be summarised as follows.

Where there are threats of serious or irreversible damage to the → environment or to human, animal or plant health, lack of full scientific certainty shall not be used as a reason for postponing cost-effective measures to prevent or reduce the possible impacts.

An important restriction for the precautionary principle is the proportionality principle, meaning that ecological benefits and economic costs of a precautionary measure must be balanced. Consequently a total exclusion of risks cannot be demanded.

Beneath the approach to minimise environmental risks of human activities the precautionary principle is increasingly used to call for a sustainable use of resources.

Putting the principle into practice, companies are requested to take a cautious approach to → development and environmental management decisions when information is uncertain, unreliable or inadequate. However, due to an increased use of the precautionary principle (especially in the EU), companies also face an increased use of product stewardship policies that require producers to be financially and legally responsible for the environmental impacts caused by their products (e.g. the EU WEEE Directive).

Andreas Hermann

PRESSURE GROUPS
→ Non-governmental organisations (NGOs)

PRIVACY
→ Consumer rights, Employee rights

Privacy refers to the ability of an individual or organisation to avoid public scrutiny of their personal affairs, and their right to control the flow of personal or confidential information about themselves.

The European Convention on Human Rights recognises a person's right to privacy, and although many privacy issues relate to government, there is growing concern about privacy issues in relation to business. This has mostly been driven by the growth of e-commerce and the 'internet age', and the way businesses use information they gather from customers, or even those who browse their websites. Privacy concerns can also create markets for particular products and services such as internet security software or tinted glass. There are a number of key principles to responsible management of customer information including:

- Notifying customers about information held, and ensuring that consent is granted for gathering, holding and disclosing information;
- Accessibility of personal information, allowing for verification of its accuracy;
- Protecting information held about customers, to reduce the risks of online → fraud or identity theft; and
- → Accountability, to ensure that there is someone within an organisation ensuring → legal compliance for data protection and adherence to responsible information management principles.

In some industries where information and privacy are central issues, such as financial services and → telecommunications, organisational roles such as 'chief privacy officer' are being established to ensure and demonstrate good privacy practice.

Privacy issues may also be relevant to companies as employers, particularly in relation to the uses to which information held about employees is put, and the steps taken to monitor employees' activities (e.g. monitoring internet usage to discourage inappropriate use).

Ken Peattie

PRIVATISATION
→ Labour issues, Public goods

From the perspective of responsible business practice, the issues surrounding the process of privatisation will generally focus on → transparency, the interests of a range of stakeholders wider than those of prospective shareholders, and the management of employee issues.

As in the UK in the 1980s, following the example of the New Zealand Government in the late 1970s, the process of privatisation addresses the transfer to the private sector of the ownership of state-owned enterprises, such as → telecommunications, postal services, → utilities, defence establishments, and increasingly services such as heath, education and correctional facilities.

In the course of this process, either a sale to a bidding buyer is agreed or an initial public offering is made for shares in the enterprise, floated on the relevant stock exchange. In some cases the government may wish to hold a 'golden share' which enables it to retain an influential say in the management of the new company – this approach tends to be more prevalent in continental → Europe.

As the underlying thesis behind privatisation is that private enterprise can do a more efficient job of running the business successfully than government, there is an inherent implication of a close scrutiny of cost structures once the process has been completed and the company has been privatised.

In most cases, significant reductions in workforces will be proposed and implemented over time. This process has generated a number of attractive euphemisms such as '→ downsizing', 'right-sizing', 'workforce re-engineering' and 'structural adjustments'.

In terms of responsible business practice, the issues to be confronted and managed will include:

- Impact on workers and their livelihoods; efforts to retrain, organise outplacements, transitional secondments, support to entrepreneurship training locally and redundancy terms are among the mechanisms responsible companies will use.

- Impact on citizens who are turned into consumers through privatisation. Rail transport, → water supply or postal services initially were government administered because affordable access to these commodities is seen as part and parcel of the social rights of citizens in a democracy. If these commodities are now delivered by private companies the pricing of and the access to these goods follow the profit-maximisation rationale of a private company. This raises serious issues, as the examples of pricing of rail services and → water or the closure of smaller 'inefficient' post offices in many countries have shown.

- The effect of 'natural monopolies'. Many privatised services were initially government administered because they are based on 'natural monopolies': the network of water pipes, telecommunication lines or rail tracks cannot easily face competition as costs of building competing networks are prohibitively high. Privatised → utilities are therefore often monopolists and next to tight regulation, it is the responsibility of these companies to make sure that they do not exploit their position and compete fairly with competitors who want to use parts of the natural monopoly.

- The impact on the local community as a whole; impact on local businesses as a result of workers' lower earning potential; effect on local suppliers of reduced spending patterns and potential off-shoring of services.

- Perception management when executive salaries rise in a manner which exacerbates wage differences and appears to reward company directors in a manner which is out of proportion to the often perceived lack of improvement in services, as for instance in the case of rail service in the UK.

- Transparency in the overall process, ensuring that there is no suggestion of insider dealing, favoured stock purchasers or other practices intended to advantage one set of investors over another.

The → BITC CR Index can be a useful tool to address issues of workplace, marketplace, community and environmental impact in the planning for privatisation in order to signpost potential challenges and mistakes.

David Halley

PRODUCT STEWARDSHIP
→ Stewardship

Product stewardship is the product-centred approach to environmental management. Product stewardship is a relatively new phenomenon as it emerged only during the last decade of the 20th century. Formerly, most of the attention paid to social and environmental impacts was related to the production process. Product stewardship aims at improving the environmental performance of a product throughout its complete life cycle. Of course, this involves looking at the production processes too. Through product stewardship a company accepts the responsibility for a product after it leaves the premises of the company. This calls for collaboration between manufacturers, retailers, users, and disposers, thereby distinguishing product stewardship from internally oriented environmental management. It also implies that product stewardship is more complex as a company has to deal with many parties, including those over which the company has little control.

Theo de Bruijn

PRODUCT TAKE-BACK SCHEMES
→ CSR in the personal and household goods sector, Recycling, Waste management

Product take-back schemes require companies to take responsibility for the → waste that is created when their products are thrown away. Traditionally, manufacturers carried little responsibility for a product once it left the company. More and more, one sees a development towards extended producer responsibility. In some cases it concerns only the product packaging (e.g., a bottle), while in others, it involves the complete product (e.g., cars, electronic equipment).

The most extended form of a product take-back scheme is the one in which the company must physically collect and accept the product after being used. The big advantage of this is that it confronts the company with the possibilities for reuse or recycling. This is expected to lead to improved product designs. Usually, though, producers are required to pay for the treatment of → waste or they must form a joint organisation that takes care of the → waste.

An important development in → Europe is the adoption of the → EU Directive on Waste Electrical and Electronic Equipment (WEEE). This directive intends to fight the rapidly increasing waste stream of electrical and electronic equipment. Producers will be responsible for taking back and recycling electrical and electronic equipment. This is thought to provide incentives to the environmentally sound design of electrical and electronic equipment. Consumers will be able to return their equipment free of charge. The expectation is that in the near future we will see many more initiatives to regulate product take-back.

Theo de Bruijn

PUBLIC AFFAIRS

→ Green marketing, Greenwash, Marketing ethics, Reporting, Reputation

Public affairs is the effective management of an organisation's business environment. Companies commonly use CSR as a public affairs tool to influence relevant public policy, engage stakeholders, and enhance their reputation. In fact, many companies house CSR in their public affairs departments. However, this often leads to accusations of → greenwash, i.e. insincere commitment to social and environmental responsibility.

The rise of CSR as a public affairs issue points to both an increasingly media dominated world, as well as greater acknowledgement of the legitimate role of various stakeholder groups over and above the demands of shareholders. Maintaining good relations with these stakeholders (often referred to as obtaining a social '→ licence to operate') is the purpose of good corporate public affairs.

Paula Ivey

PUBLIC GOODS
→ Development, Externalities, Privatisation, Tragedy of the commons

Public goods are common resources where consumption by one person does not reduce the amount available to others, and in which it is not possible to allocate property rights. An example of this is clean air; it is in everyone's interest to have clean air but in no one's individual interest to pay for it, as the cost would be individual but the benefit would be shared by all. Conversely, the adverse effects of air pollution are felt by everyone, while the costs saved by the polluter are individual.

This is an example of the → global commons where straightforward market mechanisms are of limited value unless there is a mechanism to internalise the → externalities of the use of these public goods. Solutions to this dilemma could either come from collective solutions, in particular artificial pricing of public goods (such as eco-taxes) or artificial property rights (as those issued by the → EU Greenhouse Gas Emission Trading Scheme) or they can be approached by individual companies making responsible use of public goods an element of their CSR policies.

Ruth Findlay-Brooks

PUBLIC INTEREST

→ Regulation

CSR is often conceived as the way in which business demonstrates that it is operating in the public interest, or the 'common good'. This is a shift from Adam Smith's original proposition that the 'invisible hand' of the free market automatically ensures that companies operate in the public interest. Subsequently, critics of the free market ideology have argued that, in the case of public goods (like clean air, → water and a healthy environment), markets tend to fail.

In economic terms, this is often expressed as the failure of companies to internalise the → externalities (social and environmental costs or benefits) of their activities. Hence, there is the need for market intervention in the form of either regulation, or → market-based instruments (such as → eco-taxes and → eco-subsidies) in order to protect the public interest.

CSR is often proposed by business as a counter-argument to such government intervention in the market, to the extent that CSR demonstrates that companies can voluntarily act in the public interest. This position is often backed up by the notion of a → business case for CSR, i.e. that pursuing social responsibility and economic profitability are mutually reinforcing rather than necessarily a trade-off.

Wayne Visser

PUBLIC PARTICIPATION

→ Stakeholder engagement

PUBLIC–PRIVATE PARTNERSHIPS (PPP)

→ Partnerships

PUBLIC RELATIONS

→ Public affairs

QUALITY MANAGEMENT

→ Continual improvement, ISO 9000 Series of Standards on Quality Management

Before considering the term 'quality management', it is important to consider related terminology in order to understand the concept of quality management in the appropriate context. The word quality is generally used to describe a distinguishing characteristic or attribute of a person or article. It is also used to indicate a standard of excellence and can be used to indicate that something is superior. The subtle difference between the general meaning of the term and the way in which it is used in the context of quality management as a discipline in industry has caused some confusion.

Quality management in the context of → ISO 9001:2000 is most similar to what is generally referred to as consistency – defined as the degree to which a set of inherent characteristics fulfils requirements. The term 'quality' can be used with adjectives such as poor, good or excellent. 'Inherent', as opposed to 'assigned', quality implies an intrinsic, permanent characteristic. 'Requirements' as used in the definition above refers to a need or expectation that is stated, generally implied or obligatory, while 'generally implied' means that it is custom or common practice for the organisation, its customers and other interested parties.

A quality management system is defined as a management system to direct and control an organisation with regard to quality. Central to a quality management system is the quality policy that includes the overall intentions and direction of the organisation related to quality, as formally expressed by the top management of an organisation. A quality policy will generally provide a framework for the setting of quality objectives and quality management principles. → ISO 9001, the International Standard for Quality Management Systems, can form a basis for the establishment of a quality policy.

quality management, then, refers to coordinated activities to direct and control an organisation with regard to quality, while direction and control with regard to quality generally includes establishment of the quality policy and quality objectives, quality planning, quality control, quality → assurance and quality improvement.

The various components of quality management can be defined as follows:

- Quality planning is part of quality management focused on setting quality objectives and specifying necessary operational processes and related resources to fulfil the quality objectives;
- Quality control refers to that part of quality management focused on fulfilling quality requirements;
- Quality → assurance refers to that part of quality management focused on providing confidence that quality requirements will be fulfilled; and
- Quality improvement refers to that part of quality management focused on increasing the ability to fulfil quality requirements, including effectiveness, efficiency or → traceability.

Johann Möller

RACE TO THE BOTTOM
→ Anti-globalisation, Development, Fairtrade

The 'race to the bottom' is a metaphor used to describe the competition of countries for foreign direct investment through offering investors the lowest level of taxation, environmental obligations and social standards. Unlike on markets for goods and services, on this market for direct investment there is no anti-trust law which defines the rules of the competition and no authority to enforce such rules. As an incentive to lure or retain business investment, developed countries tend to lower taxes and compromise the social safety net, while → developing countries have an incentive to relax social and environmental standards. Some authors fear that this competition may lead to a 'race to the bottom' in social and environmental standards. Others suggest that the competition of locations and their legal systems will lead to an optimum level of regulation. Though the empirical evidence is as yet inconclusive, some authors suggest the definition of a level playing field in order to define minimum standards which all countries should abide by.

Andreas Georg Scherer

RAINFOREST ALLIANCE CERTIFICATION
→ Labelling
✋ www.rainforest–alliance.org

Rainforest Alliance Certification is a → conservation tool based on independent → auditing and → labelling, whereby a third party awards a mark of approval showing consumers that the manufacture of products conforms to a specific set of criteria balancing ecological, economic and social considerations.

The Rainforest Alliance Certification programme promotes improvements in agriculture, forestry and tourism through independent → auditing and → labelling of products flowing from approved practices. A team of Rainforest Alliance-trained experts assesses compliance with a set of standards protecting the → environment, wildlife, workers and local communities. The team writes a report which is reviewed by an independent committee of outside experts. Based on the assessment and peer reviews of the report, the team decides whether the applicant is permitted to display the Rainforest Alliance Certification seal.

In forestry, the Rainforest Alliance-operated SmartWood programme certifies forest management units that meet the principles and criteria of the → Forest Stewardship Council. The Rainforest Alliance works with other partners to help farmers meet recognised standards for sustainable agriculture and to facilitate the spread of sustainable tourism → certification.

Lars H. Gulbrandsen

RECYCLING
→ EU Directive on Waste Electrical and Electronic Equipment (WEEE), Life cycle assessment, Waste management

Recycling is the reprocessing of materials into new products. It involves a series of activities that includes collecting recyclable materials that would otherwise be considered → waste, sorting and processing them into raw materials and remanufacturing these into new products. Recycling should not be confused with reuse. Recycling means breaking down a used item into its raw materials, such as glass, paper, metals, plastics or organic material. This breaking down distinguishes it from reuse. Using a bottle more than once to carry a fluid is reuse. Breaking it down to pieces to produce new glass products, either a bottle or something else, is recycling.

In the → waste hierarchy, reuse is to be preferred over recycling. Recycling limits the use of new materials and limits the pollution caused by → waste too: by separating waste into different waste streams, the amount of waste that in the end has to be burned or put into landfill is minimised. As recycled material has an economic value the costs of → waste management can be lowered. One major concern, though, is the amount of energy that is needed in order to make waste fit for another use. A life cycle analysis, which looks at waste, raw materials and energy use throughout the production chain, will have to shed light on what the preferred option is in a specific situation from an environmental point of view.

Theo de Bruijn

REGULATION
→ Civil regulation, Legal compliance, Self-regulation

Regulation describes the entirety of rules, laws and codified norms which are part of the legal framework of business and which govern its ethical, social and environmental responsibilities. Regulation is normally issued by governmental bodies or supranational institutions with governmental authority, such as the EU or the → World Trade Organisation (WTO).

On a generic level, one could argue that complying with regulation (legal responsibilities) is an intrinsic part of → CSR (alongside economic, ethical and philanthropic responsibilities in the Carroll model). CSR then has a quite close, though multifaceted, relationship with regulation.

- First, on the surface of it one could say governmental regulation and CSR have a mutually exclusive relation: CSR as a voluntary business activity takes place in areas where regulation either does not exist or is insufficiently enforced. Addressing → sweatshop working conditions or voluntary programmes for greenhouse gas reduction are cases in point. In many instances, governments refrain from legislating to free business from over-regulation or 'red tape' and leave companies more discretion in the area of CSR. An example would be the conversion of the prospective mandatory → operating and financial review in the UK in 2006 into a voluntary exercise.
- Second, there is the view that CSR and regulation are synonymous: many CSR activities take place in regimes of voluntary self-regulation, such as → codes of conduct, the → Forest Stewardship Council or the regulations of the → Fairtrade label. Basically, CSR here consists of complying with these self-regulatory environments.
- A third view would be to see CSR as orchestrated by governmental regulation. An example would be the → EU which in its Green and White Papers as well as through the → European Alliance on CSR has attempted to provide a broader frame of incentives and procedures which aim at encouraging more CSR

in → Europe. In a similar vein the UK Government has a minister for CSR and used to run a → CSR Academy with the aim of proliferating CSR practices in industry. In this view, then, regulatory frameworks by governments – though not prescribing CSR as mandatory – aim at managing a wider economic and political process towards more responsible business practices.

- Fourth, one could think of CSR as preceding regulation. A number of initiatives by CSR proactive companies have led governments to make these activities mandatory for business in general. An example would be the EU Accounts Modernisation Directive, requiring the incorporation of non-financial performance indicators (social and environmental) in the annual financial review – an activity which CSR leaders have been practising for a long time. Equally, a good deal of environmental legislation has followed the examples of companies who proactively showed that more sustainable approaches to business are feasible.

- Finally, we may think of CSR as being implicit in regulation. CSR as an explicit management idea has only come on the agenda of business outside of North America fairly recently. The responsibilities of business to wider society, for instance in → Europe, are still largely part of a negotiated, consensus-driven approach between governments, corporations, business associations and powerful trade unions. No German or French company needed to concern themselves with a formal 'CSR policy' with regard to their workers' health plans or their emission levels – these issues were implicitly part of the wider regulatory framework. Similar examples could be cited from industrialised democracies in other parts of the world, such as Japan or South Korea.

Given these various relations between CSR and regulation, Matten and Moon (*Academy of Management Review*, 2008) have suggested that CSR can be framed in two different ways: 'explicit CSR' (largely the topic of this book) is CSR in the sense of voluntary corporate policies, programmes and strategies; and 'implicit

CSR' (largely synonymous with regulation) consists of → values, norms and rules which result in (often codified and mandatory) requirements for corporations. From this perspective, then, CSR and regulation are in a complementary relationship. They are two different ways of achieving the same goal: that business assumes and lives up to its societal expectations.

Dirk Matten

RENEWABLE RESOURCES
→ Sustainable development, Utilities sector

Renewable resources are natural resources which can potentially be used or drawn upon without their total quantity being depleted. They include fresh → water, air, energy sources such as biomass, wind and solar, many natural sources of → food, and commodities like paper and wood. This contrasts with non-renewable resources, such as fossil fuels, which have only a finite quantity and will eventually run out.

However, if rates of extraction or use exceed nature's ability to replace the resource, they can cease to be renewable. Examples of this are overfishing above the replacement rate, and → water extracted from aquifers more rapidly than it can be replaced, often resulting in permanent contamination.

The problems of overuse and overextraction can result from the '→ tragedy of the commons', or from the tendency of the market to value resources only when they are exploited. A forest, for example, has a market value when it is cut down and turned into timber and farmland, but not while it is growing and providing environmental benefits such as clean air, → water preservation and → biodiversity. In order to maintain renewable resources for future generations, therefore, CSR needs to balance immediate economic drivers with longer-term responsible use of the resource.

Ruth Findlay-Brooks

REPORTING
→ Non-financial reporting

REPORT VERIFICATION
→ Auditing, Non-financial reporting

In relation to CSR, report verification can be generally defined as a process of independently obtaining and evaluating objective evidence in order to confirm whether an assertion made by an organisation about its environmental, social or economic performance is correct. The results of the verification process are reported to interested third parties in the form of an independent 'verification statement'.

The collection of verification evidence through interviews, documentation review and site inspections is based on a detailed assessment of the risk that the information in the report may contain potential errors or omissions that may influence the decisions or behaviour of the users of the information.

CSR report verification often examines and reports on the reliability not only of the performance data (e.g. on environmental impacts and human resources), but also of the assertions management makes concerning the status of policies, → codes of conduct, international agreements and performance against goals and targets over time. Ensuring balance and completeness as well as accuracy are key elements in CSR report verification.

Due to differences in interpretation of the term verification, ranging from the broader definition in EMAS for environmental matters to its specific use in accounting terminology to refer to very detailed testing involving the collection of corroborative third party evidence, it has largely been replaced by the broader term → assurance in relation to CSR reporting.

Jennifer Iansen-Rogers and George Molenkamp

REPUTATION
→ Risk management

Corporate reputation is one of the most common drivers pushing companies to address CSR issues. Likewise, CSR is a vital part of how a company is perceived. They are inextricably linked as both driver and element.

Corporate reputation is a dynamic, multidimensional concept built on the perceptions of past behaviour and a reflection of future expectations. Because no one knows for sure how corporations, or people, will act in a given situation, we use our knowledge of past events to gauge what we expect in the future. The more trust we have in a corporation, or person, the more certain we are of our expectations.

In today's modern landscape, where intangibles drive market capital, reputation enjoys an increasingly higher rank on corporate agendas. Not only has reputation seen a spike in its boardroom celebrity status, but in the past five years the very nature of corporate reputation has undergone several tectonic shifts. Both the people and the situations that can directly impact a company's reputation have changed. Hierarchical authority has given way to spheres of cross-influence. Any stakeholder with internet access can influence corporate reputation, as everyone knows everything, everywhere, all the time. A company's reputation is not only forged within its own walls, but also in supplier factories, local communities, and in consumers' trashcans. CEOs recognise that corporate reputation is more valuable and vulnerable today than it ever was in the past, and often look to CSR to help boost their company's status among various stakeholders.

Reputation, in the context of CSR, is based upon the assumption that the organisation has knowledge of and adheres to → best practices in its operations – product quality, environmental impact, supply chain management, governance, distribution, and marketing. Companies with stellar reputations strive for → best practices, acknowledge that there is always room for improvement, and consider the interests of all stakeholders when making decisions about their operations. They effectively communicate their reasoning behind difficult or controversial choices, and directly manage and learn from their mistakes.

From a business perspective, there are reputational risks and opportunities to be mitigated and taken advantage of in all operational areas. Applying astute CSR strategies in each helps to assure a positive corporate image. From an outsider's perspective, there are six broad core elements that comprise a company's reputation. In each area, companies have the opportunity to leverage CSR to positively affect their reputation.

- A company's products and services – their quality, → health and safety, life cycle design, materials, marketing, and customer satisfaction – affect the way stakeholders view a company. Is this company providing society with something good, useful, and responsible?
- Visibility is gained through strong financial performance. Considering social and environmental impacts, along with economic ones, creates a positive impression with many stakeholders. Companies that have strong CSR programmes often display envied growth potential and low risk associated with their operations.
- Vision and → leadership drive markets and the world in which we live. Companies with good reputations have the foresight to seize new opportunities and lead their industries. Companies that incorporate CSR into their vision and → leadership understand the changing business environment and the permanency of CSR.
- The amount of admiration, trust, and respect that a stakeholder gives a company constitutes emotional appeal. Consistency in corporate communications and media news, products and services, and personal experience creates trust. Respecting stakeholders engenders respect from stakeholders.

- Employees say a lot about a company. Not only do their behaviour, choices and actions represent their employer, but they also have an intimate knowledge of their organisation. When employees talk, people listen. Talking of → work–life balance, benefits, continuing education, ethical and cooperative culture – stakeholders' perceptions of a company's workplace environment impact reputation.
- Business leaders have a responsibility to their stakeholders. Product responsibility, environmental stewardship, community involvement and engagement all reflect on companies' commitment to CSR, and thus their reputation.

Maintaining a positive corporate reputation together with strong CSR benefits businesses by helping them:

- Retain and recruit top talent;
- Facilitate strong partnerships;
- Increase sales;
- Enhance shareholder value; and
- Withstand crises.

Various tools exist for measuring corporate reputation, including media analysis, statistical modelling, and stakeholder polling. Interbrand conducts research to place value on intangibles, like their 100 Best Global Brands by Value. The Reputation Institute together with Harris-Wirthlin Brand Strategy Consulting group publishes the results of their Reputation Quotient (RQ) – a survey tool (including a CSR element) that measures the reputations of the most visible companies in the US. The Annual RQ is featured in the *Wall Street Journal*.

Paula Ivey

RESEARCH
→ Corporate social responsibility, Learning

CSR has been a vibrant field of research over the last five decades. Ever since Howard Bowen published his 1953 seminal book *Social Responsibilities of the Businessman*, there has been a rich stream of work on various aspects of CSR, using, next to CSR, a variety of labels and concepts such as → business ethics, sustainability, → corporate citizenship and business and society.

Over the years one could say that there has been a clear divide between work that has appeared until the late 1990s and research that has been published after that. While the first four decades have looked at CSR mostly from the perspective of single issues of concern for society, in the last decade CSR has moved onto the agenda of business studies in a more systematic fashion. In the first category we would count business exposure to issues like doing business in foreign countries (triggered by apartheid in South Africa), business and the → environment (triggered by events like Love Canal, Harrisburg, Bhopal or Seveso), → whistleblowing, equal opportunties, supply chain issues and → ethical consumption. CSR then was seen as an approach to tackling business challenges in areas where legal institutions as yet had not been implemented or where new and sudden changes in society exposed companies to new issues.

Since the mid-1990s, however, we witness a shifting interest in CSR. First, the interest in CSR has moved significantly beyond the area of business or management studies; rather we find a growing number of publications on CSR in philosophy, political science, international relations, sociology and law. The core topics investigated more recently focus on the role of CSR as an approach to societal governance. CSR, since the advent of → globalisation, declining governance abilities of the nation state and the rise of civil society and NGOs, has put corporations in the limelight of governing a host of global political issues, such as global warming, the fight against AIDS and other diseases in the developing world, the management of key technologies (such as → genetically modified organisms (GMOs)) or, more broadly, the substitution of governmental functions by private corporations, most notably through the privatisation of many formerly state run businesses or the lack of effective governance mechanisms in many → developing countries where business plays a role.

If we look at research topics investigated one could say that academics interested in CSR – most of them are still from a management background – have been intrigued by the relationship between CSR and the financial performance of organisations. Margolis and Walsh (in *Administrative Science Quarterly*, 2003) have analysed this stream of literature and found, however, that no conclusive evidence of either a positive or a negative relation has been produced – which challenges much of the '→ business case'-related research. Next to this, another focus of research has been in the area of → ethical decision-making and the effort to understand why and how exactly managers take decisions and what the role of ethical considerations is within these decisions. Overall, most of the research from a management background has been rather functionalist, meaning: it has looked at CSR from the perspective of the corporation and how the corporation could 'manage' its interface with society in a responsible or ethical, but at the same time also profitable, manner.

CSR research has produced a sizeable amount of published work. For a quick overview, we would recommend the recent *Oxford Handbook of CSR* (2007), which is the most up-to-date and comprehensive overview of the state of the art. There is, however, also a considerable number of specialist academic journals which have published CSR-related research over the last decades. The most important ones are:

- *Business & Society* (published by Sage, starting in 1960);
- *Business and Society Review* (published by Blackwell, starting in 1972);
- *Journal of Business Ethics* (published by Springer, starting in 1982);
- *Business Ethics Quarterly* (published by Society for Business Ethics, starting in 1991);

- *Business Ethics: A European Review* (published by Blackwell, starting in 1991);
- *Journal of Corporate Citizenship* (published by Greenleaf, starting in 2001);
- *Corporate Governance: The International Journal of Business in Society* (published by Emerald, starting in 2001); and
- *Corporate Social Responsibility and Environmental Management* (published by Wiley, starting in 2002).

Analysing this body of literature, a paper by Lockett, Moon and Visser in the *Journal of Management Studies* (2006) presents empirical evidence based on publication and citation analyses of CSR research published from 1992 to 2002. The results demonstrate that, for CSR research published in management journals:

- The most popular issues investigated have been the environment and ethics;
- The empirical research has been overwhelmingly of a quantitative nature;
- The theoretical research has been primarily non-normative;
- The field is driven by agendas in the business environment as well as by continuing scientific engagement; and
- The single most important source of references for CSR articles was the management literature itself.

The debate on CSR globally is rather vibrant and much of it takes place at academic conferences. Among the most important are the annual conferences of the Academy of Management ('Social Issues in Management' Division); the → Society for Business Ethics Conference; the → International Association of Business and Society; the → European Business Ethics Network; and the → European Academy of Business in Society. Increasingly though, we see a surge of similar events organised by organisations focusing on emerging economies, such as → CSR Asia or the → African Institute for Corporate Citizenship.

Dirk Matten and Wayne Visser

RESPONSIBLE CARE PROGRAMME
→ Chemicals sector, Oil and gas sector
⌐ www.responsiblecare.org

Responsible Care® is the global chemical industry's own unique initiative which helps the worldwide chemical industry to drive → continual improvement in all aspects of health, safety and environmental performance and to be open in communication about its activities and achievements.

Responsible Care® is both an ethic and a commitment intended to build trust and confidence in an industry that is essential to improving living standards, the quality of life and → sustainable development.

A set of Global Responsible Care® Core Principles commit companies and national associations to work together. Through the sharing of information and a rigorous system of checklists, performance indicators and verification procedures, Responsible Care® enables the industry to demonstrate how it has improved over the years and to develop policies for further improvement. In these ways, Responsible Care® helps the industry to gain the trust of the public and to operate safely, profitably and with due care for future generations.

Responsible Care was launched in 1984 in Canada and is now run by the national chemical associations of 52 countries around the world under the leadership of the International Council of Chemical Associations (ICCA).

In February 2006, the Responsible Care Global Charter was launched to ensure focus on the new and important challenges facing the chemical industry and global society, including the growing public dialogue over → sustainable development, public health issues related to the use of chemical products, the need for effective management, greater industry → transparency, and the opportunity to achieve better harmonisation and consistency among the national Responsible Care programmes. Today, the initiative commits national associations and their member companies to work together to:

- Continuously improve the environmental, → health and safety knowledge and performance of technologies, processes and products over their life cycles so as to avoid harm to people and the → environment;
- Use resources efficiently and minimise → waste;
- Report openly on performance, achievements and shortcomings;
- Listen, engage and work with people to understand and address their concerns and expectations;
- Cooperate with governments and organisations in the development and implementation of effective regulations and standards, and to meet or go beyond them; and
- Provide help and advice to foster the responsible management of → chemicals by all those who manage and use them along the product chain.

Dick Robson

RESPONSIBLE COMPETITIVENESS
→ Responsible Competitiveness Index
🖑 www.accountability21.net

Responsible competitiveness (RC) is a concept first advocated by AccountAbility in 2002 and defined as the precondition for an acceptable, viable → globalisation that aligns business opportunities and roles in → development with reduction in poverty, inequality and environmental security. The basic premise behind the concept is that responsible business practices are becoming an important driver for competitiveness. Further, national and international governments have a responsibility to develop and advance public policy initiatives that create an enabling environment for responsible business practices.

AccountAbility's RC research programme explores the relationship between responsible business practices and traditional notions of national competitiveness. The key construct developed for this analysis is the Responsible Competitiveness Index (RCI) that reveals which countries are achieving sustainable economic growth based on responsible business practices. So far, two RC Indexes have been published (2003 and 2006).

The implications for the RC work going forward are to:

- Better amplify the impact of corporate responsibility practices as a means of creating real transformation in markets, thereby also allowing more responsible companies to gain sustainable business advantage.
- Develop policy and practice on how best to amplify the impact of micro-level corporate responsibility practices at sector, regional and national levels by becoming a key factor in driving their underlying productivity and competitiveness.

Maria Sillanpää

RESPONSIBLE COMPETITIVENESS INDEX
→ Responsible competitiveness
⌐ www.accountability21.net

The Responsible Competitiveness Index is constructed of two key components: the → National Corporate Responsibility Index (NCRI) and the → World Economic Forum's Growth Competitiveness Index (GCI). The NCRI has been developed by AccountAbility and Fundação Dom Cabral and assesses over 80 countries on criteria including → corruption, human capital development, civic freedom, → corporate governance and environmental management to establish a global ranking. The GCI measures the ability of countries to reach sustained medium- and long-term economic growth. The NCRI ranking is correlated with the GCI to establish the Responsible Competitiveness Index.

Highlighted by the research to date is the failure of policy-makers to understand and exploit the potential synergies between economic growth and competitiveness, and business strategies and practices that factor in social and environmental performance. AccountAbility argues that this shortfall can have serious negative consequences. First, companies who are trying to enhance their own social, economic and environmental development impacts face real limits in what they can achieve without collective efforts in realigning market competitiveness to reward these practices. Second, national and regional competitiveness strategies will fail to take advantage of opportunities to use corporate responsibility to enhance both the quantitative and qualitative aspects of competitiveness that align economic growth more closely to → sustainable development.

These two outcomes, if allowed to persist, will lead over time to corporate responsibility practices being discredited for delivering too little. They can and are increasingly leading to the drive for international competitiveness being challenged for creating unacceptable negative → externalities.

Maria Sillanpää

RETAIL SECTOR

Retailers have a particularly important and influential role in CSR as they both shape the sustainability of their supply chains and determine the range of products and services available to consumers.

Within the → food industry consolidation has meant that approximately 30 retailers have captured around one-third of the global → food market. In the UK, it is estimated that the four biggest → food retailers (Tesco, Sainsbury's, ASDA and Morrisons) control 61% of the → food and grocery market. The immense power of these retailers has predictably led to increased pressure from consumers and NGOs for greater social responsibility. Increasingly, CSR is becoming part of the competitive landscape in retailing as the companies perceive it as both integral to their attempt to connect with customers and also key to the value of their brand. The CSR agenda for retailers focuses primarily on reporting and transparency, community, ethical sourcing, and environmental performance:

- Reporting and transparency

  There is a growing demand from stakeholders, customers and non-profits for greater → transparency and improved → non-financial reporting. Retailers are responding by increasingly seeking to communicate their commitment to CSR directly to customers. This is been done through a mix of techniques such as in-store marketing campaigns, product → labelling schemes and detailed CSR reports.

  In order to substantiate their rhetoric, a number of large retailers are developing and using independently verifiable key performance indicators (KPIs) to measure, monitor, benchmark and compare their CSR performance. Other retailers have chosen to develop their own KPIs. The KPIs tend to cover areas such as regeneration, energy efficiency, recycling cardboard, organics, charitable giving, employee retention, and supply-chain labour standards.

- Community

  As a consumer facing sector, the retail sector has a large focus on community investment. This is a core part of being a 'good neighbour' and is integral to the retailers' 'licence to operate' in the locality.

  Retailers need to acknowledge their social impacts through development of CSR initiatives which create long-term impact and benefits for both their business and the community. Such initiatives would address issues such as community relations, inclusivity, → health and safety, training and staff development, and charitable giving within the community.

- Ethical sourcing

Ethical sourcing – or supply chain management – is one of the most significant challenges faced by the retail sector today. Large retailers operate within the global marketplace, where goods and services are often made in one part of the world and sold within another, and they have become increasingly aware of the need for ethical sourcing and trading policies.

Retailers are particularly aware of the implications of → human rights issues at their overseas factories and are increasingly monitoring the factories that deliver products to them. Leading retailers are working collaboratively with each other and/or their suppliers to facilitate visibility across the entire supply chain from product development stage to the shop floor. The International Association of Department Stores is an example of global cooperation on ethical sourcing.

- Environmental performance

Retailers face a range of environmental issues, including carbon footprint, energy consumption and emissions, raw material usage, → water consumption, → waste, packaging, recycling, GM foods and the use of → chemicals.

Retailers do not only face a responsibility to deliver better environmental performance in their own operations but also to encourage it among their customers. A number of retailers have begun to deploy recycling units at their stores for use by customers.

The retail industry also generates large amounts of packaging, which customers dispose of domestically. Many retailers are now seeking to redesign and simplify their packaging and eliminate plastic bags in an effort to reduce → waste. Some → food retailers have started to try to address the carbon impact of their operations by reducing → food freight and sourcing locally, and informing their customers through product → labelling.

It is not always easy for retailers to align their CSR goals. For example, when assessing whether the environmental costs of importing fresh flowers from Kenya are outweighed by the social benefits of trading with less developed economies, retailers have to make difficult trade-offs. Retailers may also face dilemmas balancing CSR goals with the everyday operational imperatives faced by their store managers who are working to achieve demanding targets in a fiercely competitive business climate. Price pressures coupled with long complex supply chains also make monitoring of low pay and poor conditions overseas extremely difficult.

Within many parts of the UK and the US, but increasingly globally, there is concern about the social impacts of giant retailers. The large retailer model characterised by superstores is being blamed by some for the decline of local shopping areas. This raises a challenge for retailers in convincing local communities that they are contributing to their well-being.

Dermot Egan

RIO DECLARATION ON ENVIRONMENT AND DEVELOPMENT
→ Sustainable development
⌐ www.unep.org

In June 1992, the United Nations Conference on Environment and Development brought together heads of state and senior officials from 179 governments for the 'Earth Summit' in Rio de Janeiro. Along with thousands of representatives from civil society, science, international organisations and the media, they sought to build on the 1972 Stockholm Declaration on the Environment.

Following on from the report of the → World Commission on Environment and Development, 'Our Common Future', the Rio Declaration on Environment and Development emphasised for the first time that sustainable economic progress is only possible if it is linked to environmental protection. The resulting 27 principles called on nations to work together to eradicate poverty, to 'equitably meet developmental and environmental needs of present and future generations', and to recognise that 'environmental protection [must] constitute an integral part of the development process and cannot be considered in isolation from it'.

Alongside the Declaration, the Rio Summit also produced → Agenda 21, a global programme of work and cooperation. The emphasis on intergenerational and → intragenerational equity, and their dependence on the preservation of the → environment, has informed much → sustainable development thinking, public sector planning and CSR policy in the decades since.

Ruth Findlay-Brooks

RIO EARTH SUMMIT
→ Rio Declaration on Environment and Development

RISK MANAGEMENT
→ Reputation, Stakeholder theory

Risk management in a CSR context can be defined as the strategies, policies and processes of addressing potential ethical, social and environmental impacts which might cause stakeholders to react in ways that harm the corporation. Many companies enter the CSR world by awakening in a rather unfriendly manner to public criticism by their → stakeholders, voiced in protests, boycotts, bad press or → shareholder resolutions. CSR then becomes primarily a tool to manage the risks of perceived socially irresponsible behaviour to the financial bottom line of the company. And in fact one will hardly find a CSR report or website of major companies which does not address in detail the inextricable link of CSR and risk. One could argue that the avoidance or the management of risk in many companies is the key way to think about the → business case for CSR: CSR is implemented as an approach to manage risks to the bottom line.

CSR-related risk management has to address two fundamentally different areas. First and foremost, a company has to manage any potential negative effects on society, such as violation of emission targets, alienation of local communities and breach of → human rights along its supply chains. One would call this the management of actual risks. Even when the probability of these risks is fairly low the corporation does not want to be taken by surprise by the occurrence of these events. The second, equally important area is what one could call the management of perceived risks. Risk is an intellectual construct, based on perceived probabilities, multiplied with perceived impact or harm. This construction process, however, is highly subjective, as comparisons between the risk perception of car → travel (perceived as low risk, but in fact a high risk activity) and air → travel (perceived as high risk, but in fact a very low risk activity) shows. Stakeholders perceive risks often in a very different way than companies think about these risks. Subjective risk perception becomes an issue in most areas of CSR, most notably in the area of nuclear power, radiation from mobile phones or the use of → genetically modified organisms (GMOs).

The management of actual risks is a complex issue. As risk is a mathematical construct of probability and harm it is highly difficult to measure it: both have to be estimated and often there is only little past data available to properly assess CSR-related risks. Good risk management approaches attempt to think creatively of all potential sources of risks, and based on their probabilities and the potential harm, prioritise management attention to the issues. A stakeholder group which has succeeded rather effectively in causing companies to actively manage their CSR-related risks are shareholders: most modern → corporate governance codes in some shape or form would require a risk management committee as a formal place in the organisation where these issues are addressed.

The management of perceived risks is primarily concerned with shaping the risk perception of stakeholders. CSR → reporting is an important tool in this process as it provides an account of the impacts the company has on many CSR issues of potential stakeholder concern. Other forms would include various forms of → stakeholder engagement where companies can learn about the perceptions, preferences and → values of their stakeholders while at the same time building trust and providing material information on the risks in question. Many mediation processes in the context of controversies around siting of hazardous facilities, such as incineration plants, follow this logic. Finally, stakeholder → partnerships, most notably with → NGOs, are an important element in the management of risk perception: the better and longer a company knows its stakeholders and the more opportunities these have to actually participate to some degree in decision-making, the more likely the risk perception of the company and its stakeholders will converge.

Many CSR-related risks are so-called lifestyle risks: rather than being the result of the activities of an individual electricity company, global warming is the result of an energy intensive, fossil fuel-based lifestyle of industrial societies. Still, individual companies or industries are often held responsible for these risks as they are the initial commercial beneficiary of the underlying activities. As governments are unwilling and often unable (in the case of global risks) to regulate these issues, we see an increasing social expectation of society addressed at companies to assume responsibility for these lifestyle risks and to come up with collective, → self-regulatory approaches to tackle these issues.

Dirk Matten

SA 8000

→ Labour issues, Supply chain

🖰 www.sa-intl.org

In 1997, Social Accountability International (SAI) was established and convened an expert, international, multi-stakeholder, Advisory Board to partner in developing standards and systems to address workers' rights. Representatives of trade unions, → human rights organisations, academia, retailers, manufacturers, contractors, as well as consulting, accounting, and → certification firms, by consensus, cooperated to develop the SA 8000 (SA 8000) Standard. Published in late 1997 and revised in 2001, the SA 8000 Standard and verification system is a credible, comprehensive and efficient tool for assuring humane workplaces. The SA 8000 system includes:

- Factory-level management system requirements for ongoing compliance and → continual improvement.
- Independent, expert verification of compliance by SAI-accredited → certification bodies.
- Involvement by stakeholders including participation by all key sectors in the SA 8000 system: workers, trade unions, companies, socially responsible investors, non-governmental organisations and government.
- Public reporting on SA 8000 certified facilities and Corporate Involvement Program (CIP) and annual progress reports through postings on the SAI website.
- Harnessing consumer and investor concern through the SA 8000 Certification and Corporate Involvement Program by helping to identify and support companies that are committed to assuring → human rights in the workplace.
- Training partnerships for workers, managers, auditors and other interested parties in effective use of SA 8000.
- Research and publication of guidance in the effective use of SA 8000.
- Complaints, appeals and surveillance processes to support the system's quality.

The SA 8000 Standard is an auditable → certification standard based on international workplace norms of International Labour

Organisation (ILO) conventions, the Universal Declaration of Human Rights and the UN Convention on the Rights of the Child. The SA 8000 Standard is available for download in various languages. A summary of the Standard elements follows:

- → Child labour
- Forced labour
- → Health and safety
- Freedom of association and right to collective bargaining
- Discrimination
- Discipline
- Working hours
- Compensation
- Management systems

SAFETY
→ Health and safety, Human security, Security

SARBANES-OXLEY ACT
→ Corporate governance
⌐ www.sec.gov

The US Sarbanes–Oxley Act of 2002 is also known as the 'Public Company Accounting Reform and Investor Protection Act'. It was passed in response to high profile business failures, such as Enron and WorldCom, in order to reinforce investment confidence and protect investors by improving the accuracy and reliability of corporate disclosure. The Act mandated a number of reforms to enhance corporate responsibility, enhance financial disclosures and combat corporate and accounting → fraud, and created the 'Public Company Accounting Oversight Board', also known as the PCAOB, to oversee the activities of the → auditing profession. Despite being a domestic regulation in the US the 'SOX', as it is often referred to, has had far reaching implications for many global companies as compliance with the Act in their US subsidiaries had fairly direct implication for the accounting and governance procedures of these companies.

SECURITY
→ Human security

SELF-REGULATION
→ Civil regulation, Legal compliance, Regulation

Corporate 'self-regulation' refers to voluntary approaches by companies to govern their own actions to benefit the greater society, as opposed to being guided by 'command and control' government regulations or economic instruments such as taxes and charges.

Japanese companies have proved themselves masters of self-regulation, usually working in broad agreement throughout corporate sectors and with government officials.

Self-regulation may come in the form of a number of companies or organisations agreeing to a set of rules or standards. For example, under the → Equator Principles, banks agree not to lend money for a project unless the borrower completes a detailed assessment that explains how it will meet criteria for → sustainable development and other social goals. These principles have been adopted by most major global financial institutions, including: Citigroup, Bank of America, HSBC and J.P. Morgan Chase.

The → Forest Stewardship Council (FSC) certifies that the operations of given companies are 'sustainable', a judgement that covers environmental and social impacts. This and other such → certification schemes are self-regulation in the sense that companies voluntarily agree to letting themselves be guided and judged by a third party.

Companies take voluntary action for a variety of reasons: to satisfy the social and environmental concerns of customers, shareholders and other stakeholders; to improve the public image of the company; or to avoid the imposition of new government regulations.

One problem with self-regulation is freeriders – those companies that save money by not regulating themselves, while also hoping to avoid government regulation because of self-regulation by others. Also, self-regulations may not go far enough to have the effects desired by society, and companies working together on self-regulation or voluntary standards for a sector may be accused of cartel-like activities.

Views on the value of self-regulation are plainly divided. The → World Business Council for Sustainable Development (WBCSD) argues that self-regulation cannot always prevail alone. And in such cases it must be complemented by rules and regulations. In general, however, self-regulation clearly carries benefits, encouraging companies to act responsibly, and simultaneously stay ahead of the development curve rather than submit to enforced regulation at a later date, and at greater cost.

Over the years, the WBCSD has run many 'sector projects' bringing together companies in a given sector to determine ways toward sustainable progress. These include work in forestry, mining, cement, mobility, electricity utilities, and tyres.

The Cement Sustainability Initiative is typical. Cement companies hired the Battelle Institute to identify its main sustainability challenges. They then divided into working groups on CO_2 emissions management, responsible use of fuels and materials, employee → health and safety, emissions monitoring and reporting, and local impacts on lands and communities. They have worked with NGOs and government bodies, reported on progress and appointed an independent body of experts to guarantee the validity of the work.

Self-regulation may prove particularly important in the area of energy and → climate change as governments find it hard to agree on ways forward. More and more companies are developing their own sophisticated systems of greenhouse gas management and internal trading of carbon dioxide.

Björn Stigson

SHAREHOLDER ACTIVISM
→ Socially responsible investment

Shareholder activism encompasses a variety of tactics through which stockowners communicate concerns to the management of corporations. Socially responsible investors use these tactics primarily to raise sustainability, economic justice, and → corporate governance issues.

Shareholder activism emerged in the 1970s as an alternative to the Wall Street Walk dictum, which stated that if you don't like corporate management sell your shares. Shareholder activists, by contrast, are committed to using their leverage as shareholders to seek change at corporations.

In one form, shareholder activism includes the filing of shareholder resolutions (primarily a North American phenomenon) and the voting by stockowners on these resolutions. Each year in the United States and Canada, religious groups, socially responsible investors, union and public pension funds, and others file hundreds of shareholder resolutions on issues such as the → environment, → human rights, racial and → gender → discrimination, militarism, and → corporate governance. Asset managers have a fiduciary duty to vote on these resolutions and, in the United States, must now disclose their voting policies and their actual votes on these issues.

In another form, shareholder activism consists primarily of dialogue between investors – or, increasingly, coalitions of investors – and corporations on specific issues, and is often referred to as engagement. For example, the → Carbon Disclosure Project is a worldwide coalition of institutional investors pressing major corporations to disclose their carbon emissions. The → Extractive Industries Transparency Initiative is a similar coalition urging disclosure of payments by companies in the extractive industries to the governments of countries in which they operate.

Most recently, both public interest, NGOs and institutional investors have increasingly turned to shareholder activism. NGOs often partner with social investors in raising social and environmental issues. Institutional investors, including pension funds and hedge funds, have increasingly used shareholder activism to call for improvements in → corporate governance or in overall financial performance.

Steve Lydenberg

SHAREHOLDER DEMOCRACY

→ Corporate governance, Shareholder activism, Stakeholder democracy

This term describes the philosophy that the relationship between investors and a company's board and management should somehow resemble the model of parliamentary democracy. The key parallels of this metaphor are that shareholders have a right to influence decision-making and have some degree of involvement in the governance of the firm, while the board and management has the duty of → accountability, → transparency and information supply to its shareholding owners. For decades investors were seen as remote and passive owners of a company's stock satisfied with seeking appreciation of the shares owned but uninvolved in the governance or decisions of the company's management and board.

With the recent wave of company scandals in the US resulting in financial harm to investors, especially institutional investors have

become much more involved in expressing opinions and holding companies accountable. To be effective in holding companies
accountable the proxy rules and means of communication between
management and investors must allow meaningful access and the
ability to challenge a company through the proxy rules if necessary.

Thus investors have been pressing for governance reforms that
would allow them to take steps like actually electing directors
requiring a majority vote, having the ability to nominate directors,
asking for compensation packages to be voted on by stockholders
in an advisory vote, having the auditors ratified annually as well
as other changes. All this builds on the belief that as the owner
shareholders need to have shareholder democracy rather than total
control being at the top by the board and management.

It is still a far cry from political democracy but it opens up the
ability to promote change in companies if the democratic process
is further expanded.

Timothy Smith

SHAREHOLDER RESOLUTION
→ Shareholder activism

A shareholder in the United States (and in other countries, depending on local regulation) is able to sponsor a resolution with a company for a vote by all investors at the annual stockholder meeting.

This resolution, filed in accordance with regulations of the Securities & Exchange Commission, must be under 500 words and be
sent to the company's corporate secretary by a date specified in the
proxy statement.

The resolution often leads to a constructive dialogue between the
sponsor(s) and the management resulting in the company changing
a policy or practice. The resolution cannot deal with issues of
'ordinary business' for the company or it can be omitted if the
company appeals to the SEC.

Resolutions on social and environmental issues started in the early 1970s while resolutions on stockholder rights and governance go back to the 1950s. Examples of specific issues dealt with in recent proxy seasons include

- The → environment and → climate change;
- → Diversity with employees;
- Disclosure of political contributions;
- → Corporate governance reforms; and
- Corporate responsibility reporting.

In 2006 over 1300 such resolutions were sponsored. Investors believe this is exercising shareholder democracy. Sponsors can range from individual investors to major pension funds to a → foundation or trade union.

In recent years votes in favour of such regulations have grown considerably since institutional investors are paying more attention to their voting of proxies. In fact, the SEC now requires that all mutual funds annually disclose their proxy voting records.

Timothy Smith

SIGMA PROJECT
→ Environmental management systems
⌐ www.projectsigma.co.uk

The SIGMA Project aims to provide clear, practical advice to organisations to help them make a meaningful contribution to → sustainable development.

The SIGMA project has developed guidelines which help organisations to:

- Effectively meet challenges posed by social, environmental and economic dilemmas, threats and opportunities; and
- Become architects of a sustainable future.

The SIGMA Project – Sustainability Integrated Guidelines for Management – was launched in 1999 with the support of the UK

Department of Trade and Industry. It is a partnership between the British Standards Institution (the leading standards organisation), Forum for the Future (a leading sustainability charity and think-tank), and AccountAbility (the international professional body for → accountability).

The Guidelines consist of:

- A set of Guiding Principles that help organisations to understand sustainability and their contribution to it; and
- A Management Framework that integrates sustainability issues into core processes and mainstream decision-making. It is structured into phases and sub-phases.

SIGMA is the first of its kind, but it links into existing management systems and frameworks such as → ISO 14001, Investors in People, the → ISO 9000 series, OHSAS 18001 and AA 1000 Framework, thus enabling compatibility with existing systems and helping organisations to build on what they already have in place.

SIN TAXES
→ Carbon tax, Eco-taxation, Externalities

Sin taxes is the slang term for taxes that seek to discourage consumers from buying products considered malign, dangerous or destructive. They form part of a taxation regime designed to influence consumer demand through the price in the market, rather than through legislative regulation. The intention is to privilege economic activity considered benign, and to discourage harmful activity.

The most widely known sin taxes were traditionally laid upon cigarettes and alcohol – hence the term – but latterly they have been incorporated into a wider fiscal philosophy sometimes called 'Taxing Bads, not Goods', or 'Taxing Value Subtracted rather than Value Added'. Sin taxes are sometimes criticised as part of the 'nanny state' – largely because not everyone agrees on what constitutes 'bads' and 'goods'. For example, proposals to introduce taxes upon carbon emissions will raise the cost of transport, and thus privilege local production. Similarly taxes upon polluting → chemicals will privilege organic production of agricultural products. These have wide political implications, and affect fundamentally the way that economies operate and which companies benefit.

Responsible companies will seek to avoid activity that will attract sin taxes.

Margaret Legum

SMALL AND MEDIUM SIZED ENTERPRISES (SMEs)
→ Leadership

Small and medium sized enterprises (SMEs) are the most common form of private business in both developed and → developing countries. There are many varied definitions, but a standard one is the European Union version which defines SMEs as having fewer than 250 employees.

There are a number of characteristics of social responsibility in SMEs which make them distinctive from the rather dominant view of CSR which takes a corporate perspective. While SMEs are themselves a varied group subject to different regional, legislative and sector-specific issues influencing social responsibility, it is possible to identify key characteristics which help us understand the different nature of small business organisations compared to large firms, including the following:

- There is a lack of codification of CSR. SMEs are unlikely to have signed up to CSR agreements, organisations and standards. As such, there is a difficulty in measuring social responsibility in SMEs.
- Personal motivation for taking socially responsible initiatives is more important than marketing, strategic or public relations approaches. SMEs are usually run by individuals who both own and manage the organisation and react on an ad hoc, personal

basis to social needs. They are unlikely to have resources to focus on strategic gains or indeed deal with the issues from a marketing or PR perspective.

- Employees are very important stakeholders in SMEs. A key characteristic of SME social responsibility is to respond to their preferences in terms of charitable support and giving, and indeed to focus efforts on ensuring the maintenance of the livelihoods of employees, managers and owners.
- Informal relationships are critical to the success of most SMEs. This is closely linked to their reputation at a local, personal level. This is closely tied to a need to act with honesty and → integrity.

It should be acknowledged that many SMEs, and indeed some larger firms, are family businesses. This brings an additional influence on social responsibility, with family commitments being very much intertwined with business → values.

The CSR sector context is particularly important for SMEs, influencing the culture in relation to social responsibility. For example, a local garage is bound to respond to issues within its local community since community members are customers, employees and neighbours, whereas an internet marketing firm is more likely to operate in a virtual environment, concerned with broader issues of → marketing ethics and responsibilities relating to new technological advancements.

SMEs often have an undeserved poor reputation in relation to social responsibility and → business ethics, perhaps due to general ignorance of the characteristics mentioned above. Research is beginning to redress this gap in understanding. Policy-makers, including the European Union, have taken note of the importance of including SMEs in the debate on CSR, giving special consideration to them in the → EU Green Paper on Corporate Social Responsibility, → EU Multi-Stakeholder Forum on CSR and the → European Alliance for CSR.

A possible reason for the lack of awareness of social responsibility approaches by SMEs is their conflation with the notion of entrepreneurship. Entrepreneurs are commonly assumed to be short-term profit maximising, uncompromising individuals. While owner-managers of SMEs may well be entrepreneurial in that they seek new markets, take calculated risks and innovate in order to survive, they are not, typically, driven by profit maximisation. The main reasons for running your own business are things like independence and challenge.

An understanding of SME issues in relation to → business ethics and social responsibility is important for the corporate sector. This is particularly pertinent in relation to managing the supply chain since often it is the case that large customers dominate the chain and dictate conditions to smaller suppliers. These may range from seeking → assurance that the SME is compliant with CSR standards, to the fairness of the treatment of the supplier (e.g. terms and conditions, timely payment). Given the comments above, large firms should be careful not to assume that formal standards are a relevant measure of CSR in SMEs. Furthermore, corporate CSR and ethics policies should cover the relationship with SME suppliers, seeking open and honest partnership rather than exploitation and short-term gain.

Laura J. Spence

SOCIAL ACCOUNTABILITY INTERNATIONAL (SAI)

→ SA 8000

Social Accountability International (SAI) is a worker's rights organisation that developed SA 8000, a widely accepted labour standard and ethical management system based on International Labour Organisation standards and United Nations → human rights conventions. Established in 1996, SAI works with workers, trade unions, companies, socially responsible investors, non-governmental organisations and government.

The SA 8000 Standard is the first certifiable labour rights standard that can be verified. Distinguishing characteristics include factory-level usage, independent verification of compliance by SAI-accredited → certification bodies, public reporting, basic needs wage requirements, applicability in China as well as across supply chains of the private, public and non-governmental sectors, training, and complaints, appeals and surveillance processes.

SAI was created out of the Council on Economic Priorities (CEP), a CSR pioneer founded in 1969 that produced notable research and publications on issues such as corporate ratings and the consumer guide *Shopping for a Better World*.

CEP arose from a study commissioned in 1968 by a pension fund in Boston that asked a securities analyst, Alice Tepper Marlin, to compile a 'peace portfolio' of corporations with the least involvement in supplying the war in Vietnam. Such information was not readily available at the time. More than 600 organisations requested the study. Responding to that demand, Tepper Marlin founded CEP, where she served for 33 years as president.

Continuing a long tradition in the relatively young CSR field, SAI ushered in the mainstreaming of labour rights standards in the formative years of development and continues to lead their integration into business practices globally.

Jonathan Cohen

SOCIAL AND ENVIRONMENTAL ACCOUNTING

→ Environmental liabilities, Non-financial reporting

Social and environmental accounting comprises a set of techniques for measuring the impact of corporate activities on the community (both local and international), employees, consumers and the physical environment. It offers a mechanism for reporting data that enables management to monitor key social and environmental opportunities and threats facing the organisation as well as providing an internal information system to support the external reporting function.

The report of the American Accounting Association's Committee on Social Costs (1975) indicates that three levels of measurement may be employed in the social and environmental accounting function. At the most basic level, activities and related impacts are identified and described. The next level involves measurement using non-monetary units, while at the highest level an attempt is made to financially quantify corporate social and environmental impacts.

Much attention in recent years has focused on the financial quantification of environmental impacts, largely as a consequence of the 'polluter pays' ethos driving much environmental legislation throughout the industrialised world. A key concern here is to charge all identifiable costs to the cause of their creation and subsequently to allocate them to products. Established management accounting techniques such as activity-based costing (ABC) and life cycle costing are increasingly being utilised towards this end. The ultimate aim is to develop a full environmental costing system that, in addition to identifying operating costs such as energy usage, $\rightarrow$ waste disposal and regulatory compliance, can encompass intangible benefits (notably improved customer satisfaction and employee motivation) resulting from achieving higher environmental performance standards as well as providing a means to internalise significant external costs. The latter aspect gives rise to severe practical problems inherent in employing non-market valuation techniques as well as raising uncomfortable questions concerning the sustainability of many current business practices.

A further focus for financial quantification has centred on attempts to provide a valuation of the organisation's human capital, i.e. its workforce. The decade from the mid-1960s to the mid-1970s witnessed much experimentation, particularly in the United States, in human resource accounting. The models developed were initially cost based, and later value based. In the case of the former, costs incurred in recruiting, training and developing or replacing employees, instead of being written off immediately, are capitalised and amortised over the expected working life of the employee. By contrast, value-based methods adopt a more forward looking economic income approach, based, for example, on discounting future salaries or future forecast earnings of the firm, in attempting to value the future economic contribution the employee may make to the organisation. Lack of significant practical applications of human resource valuation techniques caused interest in the area to fade in the late 1970s. However, the ascendance of the post-industrial knowledge economy has led to a resurgence of interest, notably in Scandinavia, in the guise of intellectual capital accounting.

In contrast to developments in accounting systems addressing environmental impact and human resources, there is a paucity of evidence suggesting that similar attention has been focused on community and consumer issues. While information clearly is collected, it would appear that it is generally not collated centrally as part of a fully developed internal management information system. A rare exception here is provided by the comprehensive social book-keeping system developed in the mid-1990s by the UK 'values-based' organisation Traidcraft, which imports products from → developing countries for sale in the domestic market. The growing popularity of 'triple-bottom line' external reporting, underpinned by rigorous reporting guidelines such as the → Global Reporting Initiative, may well focus future corporate attention on the need to introduce robust internal information gathering systems to support such initiatives.

David Owen

SOCIAL AUDITING
→ Assurance, Auditing

Social auditing encompasses different types of audit which are used to measure and report on an organisation's social and ethical impacts, policies, management systems or performance.

It is an objective, systematic and documented process of collecting and evaluating evidence against predetermined criteria to establish the social and ethical status of the organisation or confirm (verify) assertions regarding the organisation's social and ethical performance. The audit criteria may be determined by the organisation's internal policies, practices or controls; statutory regulations; conventions, voluntary → codes of conduct (e.g. ILO declarations, the → UN Global Compact), the requirements of a formally recognised social management system such as SA 8000; or internal or external → non-financial reporting guidelines.

Social auditing often focuses on the working conditions (→ health and safety), → labour relations or broader → human rights issues in an organisation's own facilities or in its supply chain, but also on responsible social behaviour (responsible advertising, responsible consumption). This type of social auditing has increased in importance as a result of → globalisation and the increasing use of outsourcing and off-shoring in both manufacturing and service industries. Social auditing may also be used to measure an organisation's social and ethical impacts or performance in relation to local communities.

The most common goal of social auditing is ultimately to improve the organisation's social and ethical performance. It is often aimed at enhancing → transparency and → accountability to the organisation's stakeholders.

Jennifer Iansen-Rogers and George Molenkamp

SOCIAL ENTERPRISE
→ Social entrepreneurship

SOCIAL ENTREPRENEURSHIP

→ Environmental entrepreneurship

Social entrepreneurship describes the discovery and sustainable exploitation of opportunities to create social and environmental benefits. This is usually done through the generation of disequilibria in market and non-market environments. The social entrepreneurship process can in some cases lead to the creation of social enterprises. These social ventures are hybrid organisations exhibiting characteristics of both the for-profit and not-for-profit sector. Individuals engaging in social entrepreneurship are usually referred to as social entrepreneurs, a term that describes resourceful individuals working to create social innovation. They do not only have to identify (or create) opportunities for social change (that so far have been unexploited), they must also muster the resources necessary to turn these opportunities into reality. A typical example is Muhammad Yunus, founder of the Grameen Bank (Bangladesh) and recipient of the Nobel Peace Prize in recognition of his contribution to poverty alleviation through the invention and popularisation of → microfinance.

Today many → foundations aim to identify and promote social entrepreneurs. Two prominent examples are Ashoka and the Skoll Foundation. These so-called venture philanthropists adopt methods from the domain of venture capital, for example, encouraging social entrepreneurs to provide detailed business plans and to measure and report systematically on their social performance. Social return on investment (S-ROI) analysis is an example of an emerging tool aimed at describing the social impact of social entrepreneurship in dollar terms, relative to the philanthropic investment made.

Kai Hockerts

SOCIAL IMPACT ASSESSMENT

→ Impact assessment

SOCIAL INNOVATION
→ Corporate social entrepreneur, Social entrepreneurship

SOCIAL JUSTICE
→ Intragenerational equity

The concept of social justice describes an ideal state of society where individuals and social groups enjoy protection of their basic → human rights and receive a just share of the benefits of social cooperation. In real societies, however, deviations from this ideal appear to be the rule rather than the exception. → Discrimination, exclusion, and inequality are causes for a continuing debate on how social justice may be realised and how the rights of individuals and minorities can be protected against the state and their fellow citizens.

This debate is mainly driven by competing political ideologies. More right wing-oriented authors stress individual liberty and suggest a restriction of state influence. They believe that social justice can be achieved as a result of voluntary exchange on free markets: due to its motivating and resource allocating effects functioning markets will lead to an optimum allocation of resources, a raise in production output, and a fair distribution of income gains. In short they argue that social injustice must be resolved by strengthening markets. Proponents of this view would see CSR as one avenue to social justice as companies might be rewarded by consumers or investors for increased socially responsible behaviour.

By contrast, more left wing authors point to → externalities and market failures. They emphasise the crucial role of the state in steering the economy towards social justice and the public good by means of regulation, income redistribution and the inclusion of minorities and suppressed voices. Here social injustice has to be resolved by the engagement of the state and a correction of market results. In political philosophy alternative conceptions of society and social justice are discussed which often are an expression of these political ideologies (e.g. liberalism, communitarism, republicanism).

Andreas Georg Scherer

SOCIALLY RESPONSIBLE INVESTMENT (SRI)

→ Shareholder activism

Socially responsible investment (SRI) is an investment practice that includes the evaluation of social, environmental, and/or ethical issues in the analysis and selection of financial products and in communications between investors and the issuers of these products.

Investors pursue SRI strategies for a number of reasons:

- To avoid investments inconsistent with their ethical precepts;
- To improve corporate behaviour on social and environmental matters;
- To identify financial risks often overlooked by traditional analysts; or
- To participate in public debate on the proper relationship between corporations – and other issuers of investment products – and society.

SRI has been variously referred to as ethical investment, sustainable investment, best-of-class investment, and triple bottom line investment. It is closely related to CSR because social investors seek to identify companies with strong CSR records for their investments and to encourage increased levels of CSR.

SRI has its roots in the investment practices of faith-based investors. On religious and moral grounds a number of religious organisations have, for many years, shunned the financial products of specific industries – e.g. producers of alcohol, gambling, tobacco, and occasionally arms manufacturers.

In the early 1970s, SRI in its modern form modified this avoidance practice by introducing three new practices:

- Use of social and environmental standards to choose among the stocks issued by corporations in the full gamut of industries;
- Use of shareholder activism to advocate specific changes in the social and environmental practices of the corporations issuing these stocks; and
- Use of investments – primarily fixed-return instruments such as deposits, loans, and bonds – to promote economic development in communities that historically had been underserved by the mainstream.

The term SRI is often applied narrowly to the process of stock selection in part because the SRI world has focused most of its research on corporations and their equities. However, both shareholder activism, and → community investing have been a part of its agenda in its modern form. In addition, over the past decade, SRI has focused increasing attention on other financial assets and issuers, including fixed income, real estate, and venture capital.

The history of SRI can be divided into two general periods, the first running from 1970 to the mid-1990s, and the second from the mid-1990s to the present.

In the first period, SRI was largely a North American phenomenon. Starting in the early 1970s, a limited number of SRI unit trusts (mutual funds) and money managers began serving retail investors and small institutions. Large institutional investors then became involved in SRI through the anti-apartheid South Africa divestment movement, which began in the 1970s and culminated in the early 1990s. Ultimately scores of US state and local pension funds, among others, screened billions of dollars in assets according to companies' labour records and levels of involvement in South Africa.

Throughout this period and continuing to today, US religious organisations have played a leading role in shareholder activism through the annual filing of hundreds of shareholder resolutions on social and environmental issues. Simultaneously, a number of community development banks, credit unions, and revolving loan funds were founded and attracted support from SRI investors.

During the second period, SRI developed into a worldwide phenomenon, starting in the United Kingdom, where it took root in the 1980s, and extending rapidly to → Europe, and then to → Asia, → Africa, and → Latin America. Its growth has paralleled the strong growth of interest in CSR throughout the world over this time.

In these regions, SRI has favoured the vocabulary of sustainability investing, triple bottom line investing, best-of-class investing, and engagement. The → triple bottom line includes environmental, social and financial concerns – sometimes referred to as people, planet, and profits. Best-of-class investing entails selection of a limited number of companies with the best sustainability records in all available industries. Engagement consists of communications with corporations through dialogue and discussion.

Among the most significant developments in this second phase are the following:

- The increasing interest of large European pension funds in SRI. In particular, since 2000, a number of the public and private pension funds in Norway, Sweden, Denmark, the Netherlands, and France have imposed a variety of social and environmental standards in the management of a part, or all, of their assets.
- The increasing interest of large British and European money managers in engagement. Since the late 1990s, many of the largest money managers in the United Kingdom have begun actively engaging with corporations on social, environmental, and → corporate governance issues on behalf of all their clients.

- The launch of SRI products in → Asia, → Africa, and → Latin America. Starting in the late 1990s, → Australia and Japan have developed active markets for SRI unit trusts (mutual funds). The stock exchanges of South Africa, Israel, and Brazil have also launched 'SRI indexes' to encourage CSR among companies listed in those countries.
- The expansion of → community investing to include → microfinance, social venture capital, and other forms of social entrepreneurship.

Reflecting the global nature of this expansion, the United Nations has become increasingly active in promoting SRI through the UN Environmental Programme's Financial Initiative, the launch in 2006 of the Principles for Responsible Investment, and the designation of 2005 as the Year of Microcredit.

Steve Lydenberg

SOCIAL REPORTING
→ Non-financial reporting

SOCIAL RESPONSIBILITY
→ Corporate social responsibility

SOCIAL VENTURE NETWORK
🖰 www.svn.org

Social Venture Network (SVN) is made up of more than 420 socially conscious business leaders in North America. Founded in 1987, SVN sees itself as a community of business leaders – company founders, private investors, social entrepreneurs and key influencers – who share a commitment to building a just and sustainable world through business. The relationships and initiatives born within the network have ranged from building personal ties between like minded individuals to investment deals to founding entire organisations. SVN supports action at three inter-related levels:

- Individual – SVN cultivates personal development by encouraging the expression of → values through work and moving beyond traditional leadership roles.
- Organisational – SVN fosters business partnerships that forge new models for social-purpose enterprise, particularly those that generate profitable opportunities in disenfranchised communities.
- Societal – SVN encourages public service and social action by leveraging the voices of business leaders to bring about positive social change.

SOCIETY FOR BUSINESS ETHICS
→ Business ethics
🖰 www.societyforbusinessethics.org

Founded in 1980, the Society for Business Ethics (SBE) is a non-affiliated international association of predominantly scholars interested in → business ethics. Membership in SBE is open to scholars and professionals from all disciplines who specialise in → business ethics. SBE provides a forum in which moral, legal, empirical, and philosophical issues of → business ethics may be openly discussed and analysed and aims at the improvement of the teaching of → business ethics in universities and organisations. SBE, among other things, conducts an annual meeting for the presentation and discussion of new research and produces the scholarly journal *Business Ethics Quarterly* which many CSR scholars consider the top journal in the field.

SPONSORSHIP
→ Philanthropy

STAKEHOLDER DEMOCRACY
→ Stakeholder theory

Traditionally the concept of democracy has been employed in relation to the corporation either in the context of industrial relations, and therefore workplace democracy, or in the context of → corporate governance, and therefore shareholder democracy. More recently, given the growing appreciation of the role of a wider set of stakeholders, the concept of stakeholder democracy is beginning to emerge. In this context the focus is on how far stakeholders have certain democratic rights in governing the corporation. In development studies a more specific construction has emerged. Here, stakeholder democracy theory proposes an ideal system of governance of a society where all stakeholders in an organisation or activity have the same opportunity to govern that organisation or activity. Stakeholder groups are key to this process, as well as also being the subjects of democratic governance. The growing interface of political theory with management studies, in light of growing societal contestation of the corporate form, is likely to make stakeholder democracy theory a vibrant conceptual field in future.

Jem Bendell

STAKEHOLDER ENGAGEMENT
→ Stakeholder theory

The past few decades have seen a shift in the role of the corporation in society. Some of the key factors causing this are the → globalisation of markets, the emergence of global social and environmental challenges like → HIV/AIDS and → climate change, as well as the decreased ability of individual national governments to address such issues by themselves. Added to this, the more than 10 fold growth in the number of international non-governmental organisations from just above 3000 to well beyond 40 000 in less than 10 years has clearly introduced an influential third sector to societal debate and decision-making. One outcome from all these → developments is an increase in the complexity and dynamics of the operating environment for all kinds of organisations, including businesses. In order to understand and address the issues emerging out of this dynamic complexity, individual actors, whether businesses, civil society organisations or governments, are becoming increasingly dependent on mutual → learning, shared knowledge and pooled capabilities.

In this changing environment, businesses now play a more important role than ever before. Their activities have economic, environmental and social impacts on society from a local through to a global scale. In many countries, businesses play an active part in the shaping of public policy and regulatory → developments. Furthermore, a wave of privatisation in many parts of the world and a growing number of public – private partnerships has increased the role of the private sector in delivering what have traditionally been seen as public services. The increased involvement of private corporations in international → development activities, often in cooperation with inter- and supranational bodies, is another significant development in this context.

In response to the enhanced role of business in society, more and more members or representatives of different social groups impacted by corporate behaviour, claim their right to be informed of, consulted on and involved in corporate decision-making. In many developed countries, these claims have been enshrined in legislation, which requires consultation before taking potential high impact decisions, for example on the location of an industrial production plant. Consequently, many corporations have come to regard engagement and dialogue with a variety of individuals and entities on social, environmental and economic issues as an important aspect of how they manage their activities.

However, the first steps in stakeholder engagement (first generation) were often driven by external pressures, undertaken in an ad-hoc manner and limited to issues that provoked conflict with stakeholders. Many businesses, realising the benefits of a more proactive, broad and ongoing dialogue, then started to develop more sophisticated and systematic approaches to stakeholder engagement. These second generation stakeholder engagement activities have proven to increase mutual understanding, mitigate risks and solve conflicts more effectively.

Today, leading companies have started to develop an appreciation that stakeholder engagement can contribute to → learning and innovation in products and processes, and enhance the sustainability of strategic decisions within and outside of the company. This third generation stakeholder engagement enables companies to align social, environmental and economic performance drivers with core business strategies and constructively renegotiate the shifting responsibility and → accountability boundaries between different societal actors. Third generation stakeholder engagement processes often involve a pooling of resources (e.g. know-how, financial, human or operational resources) that can help all parties involved to gain insights, solve problems, and reach goals that none of them could reach alone.

Despite the obvious challenges of stakeholder engagement, the outcomes of best possible practice in stakeholder engagement clearly justify the necessary efforts. Successful stakeholder engagement not only helps companies to secure leadership in an increasingly complex and ever changing business environment, but will also help to bring about systemic change towards → sustainable development.

Effective and strategically aligned stakeholder engagement can:

- Lead to more equitable and sustainable social development by giving those who have a right to be heard the opportunity to be considered in decision-making processes;
- Enable better management of risk and reputation;

- Allow for the pooling of resources (knowledge, people, money and → technology) to solve problems and reach objectives that cannot be reached by single organisations;
- Enable understanding of complex business environments, including market developments and identification of new strategic opportunities;
- Enable corporations to learn from stakeholders, resulting in product and process improvements;
- Inform, educate and influence stakeholders and the business environment to improve their decision-making and actions that impact on the company and on society; and
- Build trust between a company and its stakeholders.

Maria Sillanpää

STAKEHOLDER MANAGEMENT
→ Stakeholder theory

Stakeholder management is a practical four-level framework, developed from the insights of stakeholder theory, which executives use to create value for customers, employees, suppliers, communities, and financiers and to connect → values and ethics to the execution of their business strategy.

- The first level is about purpose and core → values, requiring executives to have clear answers to questions like: what do we stand for, and for whom do we want to create value?
- After articulating the specific ends a firm wants to serve, the second level addresses the means of achieving those goals with stakeholders. Key questions are: how are we going to manage and govern our relationships with stakeholders so that participation will continue to be fruitful for both parties, and what principles are we committed to so that stakeholders can count on our support and our actions?

- The third level addresses the wider societal context in which the firm operates. In order to take account of whether or not society appreciates and approves of the direction the firm is going, executives must ask questions like: what are our most vocal critics saying about us, and is there a way of opening a dialogue with our critics, so that we can learn from them how to realise our purpose and principles in a better way?
- The final level of stakeholder management encourages executives to see → leadership as inextricable from ethics. On this view, the very idea of → leadership cannot be stated without implied ethical judgement. Presumably, leaders are legitimate and social legitimacy begins with the idea that one is acting from an ethical point of view.

R. Edward Freeman and Bidhan Parmar

STAKEHOLDERS

→ Stakeholder engagement, Stakeholder management, Stakeholder theory

Stakeholders are those who impact and are impacted by an organisation's decisions and actions. A stake in decision-making processes allows for stakeholders to be engaged, which consequently impacts success and failure. Transparent engagement engenders trust between an institution and its stakeholders and builds relationships. Effective stakeholder engagement by institutions entails mechanisms for being responsive to concerns. A range of opinions exists between and within stakeholders, who do not necessarily agree with each other.

Stakeholders in a CSR context go beyond the strict historical focus by corporations on stock- and shareholders. Corporate stakeholders include, at the very least, employees, customers, suppliers, media, non-governmental organisations and the communities and markets in which they operate.

Effective stakeholder engagement by corporations strengthens → accountability and performance, serves as an early warning mechanism by managing risk as well as new product and service development, and improves decision-making.

Stakeholder engagement is an ongoing dialogue and crucial to the success and sustainability of corporations.

Jonathan Cohen

STAKEHOLDER THEORY
→ Stakeholder engagement, Stakeholder management

Stakeholder theory is a managerial theory about business. It asserts that business can be understood as a set of relationships among groups which have a stake in the activities of that business. Stakeholders are those individuals or groups that can affect or can be affected by the achievement of the firm's core purpose. In addition, a business is successful insofar as it creates value for and satisfies key stakeholders continually over time. Managers may find it useful to divide stakeholders in two groups: those who are foundational to the firm's activities (e.g. customers, suppliers, financiers, employees, and communities), and those secondary groups that can affect the firm's objectives (e.g. the government, the media, and interest groups).

The stakeholder concept has been traced back to the Stanford Research Institute, where in the late 1960s it was originally used to organise executives' assumptions about the environment external to their firms. The idea was employed and tested by a group of scholars and consultants at The Wharton School, one of whom eventually refined the concept into a fully fledged theory of strategic management. R. Edward Freeman's 1984 *Strategic Management: A Stakeholder Approach* set forth a new method and set of techniques for executives to use to better understand how to manage key stakeholder relationships. Based on several years of consulting experience and thousands of conversations with managers, Freeman's first book put forth a new narrative regarding what it means to be an effective executive, particularly the use of the stakeholder level of analysis to frame and categorise strategic engagements.

Stakeholder theory requires managers to see the connections between the world of business and the world of ethics. Once executives begin to think about business as creating value for stakeholders, it is easy and necessary to begin to see the process of → value creation as inherently concerned with ethics and → values. Ethics and value questions are at the core of managing for stakeholders, since executives must address the question of who are the stakeholders for whom they are creating value, and how they will create this value.

This holistic approach stands in stark contrast to traditional views of business as amoral or immoral. Reformers of business including parts of the CSR movement separate the business world from the world of ethics and → values. In these views, ethics or social concerns are seen as fundamentally alien to the amoral or immoral business mindset. Stakeholder theory rejects this overly simplistic view and places concerns for ethics at the heart of capitalism. If value is created by bringing together and satisfying various stakeholder interests, then → value creation and ethics are inseparable. In fact, without the shared → values of trust and → integrity, → value creation and trade would not be able to get off the ground. Capitalism thrives because, for the most part, people are honest, keep their promises, and satisfy stakeholder interests. In this view, business is not the vehicle of vices that needs to be curbed, but an opportunity to collectively make our lives better. Stakeholder theory provides an opportunity to reformulate CSR, to leave behind outdated assumptions about the 'objective' business world and the 'subjective' ethics world, and to help managers make better thought-out decisions. Corporate stakeholder responsibility is a way to combine the good intentions of the old CSR movement with the actual way managers make decisions.

Poor managerial decisions are one of the major causes for recent business scandals. Stakeholder theorists do not deny the scale or importance of these scandals – they differ in their diagnosis of the problem. Reformers who ascribe to the separation fallacy – the view that business and ethics are separate – call for external sanctions and concern for social responsibilities to be levied upon executives and their enterprises. Stakeholder theorists call for executives to return to their roots – in the → value creation and trade that is at the heart of capitalism. In this view, the quest of maximising shareholder returns has distorted managers' priorities and their own self-understanding. By embracing the stakeholder relationships at the core of → value creation, executives can move beyond the scandals to a sustainable prosperity that they themselves have created and must continually maintain.

Debates

Since its formal debut in *Strategic Management: A Stakeholder Approach*, a variety of scholars, particularly from the → business ethics field, have helped to refine the stakeholder concept and test its boundaries. The process has produced a variety of debates which have further obscured the pragmatic managerial roots of stakeholder theory.

Stakeholder/Stockholder debate

Most notably, stakeholder theory has been upheld as a rival to 'stockholder Theory' – a view made famous by Milton Friedman's 1970 *New York Times* magazine article, 'The Social Responsibility of Business is to Increase its Profits'. This contrast ignores the fact that shareholders are stakeholders as well and that no business can survive without making its financiers better off. In the article mentioned above, Friedman claims that 'It may be in the long-run interest of a corporation that is a major employer in a small community to devote resources to providing amenities to that community or to improving its government.' He goes on to say that it is wrong to call this social responsibility because 'they are entirely justified in its [the corporation's] self interest'. At a minimum, Friedman accepts the stakeholder view as an instrument to increase the firm's profits. Both Friedman and the stakeholder theorists reject an externally imposed social responsibility on business, and agree that stakeholder interests are closely connected to the interest of the firm. While much has been made of the stakeholder/stockholder debate, the real difference lies in the primacy that Friedman reserves for stockholder claims on the corporation.

The 'challenge' of no objective function

Another group of scholars has questioned the ability of stakeholder theory to offer managers an objective function for decision-making. For example, in Michael Jensen's view the significance of 'maximising shareholder value' is that it gives managers one simple dictum to follow which allows 'objective' business decision-making when stakeholder claims conflict. Jensen argues that claims to balance stakeholder interest over time fail to guide managerial action because they do not provide an equation for day-to-day managerial decision-making. In the stakeholder view, it is impossible to claim *a priori* which interests and considerations will be most important in a given managerial situation. While stakeholder theory does not prescribe a single magic objective, traditional stockholder-based views of the corporation are mute when asked how to maximise shareholder value. This is because there are a wide variety of ways to do so – each based in a particular company, with specific capabilities, relationships, and resources. The most useful and creative answers to these questions will come from the managers on the ground, not from any one abstract theory. Scholars who call for a single objective function assume that the financial implications of managerial action are determinable upfront, which contradicts managerial experience where actions can and do have unintended (both positive and negative) consequences.

Stakeholder theory questions the very need for an objective function. It claims that managers should start from the specific purpose and mission of their companies to resolve tensions in stakeholder claims. Managers need to use moral imagination to find ways to jointly satisfy rival stakeholder claims, and in cases where joint solutions cannot be found, they need to make sure that the same stakeholder group does not continue to be neglected. Stakeholder theory, and all theory for that matter, has its limits: no single theory can provide concrete external guidance for every managerial decision.

Where's the theory?

Colleagues in the social sciences as well as those trained in philosophy have questioned the extent to which stakeholder theory can be referred to as a theory. Social science colleagues look for a set of empirically tested and grounded observations that provide 'true' prescriptions for managers that are valid in all contexts. Stakeholder theory does not fall neatly into the positivist conception of a theory. Given its pragmatist roots, stakeholder theory creates a new narrative for executive effectiveness, one that is based firmly in managerial experience and decision-making. Unlike economic theory which aims at prediction, stakeholder theory aims to guide managerial action. Economics is about isolating the perfect model of exchange which allows reliable prediction. Stakeholder theory is about enabling better business in contexts where flesh-and-blood managers cannot always predict what will happen. There have been a variety of recent debates about whether stakeholder theory is truly a theory, a framework, or an approach. From a pragmatist perspective, these debates have little value, other than conferring some type of social legitimacy on to a narrative. The legitimacy of stakeholder theory is in its managerial point of view which is profoundly useful to executives and stakeholders in framing and maintaining their relationships.

Colleagues trained in philosophy have questioned the grounding of stakeholder theory. They want to isolate the normative foundations of the theory from its descriptive and instrumental uses. The philosophers' project assumes that once the foundational rational principles have been identified – once theory can be grounded in undeniable 'truth' then and only then are we 'really' protected from → corruption and evil – because those who have committed moral transgresses will have crossed a universally accepted line, and they will obviously be held accountable. While this may sound attractive, no such universal principles have been found and the quest for certainty continues with no end in sight. Again, from the pragmatist perspective, the only way to ensure the validity of our beliefs is to act on them, and do the work in the real world to keep them relevant and useful, as opposed to escaping to rationality where our local norms can masquerade as universals. In short, we may never find solid foundations for our beliefs but that does not mean that they are any less useful or relevant to our lives.

Both economists and philosophers judge the validity of stakeholder theory from their own disciplines' criteria and in that sense blur the practical foundations of the work. Despite their concerns about stakeholder theory, economists and philosophers express their arguments about business in stakeholder terms, further proof that the concept is an appropriate level of analysis for business.

Over the last 25 years, more and more groups connected to business have begun to find stakeholder language useful for talking about business. A wider circle of scholars have begun research using the concept. Stakeholder language enables scholars to pay attention to the real world of what managers, executives, and stakeholders are doing and saying. Stakeholder theory allows academics to interpret what is going on, and to give better, more coherent accounts of management practice, so that ultimately we can improve how we create value for each other and how we live. Most importantly, managers and executives are coming to see their enterprise in stake-holder terms and returning to the basic drivers of business, which do not separate the moral and the financial.

R. Edward Freeman and Bidhan Parmar

STEWARDSHIP
→ Sustainability

Stewardship refers to the act of assuming responsibility for the welfare of others and of interests beyond the self. It calls for an ethic of participation, care, consideration and responsibility in rela-tion to the interests, resources and concerns to which one has been entrusted. Stewardship has multiple interpretations, and its frontiers are drawn in relation to the personal value system of the steward. It may be considered to embrace responsibility for the wel-fare of the human, animal, and/or the natural world. It therefore lends itself to all forms of progressive welfare management such as healthcare, education, economic welfare, governance, peace, pro-tection, parenting, caring, counselling, mentoring, → human rights, → animal welfare, ecological → conservation and → biodiversity protection.

In the context of theology and the religious traditions, steward-ship has been adopted, in particular by Christian denominations, as a means to revive the creation-centred belief (in contrast to dominion-centred belief) that humans have been entrusted with the responsibility to care for God's creation.

In the context of the CSR and sustainability cause, there is a call for humanity's stewardship ethic to extend itself in time to embrace a duty of care for the welfare, not only for the present, but for future human generations, leading to the need for an urgent emphasis on the preservation and stewardship of the ecological welfare of planet earth today.

Kelly Lavelle

STRATEGIC IMPACT ASSESSMENT
→ Impact assessment

STOCKHOLM CONVENTION ON PERSISTENT ORGANIC POLLUTANTS (POPs)
→ Chemical sector, Persistent organic pollutants (POPs), Pollution, Waste management

🖰 www.pops.int

Delegates from 127 countries formally voted approval of the Stockholm Convention on Persistent Organic Pollutants on 22 May 2001. The Stockholm Convention is a global treaty to protect human health and the → environment from persistent organic pollutants (POPs). POPs are → chemicals that remain intact in the → environment for long periods, become widely distributed geographically, accumulate in the fatty tissue of living organisms and are toxic to humans and wildlife. POPs circulate globally and can cause damage wherever they → travel. In implementing the Convention, governments will take measures to eliminate or reduce the release of POPs into the → environment.

SUBSIDIES
→ Eco-subsidies, Externalities

Subsidies are inverse taxes: instead of levying a tax, a political authority provides a sum of money in support of an activity or product. Subsidies intend to encourage an activity, including the production of an → infrastructure, product or service. They arise generally because the unsupported operation of the market does not provide enough profit to make it worthwhile for an operator in the private sector to produce it.

Subsidies are part of the toolkit of a political authority that intends to influence the pattern of demand, and therefore the pattern of production. Subsidies privilege one form of production over another.

In a CSR context, subsidies for socially and ecologically beneficial industries or technologies (such as renewable energy or organic
farming) are designed to move business and society towards a more
sustainable model.

CSR itself can also have an affect similar to subsidies, when they
provide finance for an activity or piece of infrastructure, which
would not be created if left to the unsupported market. Poor people
and poor areas can require subsidy when the operation of the market
excludes them from participation in the life of the economy.

Margaret Legum

SULLIVAN PRINCIPLES
→ Global Sullivan Principles of Social Responsibility

SUPPLY CHAIN
→ Fairtrade, Labour issues, Off-shoring

Traditionally, supply chain management has focused on efficiently
integrating supplier and customer activities so that products are produced and distributed in the right quantities, at the right quality,
at the right prices, to the right locations, and at the right time, in
order to minimise system-wide costs while satisfying service-level
requirements. Integration of CSR aspects into supply chain management broadens the concept of quality to embrace social, ethical,
labour and environmental issues and also widens our understanding of costs. In a CSR context many companies face an extended
chain of responsibility as stakeholders do not only hold the company accountable for its own actions but also for the practices of all
those suppliers (and often their suppliers, and so on) whose goods
and services make part of the final product.

CSR risks and opportunities in the supply chain usually fall outside the direct control of the customer and therefore require a
different approach to similar issues that may be actively managed

directly at the customer's own premises. CSR risks and opportunities can be inherent in the components used to make a product – perhaps the use of a substance that is banned in the customer's own country but accepted elsewhere; or inappropriate use of a non-renewable resource. Risks can also arise from the way in which a component is obtained or processed – for example, conflict diamonds or the use of an unnecessarily polluting manufacturing process.

Some CSR issues simply come down to knowing enough about who is making the products, and how they are making them. Most companies begin with a simple review to assess what they know about the source of their products – where they come from and how they are made. Simple risk assessment techniques can be used to identify which products are likely to be associated with the most significant CSR issues. It is also generally the case that a small number of suppliers are responsible for a large proportion of the goods and services bought by the company. Such a review of the most significant products and suppliers enables a degree of prioritisation in designing the approach to assessing and managing supply chain risks.

Approaches to supply chain management can range from explicit contractual requirements in terms agreed between supplier and customer, to less direct approaches, for example where the customer seeks to influence its suppliers by raising their awareness of CSR issues and working in partnership to minimise risk.

A common technique for supply chain management is the development of purchasing policies which set out the customer's requirements to suppliers, sometimes backed up with information to support development of the supplier's understanding of what is being asked. The suppliers are then required to develop their own programmes to demonstrate compliance with the policy. The customer may use a variety of techniques to test for compliance, for example the use of self assessment questionnaires backed up by visits to test the quality of information provided.

First tier suppliers are those that have a direct relationship with the customer, and supply chain management processes often focus on these primary relationships. First tier suppliers in turn source their components and raw materials from a complex range of secondary and tertiary suppliers etc. and a customer's ability to influence its supply chain diminishes the further down the supply chain one goes. Where goods are being bought through an intermediary, for example an international buying house, efforts made to understand the source can easily be dissipated.

The nature and application of labour law varies from country to country and where a customer has cause for concern over labour standards, they may take steps to understand more about specific workplace practices to ensure that there is no use of child labour, forced labour or inhumane treatment, → discrimination or coercion, that there are acceptable → health and safety conditions and fair wages and working hours, and that there is freedom of association and speech.

Standards have been developed that can enable companies to achieve third party → certification and demonstrate that certain standards are being met in factories operated by their suppliers. Examples include the work of the Fair Labour Association (FLA) and Social Accountability International (SAI). The FLA's work is framed around its licensee companies that seek → assurance regarding the standards in their supplier factories. An annual FLA monitoring report provides feedback on the findings of unannounced visits that have happened throughout the last year across all licensee companies' supplier factories. SAI's work is framed around SA 8000, a global standard for decent working conditions which some organisations are using to support their supply chain programmes. Supplier companies can seek independent → certification to the standard. Finally, Sedex – the Suppliers Ethical Data Exchange – uses the latest → technology to enable companies to maintain and share data on labour practices in the supply chain.

The priority issues for attention at any one time tend to change dependent on current issues in the news and NGO campaigns. In recent years particular focus has been placed on the sourcing of sports apparel (labour standards), timber and timber products (deforestation), diamonds (funding military conflict), refrigerants (ozone depleting substances) and electrical equipment (rare metals).

In some specific instances, issue-specific → certification schemes have been developed that enable customers to assess compliance with their requirements – examples include the → Forest Stewardship Council for timber sourcing and the → Marine Stewardship Council for fisheries.

Mark Line

SUSTAINABILITY

→ Corporate sustainability, Sustainable development, Triple-bottom line

At one level, sustainability is simply about the ability to survive (and thrive) over a given period of time, preferably the long term. However, sustainability has come to have a much more specific meaning, linked to the human development and environmental agendas. Most popularly, sustainability is seen as a derivation of the concept of → sustainable development, which was first introduced by the United Nations' → World Commission on Environment and Development (1987) and defined as '→ development that meets the needs of present generations without compromising the ability of future generations to meet their needs.'

The ideas behind → sustainable development, however, are much older and traceable at least back to the preservation and → conservation movements of the 18th and 19th centuries. Today, sustainability remains a contested concept, which to a greater or lesser extent draws from and overlaps with notions of human development, → sustainable development, → corporate citizenship, social responsibility, social justice, environmental management, ethics and stakeholder management.

It is important to acknowledge that sustainability is in no way an objective, scientific or neutral concept, but rather a normative or subjective topic, which always contains a set of implicit or explicit → values. Hence, sustainability may be defined as a values-laden umbrella concept about the way in which the interface between the → environment and society (including its institutions and individual members) is managed to ensure that human needs are met without destroying the life supporting ecosystems on which we depend.

Wayne Visser

SUSTAINABILITY REPORTING
→ Non-financial reporting

SUSTAINABILITY REPORTING GUIDELINES
→ Global Reporting Initiative (GRI)

SUSTAINABLE CONSUMPTION
→ Consumerism, Ethical consumption, Sustainable consumption and production

Sustainable consumption denotes how and if particular aggregate patterns of consumption can be sustained globally both over time and in relation to their environmental impacts and resource intensity. The OECD in 2000 defined it as 'the use of goods and services that respond to basic needs and bring a better quality of life, while minimising the use of natural resources, toxic materials and emissions of → waste and pollutants over the life cycle, so as not to jeopardise the needs of future generations. As such it is an outcome with which many particular strategies may be associated. It does not relate only to → food but to all products and services.

Particularly key aspects of sustainable consumption relate to:

- How and whether consumption leads to industrial → waste and by-products that an ecosystem can absorb, that is, its 'carrying capacity';
- The 'de-coupling' of economic growth from environmental degradation, achieved through sustainable production processes which emphasise resource efficiency; and
- How and whether consumption processes reduce resource degradation, pollution and → waste.

From a CSR perspective there is particular interest in how to engage consumers to consume more sustainably and the role of companies more generally in promoting sustainable consumption. There are fundamental disagreements about whether this means consuming less, or whether it means consuming differently and – if the latter – how.

John Sabapathy

SUSTAINABLE CONSUMPTION AND PRODUCTION

→ Consumerism, Ethical consumption, Sustainable consumption

The idea of sustainable consumption and production found early expression in concepts like '→ eco-efficiency' (promoted by the → World Business Council for Sustainable Development), 'cleaner production' (adopted by the United Nations Environment Programme), and 'Factor-4 production' (introduced by Ernst Ulrich von Weizsäcker and Amory and L. Hunter Lovins). Sustainable Consumption and Production was clarified further by businesses, governments and NGOs at the 1992 Rio de Janeiro Earth Summit and the 2002 World Summit on Sustainable Development (WSSD) in Johannesburg.

In the UK, the government set out its goal to move to a 'one planet economy' in its 2005 *Securing the Future* → sustainable development strategy, and in its *Changing Patterns* framework on sustainable consumption and production.

Drawing from this work, sustainable consumption and production can be defined as the process of behaviour change and technological innovation required from government, business and consumers to de-couple economic development from environmental degradation in order to operate within the limits of the planet's ecosystems.

It involves rethinking current business models to develop and incorporate a wider approach to sustainability that reaches across the whole life cycle of goods, services and materials. This means that business action must extend right along the supply-chain, tackling the issues arising in the extraction of raw materials, in product design and manufacture and when consumers eventually use and discard these products and services.

Governments have a key role to play in creating the environment for business adoption of sustainable consumption and production practice through standard setting, economic incentives, regulation, voluntary agreements, business support programmes, communications and consumer policy.

Dermot Egan

SUSTAINABLE DEVELOPMENT
→ Corporate sustainability, Sustainability

The most broadly used definition of → sustainable development was coined by the → World Commission on Environment and Development's report, *Our Common Future* (1987), as '→ development that meets the needs of the present without compromising the ability of future generations to meet their own needs'. This definition implies an appropriate balance between the so-called three pillars of → sustainable development – economic development, social development, and environmental protection. IUCN provided a slightly different definition in its 1991 publication with UNEP and WWF, *Caring for the Earth*: 'Development that provides real improvements in the quality of human life and at the same time conserves the vitality and diversity of the Earth.'

Both of these definitions are very broad and leave many elements undefined. What, specifically, are the needs of the present generation? Whose needs have priority? How can we reasonably predict what future generations will need to meet their own needs, however those might be defined? While the concept has eluded a robust and practical definition, it nonetheless has proven extremely fertile, leading to numerous scholarly articles, books, and organisations.

The 2002 United Nations World Summit on Sustainable Development, in Johannesburg, South Africa, adopted a declaration on → sustainable development that committed governments to building a humane, equitable, and caring global society, cognizant of the need for human dignity for all. The world's countries assumed a collective responsibility to advance and strengthen the interdependent and mutually reinforcing pillars of → sustainable development at the local, national, regional, and global levels. They also issued a Plan of Implementation that contained detailed recommendations on various aspects of → sustainable development, after which many governments prepared strategies for → sustainable development.

Sustainable development can only be achieved by carefully balancing human development activities while maintaining a stable environment that predictably and regularly provides resources such as fresh → water, → food, clean air, wood, fisheries, and productive soils and that protects people from floods, droughts, pest infestations, and disease (these benefits to people are known as ecosystem services). Sustainable development is threatened by land cover change, overexploitation of natural resources, invasive alien species, pollution of air, soil, and water by chemical and organic wastes, and → climate change. The latter may be the most serious threat, leading to altered precipitation patterns, greater frequency of extreme weather events, rising sea levels, increased ranges for some disease vectors, and changes in ecological systems.

New and improved approaches to managing environmental resources and ecosystems are thus required for → sustainable development. Examples include using → water more efficiently, managing watersheds at a landscape scale, ensuring that any dams constructed provide equitable benefits to all affected populations, and improving agricultural production systems that both enhance productivity and use agricultural inputs (such as water, fertilisers, and pesticides) far more efficiently and benignly. These approaches also present new business opportunities, such as premium → certification schemes for timber harvested from sustainably managed forests, which can also contribute to CSR.

The → business case for addressing → sustainable development has become increasingly prominent, with companies that adopt → values consistent with economic, social, and environmental responsibility improving their → competitive advantage and long-term productivity.

Valli Moosa

SUSTAINABLE LIVELIHOODS

→ Base of the pyramid (BOP) model

Sustainable livelihoods business is the → World Business Council for Sustainable Development's (WBCSD) expression for doing business with the poor in ways that benefit the poor and benefit the company's bottom line. This is also referred to as → Base of the Pyramid (BOP) business, 'pro-poor business' and 'socially inclusive business'. A growing number of leading companies are experimenting with this type of approach.

An essential element of sustainable livelihoods business is that it is based on core business strategies. It should also serve the real needs of the local communities at affordable prices. It is not simply selling to poor communicates, but also involves including local suppliers and distributors into corporate supply chains.

Challenges to successful sustainable livelihoods business include poor framework conditions in developing nations, → corruption and lack of corporate imagination.

Björn Stigson

SWEATSHOPS
→ Labour issues, Supply chain

'Sweatshop' has become a synonym for inferior workplace conditions where basic → human rights of workers are not respected. Typical problems include unsafe or unhealthy shop floors, underage labour, → discrimination because of → gender, religion, or ethnic origin, neglect of minimum wage, forced overtime, oppression of unions, rejection of collective bargaining, or mental or physical abuse. The growth in outsourcing to → developing countries with low labour costs, low labour and environmental standards and/or weak enforcement institutions has made sweatshops an endemic phenomenon in the global south. However, sweatshops, i.e. workplaces where at least one of the basic labour rights is violated, can also be found in developed countries.

The → ILO has passed several conventions for the protection of basic labour rights. However, many countries have not yet included these conventions into their national legislations and the ILO has no mandate to enforce these conventions. The identification of sweatshop conditions has become a main task of NGOs and labour rights groups. Today these groups not only lobby against governments with poor → human rights records. They often run campaigns and force multinational corporations to take responsibility for the working conditions in their own facilities as well as for the conditions at their suppliers' production sites. As a response, many multinational companies have defined → codes of conduct with basic labour and

$\rightarrow$ human rights. Some of the leading companies have even started to enforce these standards through their supply chains by $\rightarrow$ auditing mechanisms.

Andreas Georg Scherer

TAKE-BACK SCHEMES
$\rightarrow$ Recycling, Waste management

TAX AVOIDANCE
$\rightarrow$ Legal compliance

Taxpayers can potentially minimise their tax liability in one of three ways:

- They can evade taxes by failing to make full disclosure to tax authorities (tax evasion); or
- They can avoid taxes through artificial arrangements designed to exploit loopholes in the tax laws (impermissible avoidance); or
- They can avoid taxes using lawful tax planning techniques (permissible avoidance).

In essence, evasion and impermissible avoidance are unlawful; avoidance through good planning is not.

Good $\rightarrow$ corporate citizenship and CSR seeks to integrate a set of $\rightarrow$ values in the core decision-making processes of a business. A corporate's commitment to the CSR agenda cannot simply be dusted off occasionally – the $\rightarrow$ values, beliefs and norms that underpin their CSR agenda must permeate all of the corporate's dealings and activities, including the manner in which it chooses to engage with the tax system, and with some consideration of the consequences of their behaviours (which include revenue losses, undermining the $\rightarrow$ integrity of the tax system, compelling increased complexity of tax legislation and unfairly shifting the tax burden).

While taxpayers are well within their rights to minimise their tax liability using lawful means, companies who pursue a CSR agenda cannot ethically engage in tax evasion or impermissible avoidance – to do so would be evading their → corporate social responsibility.

Telita Snyckers

TECHNOLOGY SECTOR

CSR in the technology sector can be viewed in two, inextricably linked ways – (1) the way a technology company conducts its business operations and the issues of corporate responsibility associated with those operations; and (2) the impact that technology has had in the field of CSR.

Generally, the 'technology sector' is thought to encompass companies who manufacture goods or provide services that electronically process or communicate information, or enable this functionality. Another common term for the sector is Information and Communications Technology, or 'ICT'. Traditionally, this sector has been composed of subsectors such as software, hardware and chips. As the innovations in the technology have rapidly evolved, the sector has been undergoing a major transformation. We now have media companies, → telecommunications companies and the traditional 'technology' companies converging into the technology space. Companies like Time Warner and Viacom are digitizing their content at a rapid pace, while technology brands such as Google and Yahoo! have become major media and entertainment content providers.

Although convergence is in itself an issue for the sector, other top CSR issues for the technology sector include:

- Access to technology in the developing world and underserved communities in the developed world – including issues of → gender, race, disability, socio-economic status and class. This is sometimes referred to as the '→ digital divide', 'skills divide', or 'social divide'.

- The future of technology in the workplace – how ICT is transforming productivity, the way we interact and global competitiveness.
- Use of products and services, including internet governance, net neutrality, data privacy, and freedom of expression. This use implies not only how the company chooses to implement its products and services, but also the relationships the company has with governments and other societal organisations that legislate or require certain parameters on public domain data and information.
- Off-shoring and outsourcing of labour.
- Environmental impacts of products, including issues of e-waste, toxicity, energy use, and design for the environment. Companies are being asked to look at the entire life cycle of the products they produce and take responsibility not only for designing and manufacturing more environmentally sound technologies, but also handling the end-of-life issues and recycling of products that are no longer of use or have been replaced by newer models.
- On products specifically, the most influential regulation has come from → Europe. The European Union issued a directive referred to as 'WEEE' which stands for 'Waste from Electrical and Electronic Equipment'. The 'WEEE' Directive identifies electrical and electronic equipment as a priority → waste stream; sets criteria for the collection, treatment, recycling and recovery of waste; and makes producers responsible for financing most of these activities. The RoHS legislation ('Restriction of the use of certain Hazardous Substances in Electrical and Electronic Equipment') is a 2006 European Union (EU) directive that bans, with few exemptions, the placing on the EU market of new electrical and electronic equipment containing any of six defined hazardous substances.
- Social and environmental issues in the technology supply chain – supply chain issues including labour, ethics, environmental, and → health and safety issues. Companies are also interested in

the management systems their suppliers utilise to track continued improvement on these issues. A major development for the sector has been the collaborative Electronic Industry Code of Conduct (EICC). The EICC outlines standards to ensure that working conditions in the electronics and ICT supply chain are safe, that workers are treated with respect and dignity and that manufacturing processes are environmentally responsible. Tools to implement in this work are being developed by the EICC and the Global eSustainability Initiative (GeSI) jointly.

• Finally, the social impacts of technology are always an issue, and although related to access, in particular this issue examines how technology can shape a society or change cultural norms. Similar to access, social impact analysis looks to qualify and quantify how technology can serve as a key driver for economic and social development.

Many companies are investigating creative ways to use technology to bring goods and services to those who are globally at the 'bottom of the pyramid', a term generally used to describe those who are in the largest, but poorest socio-economic group worldwide. There have been many debates among those who argue that the private sector should be investing in basic needs (→ food, → water, shelter) before bringing advanced technologies into poor areas. On the other hand, there is a large community of advocates for the '$100 computer' – a solution advocated in several circles arguing that bringing modern technology into a community encourages entrepreneurialism and fosters self-sufficiency. Most agree that technology must be adapted, supported and implemented to meet real needs in order for it to be useful. In that context, technologies such as mobile hand-held devices and cell phones can also serve as business tools as well as tools to connect a society.

Kara Hartnett Hurst

TELECOMMUNICATIONS SECTOR

The telecommunications industry has become one of the key industries of the 21st century enabling and accelerating the speed of → globalisation by providing ever cheaper, faster and efficient channels of communication around the globe. With the advent of mobile telephones as a form of mass communication, many of the CSR-related issues have recently focused on this industry, although many also apply to more traditional forms of telecommunication. As the provider of the physical infrastructure for communication and internet access, the industry faces a number of CSR challenges, such as:

- Raw materials for telecommunications equipment – apart from the fact that many raw materials for mobile phones are hazardous substances, significant controversy has ensued about the sourcing of heavy metals such as cadmium, casseterite, cobalt, coltane, lead and mercury. Many of these are mined in countries in conflict such as the Democratic Republic of Congo, with allegations that the revenues from extracting these metals directly fill the coffers of warlords and thus contribute to suffering and instability in these regions.
- Radiation and other harmful side effects of telecommunication technology – there is an ongoing scientific debate about the health risks of mobile phone use. These risks pertain, first of all, to the installation of mobile phone masts which allegedly expose people in the immediate vicinity to potential carcinogenic radiation. Combined with the fact that often schools, public buildings or economically disadvantaged neighbourhoods are susceptible to allow the construction of masts, this concern also includes a contentious social justice issue. Radiation is also an issue for the individual user as there are concerns about radiation from the phone potentially leading to brain tumours.
- Waste and disposal of used telecommunication equipment – telecommunication equipment, in particular mobile phones, are

subject to a rapid cycle of innovation, and moreover, with ever new designs and features, have become highly coveted fashion items. Many mobile phones have lifespans of less than a year, resulting in a growing → waste problem for the industry. On top of that many substances in mobile phones represent a serious hazard to the → environment if not disposed off properly.

- Responsibility for usage patterns of underage users – by far the fastest growing user segment in telecommunications are children. Estimates in the UK suggest that one in every three children between the ages of five and nine owns a mobile phone, while ownership among 10 to 14 year olds exceeds 40%. This raises allegations that companies are selling their products to customers who are often not able to afford the product or to control their use of the technology so as to avoid financial hardship for those that pay the bills. Furthermore, vulnerability to theft, bullying, 'grooming' by paedophiles and access to pornography are child protection issues faced by the industry.

- Managing the economic impact of mobile communications in the developing world – in a recent study published by Vodafone it was reported that a developing country with an extra 10 phones per 100 people between 1996 and 2003 would have had GDP growth 0.59% higher than an otherwise identical country. The impact of mobile phones in countries with poor → infrastructure has been phenomenal, improving business opportunities and general living conditions in an unprecedented manner. Mobile phone companies see themselves increasingly as a pivotal actor in a number of public policy and → development debates to overcome the → digital divide which places new CSR expectations on these private companies.

Facing these challenges, it is not surprising that in many ways the telecommunications industry has placed itself at the forefront of the CSR debate. A host of new approaches, policies, strategies and tools have been developed over the last decades, most notably the following:

- Partnerships with NGOs – mobile phone companies have joined in partnership with NGOs such as Internet Watch Foundation (which investigates internet sites that contain potentially illegal content, primarily child pornography, criminal obscenity, and incitement to racial hatred) and have substantially contributed to their funding. Companies also engage with charities, child safety campaigners, governments, law enforcement agencies, regulators, content producers, and parental groups to ensure that child protection is effective.
- Self regulation – in many countries the industry has set up codes of practice with regard to a number of the CSR issues discussed above. In the UK, the code of practice for the self-regulation of new forms of content on mobiles became effective in January 2005. This covers audiovisual content, mobile games, chat services and internet access, and institutes a rating system for adult content and a set of safeguards designed to protect members of the public, particularly children.
- New entrepreneurial initiatives – companies such as Fonebak have seized new business opportunities from the → waste problem of the industry, recycling more than 3.5 million phones since 2002 and making revenues of £60m in 2006.
- Corporate philanthropy – against the backdrop of a generally highly profitable industry, many companies have set up charitable → foundations with multimillion budgets to address wider societal needs and public policy issues, in particular in → developing countries.

Dirk Matten

TOBIN TAX
→ Anti-globalisation, ATTAC, New economics

A Tobin tax is a tax on currency trades across borders first suggested by Yale Professor and Nobel laureate economist James Tobin.

The original proposal, following the US Government's decision in 1971 to effectively end the Bretton Woods system, was designed to ensure international currency stability. The proposed tax was to be modest (between 0.1 and 0.25%) and act as a penalty on short-term currency speculation and thus reduce currency volatility.

Due to their nature, Tobin taxes, while possible to enact domestically, require multilateral cooperation to be effectively enforced and, largely because of this, the idea lay dormant for two decades.

In the 1990s, however, the concept of Tobin taxes rose up both the academic and political agendas with the emergence of → new economics and later the → anti-→ globalisation movement, as they appealed to those who believed that the power and size of speculative global capital flows had become too large. In this context, Tobin taxes have the added benefit of potentially providing a large source of income that could then be used to finance growth and projects in → developing countries which are often perceived as the biggest losers of global speculative capital flows. To date, however, Tobin taxes have not been introduced.

Nick Tolhurst

TRACEABILITY
→ Food and beverage sector

According to the European Commission traceability is the 'ability to trace and follow → food, feed, and ingredients through all stages of production, processing and distribution'. According to the International Organisation for Standardisation (ISO), traceability refers to the 'ability to trace the history, application, or location of an entity by means of recorded information'.

Although traceability relates to → food safety primarily, it also relates to a wide array of issues, including labour conditions and environmental factors. Traceability is a part of a process, an integral part of product quality. An example of traceability includes measures to track calves by the use of tags to ensure they are not affected by mad cow disease; or bar codes on fruit exports to denote pesticide use. In a CSR context traceability enables a corporation to account for the ethical, social and environmental effect of its products along their → supply chains.

Deborah Leipziger

TRAGEDY OF THE COMMONS
→ Externalities, Global commons, Public goods

The tragedy of the commons was first identified by William Forster Lloyd of Oxford University in 1832, when he observed overgrazing of common pastureland, and the concept has since been adapted to explain apparently selfish behaviour in relation to commonly owned resources and public goods.

When resources are commonly owned, there is no individual incentive to avoid exploitation. The benefits of adding one more animal to a herd accrue to an individual herdsman, while the problem of overgrazing is shared by all. Thus for each individual, there is an incentive to add to their herd beyond the carrying capacity of the land, and individual altruism will do no good as a rival herder will simply step in.

An example is the problem of overfishing; declining fish stocks affect all fishermen to a small extent, while for each individual there are major benefits in maximising their catch. Equally, polluting common resources such as air or → water saves costs for the individual polluter, while the negative impacts are shared.

A popular market solution to the tragedy of the commons is the privatisation of common resources, but this may favour the wealthy and powerful. Alternatives are a responsible approach taken through

CSR policies, or market instruments, legal restrictions and taxes imposed by governments.

Ruth Findlay-Brooks

TRANSPARENCY
→ Accountability, Corporate governance, Non-financial reporting, Transparency International

Transparency in its more literal meaning refers to the characteristic of an object or matter being able to be seen through. In recent years, however, the metaphorical use of the word has taken hold in matters relating to governance and control of organisations. In this context, the notion of → transparency denotes the quality of being clear and honest. As a principle, → transparency implies that civil servants, managers and trustees have a duty to act visibly, predictably and understandably. Sufficient information must be available so that other agencies and the general public can assess whether the relevant procedures are followed, consonant with the given mandate.

Corruption is a covert activity that thrives in environments, institutions or transactions that are marked by secrecy and subjected to opaque and arbitrary rules. The improvement of governance standards and the openness to public input and scrutiny are key factors in making societies more transparent and therefore less prone to → corruption.

The fundamental hallmark of a transparent society is its openness to consultation and public participation and the provision of mechanisms and processes to enable such participation. This includes institutional 'pillars' such as an independent and free media and a vibrant and vocal civil society. Societies where the public is better informed allow for greater citizen participation in the political process and increased opportunity to hold politicians accountable.

As the understanding grows that → transparency and good governance ward off → corruption and ultimately lead to a better and more efficient use of resources and improved economic prospects for citizens, companies are increasingly called upon by their stakeholders to consider the importance of → transparency in their contribution to the development of the societies they operate in.

Enterprises, as global citizens, have a tangible contribution to make towards the greater → transparency that in turn results in greater → accountability within society. This → transparency should begin with the enterprise itself through the disclosure of both its financial and non-financial activities and results. As responsible corporate citizens, enterprises should communicate with all their stakeholders on their activities and make this information publicly available to their stakeholders.

The rules of financial disclosure for companies are subject to well-established regulatory standards. Indeed, it is significant that stock exchanges have extensive regulations requiring public disclosures by companies in order to prevent insider trading and promote orderly markets. However, in the area of non-financial or so-called sustainability reporting (→ non-financial reporting), standards for the disclosure of meaningful information remain in the early stages via voluntary frameworks such as the → Global Reporting Initiative.

But some companies are taking their responsibility to create greater → transparency in financial transactions to a new level. Mobilised under the initiative of the → Extractive Industries Transparency Initiative (EITI), leading companies in this industry sector are taking an active role in efforts to reverse what has been dubbed the 'resource curse' whereby oil-rich countries fail to generate wealth for most of their impoverished citizens. The companies and governments participating in EITI commit respectively to the publication of oil payment and revenue figures to allow for public scrutiny that will impede the grand scale misappropriation of funds by corrupt elites − funds that could otherwise be used for → development.

Other initiatives focusing on financial → transparency aim to create greater financial literacy within civil society allowing citizens to track and challenge government budget expenditure with increased knowledge and credibility.

Transparency can also act as a deterrent to → corruption in the critical area of public procurement. Corruption in public contracting, where the public and private sectors meet, can lead to the distortion of fair competition, the → waste of scarce resources and the neglect of fundamental needs that perpetuate poverty. It is estimated that systemic → corruption can add 20–25% to the costs of government procurement, and frequently results in goods and services of inferior quality as well as unnecessary purchases.

Initiatives that create more → transparency in the procurement process can help avert the corrupt practices that are detrimental to fair competition and to ordinary citizens. The TI Integrity Pact is a no-bribes agreement that involves all parties to a public contract, including the tendering authority and all bidders for a public contract. Parties to the Integrity Pact formally agree that they will not pay, offer, demand or accept bribes; collude with competitors to obtain the contract; or engage in such abuses while carrying out the contract. The Integrity Pact includes an external monitoring system that provides for independent oversight and → accountability.

David Nussbaum and Susan Côté-Freeman

TRANSPARENCY INTERNATIONAL

→ Bribe Payers Index, Business Principles for Countering Bribery, Corruption Perception Index, Global Corruption Barometer

⌐🖰 www.transparency.org

Founded in 1993, Transparency International (TI) describes itself as the global civil society organisation leading the fight against → corruption. TI brings people together in a powerful worldwide coalition to end the devastating impact of → corruption on human beings around the world. TI's mission is to create change towards a world free of → corruption, through its global network of around 100 locally established national chapters and chapters-in-formation. The TI chapters fight → corruption in the national arena in a number of ways. They bring together relevant players from government, civil society, business and the media to promote → transparency and → accountability in elections, in public administration, in procurement and in business. TI's chapters use advocacy campaigns to make the case for anti-corruption reforms. Politically non-partisan, TI does not undertake investigations of alleged → corruption or expose individual cases, but at times will work in coalition with organisations that do. TI aims at providing the skills, tools, experience, expertise and broad participation to fight → corruption on the ground, as well as through regional and global initiatives.

David Nussbaum and Peter Wilkinson

TRAVEL AND LEISURE SECTOR
→ Eco-tourism

Travel and leisure is one of the fastest growing sectors in the world and is especially important for → developing countries. CSR in the travel and leisure sector concerns reducing the → environmental footprint, increasing the cultural sensitivity, managing the social impacts and addressing the ethical issues associated with tourism and entertainment activities. More specifically, this includes:

- Reducing the carbon footprint of travel – by making citizens aware of the → climate change impacts associated with travel, encouraging low carbon travel options (e.g. trains), investing in renewable fuels for airplanes (e.g. biofuels) and green technologies for tour buses (e.g. electric or hybrid vehicles), improving the sustainability performance of leisure facilities (e.g. in terms of energy and → water use), and encouraging travellers (for business or pleasure) to offset the greenhouse gas emissions associated with their travel activities.

- Encouraging eco-tourism and cultural tourism – by financing natural and heritage → conservation activities, protecting → biodiversity, promoting awareness of places of natural beauty and cultural diversity, and ensuring that local communities share in the management and economic benefits of resource-based tourism.
- Managing the 'social diseases' associated with tourism and leisure developments – by providing controls and support services to address the often seen increase in uncontrolled gambling, prostitution, alcohol consumption and crime in areas that attract high numbers of tourists.
- Addressing the ethics of tourism and leisure activities – by being sensitive to the impacts of foreign visitors on local cultures and communities and listening to and addressing stakeholders' ethical concerns around issues like gambling, adult entertainment and the use of → child labour in tourism.

The travel and leisure sector has begun to respond in a number of ways to these CSR issues, including, for example:

- The Green Globe → benchmarking and → certification programme that assesses and labels the sustainability performance of travel and leisure resorts, accommodation, tours and rental cars.
- The increasing promotion of Fairtrade Tourism destinations and facilities, which embrace the social equity and environmental sustainability principles of the → fair trade movement.
- The rising trend of carbon neutral tourism, which seeks to ensure that all travel and leisure activities are planned and financed in such a way as to offset the CO_2 emissions associated with any trip, usually by using low carbon travel options or paying towards emission reduction or renewable energy projects.

Wayne Visser

TRIPLE BOTTOM LINE
→ Corporate sustainability

The triple bottom line (TBL) concept underscores the fact that companies and other organisations create value in multiple dimensions. Given the nature and focus of modern accounting, the financial bottom line is generally an inadequate (and often actively misleading) expression of the total value equation. The term was introduced in 1994 by John Elkington, countering the narrower focus on the then fashionable term → eco-efficiency, which focused on the financial and environmental dimensions of performance. TBL thinking, by contrast, extended to social impacts – and to the wider economic impact issues that are rarely captured in the traditional financial bottom line. The TBL approach was discussed in detail in *Cannibals with Forks* (1997) and has been further elaborated both in hundreds of company reports aligned with the → Global Reporting Initiative (GRI) and in a growing number of books. A linked phrase, People, Planet, Profit, alternatively People, Planet, Prosperity, is based on the same concept. This phrase was adopted by Shell in its early public sustainability reporting (→ non-financial reporting), following the company's Brent Spar and Nigerian crises in 1995. Abbreviated as the 3Ps, it then became central to the → sustainable development debate in countries like the Netherlands.

John Elkington

TRIPS (TRADE RELATED ASPECTS OF INTERNATIONAL PROPERTY RIGHTS) AGREEMENT

→ Developing countries, World Trade Organisation (WTO)
🖰 www.wto.org

TRIPS, the agreement on Trade Related Aspects of Intellectual Property Rights, is an international treaty administered by the → World Trade Organisation which provides for a worldwide minimum of → intellectual property rights (IPR) protection by its member states. Advocacy by companies in favour of stricter implementation of TRIPS rules can affect their image, rendering it an important issue under CSR aspects.

The extent of IPR protection and enforcement mechanisms differed considerably throughout the world thereby threatening to obstruct free trade. Weak IPR protection in some countries might hinder IPR owners from other countries to export their products. Thus TRIPS was negotiated in connection with the General Agreement on Tariffs and Trade (GATT) of 1994 obliging all contracting states to provide a minimum level of IPR protection under national law. This includes the principles of national treatment (granting foreigners the same rights as national citizens) and the most favoured nation clause (allowances made to one member state have to be applied to each other member state too).

TRIPS was pushed for by the developed countries, namely the US, the EU and Japan. Developing countries – their IPR laws generally being weaker – have been given extra time to fulfil the obligations under TRIPS. However, the use of IPR under TRIPS has come under heavy criticism by → developing countries and NGOs as it leads to an artificial scarcity of commonly needed goods in → developing countries. → HIV/AIDS drugs, for example, have been kept at high cost levels due to their exclusive patents and their rigorous enforcement under TRIPS. Thus they have been hard to obtain for patients in African countries.

Satish Sule

UN CONFERENCE ON ENVIRONMENT AND DEVELOPMENT
→ Rio Declaration on Environment and Development

UN CONVENTION AGAINST CORRUPTION
→ Corruption
⌐ www.unodc.org

The → United Nations Convention against Corruption (UNCAC) is an international treaty that was ratified in 2003 and implemented in 2005. The UNCAC was negotiated over a two-year period at the United Nations office in Vienna by representatives of more than 100 countries from all regions. The 140 countries that are signatories to the UNCAC must implement a wide and detailed range of anti-→ corruption measures relating to laws, institutions and practices. These measures, like those of other multilateral anti-corruption treaties such as the OECD Convention against Corruption (1997) (and a number of other similar regional conventions in → Europe, → Africa and the Americas), aim to promote the prevention, detection and eradication of → corruption, as well as increase the cooperation between state parties on these matters. The UNCAC is potentially a powerful instrument because of its global coverage and the extent and detail of its provisions, including those on asset recovery and mutual legal assistance.

David Nussbaum and Peter Wilkinson

UN DECLARATION AGAINST CORRUPTION AND BRIBERY IN INTERNATIONAL COMMERCIAL TRANSACTIONS

→ Corruption

⌐ www.un.org

The UN Declaration against Corruption and Bribery in International Commercial Transactions was adopted in 1996. Together with the International Code of Conduct for Public Officials it clearly defines and prohibits conflicts of interest for public officials and the acceptance of gifts and favours commits member states to criminalise bribery of public officials. The text is in the nature of a political commitment and not a legal obligation, with actions to be taken through institutions at the national, regional and international level, and subject to each state's constitution.

UNEP FINANCE INITIATIVE

→ Banking sector

⌐ www.unepfi.org

The United Nations Environment Programme Finance Initiative (UNEP FI) is a unique global partnership between the United Nations Environment Programme (UNEP) and the private financial sector. The concept of the UNEP Finance Initiative was launched in 1991 when a small group of commercial banks, including Deutsche Bank, HSBC Holdings, Natwest, Royal Bank of Canada, and Westpac, joined forces with UNEP to catalyse the → banking industry's awareness of the environmental agenda.

Today UNEP FI works closely with over 160 financial institutions who are signatories to the UNEP FI Statements for the Banking and Insurance sectors, and a range of partner organisations to develop and promote linkages between the → environment, sustainability and financial performance. Through regional activities, a comprehensive work programme, training programmes and research, UNEP FI carries out its mission to identify, promote, and realise the adoption of best environmental and sustainability practice at all levels of financial institution operations.

UNEP INTERNATIONAL DECLARATION ON CLEANER PRODUCTION

→ Eco-efficiency, Sustainable consumption and production

⌐ www.uneptie.org/pc/cp

The International Declaration on Cleaner Production is a voluntary but public statement of commitment to the strategy and practice of cleaner production, defined as the continuous application of an integrated, preventive strategy applied to processes, products and services in pursuit of economic, social, health, safety and environmental benefits. By achieving economic, environmental and health/safety benefits, cleaner production provides a significant contribution to achieving sustainable production and consumption.

The Declaration was launched in October 1998 at Phoenix Park, South Korea, with 67 inaugural signatories. Signing ceremonies at other national and international venues are continually adding more Declaration partners to the Signatory List. The number of regional and national signatories now totals over 1700.

UNEP encourages government leaders, company presidents, NGO executive directors, business association presidents and other community leaders to publicly affirm their commitment and exercise leadership in cleaner production by signing and implementing this Declaration.

The Declaration covers statements of commitment in the following areas:

- → Leadership
- Awareness, education and training
- Integration
- Research and development
- Communication
- Implementation

UNEP STATEMENT BY BANKS ON THE ENVIRONMENT AND SUSTAINABLE DEVELOPMENT

→ Banking sector

✐ www.unepfi.org

In May 1992, in the run-up to the Rio Summit that year, the UNEP Statement by Banks on the Environment and Sustainable Development was launched in New York, and the Banking Initiative was formed.

This Initiative, which operated under the auspices of the United Nations Environment Programme, engaged a broad range of financial institutions, including commercial banks, investment banks, venture capitalists, asset managers, and multi-lateral → development banks and agencies – in a constructive dialogue about the nexus between economic development, environmental protection, and → sustainable development. The Initiative promoted the integration of environmental considerations into all aspects of the financial sector's operations and services. A secondary objective of the initiative was to foster private sector investment in environmentally sound technologies and services.

The Statement covers principles and commitments in the following areas:

- Commitment to sustainable development
- Environmental management and financial institutions
- Public awareness and communication

UNEP STATEMENT OF ENVIRONMENTAL COMMITMENT FOR THE INSURANCE INDUSTRY

⤳ www.unepfi.org

In 1995, UNEP joined forces with a group of leading insurance and reinsurance companies, including General Accident, Gerling Global Re, National Provident, Storebrand, Sumitomo Marine & Fire, Swiss Re, as well as pension funds, to launch the UNEP Statement of Environmental Commitment by the Insurance Industry. In this voluntary commitment, signatory companies pledge that they will aim at achieving a balance of economic development, the welfare of people and a sound environment.

The Statement acknowledges the principles of → sustainable development and the precautionary principle. It also calls upon insurers to incorporate environmental considerations into their internal and external business activities. In 1997, the Insurance Industry Initiative (III) was formed to fund research activities, and to sponsor awareness meetings and workshops and the annual regular meetings of the Initiative.

The Statement covers principles and commitments in the following areas:

- General principles of sustainable development
- Environmental management
- Public awareness and communications

UN GLOBAL COMPACT
⌐ www.unglobalcompact.org

In view of the fact that many people nowadays are afraid that economic → globalisation entails erosion of social, ecological and → human rights standards, but at the same time are aware that responsible business dealing can make a substantial contribution to the achievement of → development policy and social goals, the UN Secretary General, Kofi Annan, called for a global pact at the Davos → World Economic Forum in 1999. Companies, especially multinational ones, were called upon to undertake to adhere to the following 10 principles in their sphere of influence:

- Human rights
  Business is asked to:

  1. Support and respect the protection of international → human rights within their sphere of influence; and
  2. Make sure their own corporations are not complicit in → human rights abuses.

- Labour
  Business is asked to uphold:

  3. Freedom of association and the effective recognition of the right to collective bargaining;
  4. The elimination of all forms of forced and compulsory labour;
  5. The effective abolition of → child labour; and
  6. The elimination of → discrimination in respect of employment and occupation.

- Environment

  Business is asked to:

  7. Support a precautionary approach to environmental challenges;

  8. Undertake initiatives to promote greater environmental responsibility;

  9. Encourage the development and diffusion of environmentally friendly technologies.

- Anti-corruption

  Business is asked to:

  10. Work against all forms of → corruption, including extortion and bribery.

Companies that are willing to join have to (a) provide a letter from their CEO indicating a commitment to these 10 principles; and (b) share at least one example per year of how they have translated one or more of these principles into practice. In this way responsible companies, according to the UN Secretary General, can make → globalisation more socially equitable and more environmentally friendly and thus mobilise forces, resources and knowledge to achieve the → UN Millennium Development Goals. However, several NGOs and critics have argued that signing up to the 10 principles does not commit corporations to very much, since monitoring and sanctioning of their behaviour was initially not on the agenda of the UNGC. Ultimately the critics see the UN Global Compact as a cheap → bluewash for corporations.

It is the aim of the UN Global Compact (UNGC), on the one hand, to make the 10 principles an integral component of entrepreneurial activities, but at the same time dialogues and partnerships between the various stakeholders are to be encouraged and facilitated in order to generate support for the Global Compact and the other UN goals (e.g. → UN Millennium Development Goals). In international study forums, in political dialogues and, through the work of national networks, problems and opportunities of alternative methods are discussed, 'good practices' presented and recommended for emulation.

The Global Compact is a voluntary initiative and thus not a substitute for government measures, including the duty to ensure decisive laws for legal safety in sensitive areas. Nevertheless, the UNGC is aware of the different regulations that emerge in the → globalisation process and the growing ability of companies to observe these regulations in a responsible way without multiplying the levels of responsibility. The great intercultural persuasiveness of the UNGC, compared with other corporate responsibility initiatives, is that the 10 principles represent by and large the combined wisdom of the international community, e.g. the Universal Declaration of Human Rights, the basic principles and rights of the ILO and the Declaration of the Environment and Development Conference of 1992. A basic expectation made of companies is that they do not exceed the limits imposed by international standards in the exercise of their entrepreneurial freedom and rights.

The operative phase of the Global Compact began in July 2000 – by 2006 more than 3000 companies, NGOs and labour organisations had participated. Realising the importance of financial markets in pushing responsible corporate behaviour, the 'UN's principles for responsible investment' were launched by the UNGC in April 2006 and, after just three months, have been signed by institutional investors controlling more than $4 trillion in assets.

Companies are increasingly assigned moral responsibility, which for legitimacy reasons they have to take account of. The UN Global Compact describes a normative corridor for courses of action which are not negotiable for companies with → integrity. It is desirable that companies that behave in exemplary fashion in → human rights, social and ecological terms and in their work against → corruption should be evaluated with more differentiation by various actors (NGOs, media, political parties) instead of being thrown indiscriminately into a large pot along with the worst cases of malpractice. The moral prestige capital gained by this would also reward efforts of all sorts and so, with time, create a new level of competition.

Klaus Leisinger

UNION BUSTING
→ Labour relations

Union busting is when employers take action to prevent the formation of trade unions, or disempower and subvert those that already exist.

Historically, union busting brings to mind images of police and troops battling with workers, or replacement workers ('scabs') being escorted past striking workers. However, union busting has also involved infiltration and sabotage where union leaders both in the developed and developing world have turned out to be in the pay of governments or companies. One of the most common areas of union busting is the global fast → food industry, particularly within those companies that are headquartered in the US.

Overt and covert union busting continues to this day, and with growing worker unrest in fast-growing economies such as China, and the pro-labour governments in → Latin America, it is likely to become a more prominent feature of → labour relations coverage. Nowadays, in addition to direct violence, there are lawyers, → labour relations consultants, psychologists and others who specialise in undermining organised labour, and who have had significant success in weakening trade unions in some major industrialised economies.

Mick Blowfield

UN MILLENNIUM DEVELOPMENT GOALS (MDGs)
→ Development, Poverty
⌨ www.unmillenniumproject.org

The Millennium Development Goals (MDGs) bring together key aspects of human development into a set of international goals and targets that were commonly accepted as a framework for measuring → development progress by 189 member states of the United Nations in the Millennium Declaration of 18 September 2000.

The Millennium Declaration commits signatory governments to a global partnership to reduce poverty, improve health and promote peace, → human rights and environmental sustainability. The Millennium Declaration identifies human development as the key to sustaining social and economic progress in all countries, whereas the MDGs are a series of quantified targets for ending extreme poverty by 2015.

The MDGs are expressed as a set of eight goals with each one encompassing numerical and time-bound targets, most of which are linked to achievement by 2015:

- Goal 1: Eradicate extreme hunger and poverty
- Goal 2: Achieve universal primary education
- Goal 3: Promote → gender equality and empower women
- Goal 4: Reduce child mortality
- Goal 5: Improve maternal health
- Goal 6: Combat → HIV/AIDS, malaria and other diseases
- Goal 7: Ensure environmental sustainability
- Goal 8: Develop a global partnership for → development

It is important to distinguish goals from targets. The eight MDGs are general objectives (e.g. improve maternal health) whereas the 18 targets are specific aims (e.g. reduce maternal mortality by three-quarters).

Given that the global targets embodied in the MDGs are the result of intergovernmental negotiations, they are not based on rigorous analysis. They have to be customised and tailored to national circumstances. Goals have to be prioritised and targets need to be set at feasible levels.

The United Nations plays a key role in facilitating dialogue and brokering partnerships by providing a neutral space for governments and non-state actors to agree on a relevant set of national targets, ideally defined through a participatory process. Given the scale of the challenge of achieving the MDGs, the private sector is increasingly being invited by the UN and governments to become active partners in MDG-related national, regional and global initiatives.

At the World Summit of September 2005, world leaders committed to adopt, by 2006, and implement comprehensive national development strategies to achieve the MDGs and related internationally agreed → development goals and objectives. Such 'MDG-based poverty reduction strategies' were a core recommendation of *Investing in Development* (2005).

The UN Secretary-General issues a yearly report on progress toward implementation of the Millennium Declaration, including the MDGs, based on information drawn from across the UN system. The first comprehensive review was conducted in 2005.

Progress has not been uniform across the world or across the goals:

- Major disparities exist across and within countries;
- Poverty is greatest in rural areas;
- Urban poverty is also extensive, growing, and underreported;
- Sub-Saharan → Africa continues to experience → food insecurity, a rise of extreme poverty, high child and maternal mortality, large numbers of people living in slums, and a widespread shortfall for most of the MDGs;
- → Asia is making the fastest progress, but hundreds of millions of people remain in extreme poverty, and even fast-growing countries are failing to achieve some of the non-income goals; and
- There are mixed records in other regions − → Latin America, the transition economies, and the Middle East and North → Africa show slow or no progress on some of the goals and persistent inequalities undermining progress on others.

Kofi A. Annan reminds us: 'We will have time to reach the Millennium Development Goals – worldwide and in most, or even all, individual countries – but only if we break with business as usual.

We cannot win overnight. Success will require sustained action across the entire decade between now and the deadline. It takes time to train the teachers, nurses and engineers; to build the roads, schools and hospitals; to grow the small and large businesses able to create the jobs and income needed. So we must start now. And we must more than double global → development assistance over the next few years. Nothing less will help to achieve the goals.'

David F. Murphy

UN NORMS ON THE RESPONSIBILITIES OF TRANSNATIONAL CORPORATIONS AND OTHER BUSINESS ENTERPRISES WITH REGARD TO HUMAN RIGHTS
→ Human rights
⌕ www.un.org

In 2003, the UN Sub-commission on the Protection and Promotion of Human Rights adopted norms stating that 'transnational corporations   . . . , as organs of society, are also responsible for promoting and securing . . . → human rights', including the right to → development. While those norms signify an important step towards codification of corporate → accountability, they do not include binding monitoring mechanisms.

UN PRINCIPLES FOR RESPONSIBLE INVESTMENT
→ Socially responsible investment, UN Global Compact
⌕ www.unpri.org

In 2005 the UN Secretary-General invited a group of the world's largest institutional investors to join a process to develop the Principles for Responsible Investment (PRI). Individuals representing 20 institutional investors from 12 countries agreed to participate supported by a 70-person multi-stakeholder group of experts from the investment industry, intergovernmental and governmental organisations, civil society and academia. The Principles for Responsible Investment were launched in 2006 and commit the signing investors to respect six principles regarding 'environmental, social, and → corporate governance' issues in their investment decisions. The process was coordinated by the United Nations Environment Programme Finance Initiative (UNEP FI) and the → UN Global Compact. Following the launch of the Principles, Phase 2 of the process promotes adoption of the Principles by additional investors and provides comprehensive resources to assist investors in implementing the Principles.

UN UNIVERSAL DECLARATION ON HUMAN RIGHTS

→ Human rights

⌐ www.un.org

The Universal Declaration on Human Rights (UDHR) was ratified by the UN General Assembly in 1948, responding to the atrocities of WWII and the holocaust. Since then, the UDHR has been the dominant yardstick for questions of → human rights in most democracies and has been implemented in various UN → human rights treaties as well as national or regional → human rights initiatives, such as the European Convention on Human Rights. Key → human rights include:

- Non-discrimination
- Women's rights
- Life, liberty and physical integrity of a person
- Civic freedoms (e.g. expression, association, assembly, religion)

- Employees' rights
- Freedom from → child labour
- Freedom from slavery, forced and bonded labour
- Economic, social and cultural rights (e.g. → food, education, health, housing)
- Minority rights
- → Indigenous rights
- Right to information

The UDHR becomes relevant for corporations through its implementation in many national → human rights frameworks but also directly as the UDHR summons 'every individual and every organ of society' – the latter including corporations – to 'strive by teaching and education to promote respect for these rights and free-doms and ... to secure their universal and effective recognition and observance'. The respect for → human rights has entered increas-ingly the CSR agenda through → globalisation which exposes business to political regimes that may infringe → human rights, often exposing companies to allegations of complicity with these governments. Many of the self-regulatory CSR initiatives, such as the → Voluntary Principles on Security and Human Rights or campaign groups such as the → Business and Human Rights Resource Centre, are directly addressing the growing demand from stakeholders for an active corporate role in upholding and protecting → human rights as set out in the UDHR.

Dirk Matten

US FEDERAL SENTENCING GUIDELINES
→ Business ethics
⌐ www.ussc.gov

The Federal Sentencing Guidelines were developed by the United States Sentencing Commission and set out a uniform sentencing policy in the United States federal court system. They first went into effect in 1987. Of particular importance are the organisational sentencing guidelines, focused on deterrence as opposed to punishment, and achieved through sentencing benefits for organisations that have in place an 'effective programme to prevent and detect violations of law'. For a programme to be effective, the following is required by the guidelines: clear compliance standards and procedures, high-level personnel to be involved in oversight, careful delegation of discretionary authority, communication programmes, monitoring systems, and consistent enforcement. The Guidelines have subsequently led to the creation of ethics officers in many organisations and the foundation of the → Ethics and Compliance Officer Association in the US.

Petrus Marais and Daniel Malan

US SUPERFUND LEGISLATION
→ Environmental liabilities
🖱 www.epa.gov

'Superfund' is the title by which the Comprehensive Environmental Response and Liability Act (CERCLA) is more widely known. Originally enacted in 1980, and amended in 1986, CERCLA is designed to identify polluted sites and force 'responsible parties' to carry out clean-up operations. Significantly, liability for clean-up is joint and several, meaning that any party involved with the site at any time, regardless of the extent of that involvement, and indeed whether the activities carried out were perfectly legal at the time, can be held responsible for the full cost incurred. CERCLA also established a 'superfund' of $1.6 billion (increased to $8.5 billion on later amendment), of which 88% was contributed by industry, to fund clean-up operations in cases where responsible parties were unable to provide the necessary finance.

While succeeding in highlighting the extent of the problem of contaminated land, with 27 000 potential clean-up sites having been identified by 1988, the effectiveness of the Superfund Legislation has been called into question. Particular attention has been drawn to the high costs imposed, due not just to clean-up operations but also arising out of litigation, generally involving disputes between insurers. This latter development has also been responsible for causing severe delays in actually tackling the problem of cleaning up contaminated sites.

David Owen

UTILITIES SECTOR

The utilities sector meets basic needs of the public by providing → water, wastewater, electricity and gas services that are essential for human well-being, as well as economic and social development.

Companies in the utilities sector are subject to scrutiny over a broad range of CSR issues and are subject to extensive regulation to protect the → environment, customers and wider communities. Examples of specific issues include:

- Impact on → climate change – in providing essential utility services to society, companies in this sector bear the responsibility for emissions of large quantities of gases linked to → climate change (e.g. the International Energy Agency estimates that electricity generation accounts for approximately 40% of global greenhouse gas emissions). By minimising these emissions, for example through investments in renewable energy, energy efficiency, and emissions capture technologies, utility companies can reduce the → climate change impacts of society as a whole.
- Social exclusion – access to essential utility services is particularly important for poorer, remote and more vulnerable groups of people as these services contribute to economic development. Access to utilities also helps alleviate poverty through development and improvement of health and education services.

Affordability and protection for vulnerable customers are key concerns, especially for those where the costs of utilities form a significant proportion of household income. Policies towards disconnections and debt recovery need to balance the interests of the company with those of customers.

- Resource depletion – for energy companies, managing the transition to a lower carbon portfolio is key to long-term sustainability. The finite nature of fossil fuels means that as stocks are depleted, wholesale costs rise, making the economic case for investment in other energy sources, such as renewables and nuclear, more attractive. Pressure on → water resources at all levels across the world continues to grow, with competing demands for access to water leading to tension and conflict, particularly where companies are seen to be using → water to the detriment of local communities.

- Security of supply – as local resources (of fossil fuels and → water, for example) are depleted, companies are forced to look further afield, across regional and national boundaries. This can lead to the risk of interruption in supplies and restrictions being placed on use, with particular impact on vulnerable customers such as the elderly or ill. Where companies are responsible for distribution as well as supply of utility services, criticisms have been made of companies for not sufficiently anticipating resource constraints or, in the → water sector, addressing issues such as leakage. Measures to counter these issues are not adequately discussed by the world's 10 largest utility companies according to the 2006 Accountability Rating.

- Privatisation of essential services – historically, governments were responsible for providing and regulating such services but increasingly utilities are being privatised leading to competition and deregulation. Privatisation of utilities may lead to greater demand and greater environmental impacts. It can also lead to → corruption and market manipulation as seen in California in 2000 and 2001 following deregulation in 1996. Privatisation also leads to questions of who owns the resource – the public (historically → water was owned by the public) or the private company who owns the rights to clean and distribute it.

Various guidelines have been developed that are useful for the utilities sector to address global issues, including:

- WBCSD's sector project on electricity utilities, including the publications Sustainability in the Electricity Utility Sector (2002) and Powering a Sustainable Future (2006);
- The Globalisation Institute's paper, Water for Life, which argues that privatisation can help to address sustainability in → developing countries;
- The → Global Reporting Initiative (GRI) energy utility sector supplement, which can be used in conjunction with the generic Sustainability Reporting Guidelines; and
- The → ILO Tripartite Declaration of Principles concerning Multinational Enterprises and Social Policy, which is relevant to the utilities sector in terms of promoting partnerships.

Nicki Websper

VALUE CHAIN
→ Supply chain

VALUE CREATION
→ Business case

The word 'value' or '→ values' in the context of CSR is Janus faced; it is bi-valent, a duality or a dualism. In the context of CSR it refers to the range of goals and objectives set before the business enterprise. The word 'value' is defined as 'a fair or proper equivalent in money' and 'that quality of a thing according to which it is thought of as being more or less desirable, useful, estimable, important, etc.' (*Webster's New World Dictionary*). The *Shorter Oxford*

English Dictionary states that the word 'value' is used both in reference to a medium of exchange, such as money, and in ethics to indicate something that is worthy of esteem for its own sake, and has intrinsic worth.

The 'value' of the enterprise, therefore, is multifaceted and more than its income, stock price or bottom line. From the CSR perspective, the 'value' of an enterprise embraces its external impacts on customers, employees, owners, creditors, suppliers, competitors, the → environment and community. The 'value' of an enterprise measures the consequences of its actions and policies. Is wealth created? Are people employed? Are beneficial products and services provided? Do investors earn a fair return on their money? Is the → environment harmed? Are bribery, → corruption, and other abuses of political power opposed or prevented? Is the company complicit in → human rights violations?

From a CSR perspective, this understanding of business value takes the form of stakeholder analysis. A business, from the CSR perspective, is expected to take into account the concerns and interests of certain key constituencies in making its decision. These constituencies are: customers, employees, owners and other providers of finance capital, suppliers, competitors, and communities, including the → environment. Reference to all stakeholders and not merely the interests of shareholders/owners completes the calculation of enterprise value, or the → values associated with the business, in a robust and more accurate fashion.

From this CSR perspective, it can be asked: what is the value of an employee? The answer would embrace both the cost of the employee to the company, the contribution to output and profit added by the employee, the productivity or capital value of the employee, the employee's positive or negative contribution to the culture of the firm etc. Similarly, the question of how much value does the firm add to the economy and society can be measured along a number of utilitarian dimensions, some quite precise and material and others more abstract and intangible in form.

It should be noted, however, that in both senses – that of exchange or commodity price and of intrinsic estimable worth – the concept of value relies upon utilitarian perspectives of incremental worldly benefit. The notion of value cannot be understood without reference to advantage.

In the CSR contest, the advantages to be estimated are manifold and are to be contemplated from a variety of perspectives. The estimation of advantage by the board of directors, or the accountants, or the shareholders, or the CEO, standing in special isolation from other points of view provides an inadequate conception of business value. Taking into consideration a limited set of concerns truncates the resulting conclusion about the scope of value inherent in the business or the business-related action.

Market forces have several ways to set value on a company. For companies selling their stock on public exchanges, the daily stock price is not a certain estimate of the company's value. Stock markets are said frequently to undervalue or overvalue a stock. Markets for stocks and other securities include the dynamics of speculation, that is putting a price on a stock not in reference to its inherent long-term profitability, but more with a view to making a profit off the perceptions of others regarding the company as well as exogenous factors such as political events and economic ups and downs.

The value of a company is set by multiplying the net present value of its expected future earnings by a number that represents the risk associated with earning such future income. The higher the risk, the lower the value of the company. A portion of the value so calculated for the company is goodwill. Goodwill represents the intangible assets of the company that ensure or compromise its ability to earn income in the future. Goodwill includes the company's capacity to make money from managing well its relationships with its stakeholders (or to lose money if those relationships are not well managed).

Stephen B. Young

VALUES
→ Business ethics, Moral case, Moral responsibilities

Values, in a CSR context often referred to as 'moral values', comprise the set of beliefs of an individual or an organisation about right and wrong, desirable or undesirable actions or decisions. Values can have cultural, philosophical, religious or customary justifications and normally differ considerably between individuals, nations, regions and socio-economic groups. Values play a central role in CSR. Social responsibilities of business and stakeholder expectations with regard to corporate behaviour normally reflect the values held by those constituencies. Many corporations address these expectations by being transparent about their values in statements and policy documents. Values in business, in particular in multinational corporations, are normally fairly abstract and broad. The value of 'equality' may be held by such an organisation; however, it will take different shapes in different countries: in the US this might particularly address the rights of gays and lesbians; it might focus on the role of women in Saudia Arabia while in Malaysia, it might focus on the equal treatment of members of the Chinese, Indian or Malayan ethnic groups.

Dirk Matten

VERIFICATION
→ Auditing, Report verification

VOLUNTARY PRINCIPLES ON SECURITY AND HUMAN RIGHTS
→ Human rights
⌐ www.voluntaryprinciples.org

The Voluntary Principles (VPs) were launched in 2000 as the result of a consultation process which involved the governments of the USA and UK, extractive and energy companies from those countries and NGOs. The VPs are a set of standards that guide companies in maintaining the safety and security of their operations within a framework that ensures respect for → human rights and fundamental freedoms. Since 2000, several new participants have joined, including the governments of Norway and the Netherlands. Next to the governments of the four countries, 16 companies based in those countries and seven NGOs have signed the VPs.

VOLUNTARY SELF-REGULATION
→ Self-regulation

VOLUNTEERING

Employee volunteering (EV) describes an ongoing coordinated effort where businesses support and encourage their employees' involvement in social initiatives in the local community. EV manifests the social dimension of → corporate social responsibility and is one mode of corporate social investment. EV (also known as corporate volunteering) entails voluntary cooperation and building of relationships among the local community (or proxy organisations like NGOs), employees and businesses.

The approach to EV by companies has undergone a metamorphosis since its inception from 'ad hoc philanthropic' to a more 'strategic' nature of EV schemes that attempt to bridge employee, community and business needs. EV is described as a basic business strategy going beyond financial donations whose purpose could be to complement existing human resource recruitment, training and development; to complement existing corporate community initiatives; and to enhance corporate image and reputation. EV also can enhance the common good.

The management of EV schemes takes different forms from informal to formal structured programmes which are either employee led and/or employer initiated. Some examples of EV schemes include team challenges, secondments, mentoring, coaching, individual volunteering, and matched giving. There are various types of volunteering schemes:

- Team volunteering or challenges – team challenges involve a group of employees in the organisation or within departments, who work together to tackle a task, e.g. painting, landscaping, home care support. Family members also participate in such events which may be full time or part time generally concentrated over a period of one day to a week. Team challenges are good for publicity and enhance visibility in the community. Some potential challenges include sustaining commitment and the effectiveness of whole teams.

- Mentoring – there are two types of mentoring based on the nature of interaction, namely face-to-face and e-mentoring. Mentoring provides the opportunity for mentors (employees) to develop one-on-one relationships with mentees (e.g. pupils, teachers, unemployed youth, and community organisation managers). It mostly involves commitment over a long period of time.

- Development assignments – these are short and intensive (either part or full time) placements within a community organisation from around 100 hours up to three months, undertaken by individual employees or within a team. Projects are clearly defined and designed to meet the development needs of the employees while allowing the host organisation to benefit from their skills and experiences. The schemes are used to pursue training and development needs of staff. Measuring their success is sometimes integrated into job appraisals.

- Secondments – usually secondments are full time for a period between three and 24 months and undertaken at a time of significant career change often in a management or consultancy capacity. Employees carry out a general function in the collaborating organisation while still maintaining their employment. Secondments have been associated with early retirement, company restructuring or mid-career management development. They have been used to rekindle dormant skills and develop new ones that enhance people's employability.

- Individual role volunteering – employees volunteer their time and skills on an occasional or a regular basis (e.g. serving on school boards, being trustees, or joining management committees of NGOs or CBOs). This form of volunteering enables employees to associate their own interests with community needs. They have a potential of providing good visibility in the community.

Another popular form of EV are employee giving schemes which could be categorised in the following way:

- Employee donations – these include a range of tax-efficient giving schemes, e.g. payroll giving and gift aid. Payroll giving allows employees to make regular agreed-upon pre-tax donations from their gross salary to any chosen charity. Payroll giving complements other community involvement options and is an ideal scheme for those employees who would want to be involved in community initiatives but are not able to find time to volunteer. It is easy and cheap to administer. Employees have a say which causes their companies should support.
- Matched giving (time or money) – companies can match employees' time spent in the community, or money raised or donated by employees for social initiatives. For example, if an employee uses 10 hours of their own time, the company matches another 10 hours of its time giving the employee a total of 20 volunteering hours.

The different EV schemes have various features which if exploited can help achieve maximum value for the company, employees and the community. EV builds business–community partnerships by encouraging social cooperation, reciprocity, enhancing social trust, norms of generosity and resource exchange. EV strengthens stakeholder relationships which are fundamental to business success and is recommended as one way of manifesting → corporate social responsibility.

WASTE MANAGEMENT
→ Recycling

Waste is an important dimension of the environmental performance of companies and requires considerable attention throughout the production processes. Simply disposing of waste is no longer an option. There are too many environmental and financial aspects involved. In other words: waste has become one of the main topics in the environmental management of a company. Waste management is defined as the collection, transport, processing, recycling or disposal of waste materials and the activities aiming to reduce the amount of waste being produced.

Traditionally, the main approach to waste was dumping, often in a landfill as this was the cheapest option. Landfill is, however, the least preferred option in the so-called waste hierarchy. In order of desirability this hierarchy looks in principle as follows:

1. Reduce – reducing the amount of waste, for instance by changing inputs, technologies or working procedures, is the most effective way of handling waste.
2. Reuse – reusing means using an item more than once, either for the same function or for a new use.
3. Recycle – recycling means breaking down a used item into raw materials, such as glass, paper, metals or plastics. This breaking down distinguishes it from reuse. Using a bottle more than once to carry a fluid is reuse. Breaking it down to pieces to produce new glass products, either a bottle or something else, is recycling.
4. Incineration – incineration is the process through which waste gets burned. Nowadays the energy that arises from it is often used to produce energy (heat or electricity).

5. Landfill – landfilling involves the disposal of waste on the ground or, for instance, in an old mine. Landfilling can take place in a controlled way where the soil is protected from → water leakages or in an uncontrolled way (dumping).

Obviously preventing waste from being produced is the best option. Landfilling, however, is still common practice, especially in → developing countries. As the waste is put to no meaningful use, this is the least desirable option though.

The first three options can be applied within a company and are known as the 3R-approach. The last two options often take place outside the company that produced the waste in the first place. Waste management, therefore, focuses mainly on the 3R-approach.

An important aim in waste management, next to controlling waste streams, is to move up in the waste hierarchy. To this aim a number of waste minimisation techniques have been developed. One of the earliest was 3M's Pollution Prevention Pays programme. The aim of these techniques is to introduce cleaner production by rethinking production processes so that less waste (useless output) is produced, thus increasing the amount of desired output (product) per unit of raw material. In other words: these techniques aim to make a company more eco-efficient. At the core of waste minimisation techniques lies a thorough analysis of material flows through the company with special attention for inefficiencies (waste, emissions) that occur. By analysing the causes for these inefficiencies new, cleaner solutions can be considered.

Waste management is a concept that not only can be applied within a single company but also throughout the life cycle of a product in a → life cycle assessment. The aim then is to identify the most effective place for waste reduction, using an → industrial ecology approach, instead of working on suboptimal solutions within individual companies.

Theo de Bruijn

WATER MANAGEMENT

Water management is the monitoring, control and optimisation of the use of water. The aim of water management is to protect finite and vulnerable surface water and groundwater resources by limiting water use and water pollution. The goals are both qualitative (limiting pollution) and quantitative (limiting the use of water). Water is in many places around the world a major concern for the quality of life, and this is likely to become more prevalent with the effects of desertification and → climate change.

Water also has many different dimensions: on the one hand water is a scarce resource that needs to be used in a restricted manner. On the other hand the risk of flooding has and will increasingly become a reality in many places. This multidimensional perspective on water, from pollution control to efficiency to flood control, places water in an area of prime interest to companies. Measures to be taken include installing water efficient equipment, closed-loop systems, filters and safety measures to limit the damage during possible flooding. Finally, water management is also about creating a system of tasks, responsibilities and procedures through which the focus on water is ensured throughout the organisation.

Theo de Bruijn

WATER POLLUTION

→ Pollution, Water management

WHITE COLLAR CRIME

→ Corruption, Fraud

WHISTLEBLOWING

→ Corporate governance, Corruption, Employee rights, Fraud

The act of publicly raising concern about perceived wrongdoing within an organisation is referred to as whistleblowing. The term is derived from the physical act of blowing a whistle to alert others that a crime is being committed, as practised by British police officers. A concern can be raised either internally (e.g. by making use of a confidential mechanism such as a hotline) or externally (usually by approaching the media). Blowing the whistle is usually seen as a last resort, i.e. only to be used once all other avenues to address the concern (e.g. by discussing it with colleagues or reporting to a line manager) have been exhausted. Legislation will often protect whistleblowers, provided that a report was made in good faith and that proper procedures were followed. However, in practice whistleblowers are often branded as 'tell-tales' and therefore find it difficult to obtain the respect of their colleagues, although they are often praised by the public. Without adequate institutional protection whistleblowers in the past have been subject to serious sanctions, ranging from litigation, due to being made redundant, to bullying.

Daniel Malan

WOLFSBERG ANTI-MONEY LAUNDERING (AML) PRINCIPLES

→ Fraud

⌐ www.wolfsberg-principles.com

The Wolfsberg Group is an association of 12 global banks, which aims to develop financial services industry standards, and related products, for anti-money laundering and counter terrorist financing policies.

The Wolfsberg Anti-Money Laundering Principles for Private Banking were subsequently published in October 2000 (and revised in May 2002). The Group then published a Statement on the Financing of Terrorism in January 2002, and also released the

Wolfsberg Anti-Money Laundering Principles for Correspondent Banking in November 2002 and the Wolfsberg Statement on Monitoring Screening and Searching in September 2003. In 2004, the Wolfsberg Group focused on the development of a → due diligence model for financial institutions, in cooperation with Banker's Almanac, thereby fulfilling one of the recommendations made in the Correspondent Banking Principles.

In June 2006, two sets of guidance were published: Guidance on a Risk Based Approach for Managing Money Laundering Risks and AML Guidance for Mutual Funds and Other Pooled Investment Vehicles.

In early 2007, the Wolfsberg Group issued its Statement against Corruption, in close association with → Transparency International and the Basel Institute on Governance. It describes the role of the Wolfsberg Group and financial institutions more generally in support of international efforts to combat → corruption. The Statement against Corruption identifies some of the measures financial institutions may consider in order to prevent → corruption in their own operations and protect themselves against the misuse of their operations in relation to → corruption.

WORK–LIFE BALANCE
→ Employee rights, Gender issues

Work–life balance refers to the level of control over the conditions in one's workplace and its harmony with a person's private life.

Work–life balance has moved up the management agenda in recent years for a number of reasons:

- The link between productivity and hours/time worked is weaker than previously assumed.
- Acquisition, retention and motivation of skilled staff has become a (if not the) vital contributory factor for business success.

- Increased regulation faced by business with respect to → gender issues, equal opportunities, working conditions, → employee rights and business responsibilities regarding parental leave.
- The rise of teleworking and flexible work patterns has opened considerable opportunities for employees to work from home. While this might open more opportunity of spending time with the family, it often blurs the distinction between work and private spheres of an employee.

These four factors have raised the cost to business of the consequences of failing to support employees in achieving a reasonable and sustainable work–life balance. In practice maintaining a harmonious work–life balance involves reducing unnecessary and unproductive stresses on employees such as a 'long hours culture' (often little more than 'presenteeism') while increasing incentives that reward and motivate workers, such as flexible working hours or company crèches. The → business case for supporting work–life balance goes beyond → business ethics or merely being a 'good employer'. Rather, it recognises that employees are often motivated as much by the many non-financial elements to their work than the traditional view of labour as a purely time/wage transaction model assumes.

Nick Tolhurst

WORLD BUSINESS COUNCIL FOR SUSTAINABLE DEVELOPMENT (WBCSD)

⌐ www.wbcsd.org

The World Business Council for Sustainable Development (WBCSD) brings together some 180 international companies in a shared commitment to → sustainable development through economic growth, ecological balance and social progress. Its members are drawn from more than 30 countries and 20 major industrial sectors. It has a global network of 50+ national and regional business councils and partner organisations.

The council's mission is to provide business leadership as a catalyst for change toward → sustainable development, and to support the business → licence to operate, innovate and grow in a world increasingly shaped by → sustainable development issues.

Its objectives include:

- Business leadership – to be a leading business advocate on → sustainable development;
- Policy development – to help develop policies that create framework conditions for the business contribution to → sustainable development;
- The business case – to develop and promote the → business case for → sustainable development;
- Best practice – to demonstrate the business contribution to → sustainable development and share → best practices among members; and
- Global outreach – to contribute to a sustainable future for developing nations and nations in transition.

Björn Stigson

WORLD COMMISSION ON ENVIRONMENT AND DEVELOPMENT

→ Sustainable development, Rio Declaration on Environment and Development

🖰 www.un.org

The World Commission on Environment and Development (WCED) was set up by the United Nations in 1983, in response to growing concerns about the deterioration of the global environment. It became known as the Brundtland Commission after its chair, Dr Gro Harlem Brundtland, Prime Minister of Norway.

The Commission's report, Our Common Future, was issued four years later.

In contrast to earlier environmental thinking, which focused on protecting the → environment from economic development, the WCED report brought environment and → development together in the concept of → sustainable development: '→ development which meets the needs of the present without compromising the ability of future generations to meet their own needs'.

Responding to the report, the UN called on governments to make → sustainable development a central guiding principle, and to develop policies which aim to preserve peace, encourage sustainable growth, alleviate poverty, address population growth and conserve and enhance the resource base. The importance of involving both NGOs and business in working towards these goals was strongly emphasised.

The WCED's definition of → sustainable development remains a benchmark for much sustainability thinking, and the process started by the WCED and carried on through the Rio and Johannesburg Declarations continues through the UN Commission on Sustainable Development.

Ruth Findlay-Brooks

WORLD ECONOMIC FORUM

⌐ www.weforum.org

The World Economic Forum (WEF) is based in Geneva, and is a forum for business and political leaders to debate current global issues and to network. Set up in 1971, it holds annual meetings in Davos, Switzerland, as well as more frequent regional meetings. Its aim is to 'improve the state of the world by engaging leaders in partnerships to shape global, regional and industry agendas'. Key in recent years, for example, have included → Africa and ate change.

Although the majority of participants in the annual meetings are political or corporate leaders, key NGO, religious and trade union leaders are also invited, and there is a large media presence with all sessions open to journalists.

Despite its independence and its professed aims to focus on social and environmental improvements, the WEF is the subject of criticism from → anti-globalisation protestors and NGOs for being elitist and non-democratic, a 'talking shop' which gives the most powerful businesses on the planet easy access to political leaders. The NGO 'Public Eye on Davos' was set up in 1997 to voice opposition to the WEF, and for many → anti-globalisation groups, the rival → World Social Forum has become an alternative forum.

Ruth Findlay-Brooks

WORLD FEDERATION OF SPORTING GOODS INDUSTRY CODE OF CONDUCT

→ Supply chain

↗ www.wfsgi.org

The World Federation of Sporting Goods Industry Code of Conduct was launched in 1997. It is a response to massive public outcry about labour conditions in the global sports apparel and footwear industry, in particular in '→ sweatshops' in → developing countries, most notably Pakistan and Bangladesh at the time. The code is voluntary for members of the Federation and commits the organisation to source from suppliers who respect basic environmental, social and labour-related standards.

WORLD SOCIAL FORUM

↗ www.wsf2006.org

The World Social Forum (WSF) was set up in 2001 by those → anti-globalisation groups and critics of 'neo-liberal' policies, to provide a counterbalance to the → World Economic Forum (WEF). A social movement rather than an organisation, it aims to provide a meeting place for civil society organisations to share thinking, ideas and plans for action.

The WSF's focus is on peace, justice and equity, and on the provision of economic, social and → human rights. Its main meeting takes place at the same time as the WEF gathering in Davos, attracting tens of thousands to a self-organised forum for discussion about topics ranging from trade and conflict to land ownership and → HIV/AIDS. Many regional forums have grown from the WEF, with different focuses for discussion.

While it has been criticised by some for its haphazard nature and lack of structure, others see the WSF not as a group or organisation, but as a democratic forum for grassroots dialogue and change.

Ruth Findlay-Brooks

WORLD SUMMIT ON SUSTAINABLE DEVELOPMENT (WSSD)
→ Johannesburg Declaration on Sustainable Development

WORLD TRADE ORGANISATION (WTO)
→ Anti-globalisation, TRIPS Agreement
⌐ www.wto.org

The World Trade Organisation (WTO) was set up in 1995 as the successor to the GATT. Its main task is to come up with regulation for international trade between nations with the goal of facilitating the most easy and free exchange of goods and services worldwide. The WTO comes up with – often multilateral – agreements between countries about trade relations which then get adopted and ratified by the legislative bodies of the member countries. The highest organ of the WTO is the ministerial conference where the relevant ministers from the member countries meet at least every two years. The operative work is done by other bodies, based in the WTO's headquarters in Geneva. The WTO also has the power to impose sanctions to member states which are found in breach of its agreements.

In the CSR context the WTO is seen as controversial. Some of its agreements attempt at addressing certain social, ethical or environmental issues and the current round of negotiations since 2001 ('Doha Round') tries to include aspects of international → development. However, many NGOs and → anti-globalisation groups are critical of its work. They argue that the WTO is an organisation which in particular advocates the interests of rich states in the global north and infringes the interests of poorer countries in the south. A case in point is the → TRIPS Agreement which is an example of a WTO regulation protecting → intellectual property rights. Critics argue that it has been used to protect the interests of big pharmaceutical multinationals based in → Europe and North America through sanctioning poorer countries for producing or importing cheap generic drugs to address, for instance, the → HIV/AIDS pandemic.

Dirk Matten

ZEN
→ Asia

The Zen of CSR, to playfully coin a phrase, refers to a perspective on CSR as a way of being, rather than a form of doing. This echoes Matten and Moon's (*Academy of Management Review*, 2008) distinction between implicit vs explicit CSR: explicit CSR is about voluntary corporate policies, programmes and strategies that express the responsibilities of business, while implicit CSR is more about → values, norms and rules that shape the responsible business behaviour. The one is outer directed, the other inner directed.

There is a cultural element to this as well – by and large, the North and West has emphasised outer-directed, measurable CSR (witness the explosion of ethical codes and sustainability reporting (→ non-financial reporting)), while the East and South has been more content with inner-directed, intangible CSR (deeply rooted in cultural, tribal or religious traditions of community, respect and reciprocity). Examples include the Japanese concept of *kyosei* ('coexistence') and the Chinese notion of *xiaokang* ('harmonious society').

The Zen of CSR also suggests that CSR has transformative power – that both companies and individuals can be changed by engaging with CSR, which points to a newly emerging literature on CSR as a form of self-transcendence. So, for instance, Welford (→ Asia) has published work on the influence of (Zen-)Buddhist thinking on business responsibility which arguably might be of growing importance with the growth of interest in CSR in these parts of the global economy.

Wayne Visser

LIST OF ABBREVIATIONS

3Ps	People, planet, profit (or prosperity), Pollution prevention pays
3Rs	Reduce, reuse, recycle
AA	AccountAbility
AAU	Assigned Allowance Unit
ABC	Activity-based costing
AICC	African Institute for Corporate Citizenship
AIM	Alternative Investments Market
AIP	Apparel Industry Partnership
AML	Anti-money laundering
ATTAC	Association for the Taxation of Financial Transactions for the Aid of Citizens
BAM	Business AIDS Methodology
BSCI	Business Social Compliance Initiative
BEE	Black economic empowerment
BITC	Business in the Community
BOP	Base (or Bottom) of the Pyramid
BREEAM	Building Research Establishment Environmental Assessment Method
BSR	Business for Social Responsibility
CACG	Commonwealth Association for Corporate Governance
CBOs	Community-based organisations

CCI	Corporate community investment
CDFI	Community development financial institution
CDM	Clean Development Mechanism
CDP	Carbon Disclosure Project
CEDAW	Convention on the Elimination of all forms of Discrimination Against Women
CEM	Corporate environmental management
CEP	Council on Economic Priorities
CEO	Chief executive officer
CER	Certified Emissions Reduction
CERES	Coalition for Environmentally Responsible Economies
CFCs	Chlorofluorocarbons
CIP	Corporate Involvement Programme
CO_2	Carbon dioxide
COP	Conference of Parties
CPI	Corruption Perceptions Index
CR	Corporate responsibility
CRT	Caux Round Table
CSO	Civil Society Organisation
CSP	Corporate social performance
CSR	Corporate social responsibility
CSR EMS	EU Multi-Stakeholder Forum on Corporate Social Responsibility
DDT	Dichloro-diphenyl-trichloroethane
DfE	Design for the environment
DJSI	Dow Jones Sustainability Index
EABIS	European Academy for Business in Society
EBEN	European Business Ethics Network
ECOA	Ethics and Compliance Officer Association
EDC	Endocrine disrupting chemical
EFTA	European Fair Trade Association
EIA	Environmental impact assessment
EICC	Electronic Industry Code of Conduct
EIR	Extractive Industries Review
EITI	Extractive Industries Transparency Initiative
EMAS	EU Eco-Management and Audit Scheme
EMS	Environmental management system
EqIA	Equality impact assessment
ERU	Emission Reduction Unit

ESHIA	Environmental, social and health impact assessment
ETI	Economically targeted investment
ETI	Ethical Trading Initiative
ETS	Emissions Trading Scheme
EU	European Union
EUA	European Union Allowance
FAO	Food and Agriculture Organisation of the United Nations
FLA	Fair Labour Association
FLO	Fairtrade Labelling Organisations International
FSC	Forest Stewardship Council
FTA	Foreign Trade Association
FTSE	Financial Times Stock Exchange company
g/km	Grams per kilometre
GATT	General Agreement on Trade and Tariffs
GBC	Global Business Coalition on HIV/AIDS
GC	Global Compact
GDP	Gross domestic product
GeSI	Global eSustainability Initiative
GFATM	Global Fund to Fight AIDS, Tuberculosis, and Malaria
GHGs	Greenhouse gases
GIS	Geographical information systems
GM	Genetically modified
GMO	Genetically modified organism
GNP	Gross national product
GRI	Global Reporting Initiative
GSGR	Centre for the Study of Globalisation and Regionalisation
HAART	Highly active anti-retroviral therapies
HIA	Health impact assessment
HRH	His Royal Highness
IAASB	International Auditing and Assurance Standards Board
IABS	International Association for Business and Society
IAF	International Accreditation Forum
IAIA	International Association for Impact Assessment
IBLF	International Business Leaders Forum
ICC	International Chamber of Commerce
ICCA	Institute for Corporate Culture Affairs
ICFTU	International Confederation of Free Trade Unions

ICMM	International Council on Mining and Metals
ICT	Information and Communications Technology
IDB	Inter-American Development Bank
IEMA	Institute of Environmental Management and Assessment
IFAC	International Federation of Accountants
IFAT	International Fair Trade Association or International Federation for Alternative Trade
IFC	International Finance Corporation
IFOAM	International Federation of Organic Agricultural Movements
ILO	International Labour Organisation
IMF	International Monetary Fund
IOAS	International Organic Accreditation Service
IPCC	Intergovernmental Panel on Climate Change
IPRs	Intellectual property rights
ISAE	International Standard for Assurance Engagements
ISEAL	International Social and Environmental Accreditation and Labelling Alliance
ISO	International Organisation for Standardisation
ITS	International Trade Secretariats
IUCN	World Conservation Union
JI	Joint Implementation
km	Kilometres
KPIs	Key performance indicators
LBG	London Benchmarking Group
LCA	Life cycle assessment, or Life cycle analysis
LED	Local economic development
MDGs	Millennium Development Goals
MMSD	Mining and Minerals for Sustainable Development
MNCs	Multinational corporations
MNEs	Multinational enterprises
mpg	Miles per gallon
MSC	Marine Stewardship Council
MTCT	Mother-to-child transmission
NCRI	National Corporate Responsibility Index
NEPAD	New Partnership for Africa's Development
NEWS	Network of European Worldshops
NIMBY	Not in my back yard
NGO	Non-governmental organisation

OAS	Organisation of American States
OECD	Organisation for Economic Cooperation and Development
OHS	Occupational health and safety
OHSAS	Occupational Health and Safety Assessment Series
OHSMS	Occupational Health and Safety Management System
OFR	Operating and Financial Review
OSH	Occupational safety and health
P^2	Pollution prevention
PCF	Prototype Carbon Fund
POPs	Persistent organic pollutants
PPP	Public–private partnerships
PRI	Principles for Responsible Investment
RCI	Responsible Competitiveness Index
REACH	Registration, Evaluation and Authorisation of Chemicals
RSI	Repetitive strain injury
SA	Social Accountability
SAI	Social Accountability International
SBE	Society for Business Ethics
SEA	Strategic environmental assessment
SEC	Securities Exchange Commission
SIGMA	Sustainability Integrated Guidelines for Management
SMEs	Small and medium sized enterprises
SOX	Sarbanes–Oxley Act
SRI	Socially responsible investment
S-ROI	Social return on investment
SVN	Social Venture Network
TBL	Triple bottom line
TI	Transparency International
TNS	The Natural Step
TRIPS	Trade-related aspects of intellectual property rights
TPAA	Transatlantic Partners Against AIDS
UDHR	Universal Declaration on Human Rights
UK	United Kingdom
UN	United Nations
UNDP	United Nations Development Programme
UNECE	United Nations Economic Commission for Europe
UNEP	United Nations Environment Programme

UNEP FI	United Nations Environment Programme Finance Initiative
UNGC	United Nations Global Compact
UNFCCC	United Nations Framework Convention on Climate Change
UNICEF	United Nations Children's Fund
US	United States
USA	United States of America
VER	Verified Emissions Reduction
WBCSD	World Business Council for Sustainable Development
WCED	World Commission on Environment and Development
WEEE	Waste Electrical and Electronic Equipment
WEF	World Economic Forum
WRI	World Resources Institute
WSF	World Social Forum
WSSD	World Summit on Sustainable Development
WTO	World Trade Organisation

INDEX OF TERMS

CORE TERMS

Accountability	Maria Sillanpää
Business ethics	Andrew Crane and Dirk Matten
Corporate citizenship	Malcolm McIntosh
Corporate environmental management	Richard Welford
Corporate governance	Mervyn King
Corporate social responsibility (CSR)	Archie Carroll
Corporate sustainability	John Elkington
Health and safety	Deborah Leipziger
Poverty	Mark B. Milstein, Erik Simanis, Duncan Duke and Stuart Hart
Stakeholder theory	R. Edward Freeman and Bidhan Parmar

KEY TERMS

Anti-globalisation	Andreas Scherer
Auditing	George Molenkamp and Jennifer Iansen-Rogers
Base of the Pyramid model	Mark B. Milstein, Erik Simanis, Duncan Duke and Stuart Hart
Business case	Björn Stigson

DEFINITIONS

REGIONS

SECTORS

Infrastructure sector — Charles Ainger

Media sector — Kara Hartnett Hurst

Mining sector — Matt Jeschke

Oil and gas sector — Antoine Mach

Personal and household goods sector — Chris Pomfret

Pharmaceutical sector — Antoine Mach

Technology sector — Kara Hartnett Hurst

Telecommunications sector — Dirk Matten

Travel and leisure sector — Wayne Visser

Utilities sector — Nicki Websper

CODES, DECLARATIONS, GUIDELINES, INDEXES, LEGISLATION, PRINCIPLES AND STANDARDS

AA 1000 Series of Standards — Maria Sillanpää, www.accountability21.net

Agenda 21 — www.unep.org

Apparel Industry Partnership (AIP) Code of 1997 — www.itcilo.it

Basel Convention — www.basel.int

Bribe Payers Index — David Nussbaum and Peter Wilkinson, www.transparency.org

Business Principles for Countering Bribery — David Nussbaum and Peter Wilkinson, www.transparency.org

CERES Principles — www.ceres.org

Code of Labour Practices for the Apparel Industry Including Sportswear — www.cleanclothes.org

Combined Code of Corporate Governance — Daniel Malan, www.fsa.gov.uk

Commonwealth Corporate Governance Principles — Daniel Malan, www.cacg-inc.com

Corporate Responsibility Index — David Halley, www.bitc.org.uk

Greenhouse Gas Protocol — Stirling Habbitts
🖰 www.ghgprotocol.org

ICC Business Charter for Sustainable Development — 🖰 www.iccwbo.org

ICFTU Code of Labour Practice — 🖰 www.icftu.org

IFC Social and Environmental Performance Standards — Matt Jeschke
🖰 www.ifc.org

ILO Declaration on Fundamental Principles and Rights at Work — 🖰 www.ilo.org

ILO-OSH 2001 Guidelines on Occupational Safety and Health Management Systems — 🖰 www.ilo.org

ILO Tripartite Declaration of Principles Concerning Multinational Enterprises and Social Policy — Deborah Leipziger
🖰 www.ilo.org

Interfaith Declaration: A Code of Ethics on International Business for Christians, Muslims and Jews — Kelly Lavelle
🖰 astro.ocis.temple.edu/~dialogue/ Codes/cmj_codes

International Organic Accreditation Service (IOAS) — 🖰 www.ioas.org

ISAE 3000 Standard for Assurance Engagements — George Molenkamp and Jennifer Iansen-Rogers
🖰 www.ifac.org

ISO 9000 Series of Standards on Quality Management — 🖰 www.iso.org

ISO 14000 Series of Standards on Environmental Management — Johann Möller
🖰 www.iso.org

ISO 26000 Series on Corporate Social Responsibility — Jorge E. Reis Cajazeira
🖰 www.iso.org

Johannesburg Declaration on Sustainable Development — Ruth Findlay-Brooks
🖰 www.johannesburgsummit.org

UN Universal Declaration on Human Rights — www.un.org

US Federal Sentencing Guidelines — Petrus Marais and Daniel Malan — www.ussc.gov

US Superfund Legislation — David Owen — www.epa.gov

Voluntary Principles on Security and Human Rights — www.voluntaryprinciples.org

Wolfsberg Principles — www.wolfsberg-principles.com

World Federation of Sporting Goods Industry Code of Conduct — www.wfsgi.org

ORGANISATIONS

African Institute for Corporate Citizenship (AICC) — Paul Kapelus — www.aiccafrica.org

Anti-Slavery International — www.antislavery.org

ATTAC — www.attac.org

Business and Human Rights Resource Centre — www.business-humanrights.org

Business for Social Responsibility (BSR) — Aron Cramer — www.bsr.org

Business in the Community (BITC) — David Halley — www.bitc.org.uk

Business Social Compliance Initiative (BSCI) — www.bsci-eu.org

Carbon Disclosure Project — Stirling Habbitts — www.cdproject.net

Caux Round Table — Stephen B. Young — www.cauxroundtable.org

Club of Rome — www.clubofrome.org

CSR Asia — Richard Welford — www.csr-asia.com

CSR Europe — Catherine Rubbens — www.csreurope.org

Ethics and Compliance Officer Association — www.theecoa.org

Society for Business Ethics	✍ www.societyforbusinessethics.org
Transparency International	David Nussbaum and
	Peter Wilkinson
	✍ www.transparency.org
UNEP Finance Initiative	✍ www.unepfi.org
World Business Council for Sustainable Development (WBCSD)	Björn Stigson ✍ www.wbcsd.org
World Commission on Environment and Development (WCED)	Ruth Findlay-Brooks ✍ www.un.org
World Economic Forum	Ruth Findlay-Brooks ✍ www.weforum.org
World Social Forum	Ruth Findlay-Brooks ✍ www.wsf2006.org
World Trade Organisation (WTO)	✍ www.wto.org

REFERRED TERMS

3Rs	→ Recycling, Waste management
Accountability	→ AA 1000 Series of Standards
Accounting	→ Social and environmental accounting
Accreditation	→ Certification
Advertising	→ Marketing ethics
Affirmative action	→ Diversity
Agricultural sector	→ Food and beverage sector
AIDS	→ HIV/AIDS
Air pollution	→ Pollution
Animal rights	→ Animal welfare
Animal testing	→ Animal welfare
Anti-capitalism	→ Anti-globalisation
Best of class investing	→ Socially responsible investment (SRI)
Black economic empowerment	→ Empowerment
Boycotts	→ Ethical consumption
Bribery	→ Corruption

AUTHOR INDEX